The Constitutional History Of England From 1760 To 1860

by

Charles Duke Yonge

The Constitutional History Of England From 1760 To 1860
by Charles Duke Yonge

Copyright © 2023

All Rights reserved.

No part of this publication may be reproduced, stored in a retrieval system, or transmitted in any form or by any means, electronic, mechanical, photocopying or Otherwise, without the written permission of the publisher.
The author/editor asserts the moral right to be identified as the author/editor of this work.

ISBN: 978-93-59329-65-9

Published by

DOUBLE 9 BOOKS

2/13-B, Ansari Road
Daryaganj, New Delhi – 110002
info@double9books.com
www.double9books.com
Tel. 011-40042856

This book is under public domain

ABOUT THE AUTHOR

Charles Duke Yonge wrote various works of modern history and translated a number of classics. George Edward Yonge was his younger brother. On November 30, 1812, Charles Duke Yonge was born in Eton, Berkshire. On December 25, 1812, he was christened. On the 4th of December 1811, his parents married. On his father's side, his grandparents were Duke Yonge and Catherine Crawley, and on his mother's side, Joseph Lord and Corbetta Owen of Pembroke South Wales. He attended Eton College for his education. Between 1831 and 1833, he was a foundation scholar at King's College, Cambridge, at the age of eighteen. On May 17, 1834, he enrolled in St. Mary's Hall in Oxford, which was a dependency of and ultimately incorporated into Oriel College. In December 1834, he received a first-class honours B.A. in Classics. He received his M.A. from Keble College in 1874.

CONTENTS

PREFACE 7
CHAPTER I 9
CHAPTER II 38
CHAPTER III 56
CHAPTER IV 89
CHAPTER V 135
CHAPTER VI 170
CHAPTER VII 193
CHAPTER VIII 210
CHAPTER IX 245
CHAPTER X 264
CHAPTER XI 293
CHAPTER XII 313
CHAPTER XIII 334
INDEX 372

PREFACE

Mr. Hallam's "Constitutional History" closes, as is well known, with the death of George II. The Reformation, the great Rebellion, and the Revolution, all of which are embraced in the period of which it treats, are events of such surpassing importance, and such all-pervading and lasting influence, that no subsequent transactions can ever attract entirely equal attention. Yet the century which has elapsed since the accession of George III. has also witnessed occurrences not only full of exciting interest at the moment, but calculated to affect the policy of the kingdom and the condition of the people, for all future time, in a degree only second to the Revolution itself. Indeed, the change in some leading features and principles of the constitution wrought by the Reform Bill of 1832, exceeds any that were enacted by the Bill of Rights or the Act of Settlement. The only absolutely new principle introduced in 1688 was that establishment of Protestant ascendency which was contained in the clause which disabled any Roman Catholic from wearing the crown. In other respects, those great statutes were not so much the introduction of new principles, as a recognition of privileges of the people which had been long established, but which, in too many instances, had been disregarded and violated.

But the Reform Bill conferred political power on classes which had never before been admitted to be entitled to it; and their enfranchisement could not fail to give a wholly new and democratic tinge to the government, which has been visible in its effect on the policy of all subsequent administrations.

And, besides this great measure, the passing of which has often been called a new Revolution, and the other reforms, municipal and ecclesiastical, which were its immediate and almost inevitable fruits, the century which followed the accession of George III. was also marked by the Irish Union, the abolition of slavery, the establishment of the principle of universal religious toleration; the loss of one great collection of colonies, the plantation of and grant of constitutions to others of not inferior magnitude, which had not even come into existence at its commencement; the growth of our wondrous dominion in India, with its eventual transfer of all authority in that country to the crown; with a host of minor transactions and enactments, which must all be regarded as, more or less, so many changes in or developments of the constitution, as it was regarded and understood by the statesmen of the seventeenth century.

It has seemed, therefore, to the compiler of this volume, that a narrative of these transactions in their historical sequence, so as to exhibit the connection which has frequently existed between them; to show, for instance, how the repeal of Poynings' Act, and the Regency Bill of 1788, necessitated the Irish Union; how Catholic Emancipation brought after it Parliamentary Reform, and how that led to municipal and ecclesiastical reforms, might not be without interest and use at the present time. And the modern fulness of our parliamentary reports (itself one not unimportant reform and novelty), since the accession of George III., has enabled him to give the inducements or the objections to the different enactments in the very words of the legislators who proposed them or resisted them, as often as it seemed desirable to do so.

CHAPTER I

Mr. Hallam's View of the Development of the Constitution.—Symptoms of approaching Constitutional Changes.—State of the Kingdom at the Accession of George III.—Improvement of the Law affecting the Commissions of the Judges.—Restoration of Peace.—Lord Bute becomes Minister.—The Case of Wilkes.—Mr. Luttrell is Seated for Middlesex by the House of Commons.—Growth of Parliamentary Reporting.—Mr. Grenville's Act for trying Election Petitions.—Disfranchisement of Corrupt Voters at New Shoreham.

The learned and judicious writer to whom is due the first idea of a "Constitutional History of England," and of whose admirable work I here venture to offer a continuation, regards "the spirit of the government" as having been "almost wholly monarchical till the Revolution of 1688," and in the four subsequent reigns, with the last of which his volumes close, as "having turned chiefly to an aristocracy."[1] And it may be considered as having generally preserved that character through the long and eventful reign of George III. But, even while he was writing, a change was already preparing, of which more than one recent occurrence had given unmistakable warning. A borough had been disfranchised for inveterate corruption in the first Parliament of George IV.[2] Before its dissolution, the same House of Commons had sanctioned the principle of a state endowment of the Roman Catholic clergy in Ireland, and had given a third reading to a bill for the abolition of all civil restrictions affecting members of that religion. It was impossible to avoid foreseeing that the Parliamentary Reform inaugurated by the disfranchisement of Grampound would soon be carried farther, or that the emancipation, as it was termed, of all Christian sects was at least equally certain not to be long delayed. And it will be denied by no one that those measures, which had no very obscure or doubtful connection with each other, have gradually imparted to the constitution a far more democratic tinge than would have been willingly accepted by even the most liberal statesman of the preceding century, or than, in the days of the Tudors or of the Stuarts, would have been thought compatible with the maintenance of the monarchy.

When George III. came to the throne, he found the nation engaged in a war which was occupying its arms not only on the Continent of Europe, but in India and America also, and was extending her glory and her substantial power in both hemispheres. *Inter arma silent leges.* And, while the contest lasted, neither legislators in Parliament nor the people outside had much attention to spare for matters of domestic policy. Yet the first year of the new reign was not suffered to pass without the introduction of one measure limiting the royal prerogative in a matter of paramount importance to the liberty of the people, the independence of the judges. The rule of making the commissions of the judges depend on their good conduct instead of on the pleasure of the crown had, indeed, been established at the Revolution; but it was still held that these commissions expired with the life of the sovereign who had granted them; and, at the accession of Anne, as also at that of George II., a renewal of their commissions had been withheld from some members of the judicial bench. But now, even before the dissolution of the existing Parliament, the new King recommended to it such a change in the law as should "secure the judges in the enjoyment of their offices during their good behavior, notwithstanding any demise of the crown;" giving the proposal, which was understood to have been originally suggested by himself, additional weight by the very unusual step of making it the subject of a speech to the two Houses in the middle of the session. A bill to give effect to it was at once brought in, and, though the Houses sat only a fortnight longer, was carried before the dissolution.

The close of the year 1762, however, saw the restoration of peace; and the circumstances connected with the treaty which re-established it gave birth to a degree of political and constitutional excitement such as had not agitated the kingdom for more than half a century. That treaty had not been concluded by the minister who had conducted the war. When George III. came to the throne he found the Duke of Newcastle presiding at the Treasury, but the seals of one Secretary of State in the hands of Mr. Pitt, who was universally regarded as the guiding genius of the ministry. The other Secretary of State was Lord Holdernesse. But, in the spring of 1761, as soon as the Parliament was dissolved,[3] that statesman retired from office, and was succeeded by the Earl of Bute, a Scotch nobleman, who stood high in the favor of the King's mother, the Princess Dowager of Wales, but who had not till very recently been supposed to be actuated by political ambition, and who was still less suspected of any statesman-like ability to qualify him for the office to which he was thus promoted. It was presently seen, however, that he aspired to even higher dignity. He at once set himself to oppose Pitt's warlike policy; and, on the question of declaring war against Spain, he was so successful in inducing the rest of the cabinet to reject Pitt's proposals, that that statesman resigned his office in unconcealed indignation. Having got rid of the real master of the ministry, Bute's next step was to get rid of its nominal chief, and in the spring of 1762 he managed to drive the Duke of Newcastle from the Treasury, and was himself placed by the King at the head of the administration. So rapid an elevation of a man previously unknown as a politician could hardly fail to create very widespread dissatisfaction, which was in some degree augmented by the nationality of the new minister. Lord Bute was a Scotchman, and Englishmen had not wholly forgiven or forgotten the Scotch invasion of 1745. Since that time the Scotch had been regarded with general disfavor; Scotch poverty and Scotch greediness for the good things of England had furnished constant topics for raillery and sarcasm; and more than one demagogue and political writer had sought popularity by pandering to the prevailing taste for attacks on the whole nation. Foremost among these was Mr. John Wilkes, member for Aylesbury, a man of broken fortunes and still more damaged character, but of a wit and hardihood that made his society acceptable to some of high rank and lax morality, and caused his political alliance to be courted by some who desired to be regarded as leaders of a party; many of the transactions of the late reign having, unfortunately, not been favorable to the maintenance of any high standard of either public or private virtue. On Lord Bute's accession to office, Wilkes had set up a periodical paper, whose object and character were sufficiently indicated by its title, *The North Briton*, and in which the diligence of Lord Bute in distributing places among his kinsmen and countrymen furnished the staple of almost every number; while in many the Princess of Wales herself was not spared, as the cause, for motives not obscurely hinted at, of his sudden elevation. So pertinacious and virulent were the attacks thus launched at him, coinciding as they did, at least in one point, with the prejudices of the multitude, that they were commonly believed to have had some share in driving Lord Bute from office, which, in the spring of 1763, he suddenly resigned, hoping, as it might almost seem, thus to throw on his successor the burden of defending his measures. The most important of these measures had been the conclusion of the Treaty of Versailles, which, when it was first announced to Parliament, had been vehemently attacked in both Houses by Pitt and his followers, but had been approved by large majorities. Wilkes, however, not without reason, believed it to be still unpopular with the nation at large, and, flushed with his supposed victory over Lord Bute, was watching eagerly for some occasion of re-opening the question, when such an opportunity was afforded him by the King's speech at the prorogation of the Parliament, which took place a few days after Lord Bute's resignation.

Lord Bute had been succeeded by Mr. George Grenville, who had for a time been one of his colleagues as Secretary of State; and on him, therefore, the duty devolved of framing the royal speech the opening sentences of which referred to "the re-establishment of peace" in terms of warm self-congratulation, as having been effected "upon conditions honorable to the crown and beneficial to the people." Wilkes at once caught at this panegyric, as affording him just such an opportunity as he had been seeking of renewing his attacks on the government, which he regarded as changed in nothing but the name of the Prime-minister.[4] And, four days after the prorogation,[5] he accordingly issued a new number of *The North Briton* (No. 45), in which he heaped unmeasured sarcasm and invective on the peace itself, on the royal speech, and on the minister who had composed it. As if conscious that Mr. Grenville was less inclined by temper than Lord Bute to suffer such attacks without endeavoring to retaliate, he took especial pains to keep within the law in his strictures, and, accordingly, carefully avoided saying a disrespectful word of the King himself, whom he described as "a prince of many great and amiable qualities," "ever renowned for truth, honor, and unsullied virtue." But he claimed a right to canvass the speech "with the utmost freedom," since "it had always been considered by the Legislature and by the public at large as the speech of the minister." And he kept this distinction carefully in view through the whole number. The speech he denounced with bitter vehemence, as "an abandoned instance of ministerial effrontery," as containing "the most unjustifiable public declarations" and "infamous fallacies." The peace he affirmed to be "such as had drawn down the contempt of mankind on our wretched negotiators." And he described the present minister as a mere tool of "the favorite," by whom "he still meditated to rule the kingdom with a rod of iron." But in the whole number there was but one sentence which could be represented as implying the very slightest censure on the King himself, and even that was qualified by a personal eulogy. "The King of England," it said, "is not only the first magistrate of the country, but is invested by the law with the whole executive power. He is, however, responsible to his people for the due execution of the royal functions in the choice of ministers, etc., equally with the meanest of his subjects in his particular duty. The personal character of our present amiable sovereign makes us easy and happy that so great a power is lodged in such hands; but the favorite has given too just cause for him to escape the general odium. The prerogative of the crown is to exert the constitutional power intrusted to it in such a way, not of blind favor and partiality, but of wisdom and judgment. This is the spirit of our constitution. The people, too, have their prerogative; and I hope the fine words of Dryden will be engraven on our hearts, 'Freedom is the English subject's prerogative.'"

These were the last sentences of No. 45. And in the present day it will hardly be thought that, however severe or even violent some of the epithets with which certain sentences of the royal speech were assailed may have been, the language exceeds the bounds of allowable political criticism. With respect to the King, indeed, however accompanied with personal compliments to himself those strictures may have been, it may be admitted that in asserting any responsibility whatever to the people on the part of the sovereign, even for the choice of his ministers, as being bound to exercise that choice "with wisdom and judgment," it goes somewhat beyond the strict theory of the constitution. Undoubtedly that theory is, that the minister chosen by the King is himself responsible for every circumstance or act which led to his appointment. This principle was established in the fullest manner in 1834, when, as will be seen hereafter, Sir Robert Peel admitted his entire responsibility for the dismissal of Lord Melbourne by King William IV., though it was notorious that he was in Italy at the time, and had not been consulted on the matter. But as yet such questions had not been as accurately examined as subsequent events caused them to be; and Wilkes's assertion of royal responsibility to this extent probably coincided with the general feeling on the subject.[6] At all events, the error contained in it, and the insinuation that due wisdom and judgment had not been displayed in the appointment of Mr. G. Grenville to the Treasury, were not so derogatory to the legitimate authority and dignity of the crown as to make the writer a fit subject for a criminal prosecution. But Mr. Grenville was of a bitter temper, never inclined to tolerate any strictures on his own judgment or capacity, and fully imbued with the conviction that the first duty of an English minister is to uphold the supreme authority of the Parliament, and to chastise any one who dares to call in question the wisdom of any one of its resolutions. But *The North Briton* had done this, and more. No. 45 had not only denounced the treaty which both Houses had approved, but had insinuated in unmistakable language that their approval had been purchased by gross corruption (a fact which was, indeed, sufficiently notorious). And, consequently, Mr. Grenville determined to treat the number which contained the denunciation as a seditious libel, the publication of which was a criminal offence; and, by his direction, Lord Halifax, as Secretary of State, issued what was termed a general warrant—a warrant, that is, which did not name the person or persons against whom it was directed, but which commanded the apprehension of "the authors, printers, and publishers" of the offending paper, leaving the officers who were charged with its execution to decide who came under that description, or, in other words, who were guilty of the act charged, before they had been brought before any tribunal. The warrant was executed. Wilkes and some printers were apprehended; Wilkes himself, as if the minister's design had been to make the charge ridiculous by exaggeration, being consigned to the great state-prison of the Tower, such a use of which was generally limited to those impeached of high-treason. And, indeed, the commitment did declare that No. 45 of *The North Briton* was "a libel tending to alienate the affections of the people from his Majesty, and to excite them to traitorous insurrections against the government." Wilkes instantly sued out a writ of *habeas corpus*, and was without hesitation released by the Court of Common Pleas, on the legal ground that, "as a member of the House of Commons, he was protected from arrest in all cases except treason, felony, or a breach of the peace;" a decision which, in the next session of Parliament, the minister endeavored to overbear by inducing both Houses to concur in a resolution that "privilege of Parliament did not extend to the case of publishing seditious libels."

In his life of Lord Camden,[7] who was Chief-justice of the Common Pleas at the time, Lord Campbell expresses a warm approval of this resolution, as one "which would now be considered conclusive evidence of the law." But, with all respect to the memory of a writer who was himself a Chief-justice, we suspect that in this case he was advancing a position as an author engaged in the discussion of what had become a party question, which he would not have laid down from the Bench.[8] The resolution certainly did not make it law, since it was not confirmed by any royal assent; and to interpret the law is not within the province of the House of Commons, nor, except when sitting as a Court of Appeal, of the House of Lords. We may, however, fully agree with the principle which Lord Campbell at the same time lays down, that "privilege of Parliament should not be permitted to interfere with the execution of the criminal law of the country." And this doctrine has been so fully acquiesced in since, that members of both Houses have in more than one instance been imprisoned on conviction for libel.

The legality of the species of warrant under which Wilkes had been arrested was, however, a question of far greater importance; and on that no formal decision was pronounced on this occasion, the Lieutenant of the Tower, in his return to the writ of *habeas corpus*, and the counsel employed on both sides, equally avoiding all mention of the character of the warrant. But it was indirectly determined shortly afterward. The leaders of the Opposition would fain have had the point settled by what, in truth, would not have settled it—another resolution of the House of Commons. But, though it was discussed in several warm debates, Grenville always contrived to baffle his adversaries, though on one occasion his majority dwindled to fourteen.[9] What, however, the House of Commons abstained from affirming was distinctly, though somewhat extra-judicially, asserted by Lord Camden, as Chief-justice of the Common Pleas. Wilkes, with some of the printers and others who had been arrested, had brought actions for false imprisonment, which came to be tried in his court; and they obtained such heavy damages that the officials who had been mulcted applied for new trials, on the plea of their being excessive. But the Chief-justice refused the applications, and upheld the verdict, on the ground that the juries, in their assessment of damages, had been "influenced by a righteous indignation at the conduct of those who sought to exercise arbitrary power over all the King's subjects, to violate Magna Charta, and to destroy the liberty of the kingdom, by insisting on the legality of this general warrant." Such a justification would hardly be admitted now. But, in a subsequent trial, a still higher authority, the Chief-justice of the King's Bench, Lord Mansfield, held language so similar, that, once more to quote the words of Lord Campbell, "without any formal judgment, general warrants have ever since been considered illegal."

However, the release of Wilkes on the ground of his parliamentary privilege gave him but a momentary triumph, or rather respite. The prosecution was not abated by the decision that he could not be imprisoned before trial; while one effect of his liberation was to stimulate the minister to add another count to the indictment preferred against him, on which he might be expected to find it less easy to excite the sympathy of any party. Wilkes had not always confined his literary efforts to political pamphlets. There was a club named the Franciscans (in compliment to Sir Francis Dashwood, Lord Bute's Chancellor of the Exchequer, who, as well as Lord Sandwich, the First Lord of the Admiralty, was one of its members), which met at Medmenham Abbey, on the banks of the Thames, and there held revels whose license recalled the worst excesses of the preceding century. To this club Wilkes also belonged; and, in indulgence of tastes in harmony with such a brotherhood, he had composed a blasphemous and indecent parody on Pope's "Essay on Man," which he entitled "An Essay on Woman," and to which he appended a body of burlesque notes purporting to be the composition of Pope's latest commentator, the celebrated Dr. Warburton, Bishop of Gloucester. He had never published it (indeed, it may be doubted whether, even in that not very delicate age, any publisher could have been found to run the risk of issuing so scandalous a work), but he had printed a few copies in his own house, of which he designed to make presents to such friends as he expected to appreciate it. He had not, however, so far as it appears, given away a single copy, when, on the very first day of the next session of Parliament, Lord Sandwich himself brought the parody under the notice of the House of Lords. If there was a single member of the House whose delicacy was not likely to be shocked, and whose morals could not be injured by such a composition, it was certainly Lord Sandwich himself; but his zeal as a minister to support his chief kindled in him a sudden enthusiasm for the support of virtue and decency also;

and, having obtained a copy by some surreptitious means, he now made a formal complaint of it to the House, contending that the use of the name of the Bishop of Gloucester as author of the notes constituted a breach of the privileges of the House. And he was seconded by the bishop himself, whose temper and judgment were, unhappily, very inferior to his learning and piety. It is recorded that he actually compared Wilkes to the devil, and then apologized to Satan for the comparison. But the Lords were in a humor to regard no violence against Wilkes as excessive; and, submitting to the guidance of the minister and the prelate, resolved that the "Essay on Woman,"[10] as also another poem by the same writer, a paraphrase of the "Veni Creator," was "a most scandalous, obscene, and impious libel," and presented an address to the King, requesting his Majesty "to give the most effectual orders for the immediate prosecution of the author." And, in the course of the next few weeks, the House of Commons outran the peers themselves in violence and manifest unfairness. They concurred with the Lords in ordering No. 45 of *The North Briton* to be burnt by the common hangman, an order which was not carried out without great opposition on the part of the London populace, who made it the occasion of a very formidable riot, in which the sheriffs themselves incurred no little danger; and, by another resolution, they ordered Wilkes to attend in his place to answer the charge of having published the two works. But at the time when they made this order it was well known that he could not obey it. A few days before he had been challenged by a Mr. Martin, who till very recently had been one of the Secretaries of the Treasury, and who was generally believed to have prepared himself for the conflict by diligent practice with a pistol; and in the duel which ensued Wilkes had been severely wounded. It was not only notorious that he had been thus disabled, but he sent a physician and surgeon of admitted eminence in their profession, and of unquestioned honor, to testify to the fact at the bar of the House; and subsequently he forwarded written certificates to the same purport from some French doctors who had special knowledge of gunshot wounds. But the Commons declined to accept this evidence as sufficient, and directed two other doctors to examine him. Wilkes, however, refused to admit them: his refusal was treated as a sufficient ground for pronouncing him "guilty of a contempt of the authority of the House," and for deciding on his case in his absence; and, on the 19th of January, before the case had come on for trial, a resolution was carried that "Mr. Wilkes was guilty of writing and publishing *The North Briton* (No. 45), which this House had voted to be a false, scandalous, and seditious libel, and that, for the said offence, he be expelled the House." At a later period of the year, he was tried on the two charges of publishing No. 45 and the "Essay on Woman," was found guilty of both, and, as he did not appear to receive judgment, in November, 1764, he was outlawed.

which came to be tried in his court; and they obtained such heavy damages that the officials who had been mulcted applied for new trials, on the plea of their being excessive. But the Chief-justice refused the applications, and upheld the verdict, on the ground that the juries, in their assessment of damages, had been "influenced by a righteous indignation at the conduct of those who sought to exercise arbitrary power over all the King's subjects, to violate Magna Charta, and to destroy the liberty of the kingdom, by insisting on the legality of this general warrant." Such a justification would hardly be admitted now. But, in a subsequent trial, a still higher authority, the Chief-justice of the King's Bench, Lord Mansfield, held language so similar, that, once more to quote the words of Lord Campbell, "without any formal judgment, general warrants have ever since been considered illegal."

However, the release of Wilkes on the ground of his parliamentary privilege gave him but a momentary triumph, or rather respite. The prosecution was not abated by the decision that he could not be imprisoned before trial; while one effect of his liberation was to stimulate the minister to add another count to the indictment preferred against him, on which he might be expected to find it less easy to excite the sympathy of any party. Wilkes had not always confined his literary efforts to political pamphlets. There was a club named the Franciscans (in compliment to Sir Francis Dashwood, Lord Bute's Chancellor of the Exchequer, who, as well as Lord Sandwich, the First Lord of the Admiralty, was one of its members), which met at Medmenham Abbey, on the banks of the Thames, and there held revels whose license recalled the worst excesses of the preceding century. To this club Wilkes also belonged; and, in indulgence of tastes in harmony with such a brotherhood, he had composed a blasphemous and indecent parody on Pope's "Essay on Man," which he entitled "An Essay on Woman," and to which he appended a body of burlesque notes purporting to be the composition of Pope's latest commentator, the celebrated Dr. Warburton, Bishop of Gloucester. He had never published it (indeed, it may be doubted whether, even in that not very delicate age, any publisher could have been found to run the risk of issuing so scandalous a work), but he had printed a few copies in his own house, of which he designed to make presents to such friends as he expected to appreciate it. He had not, however, so far as it appears, given away a single copy, when, on the very first day of the next session of Parliament, Lord Sandwich himself brought the parody under the notice of the House of Lords. If there was a single member of the House whose delicacy was not likely to be shocked, and whose morals could not be injured by such a composition, it was certainly Lord Sandwich himself; but his zeal as a minister to support his chief kindled in him a sudden enthusiasm for the support of virtue and decency also;

and, having obtained a copy by some surreptitious means, he now made a formal complaint of it to the House, contending that the use of the name of the Bishop of Gloucester as author of the notes constituted a breach of the privileges of the House. And he was seconded by the bishop himself, whose temper and judgment were, unhappily, very inferior to his learning and piety. It is recorded that he actually compared Wilkes to the devil, and then apologized to Satan for the comparison. But the Lords were in a humor to regard no violence against Wilkes as excessive; and, submitting to the guidance of the minister and the prelate, resolved that the "Essay on Woman,"[10] as also another poem by the same writer, a paraphrase of the "Veni Creator," was "a most scandalous, obscene, and impious libel," and presented an address to the King, requesting his Majesty "to give the most effectual orders for the immediate prosecution of the author." And, in the course of the next few weeks, the House of Commons outran the peers themselves in violence and manifest unfairness. They concurred with the Lords in ordering No. 45 of *The North Briton* to be burnt by the common hangman, an order which was not carried out without great opposition on the part of the London populace, who made it the occasion of a very formidable riot, in which the sheriffs themselves incurred no little danger; and, by another resolution, they ordered Wilkes to attend in his place to answer the charge of having published the two works. But at the time when they made this order it was well known that he could not obey it. A few days before he had been challenged by a Mr. Martin, who till very recently had been one of the Secretaries of the Treasury, and who was generally believed to have prepared himself for the conflict by diligent practice with a pistol; and in the duel which ensued Wilkes had been severely wounded. It was not only notorious that he had been thus disabled, but he sent a physician and surgeon of admitted eminence in their profession, and of unquestioned honor, to testify to the fact at the bar of the House; and subsequently he forwarded written certificates to the same purport from some French doctors who had special knowledge of gunshot wounds. But the Commons declined to accept this evidence as sufficient, and directed two other doctors to examine him. Wilkes, however, refused to admit them: his refusal was treated as a sufficient ground for pronouncing him "guilty of a contempt of the authority of the House," and for deciding on his case in his absence; and, on the 19th of January, before the case had come on for trial, a resolution was carried that "Mr. Wilkes was guilty of writing and publishing *The North Briton* (No. 45), which this House had voted to be a false, scandalous, and seditious libel, and that, for the said offence, he be expelled the House." At a later period of the year, he was tried on the two charges of publishing No. 45 and the "Essay on Woman," was found guilty of both, and, as he did not appear to receive judgment, in November, 1764, he was outlawed.

So far, it may be said to have been a drawn battle. If, on the one hand, the minister had procured the expulsion of Wilkes, on the other hand Wilkes had gained great notoriety and a certain amount of sympathy, and had, moreover, enriched himself by considerable damages; and again, if the nation at large was a gainer by the condemnation of general warrants, even that advantage might be thought to be dearly gained by the discredit into which the Parliament had fallen through its intemperance. But the contest between Wilkes and the ministry was only closed for a time; and when it was revived, a singular freak of fortune caused the very minister who had led the proceedings against him on this occasion to appear as his advocate. To avoid the consequences of his outlawry, he had taken up his abode in Paris, waiting for a change of ministry, which, as he hoped, might bring into power some to whom he might look for greater favor. But when, though in the course of the next two years two fresh administrations were formed, it was seen that neither Lord Rockingham, the head of the first, nor the Duke of Grafton and Mr. Pitt (promoted to the Earldom of Chatham), the heads of the second, had any greater sympathy with him than Mr. Grenville, he became desperate, and looked out for some opportunity of giving effect to his discontent. He found it in the dissolution of Parliament, which took place in the spring of 1768. In spite of his outlawry, he instantly returned to England, and offered himself as a candidate for London. There, indeed, he did not succeed, though the populace was uproarious in his support, and drew his carriage through the streets as if in triumph. But, before the end of the month, he was returned at the head of the poll for Middlesex, when the mob celebrated his victory by great riot and outrages, breaking the windows of Lord Bute, as his old enemy, and of the Lord Mayor, as the representative of the City of London, which had rejected him, and insulting, and even in some instances beating, passers-by who refused to join in their cheers for "Wilkes and Liberty."

He had already pledged himself to take the necessary steps to procure the reversal of his outlawry; and, in pursuance of his promise, he surrendered in the Court of King's Bench. But his removal to prison caused a renewal of the tumults with greater violence than before. The mob even rescued him from the officers who had him in custody; and when, having escaped from his deliverers, he, with a parade of obedience to the law, again surrendered himself voluntarily at the gate of the King's Bench Prison, they threatened to attack the jail itself, kindled a fire under its walls, which was not extinguished without some danger, and day after day assembled in such tumultuous and menacing crowds, that at last Lord Weymouth, the Secretary of State, wrote a letter to the Surrey magistrates, enjoining them to abstain from no measures which might seem necessary for the preservation of peace, even if that could only be effected by the employment of the soldiery. The riots grew more and more formidable, till at last the magistrates had no resource but to call out the troops, who, on one occasion, after they had been pelted with large stones, and in many instances severely injured, fired, killing or wounding several of the foremost rioters. So tragical an event seemed to Wilkes to furnish him with exactly such an opportunity as he desired to push himself into farther notoriety. He at once printed Lord Weymouth's letter, and circulated it, with an inflammatory comment, in which he described it as a composition having for its fruit "a horrid massacre, the consummation of a hellish plot deliberately planned." Too angry to be prudent, Lord Weymouth complained to the House of Lords of this publication as a breach of privilege, and the Lords formally represented it to the House of Commons as an insult deliberately offered to them by one of its members. There could be no doubt that such language as Wilkes had used was libellous. In its imputation of designs of deliberate wickedness, it very far exceeded the bitterest passages of *The North Briton*; and Lord Weymouth's colleagues, therefore, thought they might safely follow the precedent set in 1764, of branding the publication as a libel, and again procuring the expulsion of the libeller from the House of Commons. There were circumstances in the present case, such as the difference between the constituencies of Aylesbury and Middlesex, and the enthusiastic fervor in the offender's cause which the populace of the City had displayed, which made it very doubtful whether the precedent of 1764 were quite a safe one to follow; but the ministers not only disregarded every such consideration, but, as if they had wantonly designed to give their measure a bad appearance, and to furnish its opponents with the strongest additional argument against it, they mixed up with their present complaint a reference to former misdeeds of Wilkes with which it had no connection. On receiving the message of the Lords, they had summoned him to appear at the bar of the House of Commons, that he might be examined on the subject; but this proceeding was so far from intimidating him, that he not only avowed the publication of his comment on Lord Weymouth's letter, but gloried in it, asserting that he deserved the thanks of the people for bringing to light the true character of "that bloody scroll." Such language was regarded as an aggravation of his offence, and the Attorney-general moved that his comment on the letter "was an insolent, scandalous, and seditious libel;" and, when that motion had been carried, Lord Barrington followed it up with another, to the effect that "John Wilkes, Esq., a member of this House, who hath at the bar of this House confessed himself to be the author and publisher of what the House has resolved to be an insolent, scandalous, and seditious libel, and who has been convicted in the Court of King's Bench of having printed and published a seditious libel, and three[11] obscene and impious libels, and by the judgment of the said

Court has been sentenced to undergo twenty-two months' imprisonment, and is now in execution under the said judgment, be expelled this House." This motion encountered a vigorous opposition, not only from Mr. Burke and the principal members of the Rockingham party, which now formed the regular Opposition, but also from Mr. Grenville, the former Prime-minister, who on the former occasion, in 1764, had himself moved the expulsion of the same offender. His speech on this occasion is the only one which is fully reported; and it deserved the distinction from the exhaustive way in which it dealt with every part of the question. It displayed no inclination to extenuate Wilkes's present offence, but it pointed out with great force the circumstance that the supporters of the motion were far from agreement as to the reasons by which they were guided; that some members of the greatest authority in the House, while they had avowed their intention of voting for the expulsion, had at the same time been careful to explain that the comment on Lord Weymouth's letter was not the ground of their vote; that so great a lawyer as Mr. Blackstone had asserted that that comment "had not been properly and regularly brought before the House," but had founded his intention to vote for the expulsion solely "upon that article of the charge which related to the three obscene and impious libels mentioned in it, disavowing in the most direct terms all the other articles." That, on the other hand, other members of deserved weight and influence, such as Lord Palmerston and Lord F. Campbell, had disdained the idea of regarding "the article of the three obscene and impious libels as affording any ground for their proceeding." So practised a debater as Mr. Grenville had but little difficulty, therefore, in arguing against the advocates of expulsion, when they were so divided that one portion of them did, in fact, reply to the other. But it would be superfluous here to enter into the arguments employed on either side to justify the expulsion, or to prove it to be unjustifiable, from a consideration of the character of either Wilkes or his publication. The strength and importance of Mr. Grenville's speech lay in the constitutional points which it raised.

Some supporters of the ministers had dwelt upon the former expulsion, insisting that "a man who had been expelled by a former House of Commons could not possibly be deemed a proper person to sit in the present Parliament, unless he had some pardon to plead, or some merit to cancel his former offences." By a reference to the case of Sir R. Walpole, Mr. Grenville proved that this had not been the opinion of former Parliaments; and he contended, with unanswerable logic, that it would be very mischievous to the nation if such a principle should be now acted on, and such a precedent established, since, though employed in the first instance against the odious and the guilty, it might, when once established, be easily applied to, and made use of against, the meritorious and the innocent; and so the most eminent and deserving members of the state, under the color of such an example, by one arbitrary and discretionary vote of one House of Parliament, the worst species of ostracism, might be excluded from the public councils, cut off and proscribed from the rights of every subject of the realm, not for a term of years alone, but forever. He quoted from "L'Esprit des Lois" an assertion of Montesquieu, that "one of the excellences of the English constitution was, that the judicial power was separated from the legislative, and that there would be no liberty if they were blended together; the power over the life and liberty of the citizens would then be arbitrary, for the judge would be the legislator." And, having thus proved that it would be a violation of the recognized constitution to found a second expulsion on the first, he proceeded to argue that to expel him for this new offence would be impolitic and inexpedient, as a step which would inevitably lead to a contest with the constituency which he represented, since, "in the present disposition of the county of Middlesex, no one could entertain a doubt that Wilkes would be re-elected. The House would then probably think itself under a necessity of again expelling him, and he would as certainly be again re-elected. The House might, indeed, refuse to issue a new writ, which would be to deprive the freeholders of Middlesex of the right of choosing any other representative; but he could not believe that the House would think it fit to inflict such a punishment on the electors of a great county. Should it not do so, the other alternative would be to bring into the House as representative and knight of the shire for Middlesex a man chosen by a few voters only, in contradiction to the declared sense of a great majority of the freeholders on the face of the poll, upon the supposition that all the votes of the latter were forfeited and thrown away on account of the expulsion of Mr. Wilkes." It seemed premature to discuss that point before it arose, and therefore the Speaker contented himself for the present with saying that "he believed there was no example of such a proceeding; and that, if it should appear to be new and unfounded as the law of the land, or even if any reasonable doubt could be entertained of its legality, the attempt to forfeit the freeholders' votes in such a manner would be highly alarming and dangerous."

Few prophecies have been more exactly fulfilled. The House did expel Mr. Wilkes; he did offer himself for re-election, and was re-elected; and the minister, in consequence, moved and carried a resolution that "John Wilkes, Esq., having been, in this session of Parliament, expelled this House, was and is incapable of being elected a member to serve in this present Parliament." And, in pursuance of this vote, a writ was again issued. At the end of another month the proceeding required to be repeated. Wilkes had again offered himself for re-election. No other candidate had presented himself, and, in answer to an inquiry, the under-sheriff reported that "no other candidate had been proposed but John Wilkes, Esq., and that no elector had given or tendered his vote for any other person." Once more the House resolved that he was "incapable of being elected," and issued a new writ. But on this second occasion the ministry had provided a rival candidate in the person of the Honorable H.K. Luttrell. He was duly proposed and seconded; a poll was taken and kept open for several days, and, as it appeared at the close that 1143 votes had been given for Wilkes and 296 for Mr. Luttrell, the sheriff again returned Wilkes as duly elected.

A debate of singularly angry excitement arose on the reception of this return. Even lawyers, such as Mr. De Grey, the Attorney-general, and Sir Fletcher Norton, who had been Attorney-general, were not ashamed to denounce the conduct of the sheriff in returning Mr. Wilkes as "highly improper and indecent," as "a flying in the face of a resolution of the House of Commons;" and Sir Fletcher even ventured to advance the proposition that, "as the Commons were acting in a judicial capacity, their resolutions were equal to law." Lord North, too, the Chancellor of the Exchequer, as we learn from the "Parliamentary History," "spoke long, but chiefly to the passions. He described Mr. Wilkes and his actions in a lively manner; showed the variety of troubles which he had given the ministry; and that unless, by voting in Mr. Luttrell, an end were put to this debate, the whole kingdom would be in confusion; though he owned that he did not think that measure would put an end to the distractions. He spoke much more to the expediency than to the legality of the measure proposed."

On the other side, it was contended by several members, Burke and Mr. Grenville being of the number, that "the House of Commons alone could not make a law binding any body but themselves. That, if they could disqualify one person, they could disqualify as many as they pleased, and thus get into their own hands the whole power of the government;" and precedents were produced to prove that votes of the House of Lords, and also of the House of Commons, regarding their own members, had been disregarded by the judges of the Court of King's Bench as being contrary to law. But the minister was secure of the steadiness of his adherents, and a majority of 221 to 152 declared that Mr. Luttrell had been duly elected.

But Lord North was correct in his anticipation that their vote would not put an end to the agitation on the question, and it was renewed in the next session in a manner which at one time threatened to produce a breach between the two Houses.

The "Parliamentary History" closes its report of the debate on the resolution by which Mr. Luttrell was seated with a summary of the arguments used in it, taken from the "Annual Register," which, as is universally known, was at this time edited by Mr. Burke. It is a very fair and candid abstract, which, in fact, puts the whole question on one single issue, "that the House of Commons is the sole court of judicature in all cases of election, and that this authority is derived from the first principles of our government, viz., the necessary independence of the three branches of the Legislature." But, though that doctrine was fully admitted by the Opposition, they made "that very admission a ground for reviving the question in the next session, by moving for a resolution which should declare that, 'being a Court of Judicature, the House of Commons, in deciding matters of election, was bound to judge according to the law of the land, and the known and established law of Parliament, which was part thereof.'" It was understood that this resolution, if carried, was intended as a stepping-stone to others which should condemn the decision of the previous session; yet it seemed such a truism that even the ministers could not venture to deny it; but they proposed to defeat the object of its framers by adding to it a declaration that the late decision was "agreeable to the said law of the land." And we might pass on to the subsequent debate, in which the constitutional correctness of that addition was distinctly challenged, did it not seem desirable to notice two arguments which were brought forward against the motion, one by an independent member, Mr. Ongley, the other by the Attorney-general. Mr. Ongley contended that "a power of preserving order and decency is essentially necessary to every aggregate body; and, with respect to this House, if it had not power over its particular members, they would be subject to no control at all." The answer to this argument is obvious: that a right on the part of the House to control the conduct of its members is a wholly different thing from a right to determine who are or ought to be members; and that for the House to claim this latter right, except on grounds of qualification or disqualification legally proved, would be to repeat one of the most monstrous of all Cromwell's acts of tyranny, when, in 1656, he placed guards at the door of the House, with orders to refuse admission to all those members whom, however lawfully elected, he did not expect to find sufficiently compliant for his purposes. Mr. De Grey's argument was of a different character, being based on what he foretold would be the practical result of a decision that expulsion did not involve an incapacity to be re-elected. If it did not involve such incapacity, and if, in consequence, Mr. Wilkes should be re-elected, he considered that the House would naturally feel it its duty to re-expel him as often as the constituency re-elected him. But one answer given to this argument was, that to expel a second time would be to punish twice for one offence, a proceeding at variance not only with English law but with every idea of justice. Another, and one which has obtained greater acceptance, was, that the legitimate doctrine was, that the issue of a new writ gave the expelled member an appeal from the House to the constituency, and that the constituency had a constitutional right to overrule the judgment of the House, and to determine whether it still regarded the candidate as its most suitable representative.

The ministers, however, were, as before, strong enough in the House to carry their resolution. But the Opposition returned to the charge, taking up an entirely different though equally general position, "That, by the law of the land and the known law and usage of Parliament, no person eligible by common right can be incapacitated by vote or resolution of this House, but by act of Parliament only." It is remarkable that, in the debate which ensued, two members who successively rose to the dignity of Lord Chancellor, Mr. Thurlow and Mr. Wedderburn, took different sides; but nothing could shake the ministerial majority. The resolution was rejected. And when Lord Rockingham proposed the same resolution in the House of Lords, though it was supported by all the eloquence of Lord Chatham, he was beaten by a majority of more than two to one, and the ministers even carried a resolution declaring "that any interference of the House of Lords with any judgment of the House of Commons, in matters of election, would be a violation of the constitutional rights of the Commons."

Even these decisive defeats of the Opposition did not finally terminate the struggle. The notoriety which Wilkes had gained had answered his purpose to no slight extent. The City had adopted his cause with continually increasing earnestness and effect. It had made him Sheriff, Alderman, Lord Mayor, and had enriched him with the lucrative office of City Chamberlain; and, as one of the City magistrates, he subsequently won the good opinion of many who had previously condemned him, by his conduct during the Gordon Riots, in which he exerted his authority with great intrepidity to check and punish the violence of the rioters. And when, in 1782, Lord Rockingham became, for the second time, Prime-minister, he thought he might well avail himself of the favor he had thus acquired, and of the accession to office of those whom the line which they had formerly taken bound to countenance him, to bring forward a motion for the expunction of the resolutions against him which had been passed in 1770. It was carried by a largo majority; and though this was as evidently a party division as those had been by which he had been defeated twelve years before, still, as the last resolution on the subject, it must be regarded as decisive of the law and practice of Parliament, and as having settled the doctrine that expulsion does not incapacitate a member who has been expelled from immediate re-election.[12]

The establishment of this rule, and the abolition of general warrants, were, however, not the only nor the most important result of these proceedings. They led indirectly to an innovation which, it is hardly too much to say, has had a greater influence on the character and conduct of Parliament, and indeed on the whole subsequent legislation of the country, than can be attributed to any other single cause. Hitherto the bulk of the people had enjoyed but very scanty and occasional means of acquiring political education. At times of vehement political excitement, or any special party conflict, pamphlets and periodical essays had enlightened their readers—necessarily a select and small body—on particular topics. But standing orders of both Houses, often renewed, strictly forbade all publication of the debates which took place in either. To a certain extent, these orders had come to be disregarded and evaded. Almost ever since the accession of the House of Brunswick, a London publisher had given to the world an annual account of the Parliamentary proceedings and most interesting discussions of the year; and before the middle of the reign of George II, two monthly magazines had given sketches of speeches made by leading members of each party. The reporters, however, did not venture to give the names of the speakers at full length, but either disguised them under some general description, or at most gave their initials; and sometimes found that even this profession of deference to the standing orders did not insure them impunity. As late as the year 1747, Cave, the proprietor and editor of the *Gentleman's Magazine*, was brought to the bar of the House of Commons for publishing an account of a recent debate, and only obtained his release by expressions of humble submission and the payment of heavy fees. The awe, however, which his humiliation and peril had been intended to diffuse gradually wore off; the keen interest which was awakened by the ministerial changes at the beginning of the reign of George III., which have been already mentioned, naturally prompted a variety of efforts to gratify it by a revelation of the language concerning them which was held by statesmen of different parties; and these revelations were no longer confined to yearly or monthly publications. More than one newspaper had of late adopted the practice of publishing what it affirmed to be a correct report of the debates of the previous day, though, in fact, each journal garbled them to suit the views of the party to which it belonged, and, to quote the words of the historian of the period, "misrepresented the language and arguments of the speakers in a manner which could hardly be considered accidental."[13] The speakers on the ministerial side in the debates on the Middlesex election had been especial objects of these misrepresentations; and, at the beginning of 1771, one of that party, Colonel Onslow, M.P. for Guilford, brought the subject before the House, complaining that many speeches, and his own among them, had been misrepresented by two newspapers which he named, and that "the practice had got to an infamous height, so that it had become absolutely necessary either to punish the offenders or to revise the standing orders."[14] And he accordingly moved "that the publication of the newspapers of which he complained was a contempt of the orders and a breach of the privileges of the House, and that the printers be ordered to attend the House at its next sitting." The habitual unfairness of the reports was admitted by the Opposition; but the publishers complained of evidently felt assured of their sympathy (which, indeed, was sufficiently, and not very decorously, shown by its leaders inflicting on the House no fewer than twenty-three divisions in a single night), and, relying on their countenance, they paid no attention to the order of the House. A fresh order for their arrest having been issued, the Sergeant-at-arms reported that he had been unable to execute it, by reason of their absence from their homes; on which the House, not disposed to allow itself to be thus trifled with, now addressed his Majesty with a request that he would issue his royal proclamation for their apprehension. And Colonel Onslow made a fresh motion, with a similar complaint of the publishers of six more newspapers— "three brace," as he described them in language more sportsman like than parliamentary. Similar orders for their appearance and, when these were disregarded, for their apprehension, were issued. And at last one of those who had been mentioned in the royal proclamation, Mr. Wheble, printer of the *Middlesex Journal*, was apprehended by an officer named Carpenter, and carried before the sitting magistrate at Guildhall, who, by a somewhat whimsical coincidence, happened to be Alderman Wilkes. Wilkes not only discharged him, on the ground that there was "no legal cause of complaint against him," but when Wheble, in retaliation, made a formal complaint of the assault committed on him by Carpenter in arresting him, bound Wheble over to prosecute, and Carpenter to answer the complaint, at the next quarter sessions, and then reported what he had done in an official Letter to the Secretary of State. Thomson, another printer, was in like manner arrested; and, when brought before Mr. Oliver, another alderman, was discharged by him. And when, a day or two afterward, a third (Mr. Miller) was apprehended by Whetham, a messenger of the House of Commons, Mr. Brass Crosby, the Lord Mayor, and the two Aldermen, signed a warrant committing Whetham to prison for assaulting Miller. Whetham was bailed by the Sergeant-at-arms, who reported what had occurred to the House; and the House, as the Lord Mayor and Alderman Oliver were members of it, as representatives for London and Honiton, ordered that they should attend the House in their places, to explain their conduct, and that Mr. Wilkes should attend at the bar of the House. Wilkes, declining to recognize the validity of the resolutions which had seated Colonel Luttrell for Middlesex, refused compliance with such an order, writing a letter to the Speaker, in which he "observed that no notice was taken of him as a member of the House; and that the Speaker's order did not require him to attend in his place." And he "demanded his seat in Parliament, and promised, when he had been admitted to his seat, to give the House a most exact detail of his conduct." But the Lord Mayor pleaded the charters of the City as a justification of his act in releasing a citizen of London who had been arrested on a warrant which had not been backed by a City magistrate, and demanded to be heard by counsel in support of his plea. His demand, however, was refused, and he and Alderman Oliver were committed to the Tower; but, as if the ministers were afraid of re-opening the question of Colonel Luttrell's election for Middlesex, they evaded taking notice of Wilkes's disobedience to their order by a singularly undignified expedient, issuing a fresh order for his appearance on the 8th of April, and adjourning till the 9th.

The ministers now moved the appointment of a select committee to investigate the whole affair; and the committee, before the end of the month, made an elaborate report, which, however, abstained from all mention of the offence committed by the printers, and confined itself to an assertion that "the power and authority of the House to compel the attendance of any commoner had ever extended as well to the City of London, without exception on account of charters from the crown or any pretence of separate jurisdiction, as to every other part of the realm." And this assertion may be regarded as having been uphold by the refusal of the judges to release the Lord Mayor and Alderman when they sued out writs of *habeas corpus*; and they consequently remained prisoners in the Tower till they were released by the prorogation.

But with this report of the committee the matter was suffered to drop. The transaction had caused almost unprecedented excitement, which was not confined to the City, for the grand-juries of many English counties and a committee of the Dublin merchants showed their sympathy with the Opposition by sending up addresses to the imprisoned City magistrates; and the ministers had a prudent fear of keeping alive an agitation which had not been always free from danger to the public tranquillity.[15] In effect, the victory remained with the Opposition. No farther attempt was made to punish any of the printers; and, though the standing orders which forbid such publication have never been formally repealed, ever since that time the publishers of newspapers and other periodicals have been in the constant habit of giving regular details of the proceedings of both Houses of Parliament. And one enterprising publisher, Mr. Hansard, has for many years published a complete record of the debates in both Houses, which is continually appealed to in the Houses themselves, by members of both parties, as a manual of political and parliamentary history.

The practice, as it now prevails, is one of the many instances of the practical wisdom with which this nation often deals with difficult subjects.

The standing order is retained as an instrument which, in certain cases, it may possibly be expedient to employ; as, in fact, it has been employed in one or two instances in the present reign, when matters have been under consideration which, however necessary to be discussed, were of such a nature that the publication of the details into which some speakers deemed it desirable to go was regarded by others as calculated to be offensive to the taste, if not injurious to the morals, of the community at large. But the very fact of such an occasional enforcement of the standing orders under very peculiar circumstances implies a recognition of the propriety of its more ordinary violation; of the principle that publication ought to be the general rule, and secrecy the unusual exception. And, indeed, it is, probably, no exaggeration to say that such publication is not only valuable, as the best and chief means of the political education of the people out-of-doors, but is indispensable to the working of our parliamentary system such as it has now become. The successive Reform Bills, which have placed the electoral power in the hands of so vast a body of constituents as was never imagined in the last century, have evidently regarded the possession by the electors of a perfect knowledge of the language held and the votes given by their representatives as indispensable to the proper exercise of the franchises which they have conferred. And, even if there had previously been no means provided for their acquisition of such information, it is certain that the electors would never have consented to be long kept in the dark on subjects of such interest. In another point of view, the publication of the debates is equally desirable, in the interest of the members themselves, whether leaders or followers of the different parties. Not to mention the stimulus that it affords to the cultivation of eloquence—an incentive to which even those least inclined or accustomed to put themselves forward are not entirely insensible—it enables the ministers to vindicate their measures to the nation at large, the leaders of the Opposition to explain their objections or resistance to those measures in their own persons, and not through the hired agency of pamphleteers, and each humbler member to prove to his constituents the fidelity with which he has acted up to the principles his assertion of which induced them to confide their interests and those of the kingdom to his judgment and integrity. Secrecy and mystery may serve, or be supposed to serve, the interests of arbitrary rulers; perfect openness is the only principle on which a free constitution can be maintained and a free people governed.

It seems convenient to take all the measures which, in this first portion of the reign before us, affected the proceedings or constitution of Parliament together; and, indeed, one enactment of great importance, which was passed in 1770, it is hardly unreasonable to connect in some degree with the decision of the House which adjudged the seat for Middlesex to Colonel Luttrell. Ever since the year 1704 it had been regarded as a settled point that the House of Commons had the exclusive right of determining every question concerning the election of its members. But it was equally notorious that it had exercised that right in a manner which violated every principle of justice and even of decency. Election petitions were decided by the entire House, and were almost invariably treated as party questions, in which impartiality was not even professed. Thirty years before, the Prime-minister himself (Sir Robert Walpole) had given notice to his supporters that "no quarter was to be given in election petitions;" and it was a division on one petition which eventually drove him from office. There was not even a pretence made of deciding according to evidence, for few of the members took the trouble to hear it. A few years after the time of which we are speaking, Lord George Germaine thus described the mode of proceeding which had previously prevailed: "The managers of petitions did not ask those on whose support they calculated to attend at the examination of witnesses, but only to let them know where they might be found when the question was going to be put, that they might be able to send them word in time for the division." The practice had become a public scandal, by which the constituencies and the House itself suffered equally—the constituencies, inasmuch as they were liable to be represented by one who was in fact only the representative of a minority; the House itself, since its title to public confidence could have no solid or just foundation but such as was derived from its members being in every instance the choice of the majority. Yet, so long as petitions were judged by the whole House, there seemed no chance of the abuse being removed, the number of judges conferring the immunity of shamelessness on each individual. To remedy such a state of things, in the spring of 1770 Mr. G. Grenville brought in a bill which provided for the future trial of all such petitions by a select committee of fifteen members, thirteen of whom should be chosen by ballot, one by the sitting member whose seat was petitioned against, and one by the petitioner. The members of the committee were to take an oath to do justice similar to that taken by jurymen in the courts of law; and the committee was to have power to compel the attendance of witnesses, to examine them on oath, and to enforce the production of all necessary papers; it was also to commence its sittings within twenty-four hours of its appointment, and to sit from day to day till it should be prepared to present its report. It was not to the credit of the ministers that they made the passing of such a bill a party question. The abuse which it was designed to remedy was notorious, and Mr. Grenville did not exaggerate its magnitude when he declared that, "if it were not checked, it must end in the ruin of public liberty." He was supported by Burke, and by two lawyers, Mr. Dunning and Mr. Wedderburn, both destined to rise to some of the highest offices in their profession; but he was opposed by the Attorney-general, by Lord North, as leader of the House, and by Mr. Fox—not yet turned into a patriot by Lord North's dismissal of him from office. The debates, both in the whole House and in committee, were long and earnest. Some of the ministerial underlings were not ashamed to deny the necessity of any alteration in the existing practice; but their more favorite argument was founded on the impropriety of the House "delegating its authority to a committee," which was asserted to be "an essential alteration of the constitution of the House of Commons." Lord North himself had too keen an instinct of propriety to deny the existence of a great evil, and contented himself with pleading for time for farther consideration; while the Attorney-general confined his objections to some details of the bill, which it would be easy to amend. Others, with too accurate a foresight, doubted the efficacy of the measure, and prophesied that the additional sanction of the oath, by which its framer hoped to bind the committees to a just and honest decision, would, "like oaths of office and Custom-house oaths, soon fall into matters of form, and lose all sanction, and so make bad worse." On the other hand, besides the arguments founded on the admitted greatness of the evil to be remedied, it was shown that the institution of committees, such as the bill proposed the appointment of, was sanctioned by numerous precedents; and though the committees—sometimes consisting of as many as two hundred members—were by far too large to make it probable that all would bestow a careful attention on the whole case, there was "nothing in the journals of the House to show that their decisions were not regarded as final, or as requiring no subsequent confirmation from the whole House." Generally speaking, Lord North could trust the steadiness of his majority; but, to his great surprise, on this occasion he found himself deserted by the country gentlemen, who voted in a body for the bill, although their spokesman, Sir W. Bagot, had been in no slight degree offended by some remarks of Burke, who, with a strange imprudence, had claimed a monopoly of the title of "friends of the constitution" for himself and his party, and had sneered at the country gentlemen, as "statesmen of a very different description, though, by a late description given of them, a Tory was now the best species of Whig." And the union of the two bodies proved irresistible; the bill was carried by a majority of sixty-two, and the government did not venture to carry on their resistance to it in the House of Lords, any interference by which would, indeed, have been resented by the Commons, as a violation of their privileges.

At first the duration of the bill was limited to seven years; but in 1774 it was made perpetual by a still larger majority, the experience of its working having converted many who had at first opposed it, but who now bore willing testimony to its efficacy. Unhappily, though the House could make the bill perpetual, at least till formally repealed, it could not invest its good effects with equal durability. After a time, the same complaints were advanced against the decision of election committees that had formerly been employed to discredit the judgments of the whole House. The success or failure of a petition again became a party question; and as in a committee of an odd number the ministerialists or the Opposition must inevitably have a majority of at least one member, before the end of the reign it had become as easy to foretell the result of a petition from the composition of the committee as it had been in the time of Walpole. And it was with the approval of almost all parties—an approval extorted only by the absolute necessity of the case—that, after one or two modifications of Mr. Grenville's act had been tried, Mr. Disraeli induced the House to surrender altogether its privilege of judging of elections, and to submit the investigations of petitions on such subjects to the only tribunal sufficiently above suspicion to command and retain the confidence of the nation, the judges of the high courts of law.

We shall probably be doing the House of Commons of the day no injustice, if we surmise that the degree in which public attention had recently been directed to the representation, and the interest which the people were beginning to show in the purity of elections, as the principle on the maintenance of which the very liberties of all might depend, had some share in leading the House to establish the wholly new, though most necessary, precedent of punishing a constituency for habitual and inveterate corruption. It may be called the first fruits of Mr. Grenville's act. At the end of the same year in which that statute had been passed, a select committee had sat to try the merits of a petition which complained of an undue return for the borough of New Shoreham. And its report brought to light an organized system of corruption, which there was too much reason to fear was but a specimen of that which prevailed in many other boroughs as yet undetected. It appeared from the report, founded as it was on the evidence and confession of many of the persons inculpated, that a society had long existed in New Shoreham, entitled the Christian Club, which, under this specious name, was instituted, as they frankly acknowledged, for the express purpose of getting as much money as possible at every election from the candidates they brought in. The members of the club were under an oath and bond of £500 not to divulge the secrets of the club, and to be bound by the majority. On every election, a committee of five persons was nominated by the club to treat with the candidates for as much money as they could get. And, in pursuance of this system, when, on the death of Sir Stephen Cornish, one of the members for the borough, five candidates offered themselves to supply the vacancy, this committee of five opened negotiations with them all. The offers of the rival purchasers were liberal enough. One (General Smith) proposed to buy the entire club in the lump for £3000, adding a promise to build 600 tons of shipping in the town. A second (a Mr. Rumbold) was willing to give every freeman £35; and his offer was accepted by the committee, who, however, cautioned him that no freeman was entitled to the money who was not a member of the Christian Club. He willingly agreed to this limitation of his expenditure, and both he and the club regarded the matter as settled. He paid every freeman who belonged to the club his stipulated bribe, and on the polling day they tendered eighty-seven votes in his favor, the entire constituency being something under one hundred and fifty. The general, finding his £3000 declined, did not go to the poll; but a Mr. Purling and Mr. James did, the latter polling only four votes, the former only thirty-seven. What bribe Mr. Purling had given was never revealed; but by some means or other he had contrived to render himself the most acceptable of all the candidates to Mr. Roberts, the returning officer. Roberts had himself been a member of the Christian Club, but had quarrelled with it, and on the day of the election, as Rumbold's voters came up, he administered to each of them the oath against bribery. They took it without scruple; but he took it on himself to pronounce seventy-six of them disqualified, and to refuse their votes; and, having thus reduced Mr. Rumbold's voters to eleven, he returned Mr. Purling as duly elected.

Mr. Rumbold, not unnaturally, petitioned against such a return; when Mr. Roberts admitted the facts alleged against him, but pleaded that he had acted under the advice of counsel, who had assured him that it was within his own discretion to admit or to refuse any votes that might be tendered, and that he might lawfully refuse any "which in his own mind he thought illegal." It is a striking proof of the laxity which prevailed on every quarter in electioneering practices, that the House, to a great extent, admitted his justification or excuse as valid. By a strange stretch of lenity, they gave him credit for an honest intention, and contented themselves with ordering him to be reprimanded by the Speaker. But the case of the bribed freemen and of the borough generally was too gross to be screened by any party. All agreed that the borough must be regarded as incurably corrupt, and deserving of heavy punishment. The Attorney-general was ordered to prosecute the five members of the managing committee for "an illegal and corrupt conspiracy;" and a bill was brought in to disfranchise and declare forever incapable of voting at any election eighty-one freemen who had been proved to have received bribes, and to punish the borough itself, by extending the right of voting at future elections to all the freeholders in the rape of Bramber, the district of Sussex in which New Shoreham lies, an arrangement which reduced the borough itself to comparative insignificance. Mr. Fox opposed the bill, on the ground that the offence committed could be sufficiently punished by the ordinary courts of law. But he stood alone in his resistance; the bill was passed, and a salutary precedent was established; the penalty inflicted on New Shoreham being for many years regarded as the most proper punishment for all boroughs in which similar practices were proved to prevail.

And it might have continued to be thought so, had corruption been confined to the smaller boroughs; but there was no doubt that in many large towns corruption was equally prevalent and inveterate, while there were also many counties in which the cost of a contest was by far too large to be accounted for by any legitimate causes of expenditure. And consequently, as time wore on, severer measures were considered necessary. Some boroughs were deprived of the right of election altogether; in others, whose population or constituency was too numerous to make their permanent disfranchisement advisable, the writ was suspended for a time, that its suspension might serve both as a punishment and as a warning, a practice which is still not unfrequently adopted. But no plan could be devised for dealing with the evil in counties, till what seemed hopeless to achieve by direct legislation was, in a great degree, effected by the indirect operation of the Reform Bill of 1832. The shortening of the duration of an election, which was henceforth concluded in a single day, and the multiplication of polling places, which rendered it impossible to ascertain the progress of the different candidates till the close of the poll, were provisions having an inevitable and most salutary effect in diminishing alike the temptation to bribe on the part of the candidate, and the opportunity of enhancing the value of his vote by the elector. The vast increase of newspapers, by diffusing political education and stimulating political discussion, has had, perhaps, a still greater influence in the same direction. And, as bribery could only be brought to bear on electors too ignorant to estimate the importance of the exercise of the franchise by any higher test than the personal advantage it might bring to themselves, it is to the general diffusion of education among the poorer classes, and their gradually improved and improving intelligence that a complete eradication of electoral corruption can alone be looked for.

Notes:

[Footnote 1:] "Constitutional History," vol. iii., p. 380; ed. 3, 1832. The first edition was published in 1827.

[Footnote 2:] Grampound. Corrupt voters had been disfranchised in New Shoreham as early as 1771, and the franchise of the borough of Cricklade had been transferred to the adjoining hundreds in 1782.

[Footnote 3:] Parliament was dissolved March 19. Lord Bute succeeded Lord Holdernesse March 25.

[Footnote 4:] The greater part of Lord Bute's colleagues did, in fact, retain their offices. Lord Egremont and Lord Halifax continued to be Secretaries of State; Lord Henley (afterward Lord Northington) retained the Great Seal; Lord North and Sir John Turner remained as Lords of the Treasury; and Mr. Yorke and Sir Fletcher Norton were still Attorney and Solicitor General.

[Footnote 5:] Parliament was prorogued April 19, and *The North Briton* (No. 45) was published April 23.

[Footnote 6:] A letter of the Prince Consort examines the principle of ministerial responsibility with so remarkable a clearness of perception and distinctness of explanation, that we may be excused for quoting it at length: "The notion that the responsibility of his advisers impairs the monarch's dignity and importance is a complete mistake. Here we have no law of ministerial responsibility, for the simple reason that we have no written constitution; but this responsibility flows as a logical necessity from the dignity of the crown and of the sovereign. 'The King can do no wrong,' says the legal axiom, and hence it follows that somebody must be responsible for his measures, if these be contrary to law or injurious to the country's welfare. Ministers here are not responsible *quâ* ministers, that is, *quâ* officials (as such they are responsible to the crown), but they are responsible to Parliament and the people, or the country, as 'advisers of the crown.' Any one of them may advise the crown, and whoever does so is responsible to the country for the advice he has given. The so-called accountability of ministers to Parliament does not arise out of an abstract principle of responsibility, but out of the practical necessity which they are under of obtaining the consent of Parliament to legislation and the voting of taxes, and, as an essential to this end, of securing its confidence. In practice, ministers are liable to account for the way and manner in which they have administered the laws which they, conjointly with the Parliament, have made, and for the way they have expended the moneys that have been voted for definite objects. They are bound to furnish explanations, to justify their proceedings, to satisfy reasonable scruples, and the answer, 'We have, as dutiful subjects, obeyed the sovereign,' will not be accepted. 'Have you acted upon conviction, or have you not?' is the question. 'If you have not, then you are civil servants of the crown, who counsel and do what you consider wrong or unjust, with a view to retain your snug places or to win the favor of the sovereign.' And this being so, Parliament withdraws its confidence from them. Herein, too, lies that ministerial power of which sovereigns are so much afraid. They can say, 'We will not do this or that which the sovereign wishes, because we cannot be responsible for it.' But why should a sovereign see anything here to be afraid of? To him it is, in truth, the best of safeguards. A really loyal servant should do nothing for which he is not prepared to answer, even though his master desires it. This practical responsibility is of the utmost advantage to the sovereign. Make independence, not subservience, the essential of service, and you compel the minister to keep his soul free toward the sovereign, you ennoble his advice, you make him staunch and patriotic, while time-servers, the submissive instruments of a monarch's extreme wishes and commands, may lead, and often have led, him to destruction.

"But to revert to the law of responsibility. This ought not to be in effect a safeguard for law itself. As such, it is superfluous in this country, where law reigns, and where it would never occur to any one that this could be otherwise. But upon the Continent it is of the highest importance;

as, where the government is an outgrowth of a relation of supremacy and subordination between sovereign and subject, and the servant, trained in ideas natural to this relation, does not know which to obey, the law of the sovereign, the existence of such a law would deprive him of the excuse which, should he offend the law, and so be guilty of a crime, is ready to his hand in the phrase, 'The sovereign ordered it so, I have merely obeyed,' while it would be a protection to the sovereign that his servants, if guilty of a crime, should not be able to saddle him with the blame of it." —*Life of the Prince Consort*, v., 262.

[Footnote 7:] "Lives of the Lord Chancellors," c. cxliii.

[Footnote 8:] Indeed, the opinion which Lord Campbell thus expresses is manifestly at variance with that which he had previously pronounced in his life of Lord Northington, where he praised the House of Lords for "very properly rejecting the bill passed by the Commons declaring general warrants to be illegal, leaving this question to be decided (as it was, satisfactorily) by the Courts of Common Law."

[Footnote 9:] From a speech of Mr. Grenville delivered at a later period (February 3, 1769, "Parliamentary History," xvi., 548), it appears that the Secretaries of State who signed this general warrant did so against their own judgment. "They repeatedly proposed to have Wilkes's name inserted in the warrant of apprehension, but were overruled by the lawyers and clerks of the office, who insisted that they could not depart from the long-established precedents and course of proceeding." And in one of these debates, Mr. Pitt, while denouncing with great severity Grenville's conduct in procuring the issue of this particular warrant, was driven to a strange confession of his own inconsistency, since he was forced to admit that, while Secretary of State, he had issued more than one general warrant in exactly similar form.

[Footnote 10:] Strange to say, it does not seem absolutely certain that Wilkes was the author of the "Essay on Woman." Horace Walpole eventually learned, or believed that he had learned, that the author was a Mr. Thomas Potter. (See Walpole's "George III.," i., 310; and Cunningham's "Note on his Correspondence," iv., 126.)

[Footnote 11:] These are the words of the resolution.—*Parliamentary History*, xvi., 537. But it does not appear what the three libels were. The "Essay on Woman" was one, the paraphrase of "Veni Creator" was a second; no third of that character is mentioned.

[Footnote 12:] The last resolution is approved by Mr. Hallam. "If a few precedents were to determine all controversies of constitutional law, it is plain enough from the journals that the House has assumed the power of incapacitation. But as such authority is highly dangerous and unnecessary for any good purpose, and as, according to all legal rules, so extraordinary a power could not be supported except by a sort of prescription that cannot be shown, the final resolution of the House of Commons, which condemned the votes passed in times of great excitement, appears far more consonant to first principles."—*Constitutional History*, iii., 357.

[Footnote 13:] Adolphus, "History of England," i., 484.

[Footnote 14:] An idea of the license which the newspapers complained of had permitted themselves at this time may be derived from the manner in which one of them had introduced a speech of Mr. Jeremiah Dyson, M.P. for Weymouth, and a Commissioner of the Treasury: "Jeremiah Weymouth, the d——n of the kingdom, spoke as follows." And it may seem that the Opposition (for the affair was made a party question) can hardly be acquitted of a discreditable indifference to the dignity of the House in supporting a resolution of Colonel Barré, that "Jeremiah Weymouth, the d——n of this kingdom, is not a member of this House." On which the previous question was moved by the ministers, and carried by 120 to 38.—*Parliamentary History*, xvii., 78. And an instance of rather the opposite kind, of the guarded way in which the most respectable publications were as yet accustomed to relate the transactions of Parliament, may be gathered from the account of the proceedings in the case of Wilkes, given in the "Annual Register" for 1770—drawn up, probably, by Burke himself—in which Lord Camden is only mentioned as "a great law lord;" Lord Chatham as "Lord C——m;" Lord Rockingham as "a noble Marquis who lately presided at the head of public affairs;" the King as "the K——;" Parliament as "P.;" and the House of Commons as the "H. of C."—*Annual Register*, 1770, pp. 59-67.

[Footnote 15:] On more than one occasion there had been disturbances in the City, and in the streets adjacent to the Houses of Parliament, which were little short of riot. One day the mob paraded effigies of the principal ministers, which, after hanging and beheading them, they committed to the flames with great uproar. On another day Mr. Charles Fox (as yet a vehement Tory) complained to the House that the mob in Palace Yard had insulted him, breaking the glasses of his chariot, and pelting him with oranges, stones, etc.—*Parliamentary History*, xvii., 163.

CHAPTER II

The Regency Bill.—The Ministry of 1766 lay an Embargo on Corn.—An Act of Indemnity is Passed.—The *Nullum Tempus* Act concerning Crown Property; it is sought to Extend it to Church Property, but the Attempt fails.—The Royal Marriage Act.—The Lords amend a Bill imposing Export Duties, etc., on Corn.

    The prosecution of Wilkes was not the only act of Mr. Grenville's administration which excited both the Parliament and the people. In 1764 the King was attacked by a serious illness, and, as the Prince of Wales was an infant scarcely two years old, it was manifestly necessary to make arrangements for a Regency, in the event of the throne becoming vacant while the heir was still a minor. A similar necessity had arisen in the preceding reign on the death of the present King's father, and a bill had accordingly been introduced by Mr. Pelham, the minister of the day, which, in the event of the reigning sovereign dying during the minority of the boy who had now become the immediate heir to the throne, vested both the guardianship of his person and the Regency of the kingdom in his mother, the Princess Dowager of Wales, who, however, in the latter capacity, was only to act with the advice of a council, composed of her brother-in-law, the Duke of Cumberland, and nine principal officers of state. It was not concealed by either the King or the Duke that they would have preferred a different arrangement, one which would have conferred an uncontrolled Regency on the Duke himself; but the bill was passed by great majorities in both Houses, and served in some respects as a model for that which was now to be brought forward, the difference being that the Regent was not to be expressly named in it. To quote the words of the royal speech, the King "proposed to the consideration of the two Houses whether, under the present circumstances, it would not be expedient to vest in him the power of appointing from time to time, by instrument in writing under his sign-manual, either the Queen or any other member of the royal family usually residing in Great Britain, to be the guardian of the person of his successor, and the Regent of these kingdoms, until such successor should attain the age of eighteen years, subject to such restrictions and regulations as were specified and contained in an act passed on a similar occasion in the fourteenth year of the late King; the Regent so appointed to be assisted by a council, composed of the several persons who, by reason of their dignities and offices, were constituted members of the council established by that act, together with those whom the Parliament might think proper to leave to his nomination."

It may be doubted whether such a power as his Majesty desired was quite consistent with the principles of the constitution. Parliament had, indeed, granted Henry VIII. the still greater power of nominating a series of successors; but the appointment which he consequently made by will was eventually superseded, when, on the failure of his immediate descendants, the representative of his elder sister, whom he had passed over, was seated on the throne, to the exclusion of the descendants of his younger sister, to whom he had given the preference. In France, the last two kings, Louis XIII. and XIV., had both, when on their death-beds, assumed the right of making the arrangements for the Regency which would become necessary, the heir to the throne being in each case a minor; but in each instance the arrangements which they had made were disregarded.

However, on the present occasion the minister (who must be taken to have framed the King's speech) and the Parliament agreed in the propriety of conferring the nomination of the Regent on the King himself;[16] and the bill might have passed almost without notice, had it not been for a strange display of the Prime-minister's ill-temper and mismanagement. Mr. Grenville was at all times uncourtly and dictatorial in his manner, even to the King himself; he was also of a suspicious disposition; and though he was universally believed to have owed his promotion to his present office to the recommendation of Lord Bute,[17] he was extremely jealous of his predecessor. He professed to believe, and probably did believe, that the King was still greatly under Lord Bute's influence (though, in fact, they had never met since that minister had quitted the Treasury), that Lord Bute was still as closely connected with the Princess of Wales as scandal had formerly reported him to be, and that George III., under the pressure of their combined influence, would be induced to name his mother rather than his wife as the future Regent. And he was so entirely swayed by this ridiculous and wholly groundless fear, that, when the bill to give effect to the royal recommendation was introduced into the House of Lords, he instigated one of his friends to raise the question who were included in the general term "the royal family," which Lord Halifax, as Secretary of State, answered by saying that he regarded it as meaning "those only who were in order of succession to the throne." Such a definition would have excluded the Queen as effectually as the Princess Dowager; and when Mr. Grenville found the peers reluctant to accept this view (which, indeed, his own Lord Chancellor pronounced untenable), he then sent another of his colleagues to represent to the King that his mother was so unpopular that, even if the Lords should pass the bill in such a form as rendered her eligible for nomination, the Commons would introduce a clause to exclude her by name. With great unwillingness, and, it is said, not without tears, George III. consented to the bill being so drawn as to exclude her, and it passed the Lords in such a form. But when it reached the Commons it was found that if the leaders of the Opposition hated Bute much, they hated Grenville more. They moved the insertion of the name of the Princess Dowager as one of the members of the royal family whom the King might nominate Regent, if it should please him. Even Grenville had not the boldness publicly to disparage his royal master's royal mother; the Princess's name was inserted by a unanimous vote in the list of those from whom the King was empowered to select the Regent, and the amendment was gladly accepted by the House of Lords.[18]

In spite, however, of the unanimity of the two Houses on the question, it will probably be thought that the authors of the amendment, by which it was proposed to address the King with an entreaty to name in the bill the person to whom he desired to intrust the Regency, acted more in the spirit of the constitution than those who were contented that the name should be omitted; indeed, that statesmen of the present century agree in holding that an arrangement of such importance should be made by the Houses of Parliament, in concurrence with the sovereign, and not by the sovereign alone, is shown by the steps taken to provide for a Regency in the event of the demise of the reigning sovereign while the heir was a minor, in the last and in the present reign, the second bill (that of 1840) being in this respect of the greater authority, since Lord Melbourne, the Prime-minister, did not propose it without previously securing the approval of the Duke of Wellington, in his character of leader of the Opposition.

We pass over for a moment the administration of Lord Rockingham, as we have already passed over the taxation of our North American Colonies by Mr. Grenville, because it will be more convenient to take all the transactions relating to that subject together when we arrive at the time when the troubles arising out of the policy of the different administrations toward those Colonies were brought to a head by the breaking out of civil war. Lord Rockingham's ministry, which succeeded Mr. Grenville's, had, as is well known, but a brief existence, and was replaced by the cabinet so whimsically composed by Mr. Pitt, who reserved to himself the office of Privy Seal, with the Earldom of Chatham; the Duke of Grafton being the nominal head of the Treasury, but the direction of affairs being wholly in the hands of the new Earl, till the failure of his health compelled his temporary retirement from public life. Lord Chatham was brother-in-law to Mr. Grenville, to whom in the occasional arrogance and arbitrariness of his disposition he bore some resemblance; and one of the earliest acts of his administration, when coupled with the language which he held on the subject in the House of Lords, displayed that side of his character in a very conspicuous light.

The summer of 1766 had been unusually wet and cold, both at home and abroad, and the harvest had, in consequence, been so deficient as to cause a very general apprehension of scarcity, while rumors were spread that the high prices which the shortness of the crops could not fail to produce were artificially raised by the selfish covetousness of some of the principal corn-dealers, who were buying up all the grain which came into the market, and storing it, with the object of making an exorbitant profit out of the necessities of the consumer, not only at home but abroad. The poorer classes, seeing themselves, as they believed, threatened with famine, rose in riotous crowds, in some places attacking the barns in which the corn was stored, and threatening destruction to both the storehouses and the owners. The ministry first tried to repress the discontent by the issue of a proclamation against "forestallers and regraters," framed in the language and spirit of the Middle Ages; and, when that proved ineffectual to restore confidence, they issued an Order in Council absolutely prohibiting the exportation of any kind of grain, and authorizing the detention of any vessels lying in any British harbor which might be loaded with such a cargo. Our annals furnished no instance of such an embargo having been laid on any article of commerce in time of peace; but the crisis was difficult, the danger to the tranquillity of the kingdom was great and undeniable, the necessity for instant action seemed urgent, and probably few would have been inclined to cavil at Lord Chatham's assertion, that the embargo "was an act of power which, during the recess of Parliament, was justifiable on the ground of necessity," had the ministry at once called Parliament together to sanction the measure by an act of indemnity. But Lord Chatham was at all times inclined to carry matters with a high hand, and willingly adopted the opinion advanced by the Chancellor (Lord Northington), that "the measure was strictly legal, and that no indemnity was necessary." Lord Northington's language on the subject Lord Campbell describes as "exhibiting his characteristic rashness and recklessness, which seemed to be aggravated by age and experience,"[19] and the censure does not seem too severe, since he presently "went so far as to maintain that the crown had a right to interfere, even against a positive act of parliament, and that proof of the necessity amounted to a legal justification." But, however ill-considered his language may have been, Lord Chatham adopted it, and acted on it so far as to decline calling the Parliament together before the appointed time, though, when the Houses did meet, he allowed General Conway, as Secretary of State, to introduce a bill of indemnity in the House of Commons. It was warmly opposed in that House, partly on the ground that, if such a measure as the embargo had been necessary, it would have been easy to have assembled Parliament before the Order in Council was issued (for, in fact, the proclamation against forestallers and regraters had been issued on the 10th of September, when Parliament, if not farther prorogued, would have met within a week). But on that same day Parliament was farther prorogued from the 16th of September till the 11th of November,[20] and it was not till after that prorogation, on the 24th of September, that the Order in Council was issued.

In the House of Lords it seems to have been admitted that the embargo was, under all the circumstances, not only desirable, but "indispensably necessary."[21] But the Opposition in that House, being led by a great lawyer (Chief-justice Lord Mansfield), took a wider view of the whole case; and, after denouncing the long prorogation of Parliament as having been so culpably advised that there was no way left of meeting the emergency but by an interposition of the royal power, directed the principal weight of their argument against the doctrine of the existence of any dispensing power. It was urged that the late Order in Council could only be justified by "the general proposition that of any, and, if of any, of every, act of parliament the King, with the advice of the Privy Council, may suspend the execution and effect whenever his Majesty, so advised, judges it necessary for the immediate safety of the people." And this proposition was denounced as utterly inconsistent with the principles of the Revolution, which had been "nothing but a most lawless and wicked invasion of the rights of the crown," if such a dispensing power were really one of the lawful prerogatives of the sovereign. Reference was made to the powers in more than one instance, and especially in the case of ship-money claimed and exercised by Charles I.; and it was affirmed that "the dispensing and suspending power, and that of raising money without the consent of Parliament, were precisely alike, and stood on the very same ground. They were born twins; they lived together, and together were buried in the same grave at the Revolution, past all power of resurrection." It was even argued that the dispensing or suspending power was yet more dangerous than that of raising money without a Parliamentary vote, since it was a power which might do the most mischief, and with the greatest speed, so many were the subjects which it included. It would be a return to the maxims of the idolators of prerogative as understood in those earlier days, that is, of absolute and arbitrary power, *a Deo Rex, a Rege Lex*. It was farther argued that, unless it could be said that the moment Parliament breaks up the King stands in its place, and that the continuance of acts is consigned into his hands, he cannot of right suspend any more than he can make laws, both acts requiring the same power. The law is above the King, and the crown as well as the subject is bound by it as much during the recess as in the session of Parliament; and therefore the wisdom of the constitution has excluded every discretion in the crown over a positive statute, and has emancipated Parliament from the royal prerogative, leaving the power of suspension, which is but another name for a temporary repeal, to reside where the legislative power is lodged—that is, in King, Lords, and Commons, who together constitute the only supreme authority of this government. Precedents were cited to prove that in former times different ministries had avoided thus taking the law into their own hands, as when, in 1709 and again in 1756, there was a similar apprehension of scarcity, even though both those years were years of war. And the Bill of Rights was quoted as the statute in which every sort of dispensing power was condemned, though, as exercised by James II., it had only been exerted in dispensing with penal laws and remitting penalties.

"Finally," said one speaker, who perhaps was Lord Mansfield himself, "he is not a moderate minister who would rashly decide in favor of prerogative in a question where the rights of Parliament are involved, nor a prudent minister who, even in a doubtful case, commits the prerogative, by a wanton experiment, to what degree the people will bear the extent of it. The opposite course was that by which a minister would consult the best interests of the crown, as well as of the people. The safety of the crown, as well as the security of the subject, requires the closing up of every avenue that can lead to tyranny."[22]

These arguments prevailed, and the indemnity bill was passed, to quote the words of the "Annual Register"—at that time written by Burke—"very much to the satisfaction of the public." And that it should have been so accepted is creditable to the good-sense of both parties. The precedent which was thus established does, indeed, seem to rest on a principle indispensable to the proper working of a constitutional government. In so extensive an empire as ours, it is scarcely possible that sudden emergencies, requiring the instant application of some remedy, should not at times arise; and, unless Parliament be sitting at the time, such can only be adequately dealt with if the ministers of the crown have the courage to take such steps as are necessary, whether by the suspension of a law or by any other expedient, on their own responsibility, trusting in their ability to satisfy the Parliament, instantly convoked to receive their explanation, of the necessity or wisdom of their proceedings; and in the candor of the Parliament to recognize, if not the judiciousness of their action, at all events the good faith in which it has been taken, and the honest, patriotic intention which has dictated it.

The establishment of the obligation instantly to submit the question to the judgment of Parliament will hardly be denied to be a sufficient safeguard against the ministerial abuse of such a power; and the instances in which such a power has since been exercised, coupled with the sanction of such exercise by Parliament, are a practical approval and ratification by subsequent Parliaments of the course that was now adopted.[23]

The next year a not very creditable job of the ministry led to the enactment of a statute of great importance to all holders of property which had ever belonged to the crown. In the twenty-first year of James I. a bill had been passed giving a secure tenure of their estates to all grantees of crown lands whose possession of them had lasted sixty years. The Houses had desired to make the enactment extend to all future as well as to all previous grants. But to this James had refused to consent; and, telling the Houses that "beggars must not be choosers," he had compelled them to content themselves with a retrospective statute. Since his time, and especially in the reigns of Charles II. and William III., the crown had been more lavish and unscrupulous than at any former period in granting away its lands and estates to favorites. And no one had been so largely enriched by its prodigality as the most grasping of William's Dutch followers, Bentinck, the founder of the English house of Portland. Among the estates which he had obtained from his royal master's favor was one which went by the name of the Honor of Penrith. Subsequent administrations had augmented the dignities and importance of his family. Their Earldom had been exchanged for a Dukedom; but the existing Duke was an opponent of the present ministry, who, to punish him, suggested to Sir James Lowther, a baronet of ancient family, and of large property in the North of England, the idea of applying to the crown for a grant of the forest of Inglewood, and of the manor of Carlisle, which hitherto had been held by Portland as belonging to the Honor of Penrith, but which, not having been expressly mentioned in the original grant by William III., it was now said had been regarded as included in the honor only by mistake. It was not denied that Portland had enjoyed the ownership of these lands for upward of seventy years without dispute; and, had the statute of James been one of continual operation, it would have been impossible to deprive him of them. But, as matters stood, the Lords of the Treasury willingly listened to the application of Sir James Lowther; they even refused permission to the Duke to examine the original deed and the other documents in the office of the surveyor, on which he professed to rely for the establishment of his right; and they granted to Sir James the lands he prayed for at a rent which could only be regarded as nominal. The injustice of the proceeding was so flagrant, that in the beginning of 1768 Sir George Savile brought in a bill to prevent any repetition of such an act by making the statute of James I.

perpetual, so that for the future a possession for sixty years should confer an indisputable and indefeasible title. The ministers opposed it with great vehemence, even taking some credit to themselves for their moderation in not requiring from the Duke a repayment of the proceeds of the lands in question for the seventy years during which he had held them. But the case was so bad that they could only defeat Sir George Savile by a side-wind and a scanty majority, carrying an amendment to defer any decision of the matter till the next session. Sir George, however, was not discouraged; he renewed his motion in 1769, when it was carried by a large majority, with an additional clause extending its operation to the Colonies in North America; and thus, in respect of its territorial rights, the crown was placed on the same footing as any private individual, and the same length of tenure which enabled a possessor to hold a property against another subject henceforth equally enabled him to hold it against the crown. The policy not less than the justice of such an enactment might have been thought to commend it to every thinking man as soon as the heat engendered by a party debate had passed away. It had merely placed the sovereign and the subject on the same footing in respect of the security which prescription gave to possession. And it might, therefore, have been thought that the vote of 1769 had settled the point in every case; since what was the law between one private individual and another, and between the sovereign and a subject, might well have been taken to be of universal application. But the ministry were strangely unwilling to recognize such a universal character in the late act, and found in the peculiar character of ecclesiastical bodies and ecclesiastical property a pretext for weakening the force of the late enactment, by denying the applicability of the principle to the claims of ecclesiastical chapters. In 1772 Mr. Henry Seymour, one of the members for Huntingdon, moved for leave to bring in a bill, which he described as one "for quieting the subjects of the realm against the dormant claims of the Church;" or, in other words, for putting the Church on the same footing with respect to property which had passed out of its possession as the crown had been placed in by the act of 1769. He contended that such a bill ought to be passed, not only on the general principle that possessors who derived their property from one source ought not to be less secure than they who derived it from another, but also on the grounds that, as ecclesiastical bodies occasionally used their power, "length of possession, which fortified and strengthened legal right and just title in every other case, did in this alone render them more weak and uncertain," from the difficulty which often occurred in finding documentary proof of very ancient titles; and that this was not an imaginary danger, since a member of the House then present had recently lost £120,000 by a bishop reviving a claim to an estate after the gentleman's family had been in undisturbed possession of it above a hundred years. The defence of the Church, however, was taken up by Mr. Skinner, Attorney-general for the Duchy of Lancaster, who argued that though, in the case of the crown, the *nullum tempus* which it had formerly claimed, and which had been put an end to in 1769, was "an engine in the hands of the strong to oppress the weak, the *nullum tempus* of the Church was a defence to the weak against the strong," as its best if not its sole security "against the encroachment of the laity." The "Parliamentary History" records that in the course of a long debate Lord North opposed the bringing in of the bill, as did "the Lord-advocate of Scotland, who gave as a reason in favor of the bill, though he voted against it, that a law of similar nature had passed in Scotland, and that the whole kingdom, clergy as well as laity, found the very best effects from it."[24] Burke argued in favor of the bill with great force, declaring that in so doing "he did not mean anything against the Church, her dignities, her honor, her privileges, or her possessions; he should wish even to enlarge them all; but this bill was to take nothing from her but the power of making herself odious." But the ministerial majority was too well disciplined to be broken, and Mr. Seymour could not even obtain leave to bring in the bill.

The year 1772 was marked by the discussion of a measure which the King seems to have regarded as one of private interest only, affecting his personal rights over his own family. But it is impossible to regard transactions which may affect the right of succession to the throne as matters of only private interest. And indeed the bill was treated as one involving a constitutional question by both sides of both Houses, and as such was discussed with remarkable earnestness, and with vehemence equalling that of any other debate which had as yet taken place since the commencement of the reign. The bill had its origin in the personal feelings of the King himself, who had been greatly annoyed at the conduct of his brother, the Duke of Cumberland, in marrying a widow of the name of Horton, daughter of Lord Irnham, and sister of the Colonel Luttrell whom the vote of the House of Commons had seated as member for Middlesex; and perhaps still more at the discovery that his other brother, the Duke of Gloucester, to whom he was greatly attached, had married another subject, the widowed Lady Waldegrave. His Majesty's dissatisfaction was, perhaps, heightened by the recollection that he himself, in early manhood, had also been strongly attracted by the charms of another subject, and had sacrificed his own inclinations to the combined considerations of pride of birth and the interests of his kingdom. And, though there was a manifest difference between the importance of the marriage of the sovereign himself and that of princes who were never likely to become sovereigns, he thought it not unreasonable that he should be empowered to exercise such a general guardianship over the entire family, of which he was the head, as might enable him to control its members in such arrangements, by making his formal sanction indispensable to the validity of any matrimonial alliances which they might desire to contract. A somewhat similar question had been raised in 1717, when George I., having quarrelled with the Prince of Wales (afterward George II.), asserted a claim to control and direct the education of all the Prince's children, and, when they should be of marriageable age, to arrange their marriages. The Prince, on the other hand, insisted on his natural and inalienable right, as their father, to have the entire government of his own offspring, a right which, as he contended, no royal prerogative could be enabled or permitted to override. That question was not, however, brought before Parliament, to which, at that time, the King could, probably, not have trusted for any leanings in his favor; but he referred it, in an informal way, to the Lord Chancellor (Lord Cowper) and the Common-law Judges. They investigated it with great minuteness. A number of precedents were adduced for the marriage and education of the members of the royal family being regulated by the sovereign, beginning with Henry III., who gave his daughter Joan, without her own consent, in marriage to the King of Scotland, and coming down to the preceding century, at the commencement of which the Council of James I. committed the Lady Arabella Stuart and Mr. Seymour to the Tower for contracting a secret marriage without the King's permission, and at the end of which King William exercised the right of selecting a tutor for the Duke of Gloucester, the son of the Princess Anne, without any consultation with the Princess herself; and finally the judges, with only two dissenting voices, expressed their conviction that the King was entitled to the prerogative which he claimed. The case does not, however, seem to have been regularly argued before them; there is no trace of their having been assisted in their deliberations by counsel on either side, and their extra-judicial opinion was clearly destitute of any formal authority;[25] so that it came before Parliament in some degree as a new question.

But George III. was not of a disposition to allow such matters to remain in doubt, and, in compliance with his desire, a bill was, in 1772, introduced by Lord Rochfort, as Secretary of State, which proposed to enact that no descendants of the late King, being children or grandchildren, and presumptive heirs of the sovereign, male or female, other than the issue of princesses who might be married into foreign families, should be capable of contracting a valid marriage without the previous consent of the reigning sovereign, signified under his sign-manual, and that any marriage contracted without such consent should be null and void. The King or the ministers apparently doubted whether Parliament could be prevailed on to make such a prohibition life-long, and therefore a clause was added which provided that if any prince or princess above the age of twenty-five years should determine to contract a marriage without such consent of the sovereign, he or she might do so on giving twelve months' notice to the Privy Council; and such marriage should be good and valid, unless, before the expiration of the twelve months, both Houses of Parliament should declare their disapproval of the marriage. The concluding clause of the bill made it felony "to presume to solemnize, or to assist, or to be present, at the celebration of any such marriage without such consent being first obtained."

The bill was stoutly resisted in both Houses at every stage, both on the ground of usage and of general principle. It was positively denied that the "sovereign's right of approving of all marriages in the royal family," which was asserted in the preamble of the bill, was either founded in law, or established by precedent, or warranted by the opinion of the judges. And it was contended that there never had been a time when the possession of royal rank had been considered necessary to qualify any one to become consort of an English prince or princess. It had not even been regarded as a necessary qualification for a queen. Three of the wives of Henry VIII. had been English subjects wholly unconnected with the royal family; nor had the Parliament nor the people in general complained of any one of those marriages; moreover, two of his children, who had in their turn succeeded to the crown, had been the offspring of two of those wives; and in the last century James II., while Duke of York, had married the daughter of an English gentleman; and, though it had not been without notorious reluctance that his royal brother had sanctioned that connection, it was well known that Charles II. himself had proposed to marry the niece of Cardinal Mazarin. In the House of Peers, Lord Camden especially objected to the clause annulling a marriage between persons of full age; and in the Commons, Mr. Dowdeswell, who had been Chancellor of the Exchequer in Lord Rockingham's administration, dwelt with especial vigor on the unreasonableness of the clause which fixed twenty-five as the age before which no prince or princess could marry without the King's consent. "Law, positive law," he argued, "and not the arbitrary will of an individual, should be the only restraint. Men who are by law allowed at twenty-one[26] to be fit for governing the realm may well be supposed capable of choosing and governing a wife."[27] Lord Folkestone condemned with great earnestness the expression in the preamble that the bill was dictated "by the royal concern for the honor and dignity of the crown," as implying a doctrine that an alliance of a subject with a branch of the royal family is dishonorable to the crown—a doctrine which he denounced as "an oblique insult" to the whole people, and which, as such, "the representatives of the people were bound to oppose." And he also objected to the "vindicatory part," as he termed the clause which declared those who might assist, or even be present, at a marriage contracted without the royal permission guilty of felony.[28]

The ministry, however, had a decided majority in both Houses, and the bill became and remains the law of the land, though fourteen peers, including one bishop, entered a protest against it on nine different grounds, one of which condemned it as "an extension of the royal prerogative for which the great majority of the judges found no authority;" while another, with something of prophetic sagacity, urged that the bill "was pregnant with civil discord and confusion, and had a natural tendency to produce a disputed title to the crown."

It may be doubted whether the circumstances which had induced George III. to demand such a power as that with which the bill invested him justified its enactment. He was already the father of a family so numerous as to render it highly improbable that either of his brothers or any of their children would ever come to the throne; while, as a previously existing law barred any prince or princess who might marry a Roman Catholic from the succession, the additional restraint imposed by the new statute practically limited their choice to an inconveniently small number of foreign royal houses, many of which, to say the least, are not superior in importance or purity of blood to many of our own nobles.

Nor can it be said to have been successful in accomplishing his Majesty's object. It is notorious that two of his sons, and very generally believed that one of his daughters, married subjects; the Prince of Wales having chosen a wife who was not only inferior in rank and social position to Lady Waldegrave or Mrs. Horton, but was moreover a Roman Catholic; and that another of his sons petitioned more than once for permission to marry an English heiress of ancient family. And our present sovereign may be thought to have pronounced her opinion that the act goes too far, when she gave one of her younger daughters in marriage to a nobleman who, however high in rank, has no royal blood in his veins. The political inconvenience which might arise from the circumstance of the reigning sovereign being connected by near and intimate relationship with a family of his British subjects will, probably, always be thought to render it desirable that some restriction should be placed on the marriage of the heir-apparent; but where the sovereign is blessed with a numerous offspring, there seems no sufficient reason for sending the younger branches of the royal house to seek wives or husbands in foreign countries. And as the precedent set in the case of the Princess Louise has been generally approved, it is probable that in similar circumstances it may be followed, and that such occasional relaxation of the act of 1772 will be regarded as justified by and consistent with the requirements of public policy as well as by the laws of nature.

[29] Generally speaking, the two Houses agreed in their support of the ministerial policy both at home and abroad; but, in spite of this political harmony, a certain degree of bad feeling existed between them, which on one occasion led to a somewhat singular scene in the House of Commons. The Commons imputed its origin to the discourtesy of the Lords, who, when members of the Commons were ordered by their House to carry its bills up to the peers, sometimes kept them "waiting three hours in the lobby among their lordships' footmen before they admitted them." Burke affirmed that this had happened to himself, and that he "spoke of it, not out of any personal pride, nor as an indignity to himself, but as a flagrant disgrace to the House of Commons, which, he apprehended, was not inferior in rank to any other branch of the Legislature, but co-ordinate with them." And the irritation which such treatment excited led the Commons, perhaps not very unnaturally, to seek some opportunity to vindicate their dignity. They found it in an amendment which the Lords made on a corn bill. In the middle of April, 1772, resolutions had been passed by the Commons, in a committee of the whole House, imposing certain duties on the importation of wheat[30] and other grain when they were at a certain price, which was fixed at 48s., and granting bounties on exportation when the price fell below 44s. The Lords made several amendments on the bill, and, among others, one to strike out the clause which granted bounties. But when the bill thus amended came back to the Commons, even those who disliked the principle of bounties resented this act of the Lords in meddling with that question, which they regarded as a violation of their peculiar and most cherished privilege, the exclusive right of dealing with questions of taxation. Governor Pownall, who had charge of the bill, declared that the Lords had forgotten their duty when they interfered in raising money by the insertion of a clause that "no bounty should be paid upon exported corn." And on this ground he moved the rejection of the bill.[31] In the last chapter of this volume, a more fitting occasion for examining the rights and usages of the House of Lords with respect to money-bills will be furnished by a series of resolutions on the subject, moved by the Prime-minister of the day. It is sufficient here to say that the power of rejection is manifestly so different from that of originating grants—which is admitted to belong exclusively to the Commons—and that there were so many precedents for the Lords having exerted this power of rejection in the course of the preceding century, that they probably never conceived that in so doing now they were committing any encroachment on the constitutional rights and privileges of the Lower House. But on this occasion the ill-feeling previously existing between the two Houses may be thought to have predisposed the Commons to seek opportunity for a quarrel. And there never was a case in which both parties in the House were more unanimous. Governor Pownall called the

rejection of the clause by the Lords "a flagrant encroachment upon the privileges of the House," and affirmed that the Lords had "forgotten their duty." Burke termed it "a proof that the Lords did not understand the principles of the constitution, an invasion of a known and avowed right inherent in the House as the representatives of the people," and expressed a hope that "they were not yet so infamous and abandoned as to relinquish this essential right," or to submit to "the annihilation of all their authority." Others called it "an affront which the House was bound to resent, and the more imperatively in consequence of the absence of a good understanding between the two Houses." And the Speaker, Sir John Cust, went beyond all his brother members in violence, declaring that "he would do his part in the business, and toss the bill over the table." The bill was rejected *nem. con.*, and the Speaker tossed it over the table, several of the members on both sides of the question kicking it as they went out;[32] and to such a pitch of exasperation had they worked themselves up, that "the Game Bill, in which the Lords had made alterations, was served in a similar manner," though those alterations only referred to the penalties to be imposed for violations of the Game-law, and could by no stretch of ingenuity be connected with any question of taxation.

Notes:

[Footnote 16:] A motion was, indeed, made (but the "Parliamentary History," xvi., 55, omits to state by whom) that the House should "humbly entreat his Majesty, out of his tender and paternal regard for his people, that he would be graciously pleased to name the person or persons whom, in his royal wisdom, he shall think fit to propose to the consideration of Parliament for the execution of those high trusts, this House apprehending it not warranted by precedent nor agreeable to the principles of this free constitution to vest in any person or persons not particularly named and approved of in Parliament the important offices of Regent of these kingdoms and guardian of the royal offspring heirs to the crown." But "it passed in the negative," probably, if we may judge by other divisions on motions made by the same party, by an overwhelming majority.]

[Footnote 17:] No one doubted that this choice had been made under the influence of Lord Bute, and was designed for the preservation of that influence.—Lord Stanhope, *History of England*, v., 41.]

[Footnote 18:] In his speech in the House of Lords on the Regency Bill of 1840, the Duke of Sussex stated that George III. had nominated the Queen as Regent in the first instance, and, in the event of her death, the Princess Dowager.]

[Footnote 19:] "Lives of the Chancellors," c. cxli.]

[Footnote 20:] It appears from these dates that it was not yet understood that Parliament could not be prorogued for a longer period than forty days.]

[Footnote 21:] These words occur in a speech attributed to Lord Mansfield. There is no detailed account of the debates on this subject in either House. All that exists in the "Parliamentary History" is a very brief abstract of the discussion in the Commons, and a document occupying above sixty pages of the same work (pp. 251-314), entitled "A Speech on behalf of the Constitution against the Suspending and Dispensing Prerogative," etc., with a foot-note explaining that "this speech was supposed to be penned by Lord Mansfield, but was, in fact, written by Mr. Macintosh, assisted by Lord Temple and Lord Lyttleton." It certainly seems to contain internal evidence that it was not written by any lawyer, from the sneers at and denunciations of lawyers which it contains, as a class of men who "have often appeared to be the worst guardians of the constitution, and too frequently the wickedest enemies to, and most treacherous betrayers of, the liberties of their country." But, by whomsoever it was "penned" and published, the arguments which it contains against the dispensing power were, probably, those which had been urged by the great Chief-justice, and as such I have ventured to cite them here.]

[Footnote 22:] In his "Lives of the Chief-justices" (c. xxxvi., life of Lord Mansfield), Lord Campbell says, with reference to this case: "The Chief-justice's only considerable public exhibition during this period was his attack on the unconstitutional assertion of Lord Chatham and Lord Camden, that, in a case of great public emergency, the crown could by law dispense with an act of parliament. The question arising from the embargo on the exportation of corn, in consequence of apprehended famine, he proved triumphantly that, although the measure was expedient and proper, it was a violation of law, and required to be sanctioned by an act of indemnity." And Lord Campbell adds, in a note: "This doctrine, acted upon in

1827, during the administration of Mr. Canning, and on several subsequent occasions, is now universally taken for constitutional law" (ii., 468).]

[Footnote 23:] To adduce a single instance, worthy of remark as affecting the personal liberty of the subject, in 1818 a bill of indemnity was passed to sanction the action of the ministry in arresting and detaining in prison, without bringing them to trial, several persons accused of being implicated in seditious proceedings (*vide infra*).]

[Footnote 24:] Vol. xvii., 304.]

[Footnote 25:] The case is mentioned by Lord Campbell in his "Lives of the Chancellors," c. cxxi. (life of Lord Macclesfield) and c. cxxiv. (life of Lord Chancellor King).]

[Footnote 26:] In fact, however, the age at which a young prince was considered competent to exercise the royal authority in person had been fixed at eighteen; and it is so stated in the speech in which the King, in 1765, recommended the appointment of a Regent to Parliament.—*Parliamentary History*, xvi., 52.]

[Footnote 27:] This idea was expanded into an epigram, which appeared in most of the daily papers, and has been thought worthy of being preserved in the "Parliamentary History," xvii., 401 (note):

"Quoth Dick to Tom, 'This act appears
   Absurd, as I'm alive,
To take the crown at eighteen years,
   A wife at twenty-five.
The mystery how shall we explain?
   For sure, as Dowdeswell said,
Thus early if they're fit to *reign*,
   They must be fit to *wed*.'
Quoth Tom to Dick, 'Thou art a fool,
   And nothing know'st of life;
Alas! it's easier far to rule
   A kingdom than a wife.'"]

[Footnote 28:] It is remarkable that this clause on one occasion proved an obstacle to the punishment of the abettors of such a marriage. In 1793 the Duke of Sussex married Lady Augusta Murray, first at Rome, and afterward, by banns, at St. George's, Hanover Square. And when the affair came to be investigated by the Privy Council, Lord Thurlow denounced the conduct of the pair in violent terms, and angrily asked the Attorney-general,

Sir John Scott, why he had not prosecuted all the parties concerned in this abominable marriage. Sir John's reply, as he reported it himself, was sufficiently conclusive: "I answered that it was a very difficult business to prosecute; that the act, it was understood, had been drawn by Lord Mansfield, the Attorney-general Thurlow, and the Solicitor-general Wedderburn, who, unluckily, had made all persons present at the marriage guilty of felony. And as nobody could prove the marriage except a person who had been present at it, there could be no prosecution, because nobody present could be compelled to be a witness." — Thorp's *Life of Eldon*, i., 235.]

[Footnote 29:] A protest against the bill, entered by fourteen peers, including one bishop (of Bangor), denounced it, among other objections, as "contrary to the original inherent rights of human nature ... exceeding the power permitted by Divine Providence to human legislation ... and shaking many of the foundations of law, religion, and public security."—*Parliamentary History*, xvii., 391.]

[Footnote 30:] The import duty on wheat was fixed at 6*d.* a quarter on grain, and 2*d.* per cwt. on flour, when the price of wheat in the kingdom should be at or above 48s.; when it was at or above 44s., the exportation was to be altogether prohibited.—*Parliamentary History*, xvii., 476.]

[Footnote 31:] See Hallam, "Constitutional History," iii., 38-46, ed. 1833, where, as far as the imperfection of our early Parliamentary records allows, he traces the origin of the assertion of this peculiar privilege by the Commons, especially referring to a discussion of the proper limits of this privilege in several conferences between the two Houses; where, as on some other occasions, he sees, in the assertion of their alleged rights by the Commons, "more disposition to make encroachments than to guard against those of others." A few years before (in 1763), the House of Lords showed that they had no doubt of their right to reject a money-bill, since they divided on the Cider Bill, which came under that description. As, however, the bill was passed, that division was not brought under the notice of the House. But in 1783, in the time of the Coalition Ministry, the peers having made amendments on the American Intercourse Bill, "the Speaker observed that, as the bill empowered the crown to impose duties, it was, strictly speaking, a money-bill, and therefore the House could not, consistently with its own orders, suffer the Lords to make any amendments on it, and he recommended that the consideration of their amendments should be postponed for three months, and in the mean time a new bill framed according to the Lords' amendments should be passed." The recommendation was approved by Mr. Pitt, as leader of the Opposition, and approved and acted on by Mr. Fox, as leader of the ministry in that House. But, at the same time, Mr. Fox fully admitted the right of the Lords to discuss such questions, "for it would be very absurd indeed to send a loan bill to the Lords for their concurrence, and at the same time deprive them of the right of deliberation. To lay down plans and schemes for loans belonged solely to the Commons; and he was willing, therefore, that the amended bill should be rejected, though he was of opinion that the order of the House respecting money-bills was often too strictly construed." And he immediately moved for leave to bring in a new bill, which was verbatim the same with the amended bill sent down by the Lords.— *Parliamentary History*, xxiii., 895. The question was revived in the present reign, on the refusal of the Lords to concur in the abolition of the duty on paper, when the whole subject was discussed with such elaborate minuteness, and with so much more command of temper than was shown on the present occasion, that it will be better to defer the examination of the principle involved till we come to the history of that transaction.]

[Footnote 32:] "Parliamentary History," xvii., 515.]

CHAPTER III

Mr. Grenville imposes a Duty on Stamps in the North American Colonies.—Examination of Dr. Franklin.—Lord Rockingham's Ministry Repeals the Duty.—Lord Mansfield affirms a Virtual Representation in the Colonies.—Mr. C. Townsend imposes Import Duties in America.—After some Years, the Civil War breaks out.—Hanoverian Troops are sent to Gibraltar.—The Employment of Hanoverian Regiments at Gibraltar and Minorca.—End of the War.—Colonial Policy of the Present Reign.—Complaints of the Undue Influence of the Crown.—Motions for Parliamentary Reform.—Mr. Burke's Bill for Economical Reform.—Mr. Dunning's Resolution on the Influence of the Crown.—Rights of the Lords on Money-bills.—The Gordon Riots.

But during these years another matter had been gradually forcing its way to the front, which, though at first it attracted but comparatively slight notice, when it came to a head, absorbed for several years the whole attention, not only of these kingdoms, but of foreign countries also. It was originally—in appearance, at least—merely a dispute between Great Britain and her Colonies in North America on the mode of obtaining a small revenue from them. But, in its progress, it eventually involved us in a foreign war of great magnitude, and thus became the one subject of supreme interest to every statesman in Europe. England had not borne her share in the seven years' war without a considerable augmentation of the national debt, and a corresponding increase in the amount of yearly revenue which it had become necessary to raise;[33] and Mr. Grenville, as Chancellor of the Exchequer, had to devise the means of meeting the demand. A year before, he had supported with great warmth the proposal of Sir Francis Dashwood, his predecessor at the Exchequer, to lay a new tax upon cider. Now that he himself had succeeded to that office, he cast his eyes across the Atlantic, and, on the plea that the late war had to a certain extent been undertaken for the defence of the Colonies in North America, he proposed to make them bear a share in the burden caused by enterprises from which they had profited. Accordingly, in March, 1764, he proposed a series of resolutions imposing a variety of import duties on different articles of foreign produce imported into "the British Colonies and plantations in America," and also export duties on a few articles of American growth when "exported or conveyed to any other place except to Great Britain." Another resolution affirmed "that, toward defraying the said expense, it might be proper to charge certain stamp-duties in the said Colonies and plantations."

The resolutions imposing import and export duties were passed by both Houses almost without comment. That relating to a stamp-duty he did not press at the moment, announcing that he postponed it for a year, in order to ascertain in what light it would be regarded by the Colonists themselves; and as most, if not all, of the Colonies had a resident agent in London, he called them together, explained to them the object and anticipated result of the new imposition (for such he admitted it to be), and requested them to communicate his views to their constituents, adding an offer that, if they should prefer any other tax likely to be equally productive, he should be desirous to consult their wishes in the matter.

He probably regarded such language on his part as a somewhat superfluous exercise of courtesy or conciliation, so entire was his conviction of the omnipotence of Parliament, and of the impossibility of any loyal man or body of men calling its power in question. But he was greatly deceived. His message was received in America with universal dissatisfaction. Of the thirteen States which made up the body of Colonies, there was scarcely one whose Assembly did not present a petition against the proposed measure, and against any other which might be considered as an alternative. Grenville, however, was not a man to be moved by petitions or remonstrances. He was rather one whom opposition of any kind hardened in his purpose; and, as no substitute had been suggested, at the opening of the session of 1765 he proposed a series of resolutions requisite to give effect to the vote of the previous year, and imposing "certain stamp-duties and other duties" on the settlements in America, perhaps thinking to render his disregard of the objections which had been made less unpalatable by the insertion of words binding the government to apply the sums to be thus raised to "the expenses of defending, protecting, and securing" the Colonies themselves. The resolutions were passed, as the "Parliamentary History" records, "almost without debate," on the 6th of March.[34] But the intelligence was received in every part of the Colonies with an indignant dissatisfaction, which astonished even their own agents in England.[35] Formidable riots broke out in several provinces. In Massachusetts the man who had been appointed Distributor of Stamps was burnt in effigy; the house of the Lieutenant-governor was attacked by a furious mob, who avowed their determination to murder him if he fell into their hands; and resolutions were passed by the Assemblies of the different States to convene a General

Congress at New York in the autumn, to organize a resistance to the tax, and to take the general state of affairs into consideration.

Before, however, that time came, a series of events having no connection with these transactions had led to a change of ministry in England, and the new cabinet was less inclined to carry matters with a high hand. Indeed, even the boldest statesman could hardly have learned the state of feeling which had been excited in America without apprehension, and those who had the chief weight in the new administration were not men to imperil the state by an insistence on abstract theories of right and prerogative. Accordingly, when, after Lord Rockingham had become Prime-minister, Parliament met in December, 1765, the royal speech recommended the state of affairs in America to the consideration of Parliament (a recommendation which manifestly implied a disposition on the part of the King's advisers to induce the House of Commons to retrace its steps), papers were laid before Parliament, and witnesses from America were examined, and among them a man who had already won a high reputation by his scientific acquirements, but who had not been previously prominent as a politician, Dr. Benjamin Franklin. He had come over to England as agent for Pennsylvania, and his examination, as preserved in the "Parliamentary History," may be taken as a complete statement of the matter in dispute from the American point of view, and of the justification which the Colonists conceived themselves to have for refusing to submit to pay such a tax as had now been imposed upon them. At a later day he was one of the most zealous, as he was probably one of the earliest, advocates of separation from England; but as yet neither his language nor his actions afforded any trace of such a feeling.

He affirmed[36] the general temper of the Colonists toward Great Britain to have been, till this act was passed, the best in the world. They considered themselves as a part of the British empire, and as having one common interest with it. They did not consider themselves as foreigners. They were jealous for the honor and prosperity of this nation, and always were, and always would be, ready to support it as far as their little power went. They considered the Parliament of Great Britain as the great bulwark and security of their liberties and privileges, and always spoke of it with the utmost respect and veneration. They had given a practical proof of their goodwill by having raised, clothed, and paid during the last war nearly 25,000 men, and spent many millions; nor had any Assembly of any Colony ever refused duly to support the government by proper allowances from time to time to public officers. They had always been ready, and were ready now, to tax themselves. The Colonies had Assemblies of their own, which were their Parliaments. They were, in that respect, in the same situation as Ireland. Their Assemblies had a right to levy money on the subject, then to grant to the crown, and, indeed, had constantly done so; and he himself was specially instructed by the Assembly of his own State to assure the ministry that, as they always had done, so they should always think it their duty to grant such aids to the crown as were suitable to their circumstances and abilities, whenever called upon for the purpose in a constitutional manner; and that instruction he had communicated to the ministry. But the Colonies objected to Parliament laying on them such a tax as that imposed by the Stamp Act. Some duties, they admitted, the Parliament had a right to impose, but he drew a distinction between "those duties which were meant to regulate commerce and internal taxes." The authority of Parliament to regulate commerce had never been disputed by the Colonists. The sea belonged to Britain. She maintained by her fleets the safety of navigation on it; she kept it clear of pirates; she might, therefore, have a natural and equitable right to some toll or duty, on merchandise carried through that part of her dominions, toward defraying the expenses she was at in ships to maintain the safety of that carriage. But the case of imposition of internal taxes was wholly different from this. The Colonists held that, by the charters which at different times had been granted to the different States, they were entitled to all the privileges and liberties of Englishmen. They found in the Great Charters, and the Petition and Declarations of Right, that one of the privileges of English subjects is that they are not to be taxed but by their common consent; and these rights and privileges had been confirmed by the charters which at different times had been granted to the different States. In reply to a question put to him, he allowed that in the Pennsylvania charter there was a clause by which the King granted that he would levy no taxes on the inhabitants unless it were with the consent of the Colonial Assembly, or by an act of Parliament; words which certainly seemed to reserve a right of taxation to the British Parliament; but he also demonstrated that, in point of fact, the latter part of the clause had never been acted on, and the Colonists had, therefore, relied on it, from the first settlement of the province, that the Parliament never would nor could, by the color of that clause in the charter, assume a right of taxing them till it had qualified itself to exercise such right by admitting representatives from the people to be taxed. And, in addition to objections on principle, he urged some that he regarded as of great force as to the working of this particular tax imposed by the Stamp Act. It was not an equal tax, as the greater part of the revenue derived from it must arise from lawsuits for the recovery of debts, and be paid by the lower sort of people; it was a heavy tax on the poor, and a tax on them for being poor. In the back settlements, where the population was very thin, the inhabitants would often be unable to get stamps without taking a long journey for the purpose. The scarcity of specie, too, in the country would cause the pressure to be felt with great severity, as, in his opinion, there was not gold and silver enough in the Colonies to pay the stamp-duty for a single year. In reply to another question, whether the Colonists would be satisfied with a repeal of the Stamp Act without a formal renunciation of the abstract right of Parliament to impose it, he replied that he believed they would be satisfied. He thought the resolutions of right would give them very little concern, if they were never attempted to be carried into practice. The Colonies would probably consider themselves in the same situation in that respect as Ireland. They knew that the English Parliament claimed the same right with regard to Ireland, but that it never exercised it; and they might believe that they would never exercise it in the Colonies any more than in Ireland. Indeed, they would think that it never could exercise such a right till representatives from the Colonies should be admitted into Parliament, and that whenever an occasion arose to make Parliament regard the taxation of the Colonies as indispensable, representatives would be ordered.

This last question put to the witness, like several others in the course of his examination, had been framed with the express purpose of eliciting an answer to justify the determination on the subject to which Lord Rockingham and his colleagues had come. It could not be denied that the government was placed in a situation of extreme difficulty—difficulty created, in part, by the conduct of the Colonists themselves. That, as even their most uncompromising advocate, Mr. Pitt, admitted, had been imprudent and intemperate, though it was the imprudence of men who "had been driven to madness by injustice." On the one hand, to repeal an act the opposition to which had been marked by fierce riots, such as those of Boston, and even in the Assemblies of some of the States by language scarcely short of treason,[37] seemed a concession to intimidation scarcely compatible with the maintenance of the dignity of the crown or the legitimate authority of Parliament. On the other hand, to persist in the retention of a tax which the whole population affected by it was evidently determined to resist to the uttermost, was to incur the still greater danger of rebellion and civil war. In this dilemma, the ministers resolved on a course calculated, as they conceived, to avoid both evils, by combining a satisfaction of the complaints of the Colonists with an assertion of the absolute supremacy of the British crown and Parliament for every purpose. And on February 24, 1766, the Secretary of State brought in a bill which, after declaring, in its first clause, "that the King's Majesty, by and with the consent of the Lords spiritual and temporal, and Commons of Great Britain, in Parliament assembled, had, hath, and of right ought to have, full power and authority to make laws and statutes of sufficient force and validity to bind the Colonists and people of America, subjects of the crown of Great Britain, in all cases whatsoever," proceeded to repeal the Stamp Act, giving a strong proof of the sincerity of the desire to conciliate the Colonists by the unusual step of fixing the second reading of the bill for the next day.

But in its different clauses it encountered a twofold opposition, which he had, probably, not anticipated. It is unnecessary to notice that which rested solely on the inexpediency of repealing the Stamp Act, "the compulsory enforcement of which was required by the honor and dignity of the kingdom." But the first clause was even more strenuously resisted, on grounds which its opponents affirmed to rest on the fundamental principles of the constitution. It was urged in the House of Commons by Mr. Pitt that, "as the Colonies were not represented in Parliament, Great Britain had no legal right nor power to lay a tax upon them—that taxation is no part of the governing or legislative power. Taxes," said the great orator, "are the voluntary gift and grant of the Commons alone. In legislation the three estates of the realm are alike concerned; but the concurrence of the peers and the crown to a tax is only necessary to clothe it with the form of a law; the gift and grant is in the Commons alone.... The distinction between legislation and taxation is essentially necessary to liberty."

Mr. Pitt had no claim to be considered as a great authority in the principles of constitutional law. George II., slight as was his political knowledge or wisdom, complained on one occasion of the ignorance of a Secretary of State who had never read Vattel; and in this very debate he even boasted of his ignorance of "law-cases and acts of Parliament." But his coadjutor in the House of Lords (Lord Camden, at this time Chief-justice of the Common Pleas) owed the chief part of the respect in which he was held to his supposed excellence as a constitutional lawyer, and he fully endorsed and expanded Pitt's arguments when the bill came up to the House of Lords. He affirmed that he spoke as "the defender of the law and the constitution; that, as the affair was of the greatest consequence, and in its consequences might involve the fate of kingdoms, he had taken the strictest review of his arguments, he had examined and re-examined all his authorities; and that his searches had more and more convinced him that the British Parliament had no right to tax the Americans. The Stamp Act was absolutely illegal, contrary to the fundamental laws of nature, contrary to the fundamental laws of this constitution—a constitution governed on the eternal and immutable laws of nature. The doctrine which he was asserting was not new; it was as old as the constitution; it grew up with it; indeed, it was its support. Taxation and representation are inseparably united. God hath joined them; no British government can put them asunder. To endeavor to do so is to stab our very vitals." And he objected to the first clause (that which declared the power and right to tax), on the ground that if the ministers "wantonly pressed this declaration, although they were now repealing the Stamp Act, they might pass it again in a month." He even argued that "they must have future taxation in view, or they would hardly assert their right to enjoy the pleasure of offering an insult." He was answered by Lord Northington (the Chancellor) and by Lord Mansfield (the Chief-justice), both of whom supported the motion to repeal the tax, but who also agreed in denying the soundness of his doctrine that, as far as the power was concerned, there was any distinction between a law to tax and a law for any other purpose; and Lord Mansfield farther denied the validity of the argument which it had been attempted to found on the circumstance that the Colonies were not represented in Parliament, propounding, on the contrary, what Lord Campbell calls "his doctrine of virtual representation." "There can," said he, "be no doubt but that the inhabitants of the Colonies are represented in Parliament, as the greatest part of the people of England are represented, among nine millions of whom there are eight who have no votes in electing members of Parliament. Every objection, therefore, to the dependency of the Colonies upon Parliament which arises upon the ground of representation goes to the whole present constitution of Great Britain.... For what purpose, then, are arguments drawn from a distinction in which there is no real difference of a virtual and an actual representation? A member of Parliament chosen for any borough represents not only the constituents and inhabitants of that particular place, but he represents the inhabitants of every other borough in Great Britain. He represents the City of London and all the other Commons of the land, and the inhabitants of all the colonies and dominions of Great Britain, and is in duty and conscience bound to take care of their interests."

Lord Mansfield's doctrine of a virtual representation of the Colonies must be admitted to be overstrained. The analogy between the case of colonists in a country from no part of which representatives are sent to Parliament, and that of a borough or county where some classes of the population which may, in a sense, be regarded as spokesmen or agents of the rest form a constituency and return members, must be allowed to fail; yet the last sentences of this extract are worth preserving, as laying down the important constitutional principle, subsequently expanded and enforced with irresistible learning and power of argument by Burke, that a member of the House of Commons is not a delegate, bound, under all circumstances, to follow the opinions or submit to the dictation of his constituents, but that from the moment of his election he is a councillor of the whole kingdom, bound to exercise an independent judgment for the interests of the whole people, rather than to guide himself by the capricious or partial judgments of a small section of it. But in its more immediate objects--that of establishing the two principles, that the constitution knows of no limitation to the authority of Parliament, and of no distinction between the power of taxation and that of any other kind of legislation--Lord Mansfield's speech is now universally admitted to have been unanswerable.[38]

The abstract right was unquestionably on the side of the minister and the Parliament who had imposed the tax. But he is not worthy of the name of statesman who conceives absolute rights and metaphysical distinctions to be the proper foundation for measures of government, and pays no regard to custom, to precedent, to the habits and feelings of the people to be governed; who, disregarding the old and most true adage, *summum jus summa injuria*, omits to take into his calculations the expediency of his actions when legislating for a nation which he is in the daily habit of weighing in his private affairs. The art or science of government are phrases in common use; but they would be void of meaning if all that is requisite be to ascertain the strict right or power, and then unswervingly to act upon it in all its rigor. And, therefore, while it must be admitted that the character of the power vested in King, Lords, and Commons assembled in Parliament is unlimited and illimitable, and that the legal competency to enact a statute depends in no degree whatever on the wisdom or folly, the justice or wickedness, of the statute, the advice given to a constitutional sovereign by his advisers must be guided by other considerations. To quote by anticipation the language addressed to the Commons on this subject by Burke eight years afterward, the proper policy was "to leave the Americans as they anciently stood ... To be content to bind America by laws of trade. Parliament had always done it. And this should be the reason for binding their trade. Not to burden them by taxes; Parliament was not used to do so from the beginning; and this should be the reason for not taxing. These are the arguments of states and kingdoms."[39]

The ministry were strong enough to carry their resolutions through both Houses. Their measure was divided into two acts, one known as the Declaratory Act, asserting the absolute and universal authority of Parliament; the other repealing the Stamp Act of the preceding year. And both were passed without alteration, though the Lords divided against them on both the second and third readings of the bill for repeal founded on them,[40] some of them entering long protests in the journals of the House. The right to tax was asserted, but the tax itself was repealed. And Franklin's estimate of the feelings on the subject entertained by his countrymen was fully verified by the reception which the intelligence met with in the Colonies. To quote the description of Lord Stanhope: "In America the repeal of the Stamp Act was received with universal joy and acclamation. Fireworks and festivals celebrated the good news, while addresses and thanks to the King were voted by all the Assemblies.... The words of the Declaratory Act, indeed, gave the Americans slight concern. They fully believed that no practical grievance could arise from it. They looked upon it merely as a salve to the wounded pride of England; as only that 'bridge of gold' which, according to the old French saying, should always be allowed to a retreating assailant."[41]

A recent writer, however, has condemned the addition of the declaration of the abstract right to tax with great vehemence. "Nothing," says Lord Campbell,[42] "could exceed the folly of accompanying the repeal of the Stamp Act with the statutable declaration of the abstract right to tax." But it does not seem difficult to justify the conduct of the ministry in this particular. For, besides the great weight deservedly attached to Franklin's assurance that the declaration would not be objected to by the Colonists, and besides the consideration that, on a general view, it was desirable, if not indispensable, to impress on all classes of subjects, whether at home or abroad, the constitutional doctrine of the omnipotence of Parliament, the line of argument adopted by Mr. Pitt and Lord Camden, in denying that omnipotence, left the ministers no alternative but that of asserting it, unless they were prepared to betray their trust as guardians of the constitution. Forbearance to insist on the Declaratory Act could not fail to have been regarded as an acquiescence on their part in a doctrine which Lord Campbell in the same breath admits to be false. It may be added, as a consideration of no small practical weight, that, without such a Declaratory Act, the King would have been very reluctant to consent to the other and more important Repealing Act. And, on the whole, the conduct of the ministry may, we think, be regarded as the wisest settlement both of the law and of the practice. It asserted the law in a manner which offended no one; and it made a precedent for placing the spirit of statesmanship above the letter of the law, and for forbearing to put forth in its full strength the prerogatives whose character was not fully understood by those who might be affected by them, and also could plead that Parliament itself had contributed to lead them to misunderstand it by its own conduct in never before exerting it.

For the moment, then, contentment and tranquillity were restored in the Colonies. Unhappily, they were not lasting. The same year which saw the triumph of the Rockingham administration in the repeal of the Stamp Act, witnessed also its fall before a discreditable intrigue. And the ministry which succeeded it had not been a year in office before the new Chancellor of the Exchequer, Charles Townsend, revived the discontents in America which Lord Rockingham had appeased. It cannot be said, however, that the blame should all belong to him; or that the Rockingham party in the House of Commons were entirely free from a share in it. They were—not unnaturally, perhaps—greatly irritated at the intrigue by which Lord Chatham had superseded them, and were not disinclined to throw difficulties in the way of their successors, for which the events of the next year afforded more than one opportunity. Lord Chatham, as has been mentioned, was universally recognized as the chief of the new ministry, though he abstained from taking the usual office of First Lord of the Treasury, and contented himself with the Privy Seal; but he had constructed it of such discordant elements[43] that no influence but his own could preserve consistency in its acts or harmony among its members, as nothing but his name could give it consideration either in Parliament or in the country. In the first months of the next year, 1767, he was attacked with an illness which for a time disabled him from attending the cabinet, being, apparently, the forerunner of that more serious malady which, before the end of the summer, compelled his long retirement from public life; and the Opposition took advantage of the state of disorganization and weakness which his illness caused among his colleagues, to defeat them on the Budget in the House of Commons, by an amendment to reduce the land-tax, which caused a deficiency in the supplies of half a million. This deficiency it, of course, became necessary to meet by some fresh tax; and Townsend—who, though endowed with great richness of eloquence, was of an imprudent, not to say rash, temper, and was possessed of too thorough a confidence in his own ingenuity and fertility of resource ever to be inclined to take into consideration any objections to which his schemes might be liable—proposed to raise a portion of the money which was needed by taxes on glass, paper, tea, and one or two other articles, to be paid as import duties in the American Colonies. His colleagues, and especially the Duke of Grafton himself, the First Lord of the Treasury, and as such the nominal Prime-minister, having been also, as Secretary of State, a member of Lord Rockingham's ministry, which had repealed the former taxes, did not consent to the measure without great and avowed reluctance; but yielded their own judgment to the strong feeling in its favor which notoriously existed in the House of Commons.[44] Indeed, that House passed the clauses imposing these import duties without hesitation, being, probably, influenced in no small degree by the evidence given in the preceding year by Dr. Franklin, who, as has been already seen, had explained that the Colonists drew a distinction between what he called "internal taxes" and import duties "intended to regulate commerce," and that to the latter class they were not inclined to object. And a second consideration was, that these new duties were accompanied and counterbalanced by a reduction of some other taxes; so that the ministry contended that the effect of these financial measures, taken altogether, would be to lower to the Colonists the price of the articles affected by them rather than to raise it. But one of the resolutions adopted provided that the whole of the money to be raised from these taxes should not be spent in America, but that, after making provision for certain

Colonial objects specified, "the residue of such duties should be paid into the receipt of his Majesty's Exchequer, and there reserved, to be from time to time disposed of by Parliament toward defraying the necessary expenses of defending, protecting, and securing the said Colonies and plantations." And this clause seems to have been understood as designed to provide means for augmenting the number of regular troops to be maintained in the Colonies, whose employment in the recent disturbances had made them more unpopular than formerly.[45]

At all events, the intelligence of these new taxes, though only import duties, found the Colonists in a humor to resist any addition of any kind to their financial burdens. The events of the last two years had taught them their strength. It was undeniable that the repeal of the Stamp Act had been extorted by the riots in Boston and other places, and the success of this system of intimidation could not fail to encourage its repetition. Accordingly, the news of this fresh attempt at taxation was met by a unanimous determination to resist it. Newspaper writers and pamphleteers denounced not only the duties but the ministry which imposed them. Petitions from almost every State were sent over to England, addressed to the King and to the Parliament; but the violent temper of the leaders of the populace was not content to wait for answers to them. Associations were at once formed in Boston and one or two other cities, where resolutions were adopted in the spirit of retaliation (as their framers avowed), to desist from the importation of any articles of British commerce, and to rely for the future on American manufactures. The principal Custom-house officers at Boston were badly beaten, and others were compelled to seek refuge in a man-of-war which happened to be in the harbor.

It would be painful, and at the present day useless, to trace the steps by which these local disturbances gradually grew into one general insurrection. The spirit of resistance was undoubtedly fanned by a party which from the first contemplated a total separation from England as its ultimate result,[46] if, indeed, they had not conceived the design even before Grenville had given the first provocation to discontent. But the Colonists were not without advocates in England, even among the members of the government. The Duke of Grafton, while he remained Prime-minister, was eager to withdraw all the duties of which they complained; but he was overruled by the majority of his colleagues. He prevailed, however, so far that Lord Hillsborough, the Secretary of State, was authorized to write a circular-letter to the governors of the different provinces, in which he disowned, in the most distinct language possible, "a design to propose to Parliament to lay any farther taxes upon America for the purpose of raising a revenue," and promised for the next session a repeal of all the taxes except that on tea; and when the

Duke retired from the Treasury, and was succeeded by Lord North, that statesman himself brought forward the promised repeal in an elaborate speech,[47] in which he explained that the duty on tea, which he alone proposed to retain, had been originally a boon to the Americans rather than an injury, as being accompanied by the removal of a far heavier tax. But he admitted that even that consideration was not the one which influenced him in his opinion that that duty should be maintained, so greatly was the perception that the real object of those who complained of it was, not the redress of a grievance, but the extinction of a right which was an essential part of "the controlling supremacy of England." The fact that the right to tax had been denied made it a positive duty on the part of the English minister to exert that right. "To temporize would be to yield, and the authority of the mother country, if now unsupported, would be relinquished forever." And he avowed his idea of the policy proper to be pursued to be "to retain the right of taxing America, but to give it every relief that might be consistent with the welfare of the mother country." He carried his resolution, though the minority—which on this occasion was led by Mr. Pownall, who had himself been Governor of Massachusetts, and who moved an amendment to include tea in the list of taxes proposed to be repealed—was stronger than usual.[48] But the concession failed to conciliate a single Colonist; it had become, as Burke said four years afterward, a matter of feeling,[49] and the irritation fed on itself, till, in 1773, a fresh act, empowering the East India Company to export tea to the Colonies direct from their own warehouses without its being subject to any duty in England—which Lord North undoubtedly intended as a boon to the Colonists—only increased the exasperation. The ships which brought the tea to Boston were boarded and seized by a formidable body of rioters disguised as native savages, and the tea was thrown into the sea. The intelligence was received in England with very different feelings by the different parties in the state. The ministers conceived themselves forced to assert the dignity of the crown, and proposed bills to inflict severe punishment on both the City of Boston and the whole Province of Massachusetts. The Opposition insisted on removing the cause of these disturbances by a total repeal of the tea-duty. The minister prevailed by a far larger majority than before, but his success only increased the exasperation in the Colonies; and it was an evil omen for peace that the leaders of the resistance began to search the records of the English Long Parliament "for the revolutionary precedents and forms of the Puritans of that day."[50] The next year saw fresh attempts to procure the repeal of the obnoxious tax rejected by the House of Commons; but, before the news of this division reached America, blood had already been shed.[51] Civil war began. The next year the Colonies, now united in one solid body, asserted their Independence, taking the title of the United States; and, though the government at home made more than one effort to recall the Colonists to their allegiance, and sent out commissioners of high rank, with large powers of concession; and though in one remarkable instance the mission of Mr. Penn, in the summer of 1775, with the petition to the King known as "the Olive Branch," seemed to show a desire for a maintenance of the union on the part of the Colonial Congress,[52] from the moment that the sword was drawn all hope of preserving the connection of the Colonies must have been seen by all reasonable men to be at an end.

It is beside our present purpose to recapitulate the military operations of the war, though they verified another of Burke's warnings, that, supposing all moral difficulties to be got over, the ocean remained—that could not be dried up; and, as long as it continued in its present bed, so long all the causes which weakened authority by distance must continue. In fact, distance from England was one of the main circumstances which decided the contest. The slowness of communication—almost inconceivable to the present generation—rendered impossible that regularity in the transport of re-enforcements and supplies which was indispensable to success; and, added to the strange absence of military skill shown by every one of the British generals, soon placed the eventual issue of the war beyond a doubt. But one measure by which Lord North's government endeavored to provide for the strengthening of the army employed in America was so warmly challenged on constitutional grounds, that, though the fortunate separation of Hanover from Great Britain has prevented the possibility of any recurrence of such a proceeding, it would be improper to pass it over.

In his speech at the opening of the autumnal session of 1775, the King announced to the Houses that, in order to leave a larger portion of the established forces of the kingdom available for service in North America, he "had sent a part of his Electoral troops to the garrisons of Gibraltar and Port Mahon." And the announcement aroused a vehement spirit of opposition, which found vent in the debates of both Houses on the address, and in two substantive motions condemning the measure as a violation of the constitution as established by the Bill of Rights and the Act of Settlement. It was strenuously maintained that both these statutes forbade the raising or keeping on foot a standing army in the kingdom in time of peace, and also the introduction of foreign troops into this kingdom, without the previous consent of Parliament, on any pretence whatever; and that "the fact that Gibraltar and Minorca were detached from these islands did not exclude them from the character of forming a part of the British dominion." And on these grounds Lord Shelburne, who supported Lord Rockingham on an amendment to the address, did not hesitate to denounce this employment of the Hanoverian regiments, as "fundamentally infringing the first principles of our government," and to declare it "high-treason against the constitution." He asked, "if there were a settled plan to subdue the liberties of this country, what surer means could be adopted than those of arming Roman Catholics and introducing foreign troops?"[53] and compared the measure under discussion to the case of the Dutch regiments of William III., "which the Parliament wisely refused to allow him to retain." In the House of Commons, the Opposition was led by Sir James Lowther and Governor Johnstone, the latter of whom "appealed to the clause in the Act of Settlement which enacted that no person born of other than English parents should enjoy any office or place of trust, civil or military, within the kingdom;" and argued that to employ foreign officers in the protection of a British fortress was to place them in an "office of great military trust."

The discussion brought to light strange divisions and weakness in the ministry. The ministerial lawyers differed on the grounds on which they relied, the Attorney-general, Thurlow, denying that the expression "this kingdom" in the Bill of Rights included the foreign dependencies of the crown[54] (a narrowing of its force which the Chancellor, Lord Bathurst, wholly repudiated), while the argument on which he himself insisted most strongly, that the existence of rebellion in America put end to all conditions which supposed the kingdom to be at peace, could not obtain the support of any one of his colleagues. But a plea urged by an independent member, Lord Denbigh, was regarded by some of the speakers with greater favor; his contention being that neither the Bill of Rights nor the Act of Settlement had been violated, since both those great statutes must be interpreted with reference to the time at which they were framed, and to the recent acts of James II. and William III., the recurrence of which they had been designed to prevent, acts to which the present proceeding bore no resemblance.

A stronger justification, however, might have been found in very recent precedents. In 1745 the ministers had brought over six thousand Dutch troops to re-enforce the army of the Duke of Cumberland, and their act had been subsequently approved by Parliament. And in 1756, at the commencement of the seven years' war, when the loss of Minorca had led to such a distrust of our fleets that a French invasion was very generally apprehended, both Houses presented addresses to George II., begging him to bring over some Hanoverian regiments; and, in the course of the next year, other addresses to thank him for compliance with their entreaty.

Looking at the strict law of the question, few lawyers doubt that the expression "this kingdom" in the Bill of Rights includes the entire dominions of the crown, or that that great statute was undoubtedly intended to protect the privileges of all their inhabitants, whether within the four seas or in foreign settlements. But it also seems that the clause against raising and keeping on foot a standing army without the consent of Parliament was not more violated by keeping a mixed garrison in Gibraltar and Port Mahon than garrisons consisting of native soldiers only; and undoubtedly the keeping of an armed force in both these fortresses had been sanctioned by Parliament. Nor could the colonel of a foreign regiment in garrison under the command of a British governor be fairly said to be in an office of great military trust. So far, therefore, the charge against the ministry may be thought to have failed. But the accusation of having transgressed the clause which prohibits "the introduction of foreign troops into this kingdom without the previous consent of Parliament on any pretence whatever," must, on the other hand, be regarded as proved. And, indeed, Lord North himself may be taken to have shown some consciousness that it was so, since he justified his conduct in omitting to procure that previous consent by the necessity of the case, by the plea that, as Parliament was in vacation, the time which would have been consumed in waiting for its sanction would have neutralized the advantage desired from the employment of the Hanoverians, since the regiments which they were to replace at Gibraltar and Port Mahon could not, after such delay, have reached America in time to be of service; and since he also consented eventually to ask Parliament for an Act of Indemnity, the preamble of which affirmed the existence of doubts as to the legality of the step which had been taken. And the fate of this act afforded a still more striking proof of the divisions in the ministry, since, after Lord North himself had proposed it in the House of Commons, and it had been passed there by a large majority, it was rejected in the House of Lords, where his own colleagues, Lord Gower, Lord Suffolk, and Lord Weymouth, spoke and voted against it as needless, because, in their judgment, no doubt of the state of the law on the subject could exist.

From a statesman-like point of view, the employment of the Hanoverians seems abundantly defensible, if force were still to be employed to bring back the Colonists to their obedience. The circumstance of their being subjects of our sovereign in his other character of Elector of Hanover, clearly distinguished it from the hiring of the Hessian and Brunswick mercenaries, which has been deservedly condemned. And, as the entire number fell short of two thousand,[55] Lord Shelburne's expression of fear for the liberties and religion of Englishmen was an absurd exaggeration. Moreover, the warm approval which, less than twenty years before, Parliament had given to the introduction of a far larger body of the same troops into England itself, justified the anticipation that a similar sanction would now be cheerfully given. That sanction—which, indeed, might have been thought to be invited by the announcement of the measure in the King's speech—was undoubtedly requisite. And, if it was, a Bill of Indemnity for having acted without it was equally necessary. But, as has been seen in the last chapter, for an administration, on urgent occasions, to take action on its own responsibility, and then to apply for indemnity, is a course in strict harmony with the practice of the constitution; and if in this instance the ministers are in any respect blamable, their error would seem to have been limited to their abstaining from instantly calling Parliament together to sanction their act, and being contented to wait for the ordinary time of the Houses meeting.

The war, therefore, went on. The assertion of their independence by the Colonies divided, and, so far, weakened, the advocates of their cause in Parliament, one section of whom, led by Lord Chatham, regarded any diminution of our dominion as not only treasonable, but ruinous; on the other hand, it procured them the alliance of France and Spain. But it cannot be said that either of these incidents produced any practical effect on the result of the war. Lord Chatham's refusal to contemplate their independence could not retard its establishment; and the alliance of France and Spain, which brought nothing but disaster to those countries, could not accelerate it by a single moment. For nearly six years the war continued with alternations of success, the victories gained by the British arms being the more numerous, the triumphs of the Americans being incomparably the more important, involving as they did the surrender of two entire armies, the latter of which, that of Lord Cornwallis, in 1781, did, in fact, terminate the war, and with the war the existence of the ministry which had conducted it. A singularly rapid succession of new administrations ensued—so rapid that the negotiations for peace which the first, that of Lord Rockingham, opened, were not formally completed till the third,[56] known as the Coalition Ministry, was on the point of dismissal. It would be beside our purpose to enter into the details of the treaty which constituted the United States, as they were now called, a nation by our formal recognition of their independence. Even in that recognition, which was the most important article of the treaty, no constitutional principle was involved, though it affords the only instance in our history which can seem to throw a doubt on our inheritance of that capacity for government which the Roman poet claimed as, in ancient times, the peculiar attribute of his own countrymen. It presents the only instance of a loss of territory peopled by men who came of our blood, and who still spoke our language. It was a stern and severe lesson; and yet, fraught with discredit and disaster as it was, it nevertheless bore fruit in a later age which we may be excused for regarding as an example of the generally predominating influence of sober practical sense in our countrymen, when not led away by the temporary excitement of passion, as shown in our capacity to take home to ourselves and profit by the teachings of experience. The loss of the American Colonies was caused by the submission of the Parliament and nation to men of theory rather than of practice; ideologists, as Napoleon called them; doctrinaires, to use the modern expression; men who, because Parliament had an abstract right of universal legislation, regarded it as a full justification for insisting on its exercise, without giving a thought to the feelings, or prejudices, or habits of those who might be affected by their measures. Abstractedly considered, Lord Chatham and Lord Camden were undoubtedly wrong in denying the power of Parliament to tax the Colonies; but there was better judgment in their counsels, though founded on false premises, than in those of Grenville and Townsend, though theirs was the more correct view of the constitutional power of legislation. The two peers were wrong in their principle; the two Chancellors of the Exchequer were unwise in their application of their principle; and the practical error was the more disastrous one.

It is now generally admitted that the true statesman-like course toward the Colonies was that adopted by Lord Rockingham and his colleagues in 1765—to avoid weakening the supreme power of Parliament by any disavowal of the right to tax but to avoid imperilling the sovereign authority of the King by a novel exertion of it. As much of our common English law is made up of precedent, so, in a still greater degree, are our feelings and ideas of our rights and privileges regulated by precedent. And we lost America because in 1764 and 1767 neither minister nor Parliament took men's feelings and prejudices into account. The loss of the United States, therefore, was a lesson not undeserved; and by our statesmen since that day it has been taken in the right spirit of profiting by its teaching as a guide to their own conduct. Since that day the enterprise of our people has planted our flag in regions far more distant, and has extended the dominion of our sovereign over provinces far more extensive than those which we then lost. And on some of the administrations of the present reign the duty has fallen of framing schemes of government for those new acquisitions, as also for some of those previously possessed. In how different a spirit from that which actuated the early ministers of George III.[57] those to whom the task was committed by Queen Victoria applied themselves to their task may be seen in a maxim laid down by the present Lord Grey, when he presided at the Colonial Office (1846-1852), that "the success of free institutions in any country depends far less upon the particular form of those institutions than upon the character of the people on whom they are conferred." But how he and others in the same office carried out that principle must be reserved for a later chapter.

Besides the numerous motions which were brought forward by the Opposition respecting the continuance and conduct of the war, there were several also which were indirectly prompted by it. The Opposition claimed to be on this subject not only the champions of the real interests of the nation, but also its spokesmen, who expressed the opinions and feelings of all the thinking and independent portion of the people. That their efforts were overborne they attributed to the subservience of the Parliament to the ministers, and of the ministers to the crown.[58] And consequently several motions were made by members of that party, the object of which was, in one way or another, to diminish what they regarded as the undue influence of the crown. In one instance, and that the most successful, a direct denunciation of that influence was employed, but the earlier and more frequent proposals were directed to the purification of the House of Commons, and to the strengthening of its independence. It is remarkable that of these the two which related to a subject of which the Commons are usually most especially and most rightly jealous, the interference of peers in elections, had the worst fortune. In 1780 complaints were made and substantiated that the Duke of Bolton and the Duke of Chandos (who was also Lord-lieutenant of the county) had exerted themselves actively in the last election for Hampshire. And, in support of motions that these peers "had been guilty of a breach of the privileges of the House, and an infringement of the liberties and privileges of the Commons of Great Britain," a case was adduced in which Queen Anne had dismissed the Bishop of Worcester from the office of Almoner for similar interference. Nor did Lord Nugent, a relative of the Duke of Chandos, deny the facts alleged; on the contrary, he avowed them, and adopted a line of defence which many must have thought an aggravation of the charge, since it asserted that to prevent such interference was impossible, and therefore the House would but waste its time in trying. However, on this occasion the House took the view which he thus suggested to it, postponing all farther consideration of the matter for four months; and the charge the Duke of Bolton was shelved in a somewhat similar manner.

Even had these peers and such practices been censured with the very greatest severity, the censures could have had but a very limited effect. But it was on measures of a wider scope, embracing what began to be called a Reform of Parliament, that the more zealous members of the Opposition placed their chief reliance. As far as our records of the debates can be trusted, Lord Chatham, ten years before, had given the first hint of the desirableness of some alteration of the existing system. On one occasion he denounced the small boroughs as "the rotten part of the constitution," thus originating the epithet by which they in time came to be generally described; but more usually he disavowed all idea of disfranchising them, propounding rather a scheme for diminishing their importance by a large addition to the county members. However, he never took any steps to carry out his views, thinking, perhaps, that it was not in the Upper House that such a subject should be first broached. But he had not been long in the grave, when a formal motion for a reform of a different kind was brought forward by one of the members for the City of London, Alderman Sawbridge,[59] who, in May, 1780, applied for leave to bring in "a bill for shortening the duration of Parliaments." His own preference he avowed to be for annual Parliaments; but his suspicion that the House would think such a measure too sweeping had induced him to resolve to content himself with aiming at triennial Parliaments. As leave was refused, the bill proposed to be introduced may, perhaps, be thought disentitled to mention here, were it not that the circumstance that proposals for shortening the duration of Parliaments are still occasionally brought forward seems to warrant an account of a few of the arguments by which those who took the leading parts in the debate which ensued resisted it. The minister, Lord North, declared that the Alderman had misunderstood the views of our ancestors on the subject; as their desire had been, not that Parliament should be elected annually, but that it should sit every year, an end which had now been attained. Fox, on the other hand, while avowing that hitherto he had always opposed similar motions, declared his wish now to see not only triennial but annual Parliaments, as the sole means of lessening the influence of the crown. "If any of his constituents were to ask him to what our present misfortunes were ascribable, he should say the first cause was the influence of the crown; the second, the influence of the crown; and the third, the influence of the crown." But it was replied by Burke, who usually exhausted every question he took in hand, that such a bill would rather tend to augment that influence, since "the crown, by its constant stated power, influence, and revenue, would be able to wear out all opposition at elections; that it would not abate the interest or inclination of ministers to apply that interest to the electors; on the contrary, it would render it more necessary to them, if they desired to have a majority in Parliament, to increase the means of that influence, to redouble their diligence, and to sharpen dexterity in the application. The whole effect of the bill would, therefore, be to remove the application of some part of that influence from the elected to the electors, and farther to strengthen and extend a court interest already great and powerful in boroughs. It must greatly increase the cost of a seat in Parliament; and, if contests were frequent, to many they would become a matter of expense totally ruinous, which no fortunes could bear. The expense of the last general election was estimated at £1,500,000; and he remembered well that several agents for boroughs said to candidates, 'Sir, your election will cost you £3000 if you are independent; but, if the ministry supports you, it may be done for £2000, and even less.'" And he adduced the case of Ireland, where formerly, when "a Parliament sat for the King's life, the ordinary charge for a seat was £1500; but now, when it sat for eight years, four sessions, the charge was £2500 and upward." Such a change as was proposed would cause "triennial corruption, triennial drunkenness, triennial idleness, etc., and invigorate personal hatreds that would never be allowed to soften. It would even make the member himself more corrupt, by increasing his dependence on those who could best support him at elections. It would wreck the fortunes of those who stood on their own private means. It would make the electors more venal, and injure the whole body of the people who, whether they have votes or not, are concerned in elections." Finally, it would greatly impair the proper authority of the House itself. "It would deprive it of all power and dignity; and a House of Commons without power and without dignity, either in itself or its members, is no House of Commons for this constitution."

The applicability of some of his arguments—those founded on the disorders at times of election—has been greatly diminished, if not destroyed, at the present day, by the limitation of the polling to a single day. The disfranchisement of the smaller boroughs has neutralized others; but the expense of a general election is not believed to have diminished, and that alone seems a strong objection to a system which would render them more frequent than they are at present. Mr. Sawbridge could not obtain the support of a third of his hearers.[60] But his notions had partisans in the other House who were not discouraged by such a division; and three weeks later the Duke of Richmond brought forward a Reform Bill on so large a scale that, as the "Parliamentary History" records, "it took him an hour and a half to read it," and which contained provisions for annual Parliaments and universal suffrage. But he met with even less favor than the Alderman, and his bill was rejected without a division.

Still the subject was not allowed to rest. Even after Lord North had been replaced by Lord Rockingham, the demand for Parliamentary Reform was continued; the young Mr. Pitt making himself the mouth-piece of the Reformers, and founding a motion which he made in May, 1782, on "the corrupt influence of the crown; an influence which has been pointed at in every period as the fertile source of all our miseries; an influence which has been substituted in the room of wisdom, of activity, of exertion, and of success; an influence which has grown up with our growth and strengthened with our strength, but which, unhappily, has not diminished with our diminution, nor decayed with our decay." He brought forward no specific plan, but denounced the close boroughs, and asked emphatically whether it were "representation" for "some decayed villages, almost destitute of population, to send members to Parliament under the control of the Treasury, or at the bidding of some great lord or commoner." He, however, was defeated, though by the small majority of twenty. And it is remarkable that when, the next year, he revived the subject, developing a more precise scheme—akin to that which his father had suggested, of increasing the number of county members, and including provisions for the disfranchisement of boroughs which had been convicted of systematic corruption—he was beaten by a far larger majority,[61] the distinctness of his plan only serving to increase the numbers of his adversaries. A kinsman of Pitt's, Lord Mahon, made an equally futile attempt to diminish the expenses of elections, partly by inflicting very heavy penalties on parties guilty of either giving or receiving bribes,[62] and partly by prohibiting candidates from providing conveyances for electors; and more than one bill for disfranchising revenue-officers, as being specially liable to pressure from the government, and to prevent contractors from sitting in Parliament, was brought forward, but was lost, the smallness of the divisions in their favor being not the least remarkable circumstance in the early history of Reform. It was made still more evident that as yet the zeal for Reform was confined to a few, when, two years afterward, Pitt, though now invested with all the power of a Prime-minister, was as unable as when in opposition to carry a Reform Bill, which in more than one point foreshadowed the measure of 1832; proposing, as it did, the disfranchisement of thirty-six small boroughs, which were to be purchased of their proprietors nearly on the principle adopted in the Irish Union Act, and on the other hand the enfranchisement of copyholders; but it differed from Lord Grey's act in that it distributed all the seats thus to be obtained among the counties, with the exception of a small addition to the representatives of London and Westminster. However, his supporters very little exceeded the number who had divided with him in 1783, and Lord North, who led the Opposition in a speech denouncing any change, had a majority of seventy-four. After this second defeat, Pitt abandoned the question, at all events for the time; being convinced, to quote Earl Stanhope's description of his opinion on the subject, "that nothing but the pressure of the strongest popular feeling, such as did not then exist, could induce many members to vote against their own tenure of Parliament, or in fact against themselves."[63] What, perhaps, weighed with him more, on deciding to acquiesce in this vote as final, was the perception that as yet the question excited no strong interest out-of-doors; and when, a few years later, some who sought to become leaders of the people endeavored to raise an agitation on the subject, their teachings were too deeply infected with the contagion of the French Revolution to allow a wise ruler to think it consistent with his duty to meet them with anything but the most resolute discouragement.

But, concurrently with the first of these motions for Parliamentary Reform, two more direct attacks on the royal influence, and on what was alleged to be the undue exertion of it, were made in the session of 1780. The first was made by Burke, who brought forward a measure of economical reform, demonstrating, in a speech of extraordinary power, a vast mass of abuses, arising from corrupt waste in almost every department of the state, and in every department of the royal household, without exception, and proposing a most extensive plan of reform, which dealt with royal dignities, such as the Duchy of Lancaster and the other principalities annexed to the crown; with the crown-lands, a great portion of which he proposed to sell; with the offices of the royal household, a sufficient specimen of the abuses on which was furnished by the statement, that the turnspit in the King's kitchen was a member of Parliament; and with many departments of state, such as the Board of Works and the Pay-office, etc. He was studiously cautious in his language, urging, indeed, that his scheme of reform would "extinguish secret corruption almost to the possibility of its existence, and would destroy direct and visible influence equal to the offices of at least fifty members of Parliament," but carefully guarding against any expressions imputing this secret corruption, this influence which it was so desirable to destroy, to the crown. But his supporters were less moderate; and Mr. Thomas Townsend declared that facts which he mentioned "contained the most unquestionable presumptive evidence of the influence of the crown; he meant the diverting of its revenues to purposes which dared not be avowed, in corrupting and influencing the members of both Houses of Parliament;" and he asserted that "the principle and objects of the bill were the reduction of the influence of the crown." The bill was not opposed by the ministers on its principle; but Lord North, even while consenting to its introduction, "did not pledge himself not to oppose it in some or other of its subsequent stages;" and, in fact, his supporters resisted it in almost every detail, some of them utterly denying the right of the House to interfere at all with the expenditure of the civil list; others contesting the propriety of alienating the crown-lands; and a still greater number objecting to the abolition of some of the offices which it was proposed to sweep away, such as that of the "third Secretary of State, or Secretary for the Colonies," that of "Treasurer of the Chamber," and others of a similar character. And, as the minister succeeded in defeating him on several, though by no means all, of these points, Burke at last gave up the bill, Fox warning the House at the same time that it should be renewed session after session, and boasting that even the scanty success which it had met with had been worth the struggle.

  The other direct attack was made by Mr. Dunning, who, perhaps, did not then foresee that he himself was destined soon to fill one of the offices which had come under the lash of Burke's sarcasm, and who a few days afterward, in moving that it was necessary to declare "that the influence of the crown had increased, was increasing, and ought to be diminished" rested no small portion of his argument on the treatment that Burke's bill had received. He affirmed that, though Lord North had declared that "the influence of the crown was not too great," the divisions on that bill, and on many other measures which had been under discussion, were irrefragable proofs of the contrary. He quoted Hume and Judge Blackstone as testifying to the existence and steady increase of that influence, and "could affirm of his own knowledge, and pledge his honor to the truth of the assertion, that he knew upward of fifty members in that House who always voted in the train of the noble lord in the blue ribbon,[64] but who reprobated and condemned, out of the House, the measures they had supported and voted for in it." Mr. T. Pitt even instanced "the present possession of office by Lord North as an indubitable proof of the enormous influence of the crown."

It was not strange that Lord North opposed a resolution supported by such arguments with all the power of the government, basing his own opposition chiefly on the wisdom "of maintaining the rule long since established by Parliament, never to vote abstract propositions." But he presently saw that he was in a minority, and was forced to be content with adopting and carrying an amendment of Mr. Dundas, one of the members for Edinburgh, who flattered himself that by the insertion of *now* he converted a general assertion into a temporary declaration, which might at a future time be disavowed as no longer applicable. A majority of eighteen[65] affirmed the resolution; and when the mover followed it up by a second, declaring that "it is competent to this House to examine into and to correct abuses in the expenditure of the civil list revenues, as well as in every other branch of the public revenue, whenever it shall seem expedient to the wisdom of this House to do so," though the minister, with what was almost an appeal *ad misericordiam*, "implored the House not to proceed," he did not venture to take a division, and that resolution also, with one or two others designed to give instant effect to them, were adopted and reported by the committee to the House in a single evening.[66] The first resolution did, in fact, embody a complaint, or at least an assertion, which the Rockingham party had constantly made ever since the close of the Marquis's first administration. In a speech which he had made only a few weeks before,[67] Lord Rockingham himself had declared that "it was early in the present reign promulgated as a court axiom that the power and influence of the crown alone was sufficient to support any set of men his Majesty might think proper to call to his councils." And Burke, in his "short account" of his administration of 1765, had not only imputed both its formation and its dismissal to the "express request" and "express command of their royal master," but in the sentence, "they discountenanced and, it is to be hoped, forever abolished, the dangerous and unconstitutional practice of removing military officers for their votes in Parliament," condemned with unmistakable plainness some acts of the preceding ministry which were universally understood to have been forced upon it by the King himself. General Conway had been deprived of the colonelcy of his regiment; Lord Rockingham himself, with several other peers, had been dismissed from Lord-lieutenancies, as a punishment for voting against the ministry; such dismissals being a flagrant attempt to put down all freedom of debate in Parliament, which of all its privileges is the one most essential to its usefulness, if not to its very existence. But, as Burke said, the practice had been abandoned, and the first resolution, therefore, as Lord North said, involved no practical result. It is the second resolution that confers a constitutional character and importance on this debate. And it is not too much to say that no vote of greater value had been come to for many years. It might have been considered almost as the assertion of a truism included in the power of granting supplies, to declare that the Parliament has the right and authority to examine into and correct abuses in the expenditure, if it had not been denied by more than one speaker on the ministerial side, though not by the Prime-minister himself. But that denial made the assertion of the right an imperative duty; for certainly the exclusive right of authorizing a levy of money would lose half its value, if unaccompanied by the other right of preventing the waste of the revenue thus raised.

It may likewise be said that another principle of the parliamentary constitution is, by implication, contained in Mr. Dunning's second resolution, and that the words, "it is competent to this House to examine into and to correct abuses in the expenditure," were meant to imply a denial of the competency of the other House to institute, or even to share in, such an examination. Even if that were the object of its framer, it only coincided with the view of the peers themselves, a very considerable majority[68] of whom had, a few weeks before, rejected a motion made by Lord Shelburne for the appointment of "a committee of members of both Houses to examine without delay into the public expenditure," principally on the ground urged by the Secretary of State, Lord Stormont, and by several other peers, that "to inquire into, reform, and control the public expenditure" would be an improper interference with the privileges of the Commons; the Chief-justice, Lord Mansfield, even going the length of warning his brother peers that such interference might probably lead the Commons "to dispute in their turn the power of judicature in the last resort exercised by the peers." Lord Camden, on the contrary, affirmed, as a proposition which "no noble lord present would deny, that that House had a right to inquire so far as the disposal of public moneys came under their cognizance as a deliberative body." And in the Lower House itself, Burke, in his speech in favor of his Bill for Economical Reform, went even farther than Lord Camden, and blamed the House of Lords for rejecting Lord Shelburne's motion on such a ground. "They had gone," he said, "farther in self-denial than the utmost jealousy of the Commons could have required. A power of examining accounts, of censuring, correcting, and punishing the Commons had never, that he knew of, thought of denying to the Lords. It was something more than a century ago that the Commons had voted the Lords a useless body. They had now voted themselves so." And it would seem that the Lords themselves, to a certain extent, retracted this, their self-denying vote, when, before the end of the same session, they discussed Burke's Bill for Economical Reform, and passed it, though it was a money-bill, "containing extraneous enactments," and as such contravened one of their own standing orders which had been passed in the beginning of Queen Anne's reign, when the system of "tacking," as it was called, had excited great discontent, which was not confined to themselves. The propriety of rejecting the bill on that ground was vigorously urged by the only two lawyers who took part in the debate, the Chancellor, Lord Thurlow, and Lord Loughborough, whose object was avowedly thus to give a practical proof that the Lords "had not voted themselves useless." But even those who disregarded their advice fully asserted the right of the peers "to exercise their discretion as legislators." We have noticed this matter on a previous occasion. The privilege claimed by the Commons, both as to its origin and its principle, has been carefully examined by Hallam, who has pointed out that in its full exclusiveness it is not older than Charles II., since the Convention Parliament of 1660 "made several alterations in undoubted money-bills, to which the Commons did not object."[69] And, though his attachment to Whig principles might have inclined him to take their part in any dispute on the subject, he nevertheless thinks that they have strained both "precedent and constitutional analogy" in their assertion of this privilege, which is "an anomaly that can hardly rest on any other ground of defence than such a series of precedents as establish a constitutional usage." The usage which for two centuries was established in this case by the good-sense of both parties clearly was, that the Lords could never originate a money-bill, nor insert any clause in one increasing or even altering the burden laid by one on the people, but that they were within their right in absolutely rejecting one. But such a right has a tendency to lapse through defect of exercise; and we shall hereafter see that "the disposition to make encroachments," which in this matter Hallam imputes to the Commons, has led them in the present reign to carry their pretensions to a height which at a former period had been practically ignored by the one House, and formally disclaimed by the other.

It may be remarked that Mr. Dunning's success in carrying his first resolution did in itself, to a certain extent, disprove the truth of that resolution, since, if the influence of the crown had been such as he represented it, it must have been sufficient to insure its rejection. But that resolution, and a new statute, of which in a previous session he had been one of the principal promoters, are reckoned by Lord Stanhope as among the chief causes of the disgraceful riots of 1780. In the summer of 1778 he had seconded and supported with great eloquence the repeal of some of the penal statutes against the Roman Catholics which had been passed in the reign of William III. It was the first blow at that system of religious intolerance which for nearly a century had been one of the leading principles, as it had been also the chief disgrace, of the constitution; and it was passed with scarcely any opposition by both Houses. As, however, the statute which it repealed had been enacted before the Scotch Union, the repeal did not extend to Scotland, and it was necessary, therefore, to bring in a separate measure for that kingdom. But the intelligence that such a proceeding was in contemplation excited great wrath among the Scotch Presbyterians, who, in the hope of defeating it, established a Protestant Association for the defence of what they called the Protestant interest, and elected as its president Lord George Gordon, a young nobleman whose acts on more than one occasion gave reason to doubt the soundness of his intellect. Against any relaxation whatever of the restrictions on the Roman Catholics the Association sent up petitions to the House and to the King, couched in language the wildness of which was hardly consistent with the respect due to Parliament or to the sovereign. Apparently in the hope of mitigating its opposition, the Houses the next year passed an act, similar in principle, to relax some of the restrictions still imposed on Protestant dissenting ministers by some of the subscriptions which were required of them. But, as in the reign of Charles II., the Presbyterian hatred of the Roman Catholics was too uncompromising to be appeased in such a manner. And when Lord George found the House of Commons itself acknowledging the danger with which the constitution was threatened by the influence of the crown, he saw in their vote a justification for all his alarms, since he had adopted as one of his most settled opinions the belief that George III. was himself a Papist at heart; and, under the influence of this strange idea, he drew up a petition to Parliament which he invited all the members of the Association to accompany him to present. His summons was received with enthusiasm by his followers. The number who, in obedience to it, mustered in St. George's Fields, which he had appointed as the place of rendezvous, was not reckoned by any one at less than fifty thousand, and some calculations even doubled that estimate. Whatever the number may originally have been, it was speedily swelled by the junction of large bands of the worst characters in the metropolis, who soon began to display their strength by every kind of outrage. They commenced by attacking some of the Roman Catholic chapels, which they burnt; and, their audacity increasing at the sight of their exploits, they proceeded to assault the houses of different members of Parliament who had voted for the measures which had offended them. Because the Chief-justice, Lord Mansfield, had lately presided at a trial where a Roman Catholic had been acquitted, they sacked and burnt his house, and tried to murder himself. The magistrates, afraid of exposing themselves to the fury of such a mob, kept for the most part out of the way; and though the troops had been put under arms, and several regiments from the rural districts had been brought up to London in haste, the military officers were afraid to act without orders. Left to work their pleasure almost without resistance, the rioters attacked the different prisons, burnt Newgate and released all the prisoners, and made more than one attack on the Bank of England, where, however, fortunately the guard was strong enough to repel them. But still no active measures were taken to crush the riot. The belief was general that the soldiers might not act at all, or, at all events, not fire on rioters, till an hour after the Riot Act had been read and the mob had been warned to disperse; and no magistrate could be found to brave its fury by reading it. There seemed no obstacle to prevent the rioters from making themselves masters of the whole capital, had it not been for the firmness of the King himself, who, when all the proper authorities failed, showed himself in fact as well as in name the Chief Magistrate of the kingdom.[70] He summoned a Privy Council, and urged the members to adopt instant measures of repression; and, when some of the ministers seemed to waver, he put the question himself to the Attorney-general whether the interpretation put on the Riot Act, which seemed to him inconsistent with common-sense, were justified by the law. Wedderburn unhesitatingly replied that it was not; that "if a mob were committing a felony, as by burning dwelling-houses, and could not be prevented by other means, the military, according to the law of England, might and ought to be immediately ordered to fire upon them, the reading of the Riot Act being wholly unnecessary under such circumstances."[71] The King insisted on this opinion being instantly acted on; a proclamation was issued, and orders were sent from the Adjutant-general's office that the soldiers were to act at once without waiting for directions from the civil magistrates. A few hours now sufficed to restore tranquillity. The Chief-justice, in his place in the House of Lords, subsequently declared Wedderburn's opinion, and the orders given in reliance upon it, to be in strict conformity with the common law, laying down, as the principle on which such an interpretation of the law rested, the doctrine that in such a case the military were acting, "not as soldiers, but as citizens; no matter whether their coats were red or brown, they were legally employed in preserving the laws and the constitution;"[

72] and Wedderburn, who before the end of the year became Chief-justice of the Common Pleas, repeated the doctrine more elaborately in a charge from the Bench. It was a lesson of value to the whole community. It was quite true that the constitution placed the army in a state of dependence on the civil power. But, when that doctrine was so misunderstood as to be supposed to give temporary immunity to outrage, it was most important that such a misconstruction should be corrected, and that it should be universally known that military discipline does not require the soldier to abstain from the performance of the duty incumbent on every citizen, the prevention of crime.

Notes:

[Footnote 33:] It is worth while to preserve the amount, if for no other reason, for the contrast that the expenditure and resources of the kingdom a hundred years ago present to those of the present day. The supply required in 1764 was in round numbers £7,712,000; in 1755, before the war broke out, £4,073,000, and even that included a million for the augmentation of the army and navy. In 1761, when the war was at its height, the sum voted was £19,616,000.]

[Footnote 34:] The report in the "Parliamentary History," xvi., 37, says: "This act (the Stamp Act) passed the Commons almost without debate; two or three members spoke against it, but without force or apparent interest, except a vehement harangue from Colonel Barré (date, March 6, 1765)."]

[Footnote 35:] Lord Stanhope ("History of England," v., 131) quotes a letter of Dr. Franklin to one of his friends in America, in which, after deploring the impossibility of preventing the act from being passed, he expresses a hope that "frugality and industry will go a great way toward indemnifying us." And he complied with Mr. Grenville's request to select a person to act as Distributor of Stamps in Pennsylvania whom he thought likely to be generally acceptable.]

[Footnote 36:] These statements and arguments of Franklin are taken from different parts of his examination before the House of Commons, as preserved in the "Parliamentary History," xvi., 137-160.]

[Footnote 37:] In the Assembly of Virginia, one of the members—Patrick Henry—after declaiming with bitterness against the supposed arbitrary measures of the present reign, exclaimed, "Caesar had his Brutus, Charles I. his Oliver Cromwell, and George III.—" A cry of "Treason!" was uttered. The Speaker called Mr. Henry to order, and declared he would quit the chair unless he were supported by the House in restraining such intemperate speeches.—Adolphus, *History of England*, i., 188.]

[Footnote 38:] On this point the law has been affirmed by a judge of high reputation to be still what Lord Rockingham and his colleagues asserted. In 1868, on the trial of Governor Eyre for an indictment arising out of disturbances in Jamaica, Judge Blackburne laid it down "that, although the general rule is that the Legislative Assembly has the sole right of imposing taxes in the colony, yet, when the Imperial Legislature chooses to impose taxes, according to the rule of English law they have a *right* to do it."]

[Footnote 39:] See his speech on American taxation in April, 1774.]

[Footnote 40:] The chief divisions were: in the Commons, 275 to 167; in the Lords, 105 to 71.]

[Footnote 41:] "History of England," vol. v., c. xlv., p. 218, ed. 1862.]

[Footnote 42:] "Lives of the Chancellors," c. cxliii., life of Lord Camden.]

[Footnote 43:] Every political student will recollect Burke's description of it as "a cabinet so variously inlaid, such a piece of diversified mosaic, such a tessellated pavement without cement—here a bit of black stone, there a bit of white—patriots and courtiers, King's friends and republicans, Whigs and Tories, treacherous friends and open enemies," etc.—*Speech on American Taxation.*]

[Footnote 44:] In a debate in the year 1776, on some measures adopted for the conduct of the war, the Duke of Grafton said: "In that year (1767), when the extraordinary expenses incurred on account of America were laid before the House of Commons, the House rose as one man and insisted that that country should contribute to the burdens brought on by the military establishment there, and a motion was made for bringing in a bill for that purpose. I strenuously opposed the measure, as big with the consequences it has since, unfortunately, produced. I spoke to my friends upon the occasion, but they all united in the opinion that the tide was too strong to expect either to stem or turn it, so as to prevent whatever might be offered in that shape from passing into a law. Finding that all my efforts would be vain, I was compelled to submit, but was resolved, as far as lay in my power, to prevent the effect; and, while I gave way, to do it in such a manner as would cause the least harm. I accordingly proposed the tea-duty as the most palatable; because, though it answered the main purpose of those with whom taxation was a favorite measure, it was doing America an immediate benefit, for I procured the shilling a pound duty to be taken off, and threepence to be laid on in lieu thereof; so that, in fact, it was ninepence a pound saved to America. However, the attempt was received in America as I expected it would be—it immediately caused disturbances and universal dissatisfaction."—*Parliamentary History*, xviii., 134.]

[Footnote 45:] This unpopularity had been aggravated by another measure which was among the last acts of Mr. Grenville's ministry. The Mutiny Act in the Colonies was renewed for two years at a time, and, at its renewal in the spring of 1765, a clause was added which required the Colonists to furnish the troops with "fire, candles, vinegar, salt, bedding, utensils for cooking, and liquors, such as beer, cider, and rum." The Assemblies of several States passed resolutions strongly condemning this new imposition; but, as the dissatisfaction did not lead to any overt acts of disturbance, it seems to have been unnoticed in England at the time, or the clause would probably have been repealed by Lord Rockingham; and eventually the Assembly of New York seems to have withdrawn its objections to it, presenting an address to Sir H. Moore, the Governor, in which "they declared their intention of making the required provision for the troops."—Lord E. Fitzmaurice, *Life of Lord Shelburne*, ii., 61.]

[Footnote 46:] The "Memoirs of Judge Livingstone" record his expression of opinion as early as 1773, that "it was intolerable that a continent like America should be governed by a little island three thousand miles distant." "America," said he, "must and will be independent." And in the "Memoirs of General Lee" we find him speaking to Mr. Patrick Henry, who in 1766 had been one of the most violent of all the denouncers of the English policy (see *ante*,), of "independence" as "a golden castle in the air which he had long dreamed of."]

[Footnote 47:] See the whole speech, "Parliamentary History," xvi., 853. Many of the taxes he denounced as so injurious to the British manufacturers, "that it must astonish any reasonable man to think how so preposterous a law could originally obtain existence from a British Legislature."]

[Footnote 48:] The division was: for the amendment, 142; against it, 204.]

[Footnote 49:] The words of the "preamble," on which Burke dwelt in 1774, were: "Whereas it is expedient that a revenue should be raised in your Majesty's dominions in America for making a more certain and adequate provision for defraying the charge of the administration of justice and support of civil government in such provinces where it shall be found necessary, and toward farther defraying the expenses of defending, protecting, and securing: the said dominions, be it enacted," etc.]

[Footnote 50:] "Memoirs and Correspondence of Jefferson." Quoted by Lord Stanhope, "History of England," vi., 14.]

[Footnote 51:] At Lexington, April 19, 1775.]

[Footnote 52:] Lord Stanhope, however, has reason on his side when he calls the words of this petition "vague and general," though "kindly and respectful;" and when he points to the language of extreme bitterness against England indulged in by Franklin at the very time that this petition was voted. He, however, expresses a belief that even then "the progress of civil war might have been arrested," which seems doubtful. But it is impossible not to agree with his lordship in condemning the refusal by the ministry to take any notice of the petition, on the ground that the Congress was a self-constituted body, with no claim to authority or recognition, and one which had already sanctioned the taking up arms against the King.—*History of England*, vi., 93, 95, 105.]

[Footnote 53:] It is probable, however, that the greater part of the Hanoverian soldiers were Protestants.]

[Footnote 54:] Lord Campbell, who, in his "Life of Lord Bathurst," asserts that the legality of the measure turns upon the just construction of the Act of Settlement, adduces Thurlow's language on this subject as "a proof that he considered that he had the privilege which has been practised by other Attorney-generals and Chancellors too, in debate, of laying down for law what best suited his purpose at the moment." It does not seem quite certain that the noble and learned biographer has not more than once in these biographies allowed himself a similar license in the description of questions of party politics.]

[Footnote 55:] In the debates on the subject it was stated that the number of Hanoverians quartered in the two fortresses was nineteen hundred, and the number of British troops left in them was two thousand. Moreover, as has been already remarked, though Lord Shelburne spoke of arming Roman Catholics, it is probable that the Hanoverians were mostly Protestants.]

[Footnote 56:] The Preliminary or Provisional Articles, as they were called, of which the Definitive Treaty was but a copy, were signed at Paris, November 30, 1782, during Lord Shelburne's administration. But the Definitive Treaty was not signed till the 3d of September of the following year, under the Coalition Ministry, which was turned out a few weeks afterward.]

[Footnote 57:] We shall see in a subsequent chapter that even in this reign of George III. Pitt laid down the true principles of our legislation for the colonies in his bill for the better government of Canada.]

[Footnote 58:] An admirably reasoned passage on the influence of the crown, especially in the reigns of the two first Hanoverian Kings, will be found in Hallam, "Constitutional History," c. xvi., vol. iii., p. 392, ed. 1832.]

[Footnote 59:] The "Parliamentary History" shows that he had brought forward the same motion before 1780; since Lord Nugent, who replied to him, said "the same motion had been made for some years past, and had been silently decided on." From which it seems that it was never discussed at any length till May 8, 1780.]

[Footnote 60:] On the division the numbers were: for the motion, 90; against it, 182.]

[Footnote 61:] The division in 1782 was: 161 to 141; in 1783, 293 to 149.]

[Footnote 62:] How systematic and open bribery was at this time is shown by an account of Sheridan's expenses at Stafford in 1784, of which the first item is—248 burgesses, paid £5 5s. each, £1302.—Moore's *Life of Sheridan*, i., 405.]

[Footnote 63:] "Life of Pitt," i., 359.]

[Footnote 64:] Lord North was a Knight of the Garter, the only commoner, except Sir R. Walpole, who received that distinction in the last century, and the latest, with the exception of Lord Castlereagh. on whom it has been conferred.]

[Footnote 65:] 233 to 315.]

[Footnote 66:] It is perhaps worth pointing out, as a specimen of the practical manner in which parliamentary business was transacted at that time, that this great debate—in which (the House being in committee) Mr. Dunning himself spoke three times, and Lord North, Mr. T. Pitt, Mr. Fox, the Speaker (Sir F. Norton), the Attorney-general, General Conway, Governor Pownall, the Lord-advocate, and several other members took part—was concluded by twelve o'clock.]

[Footnote 67:] February 8, 1780, on Lord Shelburne's motion for an inquiry into the public expenditure.—*Parliamentary History*, xx., 1346.]

[Footnote 68:] 101 to 55.]

[Footnote 69:] "Constitutional History," iii., 43.]

[Footnote 70:] His language is said to have been that "there was at all events one Magistrate in the kingdom who would do his duty."—Lord Stanhope, *History of England*, vii., 48.]

[Footnote 71:] "Lives of the Lord Chancellors," c. clxvii.]

[Footnote 72:] Lord Stanhope's "History of England," vii, 56.]

CHAPTER IV

Changes of Administration.—The Coalition Ministry.—
The Establishment of the Prince of Wales.—Fox's India
Bill.—The King Defeats it by the Agency of Lord Temple.—
The Ministry is Dismissed, and Succeeded by Mr. Pitt's
Administration.—Opposition to the New Ministry in the
House of Commons.—Merits of the Contest between the
Old and the New Ministry.—Power of Pitt.—Pitt's India
Bill.—Bill for the Government of Canada.—The Marriage of
the Prince of Wales to Mrs. Fitzherbert.—The King becomes
Deranged.—Proposal of a Regency.—Opinions of Various
Writers on the Course adopted.—Spread of Revolutionary
Societies and Opinions.—Bills for the Repression of
Sedition and Treason.—The Alien Act.—The Traitorous
Correspondence Act.—Treason and Sedition Bills.—Failure
of some Prosecutions under them.

The occurrences of the next year brought the question of the influence of the crown into greater prominence. Lord Rockingham's administration, unfortunately, came to a premature termination by his death at the beginning of July. With a strange arrogance, Fox claimed the right of dictating the choice of his successor to the King, making his pretensions the more unwarrantable by the character of the person whom he desired to nominate, the Duke of Portland, who, though a man of vast property and considerable borough influence, was destitute of ability of any kind, and had not even any of that official experience which in some situations may at times compensate or conceal the want of talent.[73] The King preferred Lord Shelburne, a statesman whose capacity was confessedly of a very high order, who had more than once been Secretary of State,[74] and who had been recognized as the leader of what was sometimes called the Chatham section of the Whigs, ever since the death of the great Earl. Indeed, if George III. had been guided by his own wishes and judgment alone, he would have placed him at the Treasury, in preference to Lord Rockingham, three months before. But, during the last three months, jealousies had arisen between him and Fox, his colleague in office, who charged him with concealing from him the knowledge of various circumstances, the communication of which he had a right to require. It was more certain that on one or two points connected with the negotiations with the United States there had been divisions between them, and that the majority of the cabinet had agreed with Lord Shelburne. Lord Shelburne, therefore, became Prime-minister,[75] and Fox, with some of his friends, resigned; Fox indemnifying himself by a violent philippic against "those men who were now to direct the counsels of the country," and whom he proceeded to describe as "men whom neither promises could bind nor principles of honor could secure; who would abandon fifty principles for the sake of power, and forget fifty promises when they were no longer necessary to their ends; who, he had no doubt, to secure themselves in the power which they had by the labor of others obtained, would strive to strengthen it by any means which corruption could procure."[76]

Fox at once went into what even those most disposed to cherish his memory admit to have been a factious opposition. He caballed with the very men to whom he had hitherto been most vehemently opposed for the sole object of expelling Lord Shelburne from office. And when, at the beginning of the session of 1783, the merits of the preliminary articles of peace which had been provisionally concluded with the United States came under discussion, though the peers approved of them, in the House of Commons he defeated the ministers in two separate divisions,[77] and thus rendered their retention of office impossible. He had gained this victory by uniting with Lord North and a portion of the Tory party whom, ever since his dismissal from office in 1774, he had been unwearied in denouncing, threatening Lord North himself with impeachment. And he now used it to compel the King to intrust the chief office in the government to the very man whom his Majesty had refused to employ in such an office six months before.

The transactions of the next twelve months exhibit in a striking light more than one part of the practical working of our monarchical and parliamentary constitution, not only in its correspondence with, but, what is more important to notice, in its occasional partial deviations from, strict theory. The theory has sometimes been expressed in the formula, "The King reigns, but does not govern." But, like many another terse apophthegm, it conveys an idea which requires some modification before it can be regarded as an entirely correct representation of the fact; and the King himself, especially if endowed with fair capacity and force of character, imbued with earnest convictions, and animated by a genuine zeal for the honor and welfare of his kingdom, will be likely to dwell more on the possible modifications than on the rigid theory. Even those who insist most on the letter of the theory will not deny that, if the King has not actual power, he has at least great influence; and the line between authority and influence is hard to draw. One of George the Third's earliest ministers had explained to his Majesty that the principle of the constitution was, "that the crown had an undoubted right to choose its ministers, and that it was the duty of subjects to support them, unless there were some very strong and urgent reasons to the contrary."[78] And such a doctrine was too much in harmony with the feelings of George III. himself not to be cordially accepted. For George III. was by no means inclined to be a *Roi fainéant*. No sovereign was ever penetrated with a more conscientious desire to do his duty to his people. Conscious, perhaps, that his capacity was rather solid than brilliant, he gave unremitting attention to the affairs of the nation in every department of the government; and, perhaps not very unnaturally, conceived that his doing so justified him, as far as he might be able, in putting a constraint on his ministers to carry out his views. Thus, he had notoriously induced Lord North to persevere in the late civil war in America long after that minister had seen the hopelessness of the contest; and it was, probably, only the knowledge of the strength of his feelings on that subject, and of his warm attachment to that minister, that caused the Parliament so long to withstand all the eloquence of the advocates of peace, and the still stronger arguments of circumstances. He might fairly think that he had now greater reason to adhere to his own judgment; for Fox's recommendation of the Duke of Portland in preference to Lord Shelburne was an act not only of unwarrantable presumption, but of inconceivable folly, since there was no comparison between the qualifications of the two men; and the coalition by which, six months afterward, he had, as it were, revenged himself for the rebuff, and had driven Lord Shelburne from office, was, as the King well knew, and as even Fox's own friends did not conceal from themselves, almost universally condemned out-of-doors.[79] To this combination, therefore, his Majesty tried every expedient to escape from yielding. And when Pitt's well-considered and judicious refusal of the government left him no alternative but that of submission to Fox's dictation, it would hardly have been very unnatural if his disposition and attitude toward a ministry which had thus forced itself upon him had been those attributed to him by Lord John Russell, of "an enemy constantly on the watch against it."[80] But for some time that was not the impression of the ministers themselves. In July, when they had been in office more than three months, Fox admitted that he had never behaved toward them as if he were displeased with them, and that he had no project of substituting any other administration for the present one.[81] And his temperate treatment of them was the more remarkable, because a flagrant blunder of Burke (who filled the post of Paymaster), in reinstating some clerks who had been dismissed by his predecessor for dishonesty, had manifestly weakened the ministry in the House of Commons;[82] while in another case, in which the King had clearly in no slight degree a personal right to have his opinion consulted and his wishes accepted by them as the guide for their conduct, the establishment to be arranged for the Prince of Wales, whose twenty-first birthday was approaching, Fox persuaded the Parliament to settle on the young Prince an allowance of so large an amount that some even of his own colleagues disliked it as extravagant;[83] while the King himself reasonably disapproved both of the amount and of the mode of giving it, the amount being large beyond all precedent, and the fact of its being given by Parliament rendering the Prince entirely independent of his parental control, of which his conduct had given abundant proof that he stood greatly in need.

That he presently changed his line of behavior toward them was caused by their introduction of a bill which he regarded as aimed in no small degree at his own prerogative and independence—the celebrated India Bill, by which, in the November session, Fox proposed to abrogate all the charters which different sovereigns had granted to the East India Company, to abolish all vested rights of either the Company or individuals, and to confer on a board of seven persons, to be named by Parliament, the entire administration of all the territories in any way occupied by the Company. It was at once objected to by the Opposition in the House of Commons, now led by Mr. Pitt, as a measure thoroughly unconstitutional, on the twofold ground that such an abrogation of formally granted charters, and such an extinction of vested rights, was absolutely without precedent; and also that one real, if concealed, object of the bill was to confer on the ministers who had framed and introduced it so vast an amount of patronage as would render them absolute masters of the House of Commons, and indirectly, therefore, of the King himself, who would be practically disabled from ever dismissing them. That such a revocation of ancient charters, and such an immovable establishment of an administration, were inconsistent with the principles of the constitution, was not a position taken up by Pitt in the heat of debate, but was his deliberate opinion, as may be fairly inferred from his assertion of it in a private letter[84] to his friend the Duke of Rutland. It may, however, be doubted whether the epithet "unconstitutional" could be properly applied to the bill on either ground. There is, indeed, a certain vagueness in the meaning, or at all events in the frequent use of this adjective. Sometimes it is used to imply a violation of the provisions of the Great Charter, or of its later development, the Bill of Rights; sometimes to impute some imagined departure from the principles which guided the framers of those enactments. But in neither sense does it seem applicable to this bill. To designate the infringement or revocation of a charter by such a description would be to affirm the existence of a right in the sovereign to invest a charter, from whatever motive it may originally have been granted, with such a character of inviolability or perpetuity that no Parliament should, on ever such strong grounds of public good, have the power of interfering with it. And to attribute such a power to the crown appears less consistent with the limitations affixed to the royal prerogative by the constitution, than to regard all trusts created by the crown as subject to parliamentary revision in the interests of the entire nation. On the second ground the description seems even less applicable. An arrangement of patronage is a mere matter of detail, not of principle. For the minister to propose such an arrangement as should secure for himself and his party a perpetual monopoly of power and office might be grasping and arrogant; for Parliament (and Parliament consists of the sovereign and the peers, as well as of the House of Commons) to assent to such an arrangement might be short-sighted and impolitic; but it is not clear that either the minister in proposing such an enactment, or the Parliament in adopting it, would be violating either the letter or the spirit of the constitution. Every member of the Governing Board was to be appointed by the Parliament itself; and, though unquestionably Fox would have the nomination, and though he could reckon on the support of the majority in the House of Commons for those whom he might select, still it was a strictly constitutional machinery that he was putting in motion.

A measure, however, may be very objectionable without being unconstitutional, and such a view of the India Bill the progress of the debates in the House of Commons disposed the King to take of it. In the House of Peers Lord Thurlow described the bill as one to take the crown off his head and place it on that of Mr. Fox; and, even without adopting that description to its full extent, the King might easily regard the bill as a very unscrupulous attempt to curtail his legitimate authority and influence. He became most anxious to prevent the bill from being presented to him for his royal assent. And it was presently represented to him that the knowledge of his desire would probably induce the Lords to reject it. Among the peers who had attacked the bill on its first introduction into their House was Earl Temple, whose father had taken so prominent a part in the negotiations for the formation of a new ministry in 1765, and who had himself been Lord-lieutenant of Ireland under Lord Shelburne's administration. But he had not thought it prudent to divide the House against its first reading, and felt great doubts as to his success in a division on the second, unless he could fortify his opposition by some arguments as yet untried. He had no difficulty in finding a willing and effective coadjutor. Since the retirement of Lord Bute from court, no peer had made himself so personally acceptable to the King as Lord Thurlow, who had been Lord Chancellor during the last four years of Lord North's administration, and, in consequence, as it was generally understood, of the earnest request of George III., had been allowed to retain the seals by Lord Rockingham, and afterward by Lord Shelburne. What special attraction drew the King toward him, unless it were some idea of his honesty and attachment to the King himself—on both of which points subsequent events proved his Majesty to be wholly mistaken—it is not very easy to divine; but his interest with the King at this time was notorious, and equally notorious was the deep resentment which he cherished against Fox and Lord North, of whom, as he alleged, the former had proscribed and the latter had betrayed him. To him, therefore, Lord Temple now applied for advice as to the best mode of working on the King's mind, and, with his assistance, drew up a memorial on the character of the India Bill, on its inevitable fruits if it should pass (which it described as an extinction of "more than half of the royal power, and a consequent disabling of his Majesty for the rest of his reign"), and on the most effectual plan for defeating it; for which end it was suggested that his Majesty should authorize some one to make some of the Lords "acquainted with his wishes" that the bill should be rejected.[85]

George III. eagerly adopted the suggestion, and drew up a brief note, which he intrusted to Lord Temple himself, and which stated that "his Majesty allowed Earl Temple to say that whoever voted for the India Bill was not only not his friend, but would be considered by him as his enemy. And, if these words were not strong enough, Earl Temple might whatever words he might deem stronger and more to the purpose."[86]

Lord Temple lost no time in availing himself of the permission thus granted him; and, as it was by no means his object to keep the transaction secret, his conduct was made the subject of severe comment by the Prime-minister himself the next time that the bill was mentioned in the Upper House. The Duke of Portland, indeed, professed to have learned it only from common report, and to hope that the report was unfounded, since, were it true, "he should be wanting in the duty he owed to the public as a minister if he did not take the opportunity of proposing a measure upon it to their lordships that would prove that they felt the same jealousy, the same detestation, the same desire to mark and stigmatize every attempt to violate the constitution as he did." Lord Temple, in reply, abstained from introducing any mention of the King's opinions or wishes, but avowed plainly that he had used his privilege as a peer to solicit an interview with his Majesty, and that at that interview "he had given his advice. What that advice had been he would not then say; it was lodged in the breast of his Majesty, nor would he declare the purport of it without the royal consent, or till he saw a proper occasion. But, though he would not declare affirmatively what his advice to his sovereign was, he would tell their lordships negatively what it was not. It was not friendly to the principle and objects of the bill."[87] The debate lasted till near midnight. Of the speakers, a great majority declared against the bill; and, on the division, it was rejected by a majority of nineteen.[88] This took place on the 15th of December. On the 18th, as the ministers had not resigned—not regarding a single defeat in the Upper House as a necessary cause for such a step—the King sent messengers to them to demand their resignation, and the next day it was publicly announced in the House of Commons that Pitt had accepted the office of Prime-minister.

But Fox, who had anticipated the dismissal of himself and his colleagues, was by no means inclined to acquiesce in it, or to yield without a struggle; and on the 17th one of his partisans in the House of Commons, Mr. Baker, one of the members for Hertfordshire, brought forward some resolutions on the subject of the late division in the House of Lords. He professed to rest them solely on rumors, but he urged that "it was the duty of that House to express its abhorrence even of that rumor," since by such an action as was alleged "that responsibility of ministers which was the life of the constitution would be taken away, and with it the principal check that the public had upon the crown." And he urged "the members of that House, as the guardians of the constitution, to stand forward and preserve it from ruin, to maintain that equilibrium between the three branches of the Legislature, and that independence without which the constitution could no longer exist," and with this view to resolve "that to report any opinion, or pretended opinion, of his Majesty upon any bill or other proceeding depending in either House of Parliament, with a view to influence the votes of the members, is a high crime and misdemeanor, derogatory to the honor of the crown, a breach of the fundamental privileges of Parliament, and subversive of the constitution of the country." It was opposed by Pitt, chiefly on the ground that Mr. Baker only based the necessity for such a resolution on common report, which he, fairly enough, denied to be a sufficient justification of it; and partly on the undoubted and "inalienable right of peers, either individually or collectively, to advise his Majesty, whenever they thought the situation of public affairs made such a step an essential part of their duty." But it was supported by Lord North as "necessary on constitutional principles," since the acts so generally reported and believed "affected the freedom of debate;" and by Fox, who declared that the action which was reported, if true, "struck at the great bulwark of our liberties, and went to the absolute annihilation, not of our chartered rights only, but of those radical and fundamental ones which are paramount to all charters, which were consigned to our care by the sovereign disposition of Nature, which we cannot relinquish without violating the most sacred of all obligations, to which we are entitled, not as members of society, but as individuals and as men; the right of adhering steadily and uniformly to the great and supreme laws of conscience and duty; of preferring, at all hazards and without equivocation, those general and substantial interests which members have sworn to prefer; of acquitting themselves honorably to their constituents, to their friends, to their own minds, and to that public whose trustees they were, and for whom they acted." He avowed his conviction that rumor in this instance spoke truth, and, affirming that "the responsibility of ministers is the only pledge and security the people of England possesses against the infinite abuses so natural to the exercise of royal powers," argued that, if "this great bulwark of the constitution were once removed, the people would become in every respect the slaves and property of despotism. This must be the necessary consequence of secret influence." He argued that the sole distinction between an absolute and a limited monarchy was that the sovereign in one is a despot, and may do as he pleases, but that in the other he is himself subjected to the laws, and consequently is not at liberty to advise with any one in public affairs who is not responsible for that advice, and that the constitution has clearly directed his negative to operate under the same wise restrictions. Mr. Baker's resolution was carried by a large majority; but, as we have seen, did not deter the King from dismissing the ministry.

The conduct of George III. in this transaction has been discussed by writers of both parties with such candor that the Tory historian, Lord Stanhope, while evidently desirous to defend it by implication, passes a slight censure on it in the phrase that "the course pursued by the King was most unusual, and most extreme, and most undesirable to establish as a precedent;"[89] while, on the other hand, so rigid a Whig as Lord Campbell urges in his favor "that if it be ever excusable in a King of England to cabal against his ministers, George III. may well be defended for the course he now took, for they had been forced upon him by a factious intrigue, and public opinion was decidedly in his favor."[90] But to those who regard not the excuse which previous provocation may be conceived in some degree to furnish to human infirmity, but only the strict theory and principle of the constitution on which the doctrine of the responsibility of the ministers and the consequent irresponsibility of the sovereign rests, Lord Campbell's conditional justification for the communication made through Lord Temple will hardly appear admissible. We cannot be sure how far Mr. Grenville's "Diary" is to be trusted for transactions in which he was not personally concerned, or for conversations at which he was not present; but in giving an account[91] of some of the occurrences of the spring of 1766, while Lord Rockingham was Prime-minister, we find him relating a conversation between the King and Lord Mansfield on the ministerial measure for conciliating the American Colonies by the repeal of the Stamp Act, combined, however, with an assertion of the *right* to tax. "He (Lord Mansfield) took notice of the King's name having been bandied about in a very improper manner; to which the King assented, saying he had been very much displeased at it, as thinking it unconstitutional to have his name mentioned as a means to sway any man's opinion in any business which was before Parliament; and that all those who approached him knew that to be his sentiment. Lord Mansfield said he differed from his Majesty in that opinion, for that, though it would be unconstitutional to endeavor by his Majesty's name to carry questions in Parliament, yet where the lawful rights of the King and Parliament were to be asserted and maintained, he thought the making his Majesty's opinion in support of those rights to be known was very fit and becoming." The line here alleged to have been drawn by the great Chief-justice, between proclaiming the King's opinion in support of rights, but withholding it in the case of measures, is, perhaps, too fine to be perceptible by ordinary intellects. But however the King may have understood the judge, it is clear that the doctrine thus asserted does not justify, but condemns, such an act as the communication of the King's opinion and wishes in the case under consideration. If it "would be unconstitutional to endeavor by his Majesty's name to carry questions in Parliament," it must be at least equally so to use his name to defeat them. And the case is infinitely stronger, if the measure to be defeated be one which has been introduced by his ministers. For there can be no doubt whatever that, so long as they are his ministers, they are entitled to his full and complete support on every question; alike in their general policy and on each separate measure. When he can no longer give them that support, which the very act of conferring their offices on them promised them, his only legitimate and becoming course is to dismiss them from their offices, and to abide the judgment of Parliament and the nation on that act. Thus William IV. acted in the autumn of 1834; and thus George III. himself acted at the end of the month of which we are speaking. But to retain them in their offices, and to employ an unofficial declaration of his dissent from them to defeat their policy, is neither consistent with the straightforward conduct due from one gentleman to another, nor with the principle on which the system of administration, such as prevails in this country, is founded.

As has been already mentioned, the King at once dismissed the Coalition Ministry. Mr. Pitt accepted the conduct of affairs, and by so doing accepted the responsibility for all the acts of the King which had conduced to his appointment. Lord John Russell, who in his "Memorials and Correspondence of Fox" has related and examined the whole transaction at considerable though not superfluous length, while blaming the prudence, and in some points the propriety, of Fox's conduct, at the same time severely censures Pitt as "committing a great fault in accepting office as the price of an unworthy intrigue," and affirms that "he and his colleagues who accepted office upon the success of this intrigue placed themselves in an unconstitutional position."[92] This seems to be a charge which can hardly be borne out. In dismissing his former ministry, the King was clearly acting within his right; and, if so, Pitt was equally within his in undertaking the government. The truer doctrine would seem to be, that, in so undertaking it, he assumed the entire responsibility for the dismissal of his predecessors,[93] and left it to the people at large, by the votes of their representatives, to decide whether that dismissal were justified, and whether, as its inevitable consequence, his acceptance of office were also justified or not. The entire series of transactions, from the meeting of Parliament in November, 1783, to its dissolution in the following March, may be constitutionally regarded as an appeal by the King from the existing House of Commons to the entire nation, as represented by the constituencies; and their verdict, as is well known, ratified in the most emphatic manner all that had been done. And we may assert this without implying that, if the single act of empowering Lord Temple to influence the peers by the declaration of the King's private feeling had been submitted by itself to the electors, they would have justified that. The stirring excitement of the three months' contest between the great rivals led them to pronounce upon the transaction as a whole, and to leave unnoticed what seemed for the moment to be the minor issues—the moves, if we may borrow a metaphor from the chess-table, which opened the game; and it may be observed that, though, on the 17th of December, Pitt resisted Mr. Baker's resolution with his utmost energy, in the numerous debates which ensued he carefully avoided all allusion to Lord Temple's conduct, or to the measure which had led to the dismissal of his predecessors, farther than was necessary for the explanation of the principles of his own India Bill. It may even be surmised that, if he had been inclined to recognize Lord Temple's interference as warrantable, the breach between that peer and himself, which occurred before the end of the week, would not have taken place, since it seems nearly certain that the cause of that breach was a refusal on the part of Pitt to recommend his cousin for promotion in the peerage, a step which, at such a moment, would have had the appearance of an approval of his most recent deed,[94] but which he could hardly have refused, if it had been done with his privity. The battle, as need hardly be told, was first fought among the representatives of the people in the House of Commons; for there was only one occasion on which the opinion of the Lords was invited, when they declared in favor of Pitt by a decisive majority. [95] But in the Lower House the contest was carried on for more than two months with extraordinary activity and ability, by a series of resolutions and motions brought forward by the partisans of the coalition, and contested by the youthful minister. In one respect the war was waged on very unequal terms, Pitt, who had been but three years in Parliament, and whose official experience could as yet only be counted by months, having to contend almost single-handed against the combined experience and eloquence of Lord North, Fox, and Burke. Fortunately, however, for him, their own mismanagement soon turned the advantage to his side. They were too angry and too confident to be skilful, or even ordinarily cautious. The leaders on both sides made professions in one respect similar; they both alike denied that a desire of office influenced either their conduct or their language (a denial for which Pitt's refusal of the Treasury, a year before, gained him more credit than could be expected by Fox after his coalition with Lord North), and both alike professed to be struggling for the constitution alone, for some fundamental principle which each charged his antagonist with violating; Fox on one occasion even going so far as, in some degree, to involve the King himself in his censures, declaring not only that "the struggle was, in fact, one between Pitt himself and the constitution," but that it was also one "between liberty and the influence of the crown," and "between prerogative and the constitution;" and that "Pitt had been brought into power by means absolutely subversive of the constitution."[96] But no act of which he thus accused the minister or the King showed such a disregard of the fundamental principle of the constitution of Parliament as was exhibited by Fox himself when, in the very first debate after the Christmas recess, he called in question that most undoubted prerogative of the crown to dissolve the Parliament, and, drawing a distinction which had certainly never been heard of before, declared that, though the King had an incontestable right to dissolve the Parliament after the close of a session, "many great lawyers" doubted whether he had such a right in the middle of a session, a dissolution at such a period being "a penal" one. Professing to believe that an immediate dissolution was intended, he even threatened to propose to the House of Commons "measures to guard against a step so inimical to the true interests of the country," and made a more direct attack than ever on the King himself, by the assertion of a probability that, even if Pitt did not contemplate a dissolution, his royal master might employ "secret influence" to overrule him, and might dissolve in spite of him,[97] an imputation which Lord North, with a strange departure from his customary good-humor, condescended to endorse.[98] There could be no doubt that both the doubt and the menace were of themselves distinct attacks on the constitution; and they were, moreover, singularly impolitic and inconsistent with others of the speaker's arguments, since, if the nation at large approved of his views and conduct, a dissolution—which would have placed the decision in its hands—would have been the very thing he should most have desired. On another evening, though he admitted as a principle that the sovereign had the prerogative of choosing his ministers, he not only sought to narrow the effect of that admission by the assertion that "to exercise that prerogative in opposition to the House of Commons would be a measure as unsafe as unjustifiable,"[99] but to confine the right of deciding the title of the ministers to confidence to the existing House of Commons. He accused Pitt of "courting the affection of the people, and on this foundation wishing to support himself in opposition to the repeated resolutions of the House passed in the last three weeks." Had he confined himself to urging the necessity of the ministers and the House of Commons being in harmony, even though such a mention of the House of Commons by itself were to a certain extent an ignoring of the weight of the other branches of the Legislature, he would have only been advancing a doctrine which is practically established at the present day, since there has been certainly more than one instance in which a ministry has retired which enjoyed the confidence of both the sovereign and the House of Lords, because it was not supported by a majority in the House of Commons. But when he proceeded to make it a charge against the minister that he trusted to the good-will of the people to enable him to disregard the verdict of the House of Commons, he forgot that it was only as representing the people that the House had any right to pronounce a verdict; and that, if it were true that the judgment of the people was more favorable to the minister than that of the House of Commons, the difference which thus existed was a condemnation of the existing House, and an irresistible reason for calling on the constituencies to elect another.

Pitt, therefore, had no slight advantage in defending himself against so rash an assailant. "He did not shrink," he said, "from avowing himself the friend of the King's just prerogative," and in doing so he maintained that he had a title to be regarded as the champion of the people not less than of the crown. "Prerogative had been justly called a part of the rights of the people, and he was sure it was a part of their rights which they were never more inclined to defend, of which they were never more jealous, than at that hour."[100] And he contended that Fox's objections to a dissolution betrayed a consciousness that he had not the confidence of the nation. At last, when the contest had lasted nearly two months, Fox took the matter into his own hands, and, no longer putting his partisans in the front of the battle, on the 1st of March he himself moved for an address to the King, the most essential clause of which "submitted to his Majesty's royal consideration that the continuance of an administration which did not possess the confidence of the representatives of the people must be injurious to the public service." ...

And, therefore, that "his Majesty's faithful Commons did find themselves obliged again to beseech his Majesty that he would be graciously pleased to lay the foundation of a strong and stable government by the previous removal of his present ministers." In the speech with which he introduced this address he put himself forward as especially the champion of the House of Commons. He charged the Prime-minister with an express design "to reduce the House to insignificance, to render it a mere appendage to the court, an appurtenance to the administration." He asserted the existence of a systematic "design to degrade the House, after which there was not another step necessary to complete the catastrophe of the constitution." And on this occasion he distinguished the feelings of the King from those which influenced the minister, affirming his confidence "that the King's heart had no share in the present business."[101]

Pitt, on the other hand, in reply, affirmed that he was called on by duty "to defend the rights of the other branches of the Legislature; the just and constitutional prerogative of the sovereign," upon which the Opposition was seeking to encroach, without even having shown a single reason to justify such invasion. He freely admitted that, if the House of Commons or either of the other branches of the Legislature "disapproved of an administration on proper grounds, it would not be well for that administration to retain office." But in the present instance he contended that "no ground for disapprobation had been shown." The existing administration "had, in fact, by an unaccountable obstinacy and untowardness of circumstances, been deprived of all opportunity" of showing its capacity or its intentions. "If any accusations should be made and proved against it, if any charges should be substantiated, it would, indeed be proper for the ministers to resign; and if, in such a case he were afterward to continue in office, he would suffer himself to be stigmatized as the champion of prerogative, and the unconstitutional supporter of the usurpation of the crown. But till this period arrived, he should reckon it his duty to adhere to the principles of the constitution, as delivered to us by our ancestors; to defend them against innovation and encroachment, and to maintain them with firmness." "The constitution of this country," he presently added, "is its glory; but in what a nice adjustment does its excellence consist! Equally free from the distractions of democracy and the tyranny of monarchy, its happiness is to be found in its mixture of parts. It was this mixed government which the prudence of our ancestors devised, and which it will be our wisdom to support. They experienced all the vicissitudes and distractions of a republic; they felt all the vassalage and despotism of a simple monarchy. They abandoned both; and, by blending each together, extracted a system which has been the envy and admiration of the world. This system it is the object of the present address to defeat and destroy. It is the intention of this address to arrogate a power which does not belong to the House of Commons; to place a negative on the exercise of the prerogative, and to destroy the balance of power in the government as it was settled at the Revolution."

Fox had urged that our history afforded no example of a ministry retaining office after the House of Commons had passed a resolution condemning it. Pitt, in reply, urged that our history equally failed to furnish any instance of a ministry having been called on to retire without any misconduct being alleged against them. And the result of the division showed that his arguments and his firmness were producing an impression on the House, for, though he was again defeated, the majority against him (only twelve) was far smaller than on any previous division.[102] A week later, this feeling in his favor was shown still more decidedly, when Fox, on moving for a fresh address, or, as he termed it, a representation to the King that the House had received his Majesty's reply to their address "with surprise and affliction," he could only carry it by a single vote.[103] And this division closed the struggle. Fox made no farther effort. Before the end of the month the Parliament was dissolved, and the general election which ensued sent to the House a majority to support the ministers which Pitt was fairly warranted in claiming as the full justification of the course which he had pursued.

On a review of the whole of this extraordinary transaction, or series of transactions, it is impossible to avoid regarding the issue of the struggle as an all-important element in the case, and a test almost decisive of the correctness of conduct of the rival leaders. We may leave out of the question the action of the King in his communication to Lord Temple, which, although sanctioned by the great legal authority of Lord Thurlow, we are, for reasons already given, compelled to regard as unconstitutional, but for which Mr. Pitt was only technically responsible; having, indeed, made himself so by his subsequent acceptance of office, but having had no previous suspicion of the royal intentions. Similarly, we may dismiss from our consideration the merits or demerits of Fox's India Bill, the designs which were imputed to its framers, or the consequences which, whether intended or not by them, were predicted as certain to flow from it. And we may confine ourselves to the question whether, in the great Parliamentary struggle which ensued, and which lasted for more than three months,[104] the doctrines advanced by Mr. Fox, and the conduct pursued by him, were more or less in accordance with the admitted rules and principles of the constitution.

These doctrines may be reduced to two: the first a declaration that no minister is justified in retaining office any longer than he is sustained in it by the favorable judgment of the representatives of the people. Taken by itself, this, but for one consideration, might be pronounced the superfluous assertion of a truism; superfluous, because it is obvious that a House of Commons hostile to a minister can compel his resignation by obstructing all his measures. And Pitt himself recognized this as fully as Fox, though we may hardly agree with him that the Opposition was bound to allow him time to develop his policy, and to bring forward his various measures, before it pronounced an opinion adverse to them. In 1835, when Sir R. Peel first met Parliament after his acceptance of office, consequent on the King's dismissal of Lord Melbourne's ministry, the Opposition encountered and defeated him twice in the first week of the session—on the choice of a Speaker, and on the address, though the latter had been framed with the most skilful care to avoid any necessity for objection; but no attempt was made by him to call in question the perfect right of Lord J. Russell and his followers in the House to choose their own time and field of battle. But there is one farther consideration, that the authority belonging to the judgment of the House of Commons depends on that judgment being not solely its own, but the judgment also of the constituencies which have returned it, and whose mouth-piece it is; and also that the House is not immortal, but is liable to be sent back to those constituencies, to see whether they will ratify the judgment which their representatives have expressed; whether, in other words, their judgment be the judgment of the nation also. This farther consideration was, in fact, Pitt's plea for resisting the majorities which, through January and February, so repeatedly pronounced against him. And in determining to appeal to the constituencies, as the court of ultimate resort, he was clearly within the lines of the constitution.

It follows that Fox, in protesting against a dissolution, in threatening even to take steps to prevent it, was acting in self-evident violation of all constitutional principle and precedent. He was denying one of the most universally acknowledged of the royal prerogatives. The distinction which he endeavored to draw between a dissolution at the close of a session and one in the middle of it, had manifestly no validity in law or in common-sense. The minister had a clear right to appeal from the House of Commons to the people, and one equally clear to choose his own time for making that appeal. The appeal was made, the judgment of the nation was pronounced, and its pronouncement may be, and indeed must be, accepted as a sufficient justification, in a constitutional point of view, of Pitt's conduct both in accepting and retaining office. If he retained it for three months, in opposition to the voice of the existing House of Commons, he could certainly allege that he was retaining it in accordance with the deliberate judgment of the nation.

And this is the verdict of a modern statesman, a very careful student of the theory of our Parliamentary constitution, and one whom party connection would notoriously have inclined to defend the line taken by Mr. Fox, had it been possible to do so. Indeed, he may be said to show his bias in that statesman's favor when he affirms that he would have been right in moving a resolution of censure on Pitt for "his acceptance of office," which he presently calls the result of "the success of a court intrigue,"[105] and, without a particle of evidence to justify the imputation, affirms to "have been prepared beforehand with much art and combination." But *amicus Fox, sed magis arnica veritas*; and though he thus passes censure on Pitt, where the facts on which he bases it are at least unproved, on those points as to which the facts are clear and certain he condemns Fox altogether, affirming that his "attempt to show that the crown had not the prerogative of dissolving Parliament in the middle of a session had neither law nor precedent in its support."[106] And he proceeds to lay down, with great clearness and accuracy, "the practice as well as the theory of our mixed government," which is, that "when two of the powers of the state cannot" agree, and the business of the state is stopped, the only appeal is to the people at large. Thus, when in the reign of Queen Anne the House of Lords and the House of Commons fulminated resolutions at each other, a dissolution cleared the air and restored serenity. If no case had occurred since the Revolution of a quarrel between the crown and the House of Commons, the cause is to be sought in the prudence with which every sovereign who had reigned since that event had wielded his constitutional authority. If George III. had been wanting in that prudence, it did not follow that he was debarred from the right of appealing to the people. Any other doctrine would invest the House of Commons, elected for the ordinary business of the state, with a supreme power over every branch of it. This supreme power must rest somewhere; according to our constitution it rests in the common assent of the realm, signified by the persons duly qualified to elect the members of the House of Commons; and Lord Russell, in thus expounding his ideas on this subject, was undoubtedly expressing the view that ever since the transactions of which we have been speaking has been taken of the point chiefly in dispute. Since that day there has been more than one instance of Parliament being dissolved in the middle of a session; but, though the prudence of the different ministers who advised such dissolutions may, perhaps, have been questioned—nay, though in one memorable instance it was undoubtedly a penal dissolution in the fullest sense of the word[107]—no one has ever accused the sovereign's advisers of seducing him into an unconstitutional exercise of his prerogative.

Pitt was now Prime-minister, with a degree of power in Parliament and of popularity out-of-doors that no former minister, not even his own father, had ever enjoyed. As such, by the confession of one who was certainly no friendly critic,[108] "he became the greatest master of Parliamentary government that has ever existed." His administration may be regarded as a fresh starting-point in the history of the country, as the inauguration of the principle of steady amendment, improvement, and progress, in place of the maxims which had guided all his predecessors since the Revolution, of regarding every thing as permanently settled by the arrangements made at that time, and their own duty, consequently, as binding them to keep everything in its existing condition. But, of all the ministers recorded in our annals, there is not one so greatly in advance of his time as Pitt; and from the very outset of his ministerial career he applied himself, not only to the removal or correction of admitted abuses or defects, but, in cases where the fault, being in our general system of policy, had been less conspicuous, to the establishment of new principles of action which have been the rules of all succeeding statesmen. He was not, indeed, the first raiser of the question of Parliamentary Reform, but he was the first to produce an elaborate scheme with that object, parts of which, such as the suppression of the smaller boroughs and the enfranchisement of places which had gradually become more important, have been leading features of every subsequent bill on the subject. He was the first to propose the removal of those political disabilities under which the Roman Catholics labored, which no one before him had regarded as consistent with the safety of the state, and to which he sacrificed office. He was the first to conceive the idea of developing our national industries and resources by commercial treaties with other nations, even choosing for his essay-piece a treaty with a country with which our relations for nearly five hundred years had been almost uninterruptedly hostile, and which Fox, in the heat of his opposition, objected even to consider in any other light than that of an enemy. He laid the foundation for all subsequent legislation connected with our colonies in his Bill for the Government of Canada; and he established a system for the government of our Indian dependencies on so statesman-like a principle, that all subsequent administrations concurred in upholding it, till subsequent events compelled the abolition of all the share in the government of the country previously possessed by the Company.

A great writer of the past generation,[109] who in some respects has done full justice to his genius and political virtue, has, however (partly, it can hardly be doubted, from regarding himself as a follower of his great rival, Fox), contrasted his capacity as a War-minister with that of his father, drawing a comparison on this point very disadvantageous to the son. We need not stop to examine how far the praises which he bestows on Lord Chatham's talents as a planner of military operations are deserved; but it may very fairly be contended that the disparaging views of Pitt's military policy which he has advanced are founded solely on what is in this as well as in many other instances a most delusive criterion, success. It is true, unquestionably, that in the campaigns of 1793-4-5 against the French revolutionists, while he took upon this country the entire burden of the naval war, on land he contented himself with playing a secondary part, and employing a comparatively small force (which, however, doubled that which his father had sent to Minden),[110] for the success of the military operations trusting chiefly to the far stronger Austrian and Prussian divisions, under the command of Prince Coburg and the Duke of Brunswick, to which the British regiments were but auxiliaries. It is true, also, that the result of their operations was unfortunate, and that the German generals proved wholly unable to contend with the fiery and more skilful impetuosity of Jourdan and Pichégru. But the question is not whether Pitt's confidence in the prowess of his allies was misplaced, but whether he had not abundant reason to justify him in entertaining it. And, to judge fairly on this point, we must recollect the reputation which for the last forty years the Austrian and Prussian armies had enjoyed. The result of the seven years' war had established the renown of the Prussians, and the Duke of Brunswick was understood to be a favorite pupil of the Great Frederic. The same war had shown that the Austrians were not very unequal to the Prussians; while the reputation of the French troops had fallen to the lowest ebb, the most memorable event in their annals during the same war being the rout of Rosbach, when 60,000 of them fled before Frederic and 22,000. At the breaking out of the Revolution, it might be said that De Bouille was the only French general of the slightest reputation, and since the sad journey to Varennes he had been an exile from his country. And, though again in 1803 Pitt once more trusted for success on land to Continental alliances, not only does he deserve admiration for the diplomatic talent with which he united Austria, Prussia, and Russia against France, but it can hardly be doubted that confederacy would have been triumphant, had not the incompetent vanity of Alexander ruined all its prospects by his rash disregard at Austerlitz of the experienced warnings of his own staff.[111]

The new form of government which he established for India, and to which allusion has been made, has lost the greater part of its importance in the eyes of the present generation, from the more-recent abolition of the political authority of the East India Company, though of some of the principles which he avowed he had taken for his guides it is worth while to preserve the record; with such clearness, as well as statesman-like wisdom, do they affirm the objects which every one should keep in view who applies himself to legislation for distant dependencies where the privileges and interests of foreign fellow-subjects are to be regarded with as jealous a solicitude as those of our own countrymen. These objects may be briefly described as being the reconciling the vested and chartered interests of the Company with the legitimate authority of the King's government; for, though Pitt admitted that "state necessity" might occasionally be allowed as a valid reason for the abrogation of a charter, he affirmed that nothing short of such absolute necessity could excuse such a measure, and he relied on the previous history of the Company to prove the fallacy of an observation that had sometimes been made, that commercial companies could not govern empires. There were three interests to be considered: that of the native Indians, that of the Company, and that of this country; and the problem to be solved was, "how to do the most good to India and to the East India Company with the least injury to our constitution." Some of his remarks contained unavoidable allusions to Fox's bill of the previous year, since some of the provisions of his bill were entirely opposite to those which Fox had framed, the most material point of difference being the character of the Board of Control which he proposed to establish. Fox, as has been seen, had proposed to make the commissioners to be appointed under his bill irremovable for several years, whatever changes might take place in the home government; an arrangement which the opposers of the bill suspected of being designed to prevent any change in the home government from taking place. Pitt, on the other hand, laid down as one of his leading principles that "the board could not be permanent, that it must be subordinate to the administration of the day, and that permanency would be in itself a deviation from the principles of the constitution, and would involve the board in contradictions to the executive government that could not fail to be attended with great public inconvenience. An institution to control the government of India must be either totally independent of the government of this country or subordinate to it." "The board was to consist of none but privy councillors," and instead of the vast amount of patronage which was to have been created by the bill of 1783, this board was "to create no increase of officers nor to impose any new burdens." ... "The first and leading ideas would be, to limit the subsisting patronage;" ... and so little was Pitt covetous to engross that which did and must continue to subsist, that he left even "the officers of the government of Bengal to the nomination of the Court of Directors, subject only to the negative of the crown; and the Court of Directors was also to have the nomination of the officers of all the subordinate governments, except only of the commander-in-chief, who, for various reasons, must remain to be appointed by the crown." Another very important part of the arrangement was, that "gradation and succession were to be the general rule of promotion," a regulation which of itself would be "a forcible check upon patronage, and tend greatly to its reduction." The governor of Bengal was to be the governor-general of the whole country, the governors of Madras and Bombay being subordinate to him; and each governor was to be assisted by a council of three members, of whom the commander of the forces was to be one.

The spirit in which a law or a government is administered is commonly of greater practical importance than the words in which the regulation or the system is framed or defined; and Pitt, therefore, concluded his speech by laying down a few "clear and simple principles as those from which alone a good government could arise. The first and principal object would be to take care to prevent the government from being ambitious and bent on conquest. Commerce was our object, and, with a view to its extension, a pacific system should prevail, and a system of defence and conciliation. The government there ought, therefore, in an especial manner, to avoid wars, or entering into alliances likely to create wars." It was not to forget "to pay a due regard to self-defence, or to guard against sudden hostilities from neighboring powers, and, whenever there was reason to apprehend attack, to be in a state of preparation. This was indispensably necessary; but whenever such circumstances occurred, the executive government in India was not to content itself with acting there as the circumstances of the case might require; it was also to send immediate advice home of what had happened, of what measures had been taken in consequence, and what farther measures were intended to be pursued; and a tribunal was to be established to take cognizance of such matters." The system of taking presents from the natives was to be absolutely prohibited, a regulation which he hoped would "tend effectually to check private corruption;" and, lastly, it was proposed to establish a court of criminal judicature for the trial in England of certain classes of delinquents after their return from India. The Judges of the court were to be men of the highest character; they were to be chosen by ballot, some being taken from the bench of judges, some from each House of Parliament. And they were "not to be tied down to strict rules of evidence, but to be upon their oaths to give their judgments conscientiously, and to pronounce such judgment as the common law would warrant." Such a tribunal he admitted to be an innovation; but, "unless some new process were instituted, offences shocking to humanity, opposite to justice, and contrary to every principle of religion and morality, must continue to prevail, unchecked, uncontrolled, and unrestrained, and the necessity of the case outweighed the risk and the hazard of the innovation."

These were the general outlines of the constitution which in 1784 the Parliament established for India, and the skill with which it was adapted to the very peculiar character of the settlements to be governed is sufficiently proved by the fact that it was maintained with very little alteration equally by Whig and Tory administrations for three-quarters of a century, till the great convulsion of the Mutiny compelled an entire alteration in the system, and the abolition of the governing powers of the Company, as we shall have occasion to relate in a subsequent chapter. The principles which Pitt had laid down as the guiding maxims for the governors; the avoidance of ambitious views of conquest, the preservation of peace, and the limitation of the aims of the government to the encouragement and extension of commerce, were not equally adhered to. Undoubtedly, in some instances, the wars in which, even during Pitt's too short lifetime, the Indian government was engaged, came under his description of wars which were justifiable on the ground of self-defence—wars undertaken for the preservation of what had been previously won or purchased, rather than for the acquisition of new territories at the expense of chiefs who had given us no provocation. But for others, though professedly undertaken with a view only of anticipating hostile intentions, the development of which might possibly be reserved for a distant future, it is not easy to find a similar justification; and it may be feared that in more than one case governors-general, conscious of great abilities, have been too much inclined to adopt the pernicious maxim of Louis XIV., that the aggrandizement and extension of his dominions is the noblest object which a ruler of nations can have in view. Yet, though unable on strictly moral grounds to justify all the warlike enterprises which make up so large a part of our subsequent Indian history, it is impossible, probably, for even the most rigid moralist to avoid some feelings of national pride in the genius of our countrymen, who in the short space of a single century have built up an empire of a magnitude unequalled even by the Caesars, and have governed and still are governing it in so wise and beneficent a spirit, and with such a display of administrative capacity, that our rule is recognized as a blessing by the great majority of the nations themselves, as a protection from ceaseless intestine war, from rapine, and that worst of tyrannies, anarchy, which was their normal condition before Clive established our supremacy at Plassy, and into which they would surely and speedily fall back, if our controlling authority were to be withdrawn.

India was not the only British settlement for which the growth of our empire compelled Pitt to devise a constitution. The year which saw his birth had also seen the conquest of Canada from the French; and in 1774 a system of government for the new province had been established which it is sufficient here to describe as one, which differed but little from a pure despotism, the administration being vested in a governor and Legislative Council, every member of which was to be nominated by the crown. But the working of this act had from the first proved very unsatisfactory, and had become more so as the population increased by the influx of fresh settlers from Great Britain, and also from the United States, here many of those who in the recent civil war had adhered the connection with the mother country had been exposed to constant malice and ill-treatment, and had preferred crossing the border and obtaining lands in Canada to returning to England. Pitt recognized the evil, and undertook to remedy it and in 1791 he introduced a bill to establish a constitution for Canada, which a recent historian describes as "remarkable, as recognizing for the first time the wise and generous principle of independent colonial institutions, which has since been fully developed in every dependency of the British crown capable of local self-government."[112] One peculiar difficulty in framing such a constitution arose from the circumstance of the old French colonists, who greatly outnumbered the settlers of British blood, being attached to the Roman Catholic religion; while the British settlers were nearly, or perhaps all, Protestant, though of different denominations. The difficulty was, indeed, lessened by the circumstance that the French dwelt in Quebec and the district between that city and the mouth of the St. Lawrence, and that the English had for the most part betaken themselves to the more inland region. And this local separation of the two races the minister now took for his guide in the arrangement which he devised. The most important feature in it was the division of the province into two parts, as Upper and Lower Canada, and the establishment of a distinct local Legislature for each division, a House of Assembly being created in each, and a Council, so as, in Pitt's words, "to give both divisions the full advantages of the British constitution." The Assemblies were to have the power of taxation (so that there was no room left for such perverse legislation by a British Parliament as had lately cost its sovereign the United States). The act of *habeas corpus* was extended to the province (a privilege which no one of French blood had ever enjoyed before); the tenure of land was to be the socage[113] tenure so long and happily established in England. Complete religious toleration was established, and a certain proportion of land was allotted in Upper Canada, as a provision for a Protestant clergy, and the foundation of an ecclesiastical establishment. So great was Pitt's desire to complete the resemblance between the colony and Great Britain, that he even contemplated the creation of an aristocracy, by the introduction of a provision enabling the King to grant hereditary colonial titles, the possession of which should include hereditary seats in the provincial Council. The two latter clauses were opposed by Fox, and the latter of them, though sanctioned by Parliament, was never carried out in practice. But Fox, bitter as he was at this time in his general opposition to the government, agreed cordially in the general principles of the bill, avowing his conviction that "the only method of retaining distant colonies with advantage is to enable them to govern themselves," so that each party in the British Parliament is entitled to a share of the credit for this pattern of all subsequent colonial constitutions—Pitt for the original genius for organization which his contrivance of all the complicated details of the measure displayed, and Fox for his frank adoption of the general principle inculcated by his rival, even while differing as to some of the minor details of the measure. During these years the country was increasing in prosperity, and the minister was daily rising in credit; more powerful and more popular than the most successful or the most brilliant of his predecessors. But during these same years two great constitutional difficulties had arisen, one of which, indeed, the deep sense which both parties felt of the danger of investigating it shelved almost as soon as it was seen; but the other of which, besides the importance which it derived from the degree in which it involved the principle of the supreme authority of Parliament, and brought under discussion even that which regulates the succession to the crown, imperilled the existence of the ministry, and threatened a total change in both the domestic and foreign policy of the nation.

The Prince of Wales, who had come of age in the summer of 1783, had at once begun to make himself notorious for the violence of his opposition to his father's ministers, carrying the openness of his hostility so far as, during the Westminster election to drive about the streets with a carriage and all his servants profusely decorated with Fox's colors; and, still more discreditably, by most unmeasured profligacy of all kinds. The consequence was that he soon became deeply involved in debt, so deeply that, in 1787, a member of Fox's party gave notice of his intention to move that the Parliament should pay his debts and increase his income. Pitt, without specifying his reasons, avowed that he should feel it his duty to oppose any grant of such a character; but another member of Parliament, Mr. Rolle, one of the members for Devonshire, being trammelled by no such feeling of responsibility, expressed a similar resolution in language which contained an allusion perfectly understood on both sides of the House. He said that "the question thus proposed to be brought forward went immediately to affect our constitution in Church and State." And every one knew that he was referring to a report which had recently become general, that the Prince was married to a Roman Catholic lady of the name of Fitzherbert. No direct notice was taken of this allusion at the moment, Fox himself, who had the chief share of the Prince's confidence, being accidentally absent; but a day or two afterward he referred to Rolle's speech with great indignation, declaring that it referred to a "low, malicious calumny" which had no foundation whatever, and "was only fit to impose on the lowest order of persons." Being pressed as to the precise force of his assertion, and being asked whether it meant more than that under the existing laws, such as the Royal Marriage Act, there had been no marriage, because there could have been no *legal* marriage, he declared that he meant no such evasion, but that no marriage ceremony, legal or illegal, had ever taken place; and farther, that in saying this he was speaking on the direct authority of the Prince himself. No more degrading act stains the annals of British royalty. For the fact was true—the very next evening Fox learned the deceit which the Prince had practised on him from a gentleman who had been one of the witnesses to the marriage, which had been solemnized by a Protestant clergyman fifteen months before.[114] And his indignation was such that for some time afterward he abstained from all interference in the Prince's affairs; while the language held by the Prince's other confidant, Mr. Sheridan, was so evasive as to betray a consciousness that whatever had occurred would not bear the light of day; so that there were very few to whom the truth or falsehood of the report was a subject of interest who felt any uncertainty on the subject.

It may, probably, be regarded as fortunate for the peace of the kingdom that the Prince, who eventually became King George IV., left behind him no issue from his marriage with the Princess, the failure of heirs of his body thus removing any temptation to raise the question whether he had not himself forfeited all right to succeed to the throne by his previous marriage to a Roman Catholic. A clause of the Bill of Rights provides that any member of the royal family who should marry a Roman Catholic (with the exception of the issue of princesses who may be the wives of foreign princes) shall by that marriage be rendered incapable of inheriting the crown of England. And though the Royal Marriage Act (which, as we have seen, had been recently passed) had enacted that no marriage of any member of the royal family contracted without the consent of the reigning sovereign should be valid, it by no means follows that an invalidity so created would exempt the contractor of a marriage with a Roman Catholic, which as an honorable man he must be supposed to have intended to make valid, from the penalties enacted by the Bill of Rights. It is a point on which the most eminent lawyers of the present day are by no means agreed. The spirit of the clause in that bill undoubtedly was, that no apparent or presumptive heirs to the crown should form a matrimonial connection with any one who should own allegiance to a foreign power, and that spirit was manifestly disregarded if a prince married a Roman Catholic lady, even though a subsequent law had enacted a conditional invalidity of such a marriage. We may find an analogy to such a case in instances where a man has abducted a minor, and induced her to contract a marriage with himself. The lady may not have been reluctant; but the marriage has been annulled, and the husband has been criminally prosecuted, the nullity of the marriage not availing to save him from conviction and punishment. A bigamous marriage is invalid, but the bigamist is punished. And, apart from any purely legal consideration, it may be thought that public policy forbids such a construction of law as would make the illegality or invalidity of an act (and all illegal acts must be more or less invalid) such a protection to the wrong-doer as would screen him from punishment.

Whatever may be the judgment formed on the legal aspect and merits of the case, the conduct of the Prince could not fail to give the great body of the people, justly jealous at all times of their national adherence to truthfulness and honesty, a most unfavorable impression of his character. As has been already mentioned, Fox was so indignant at having been made the instrument to assure the Parliament and the nation of a falsehood, that he for a time broke off all communication with him.[115] Yet a singular caprice of fortune, or, it would be more proper to say, a melancholy visitation of Providence, before the end of the following year led Fox to carry his championship of the same Prince who had so abused his confidence to the length of pronouncing the most extravagant eulogies on his principles, and on his right to the confidence and respect of the nation at large. In the autumn of 1788 the King fell into a state of bad health, which in no long time affected his mind, and, by the middle of November, had so deranged his faculties as to render him incapable of attending to his royal duties, or, in fact, transacting any business whatever. Parliament was not sitting, but its re-assembling had been fixed for the 4th of December, and before that day arrived the King's illness had assumed so alarming a character, and it appeared so unsafe to calculate on his immediate recovery, that the minister summoned a Privy Council, the summons being addressed to the members of the Opposition as well as to his own followers, to receive the opinions of the physicians in attendance on his Majesty, as a necessary foundation for the measures which he conceived it to be his duty to propose to Parliament. Those opinions were, that it was almost certain that the disease would not be permanent, though no one could undertake to fix its duration with the least appearance of probability. And, as the royal authority could not be left in abeyance, as it were, for an uncertain period, it was indispensable to appoint a Regent to conduct the affairs of the kingdom till the King should, happily, be once more in a condition to resume his functions.

In considering the line of conduct adopted in this emergency by Pitt and his great rival Fox, Pitt has one manifest advantage on his side, that it is impossible to attribute the course which he took to any personal motive, or any desire for the retention of official power; while it is equally impossible to doubt that Fox was in no slight degree,[116] and that Lord Loughborough, the prince's chief adviser on points of law, was wholly influenced by the hope of supplanting the ministry. Pitt had never the least doubt that on the establishment of the Regency he should be dismissed, and was prepared to return to the Bar. But his knowledge of the preference which the Prince entertained for his rival did not lead him to hesitate for a single moment as to the propriety of placing him in a situation to exercise that preference. On the reassembling of Parliament, he at once took what he conceived to be the proper parliamentary course of proceeding; at his suggestion committees in both Houses were appointed to take a formal examination of the royal physicians; and, when those committees had reported that the King was for the present incapable of discharging his royal functions, though likely at some future period to be able to resume them, he moved the House of Commons to appoint another committee, to search for "precedents of such proceedings as might have been taken in the case of the personal exercise of the royal authority being prevented or interrupted by infancy, sickness, or infirmity, with a view to provide for the same." Such a search for precedents was no novelty, and may be thought to have been especially proper in such a case as this, since history recorded the appointment of several regencies, one under circumstances strikingly resembling those now existing, when, in 1454, Henry VI. had fallen into a state of imbecility, and the Parliament appointed the Duke of York Protector[117] of the kingdom.

But Fox instantly opposed it with extreme vehemence, declaring that the appointment of such a committee would be a pure waste of time. It was notorious, he affirmed, that no precedent existed which could have any bearing on the present case, since there was in existence a person such as had never been found on any previous occasion, an heir-apparent of full age and capacity to exercise the royal authority; and he declared it to be his deliberate opinion that the Prince of Wales had "as clear and express a right to assume the reins of government, and to exercise all the powers of sovereignty, during the illness and incapacity of the sovereign, as if that sovereign were actually deceased." Such an assertion of indefeasible right was so totally at variance with the Whig doctrines which Pitt, equally with Fox, regarded as the true principles of the constitution, that Pitt at once perceived the advantage which it gave him, by enabling him to stand forward as the supporter of the supreme authority of Parliament, which Fox had by implication denied. He instantly replied that to assert an inherent indefeasible right in the Prince of Wales, or any one else, independently of the decision of the two Houses, fell little short of treason to the constitution; but, at the same time, to prevent any one pretending to misconceive his intentions, he allowed it to be seen with sufficient plainness that, when once the right of Parliament to appoint the Regent had been established, he should agree in the propriety of conferring that office on the Prince of Wales. The committee was appointed; but, even before it could report the result of its investigations, the doctrine advanced by Fox had been the subject of discussion in the House of Lords, where Lord Camden, who had presided over the meeting of the Privy Council a few days before, on moving for the appointment of a similar committee of peers, had taken occasion to declare that, if Fox had made such an assertion as rumor imputed to him, it was one which had no foundation in "the common law of the kingdom." He had never read nor heard of such a doctrine. Its assertors might raise expectations not easily laid, and might involve the country in confusion. And he contended, as Pitt had done in the Commons, that its assertion was a strong argument in favor of the appointment of a committee, that it might be at once seen whether it were warranted by any precedent whatever. The reports of the two committees bore out Fox's statement, that no precedent entirely applicable to the case before them had ever occurred. But by this time Fox had learned that the argument which he had founded on it was in the highest degree unpalatable both to Parliament and to the nation; and for a moment he sought to modify it by an explanation that, though he had claimed for the Prince "the naked right, he had not by that expression intended to maintain that that right could be reduced into possession without the consent of Parliament;" an explanation not very reconcilable to common sense, since, if a right were inherent and indefeasible, Parliament could not, without absolute tyranny, refuse to sanction its exercise; and, in fact, his coadjutor, Sheridan, on the very same evening, re-asserted his original doctrine in, if possible, still more explicit terms, warning the minister "of the danger of provoking the Prince to assert his right," while a still greater man (Burke) declared that "the minister had taken up an attitude on the question tantamount to that of setting himself up as a competitor to the Prince." Such inconsiderate violence gave a great advantage to Pitt, one of whose most useful characteristics as a debater was a readiness and presence of mind that nothing could discompose. He repelled such menaces and imputations with an equally lofty scorn, and, after a few necessary preliminaries, brought forward a series of resolutions, one of which declared the fact of the sovereign's illness, and consequent incapacity; a second affirmed it to be the right and duty of the two Houses of Parliament to provide the means for supplying the defect in the royal authority; and a third imposed on the Houses the task of deciding on the mode in which the royal assent necessary to give their resolutions the authority of law should be signified. It was impossible to object to the first; but the second was stubbornly contested by the Opposition, the chiefs of the Coalition Ministry once more fighting side by side; though Lord North contented himself with arguing that the affirmation of the right and duty of Parliament was a needless raising of a disputable point, and moving, therefore, that the committee should report progress, as the recognized mode of shelving it. Fox, however, carried away by the heat of debate, returned to the assertion of the doctrine of absolute right, overlooking his subsequent modification of it, and again gave Pitt the advantage, by condescending to impugn his motives for proposing the resolution, as being inspired, not by a zeal for the constitution, but by a consciousness that he did not deserve the confidence of the Prince, and, therefore, anticipated his instant dismissal by the Regent. The re-affirmation of the Prince's inherent right was, indeed, necessary to Fox as the foundation for the objections which he took to other parts of Pitt's scheme. For the minister, while admitting to its full extent the irresistible claim which the Prince of Wales possessed to the preference of Parliament for the Regency, proposed at the same time to impose certain limitations on his exercise of the authority, so long as there was a reasonable hope of his royal father's recovery. He was not to have the power to create peerages, nor to alienate the property of the crown, nor to grant offices in reversion; and, as the Queen was to have the care of his Majesty's person, she also was to have the appointment of all the offices in the royal household. Fox, on the other hand, objected with extreme earnestness to the impropriety of imposing any limitations whatever on the power of the Regent; and then the question whether the Prince was to derive his right to the Regency from the authority of Parliament, or from his natural position and inalienable preceding right as his father's heir, became one of practical importance. If the Parliament had the right to confer authority, it had clearly the right to limit the authority it conferred. If the Prince had an indefeasible right to the Regency, independently of the will of Parliament, then Parliament could have no pretence to limit or restrain the exercise of an authority which in no degree flowed from itself. Fox, indeed, took another objection to the imposing of limitations to the authority to be intrusted to the Regent, contending that this would be to create a power unknown to the constitution—a person in the situation of King without regal power. But, not to mention precedents drawn from the reigns of Edward III., Richard II., and Henry VI., in the twenty-fourth year of the very last reign, George II., on the death of his son, the father of the present King, had enjoined the Parliament to provide for the government, in the case of his own death, while the heir was still a minor, recommending to them the appointment of the Princess Dowager of Wales as Regent, "with such powers and limitations as might appear expedient." And, in conformity with his desire, the Parliament had appointed the Princess Regent, with a Council of Regency to assist her; and had enacted that "several portions of the regal power" should be withheld from the Regent, if she could not obtain the consent of the Council thus appointed.[118]

This part of the case was so plain, that when, after the different resolutions proposed by Pitt had been adopted in both Houses, Fox insisted that, instead of proceeding by a bill to create a Regency, and to appoint the Prince of Wales Regent, the only course which could be adopted with propriety would be to present an address to the Prince, to entreat him to assume the government, he failed to induce the House to agree with him; and finally, as if he were determined to find a battle-field in every clause, he made a vigorous resistance to the expedient by which Pitt proposed that the formal royal assent which was necessary to make the bill law should be given. Fox, on one occasion, had gone the length of denying that the two Houses had any right to be regarded as a Parliament while the King, an essential part of Parliament, was incapacitated. But such an objection could have had no force, even in the mind of him who raised it, since the proceedings of the two Convention Parliaments of 1660 and 1689 labored under a similar defect; and yet their acts had been recognized as valid, and ratified by subsequent Parliaments. And now, in reference to the expedient proposed by the minister, that the two Houses should empower and authorize the Lord Chancellor to affix the Great Seal to the bill, Burke, with great, but for him not unusual, violence, denounced both the proposal and the Chancellor, declaring that such a step would be the setting up of a phantom of sovereignty, a puppet, an idol, an idiot, to which he disclaimed all allegiance. A more perilous amendment was one proposed to another clause by Mr. Rolle, enacting that if the Regent should marry a Roman Catholic his authority should cease. Since the Bill of Rights, as we have seen, forbade a sovereign to marry a Roman Catholic without incurring the forfeiture of his crown, it was evidently reasonable that the same restriction should be imposed on every Regent; but it was hard at the moment altogether to dissociate such a clause from the discussions of the preceding year; and Mr. Rolle endeavored to give the clause a more pointed meaning by an amendment to enact that the forfeiture should be incurred by the mere celebration of any marriage ceremony, whether the marriage thus performed were legal and valid or not. His amendment, however, was unanimously rejected. The bill was passed without alteration by the House of Commons; the Prince, while protesting in an elaborate and most able letter, drawn up for him by Burke, against the restrictions imposed by the bill, nevertheless consented to sacrifice his own judgment to the general good of the kingdom, and to accept the authority, limited as it was. And by the middle of February the bill was sent up to the House of Lords. There Lord Camden had charge of it, and his position as a former Chancellor gave irresistible weight to his opinion that the mode proposed to give the final sanction to the bill was strictly in accordance with the spirit and practice of the constitution. The point with which he dealt was the previous one, how Parliament, which was to pass the bill, was to be opened, for, "circumstanced as it was, Parliament could not at present take a single step." The law, as he put it, declared that the King must be present, either in person or by a representative. When he could not attend personally, the legal and constitutional process was to issue letters-patent under the Great Seal. In the present dilemma, therefore, he recommended that the two Houses should direct letters-patent to be issued under the Great Seal, authorizing commissioners to open Parliament in the name of his Majesty. He "must use the liberty to say that those who treated this proposal with ridicule were ignorant of the laws of their country. A fiction it might be termed, but it was a fiction admirably calculated to preserve the constitution, and, by adopting its forms, to preserve its substance." The authority of the Great Seal he explained to be such that, "even if the Lord Chancellor, by caprice, put it to any commission, it could not afterward be questioned;" and he adduced a precedent of a very similar character to the course now proposed, which occurred "at the commencement of the reign of Henry VI., when, the sovereign being an infant of nine months old, the Great Seal was placed in his hand, and it was supposed to be given to him by the Master of the Rolls, whereupon many commissions were sealed by it, and the government was carried on under its authority." That precedent, he reminded the peers, had been followed as recently as the year 1754, when, during an illness of George II., Lord Chancellor Hardwicke affixed the Great Seal to a commission for opening a session of Parliament. And, finally, he concluded by moving, "That it is expedient and necessary that letters-patent for opening the Parliament should pass under the Great Seal."[119] The motion was carried, and Parliament was opened in accordance with it; and, if it had been necessary, the same expedient would have sufficed to give the requisite assent to the Regency Bill, a necessity which was escaped by the fortunate recovery of the royal patient, which was announced by his medical advisers a day or two before that fixed for the third reading of the bill in the House of Lords.

Though the question was thus left undetermined for the moment, it was revived twenty-two years afterward, when the same sovereign was attacked by a recurrence of the same disease, and the existing ministry, then presided over by Mr. Perceval, brought forward a Regency Bill almost identical with that which on this occasion had been framed by Mr. Pitt; and the Opposition, led by Lord Grey and Sir Samuel Romilly, raised as nearly as possible the same objections to it which were now urged by Fox and his adherents. The ministerial measure was, however, again supported by considerable majorities; so that the course proposed by Mr. Pitt on this occasion may be said to have received the sanction of two Parliaments assembled and sitting under widely different circumstances; and may, therefore, be taken as having established the rule which will be adopted if such an emergency should, unfortunately, arise hereafter. And indeed, though the propriety of Pitt's proposals has, as was natural, been discussed by every historical and political writer who has dealt with the history of that time, there has been a general concurrence of opinion in favor of that statesman's measure. Lord John Russell, while giving a document, entitled "Materials for a Pamphlet," in which he recognizes the handwriting of Lord Loughborough, and which "contains the grounds of the opinion advanced by him, and adopted by Mr. Fox, that, from the moment the two Houses of Parliament declared the King unable to exercise his royal authority, a right to exercise that authority attached to the Prince of Wales," does not suppress his own opinion of the "erroneousness of this or any other doctrine that attributes to any individual or any constituted authority existing in the state a strict or legal right to claim or to dispose of the royal authority while the King is alive, but incapable of exercising it."[120]

The only writer, as far as I am aware, who advocates the opposite view is Lord Campbell, who, after quoting the speech of Lord Camden, from which extracts have been made, comments on it, and on the whole transaction, in the following terms: "From the course then adopted and carried through, I presume it is now to be considered part of our constitution that if ever, during the natural life of the sovereign, he is unable by mental disease personally to exercise the royal functions, the deficiency is to be supplied by the two Houses of Parliament, who, in their *discretion*, will probably elect the heir-apparent Regent, under such restrictions as they may please to propose, but who may prefer the head of the ruling faction, and at once vest in him all the prerogatives of the crown. On the two occasions referred to in the reign of George III., the next heir being at enmity with the King and his ministers, this was considered the loyal and courtly doctrine; and, from its apparent advancement of the rights of Parliament, there was no difficulty in casting odium on those who opposed it. But I must avow that my deliberate opinion coincides with that of Burke, Fox, and Erskine, who pronounced it to be unsupported by any precedent, and to be in accordance with the principles of the Polish, not the English, monarchy. The two Houses of Parliament would be the proper tribunal to pronounce that the sovereign is unable to act; but then, as if he were naturally as well as civilly dead, the next heir ought of right to assume the government as Regent, ever ready to lay it down on the sovereign's restoration to reason, in the same way as our Lady Victoria would have returned to a private station if, after her accession, there had appeared posthumous issue of William IV. by his queen. It is easy to point out possible abuses by the next heir as Regent, to the prejudice of the living sovereign; but there may be greater abuses of the power of election imputed to the two Houses, whereby a change of dynasty might be effected. I conceive, therefore, that the Irish Parliament[121] in 1789 acted more constitutionally in acknowledging the *right* of the next heir, in scouting the fiction of a commission or royal assent from the insane sovereign, and in addressing the Prince of Wales to take on himself the government as Regent."

Though the sneers at the possibility of Parliament preferring "the head of the ruling faction" to the heir-apparent be hardly consistent with the impartial candor which is one of the most imperative duties of an historical critic, and though the allusion to the principles of the Polish monarchy be not very intelligible, yet no one will refuse to attach due weight to the deliberate opinion of one who won for himself so high a professional reputation as Lord Campbell. But, with all respect to his legal rank, we may venture to doubt whether he has not laid down as law, speaking as a literary man and an historian, a doctrine which he would not have entertained as a judge. For, if we consider the common law of the kingdom, it is certain that, in the case of subjects, if a man becomes deranged, his next heir does not at once enter on his property "as if he were naturally as well as civilly dead." And if, as in such cases is notoriously the practice, the Court of Chancery appoints a guardian of the lunatic's property, analogy would seem to require that the Houses of Parliament, as the only body which can possibly claim authority in such a matter, should exercise a similar power in providing for the proper management of the government to that which the law court would exercise in providing for the proper management of an estate; and that, therefore, the principles of constitutional[122] statesmanship, which is deeply interested in upholding the predominant authority of Parliament, must justify the assertion of the ministers that the two Houses had the entire and sole right to make regulations for the government of the kingdom during the incapacity of the sovereign; and that the next heir, even when a son of full age, can have no more right to succeed to his father's royal authority in his lifetime than, if that father were a subject, he would have to succeed to his estate.

The opposite doctrine would seem to impugn the legality of the whole series of transactions which placed William and Mary on the throne. The admission of an indefeasible right of the heir-apparent would have borne a perilous resemblance to a recognition of that divine right, every pretension to which the Revolution of 1688 had extinguished. If, again, as Fox and his followers at one time endeavored to argue, the Houses in 1789 had no right to the name or power of a Parliament, because the King had no part in their meetings, the convention that sat a century before (as, indeed, was admitted) was certainly far less entitled to that name or power, for it had not only never been called into existence by a King, but was assembled in direct defiance of the King. Similarly, it is admitted that the body which invited Charles II. to return and resume his authority was equally destitute of the validity which could only be given by a royal summons. Yet both these bodies had performed actions of greater importance than that which was looked for from this Parliament. The one had abolished the existing and usurping government, and restored to his kingdom a King who had been long an exile. The other had, as it were, passed sentence on the existing sovereign, on grounds which confessedly will not bear a strict examination, and had conferred the crown on a prince who had no hereditary claim to the title. The justification of both acts was necessity. *Salus regni suprema Lex*. And the necessity was clearly more urgent in the present case than in either of the preceding instances. For, unless the Parliament interfered to create an authority, there was absolutely none in existence which was capable of acting. It should also be remembered that this Parliament of 1789, though not opened for the session by the King, had been originally elected in obedience to his order, and had been prorogued by his proclamation to the day of meeting;[123] and, though the opening of a session by a speech from the throne is the usual form for the commencement of its proceedings, it may be doubted whether it be so indispensable a part of them that none of their acts are valid without it.

  The breaking out of the French Revolution, and the degree in which, in spite of all its atrocities and horrors, the revolutionary spirit for a time infected a large party in England, prevented Pitt from reviving the plan of Reform which he had framed with such care and genius for organization, and in which, though defeated in Parliament, both before and after he became minister, he had hitherto continued to cherish the hope of eventually succeeding. But when clubs and societies, where the most revolutionary and seditious doctrines were openly broached, were springing up in London and other large towns, and unscrupulous demagogues by speeches and pamphlets were busily disseminating theories which tended to the subversion of all legitimate authority, he not unnaturally thought it no longer seasonable to invite a discussion of schemes which would be supported in many quarters only, to quote his own words, "as a stepping-stone to ulterior objects, which they dared not avow till their power of carrying them into effect should be by this first acquisition secured." But the alarm which the spread of revolutionary ideas excited in his mind was displayed, not only passively in this abstention from the advocacy of measures the expediency of which must at all times in some degree depend on the tone of their introduction, but also in active measures of repression, some of which were not, indeed, unwarranted by precedent, but others of which can hardly be denied to have been serious inroads on the constitution, infringements of the freedom of opinion and discussion to which all Englishmen are entitled, and one of which was, to say the least, a very perilous extension of a law already sufficiently severe, the statute of treason. If the French had been content with the overthrow of their own government and institutions, much as we should have lamented the indiscriminate rashness and abhorred the atrocities with which their design was carried out, we should still have adhered to the unquestionable maxim, that no nation is justified in interfering in the internal affairs of another. But the Jacobin and Girondin demagogues, who had now the undisputed sway in Paris, did not limit their views to their own country, but openly declared themselves the enemies of all established governments in every country; and the Convention passed a formal resolution in which they proffered "fraternity and assistance" to every people which might be inclined to rise against their governments. Their resolutions were officially communicated to the sympathizing societies in England, and emissaries were secretly encouraged to cross the Channel in the hope of gaining converts. Nor were their exertions barren. Two men were convicted in Scotland of a plot to seize Edinburgh Castle, to massacre the garrison, to imprison the judges, and to rise in arms to compel the government to a change of policy. In London the King was fired at on his way to open Parliament, and on his return his carriage was attacked by a furious mob, and was only protected from serious injury by a troop of the Life Guards. Such outrages proved the existence of a new danger, against which no previous government had ever been called on to provide, and such as, in the opinion of the cabinet, could only be met by novel measures of precaution.

The first was directed against the foreign propagators of revolution. The resolutions of the Convention had been promulgated in November, 1792; and at the meeting of Parliament in December, Lord Grenville, as Foreign Secretary of State, introduced in the House of Lords an alien bill, to enable the government to deal in a summary manner with any foreign visitors whose conduct or character might seem to call for its interference. It provided that all foreigners who had arrived in the kingdom since the preceding January should give in a statement of their names and residences; that any one who should arrive in future should furnish an account of his name, his station in life, and his object in visiting England; that the King, by proclamation, order in Council, or sign-manual, might direct all foreigners to reside in such districts as might be thought suitable; that no one might quit the residence in which he first settled without a passport; and that the

Secretary of State might order any suspected foreigner to quit the kingdom instantly.

The act was to be in operation for twelve months, and Lord Grenville, in introducing it, though he admitted it to be a measure of "rather a novel nature," explained at the same time that it was so far from being new in the powers which it gave, that Magna Charta distinctly recognized "the power and right of the crown to prevent foreigners from entering or residing within the realm." All that was really new was the defining of the manner in which that power should be exercised, since it had been so rarely needed that doubts might exist as to the proper mode of putting it in action. The bill, which was adopted in both Houses by large majorities, is remarkable, among other circumstances, from the fact that its discussion furnished the first instance of a public display of the difference between the two sections of the Opposition, subsequently described by Burke in one of his most celebrated pamphlets as the Old and New Whigs; those whom he called the Old Whigs (the Duke of Portland, Sir Gilbert Elliott, Mr. Windham, not to mention Burke himself) earnestly supporting it, while Lord Lansdowne, Mr. Fox, Mr. Sheridan, and Mr. Grey resisted it with equal zeal. Lord Lansdowne took the ground that it was a suspension of the *Habeas Corpus* Act; while Fox and Grey denounced it, in more general terms, as a measure "utterly irreconcilable with the principles of the constitution," Mr. Grey apparently referring chiefly to the power given by the bill to the Secretary of State to send any foreigners from the country, which he described as "making the bill a measure of oppression, giving power for the exercise of which no man was responsible." Sir Gilbert Elliott's answer was singularly ingenious. He did not deny that the bill conferred additional power on the crown, though not more than was justified by existing circumstances; but he maintained that the right of giving extraordinary powers to the crown on occasions was so far from being inconsistent with the principles of the constitution, that to grant extraordinary powers in extraordinary emergencies was a part of it essential to the character of a free government. If such powers were at all times possessed by the crown, its authority would be too great for a free government to co-exist with it; but if such could not be at times conferred on the crown, its authority would be too small for its own safety or that of the people.

The arguments of the ministers were, no doubt, greatly recommended, both to the Parliament and the people in general, by the notoriety of the fact that foreign agents were in many of our large towns busily, and not unsuccessfully, engaged in propagating what were known as Jacobin doctrines. But, even without that aid, it was clear that every government must, for the common good of all, be at times of extraordinary emergency invested with the power of suspending laws made for ordinary circumstances. And what would be an intolerable evil, if the supreme magistrate took upon himself to exercise it, ceases to be one when the right to exercise it is conferred by the nation itself in Parliament. If the bill did, as was argued, suspend the *Habeas Corpus* Act, that statute had been enacted by Parliament, and therefore for Parliament, in a case of necessity, to suspend its operation was clearly within the spirit of the constitution.

The bills affecting our own fellow-subjects were still more warmly contested. One was known as the Traitorous Correspondence Bill, which, according to Lord Campbell, was suggested by Lord Loughborough, who had lately become Lord Chancellor. The old law of high-treason, enacted in the reign of Edward III., had been in effect greatly mitigated by later statutes, which had made acts to which that character was imputed more difficult of proof, by a stricter definition of what was admissible evidence, and other safeguards; and the practice of the courts had by degrees practically reduced the list of treasons enumerated in the old law, indictments for many of the offences contained in it forbearing to assert that the persons accused had incurred the penalty of high-treason. But this new bill greatly enlarged the catalogue. It made it high-treason to hold any correspondence with the French, or to enter into any agreement to supply them with commodities of any kind, even such as were not munitions of war, but articles of ordinary merchandise, or to invest any money in the French Funds; and it enacted farther that any person who, by "any writing, preaching, or malicious and advised speaking," should encourage such designs as the old statute of Edward made treasonable, should be liable to the penalties of high-treason.

Another bill was designed to check the growing custom of holding public meetings, by providing that no meeting, the object of which was to consider any petition to the King or Parliament, or to deliberate on any alleged grievance, should be held without those who convened it, and who must be householders, giving previous notice of it by public advertisement; and empowering any two justices of the peace, at their own discretion, to declare any such meeting an unlawful assembly, and to disperse it by force, if, from the subjects discussed, the language held, or any special circumstances, they should regard it as dangerous.

Fox, and those who still adhered to him, resisted almost every clause of these different bills. They maintained that one of the most fundamental maxims of law "in every country calling itself free was, that property was in the highest degree entitled to the protection of the law; and, if so, that the right of disposing of it or investing it in any manner must be considered under the same protection;" that any interference "with ordinary commercial transactions was equally repugnant to the spirit of the constitution;" and, taking a practical view of the question, they warned the minister that such rigorous enactments imposing such extreme penalties would defeat their own end; for "it was a general and true maxim, that excess of punishment for a crime brings impunity along with it; and that no jury would ever find a verdict which would doom a fellow-creature to death for selling a yard of cloth and sending it to France." They protested, too, against inflicting on words, whether written or spoken, penalties which had hitherto been confined to overt acts. And the clauses conferring power on magistrates to prevent or disperse public meetings encountered still more vehement opposition; Fox insisting, with great eloquence, that "public meetings for the discussion of public subjects were not only lawful, but agreeable to the very essence of the constitution; that, indeed, to them, under that constitution, most of the liberties which Englishmen now enjoyed were particularly owing." The people, he maintained, had a right to discuss their grievances. "They had an inalienable right to complain by petition, and to remonstrate to either House of Parliament, or to the King; and to make two magistrates, who might be strong partisans, irresponsible judges whether anything said or done at a meeting had a tendency to encourage sedition, was to say that a free constitution was no longer suitable to us." Pitt justified these measures, partly on the ground of the special and unprecedented danger of the times, as proved by the late attempt on the King's life, and partly by the open avowal of republican doctrines made at the meetings of different societies; partly, also, on the temporary character of the measures, since in each bill a period was fixed after which its operation should expire. And he argued, farther, that, as many of the actions specified in these bills as seditious or treasonable were by many lawyers considered capable of being reached by statutes already existing, though not universally understood, it was "humane, not cruel, to remove doubts, and to prevent men from being ensnared by the ambiguity of old laws."

And in May, 1794, he brought in another bill, founded on the report of a secret committee which, in compliance with a royal message, the House of Commons had appointed to investigate the proceedings and objects of certain societies which were known to exist in different parts of the kingdom. In obedience to a Secretary of State's warrant, founded on sworn informations, their books and papers had been seized, and, having been sealed up, were now laid before the House, with the report of the committee that they proved that several of the societies which they named had, ever since the end of the year 1791, been uniformly pursuing a settled design for the subversion of the constitution; one society, in particular, having approved a plan for assembling a Convention, in imitation of the French Assembly sitting under that title, in order to overturn the established government, and to wrest from the Parliament the power which the constitution placed in its hands.

To prevent the dissemination of such principles, and to defeat such schemes, Pitt now asked leave to bring in a bill to empower his Majesty—acting, of course, through the Secretary of State—to secure and detain such persons as he should suspect of conspiring against the King's person and government. He admitted that the power which he thus proposed to confer amounted to a suspension of the *Habeas Corpus* Act in every part of the United Kingdom; nor did he deny that it was an unusually strong measure, but he contended that it was one justified by absolute necessity, by the manifest danger of such a conspiracy as the committee had affirmed to exist to the tranquillity of the nation and the safety of the government.

Fox, it may almost be said as a matter of course, opposed the introduction of any such measure; but his opposition was hardly marked by his usual force of argument. He was hampered by the impossibility of denying either the existence of the societies which the committee and the minister had mentioned, or the dangerous character of some of their designs; but he objected to the measures of repression which were proposed, partly on the absence of all attempts at concealment on the part of the promoters of these societies, partly on the contemptible character of the Convention which it was designed to summon, and the impossibility that such an assembly should have the slightest influence. He even made their avowed hostility to the constitution a plea for a panegyric on that constitution, and on the loyal attachment to it evinced by the vast majority of the people; and from that he proceeded to found a fresh argument against the proposed measure, contending that it made a fatal inroad on that very constitution which was so highly valued by the whole nation. He described it as a measure "of infinitely greater mischief than that which it proposed to remedy, since it would give the executive authority absolute power over the personal liberty of every individual in the kingdom." He did not deny that a similar measure had been enacted under William III., again in 1715, and again in 1745; but he contended that "the present peril bore no resemblance to the dangers of those times. This measure went to overturn the very corner-stone of the constitution, and if it passed, there was an end of the constitution of England." The bill was passed in both Houses by very large majorities.[124] It was originally enacted for six months only, but was from time to time renewed till the end of the century.

If we take a general survey of all these measures together, as parts of one great defensive scheme for the preservation of the public tranquillity and the general safety of the empire, it may, probably, be thought that, though undoubtedly suspensions of the constitution, they are not open to the charge of being unconstitutional, since they were enacted, not only for the welfare of the people, but with their consent and concurrence, legitimately signified by their representatives in Parliament. It is scarcely consistent with sound reason to contend that the *habeas corpus*, which had been enacted by Parliament, could not be suspended by the authority which had enacted it; that the constitution, which exists for the benefit of the people, could not be suspended by the people; or to deny, if it was in appearance transgressed by these enactments, that it was yet transgressed by strictly constitutional acts, by the decision of the Parliament, to whose power the constitution prescribes no limits.

But it is not sufficient that in this point of view these measures may have been defensible. In judging of their statesmanship, it is almost equally to be considered whether they were expedient and politic, whether the emergency or necessity were such as to justify such rigorous methods of repression. It was fairly open to doubt whether some of them, and especially the Traitorous Correspondence and the Seditious Meetings Bills, did not treat as treasonable acts which did not go beyond sedition, and whether so to treat them were not to invest them with an importance which did not belong to them. And on this part of the question the general judgment has, we think, been unfavorable to the government; and it has been commonly allowed that the Chancellor, whose advice on legal subjects the Prime-minister naturally took for his guide, gave him impolitic counsel. In fact, it is well known that these two acts, to a great extent, failed in their object through their excessive severity, several juries having refused to convict persons who were prosecuted for treason, who would certainly not have escaped had they only been indicted for sedition; and it is deserving of remark that these two bills were not regarded with favor by the King himself, if the anecdote—which seems to rest on undeniable authority—be true, that he expressed satisfaction at the acquittal of some prisoners, on the ground that almost any evil would be more tolerable than that of putting men to death "for constructive treason." It must therefore, probably, be affirmed that these two acts, the Treason Act and the Seditious Meetings Act, went beyond the necessity of the case; that they were not only violations of the constitution—which, when the measures are temporary, as these were, are not always indefensible—but that they were superfluous, unjust, and impolitic; superfluous, when they proposed to deal with acts already visitable with punishment by the ancient laws of the kingdom; unjust, when they created new classes of offences; and impolitic, as exciting that kind of disapproval of the acts of government which in many minds has a tendency to excite a spirit of discontent with and resistance to legitimate authority. And, indeed, it must be inferred that such was the light in which these measures were regarded by a statesman who in his general policy was proud to acknowledge himself Mr. Pitt's pupil, as he was also the most skilful and successful of his more immediate successors. Twenty-five years afterward the distress caused by the reaction inevitably consequent on the termination of twenty years of war produced a political excitement scarcely inferior to that with which Pitt had now to deal, and seditious societies and meetings scarcely less formidable; but, as we shall see, Lord Liverpool, taking warning, perhaps, from the mistake into which Mr. Pitt was led on this occasion, though compelled to bring forward new and stern measures of repression, and even to suspend the *Habeas Corpus* Act for a time, kept strictly within the lines of constitutional precedent, and was careful to avoid confounding sedition with treason.

Notes:

[Footnote 73:] He had been Lord-chamberlain in Lord Rockingham's administration of 1765. He was now Lord-lieutenant of Ireland.]

[Footnote 74:] In Lord Chatham's or the Duke of Grafton's ministry of 1766, and in the later administration of Lord Rockingham.]

[Footnote 75:] It may be convenient to take this opportunity of pointing out that, in this administration, Lord Shelburne altered the old, most unreasonable, and inconvenient arrangement by which the departments of the two Secretaries of State were distinguished by the latitude, and called Northern and Southern. By a new division, one took charge of the home affairs, the other of the foreign affairs. And in 1794 a third Secretary was added for War, who, by a very singular arrangement, which continued till very recently, had charge also of the colonies. But, in the year 1855, the Colonial-office was intrusted to a separate minister; and in 1858 a fifth Secretary of State, that for India, was added, on the transfer of the government of that country from the East India Company to the Crown. When there were only two Secretaries of State, the rule was that one should sit in each House. At present it is not *necessary* that more than one should be a peer, though it is more usual for two to be members of the Upper House. And it is usual also for the Under-secretaries to be members of the House to which the Chief-secretaries do not belong, though this rule is not invariably observed.]

[Footnote 76:] "Parliamentary History," xxiii., 163.]

[Footnote 77:] The divisions were: 224 to 208, and 207 to 190.]

[Footnote 78:] Lord Stanhope, quoting from an unpublished "Life of Lord Barrington," compiled by the Bishop of Durham (meaning, I suppose, Bishop Shute Barrington).—*History of England*, v., 174.]

[Footnote 79:] Even with the first flush of triumph, the night after the second defeat of Lord Shelburne in the House of Commons, Fox's great friend, Mr. Fitzpatrick, writes to his brother, Lord Ossory: "To the administration it is *cila mors*, but not *victoria loeta* to us. The apparent juncture with Lord North is universally cried out against."—Lord J. Russell's *Memorials and Correspondence of C.J. Fox*, ii., 18.]

[Footnote 80:] Lord J. Russell's "Memorials and Correspondence of C.J. Fox," ii., 90.]

[Footnote 81:] *Ibid.*, p. 118.]

[Footnote 82:] In one division (161 to 137) they had only a majority of twenty-four.]

[Footnote 83:] In a letter to Lord Northington (Lord-lieutenant of Ireland), dated July 17, Fox himself mentions that not one of his colleagues, except the Duke of Portland and Lord Keppel (First Lord of the Admiralty), approved of it.—*Memoirs of Fox*, ii., 116.]

[Footnote 84:] November 22 he writes to the Duke of Rutland: "The bill ... is, I really think, the boldest and most unconstitutional measure ever attempted, transferring at one stroke, in spite of all charters and compacts, the immense patronage and influence of the East to Charles Fox, in or out of office."—Stanhope's *Life of Pitt*, i., 140.]

[Footnote 85:] The whole paper is given by the Duke of Buckingham, "Courts and Cabinets of George III," i., 288, and quoted by Lord Russell in his "Memorials and Correspondence of C. J. Fox," ii., 251. It is endorsed, "Delivered by Lord Thurlow, December 1, 1783. Nugent Temple."]

[Footnote 86:] "Life of Pitt," i., 148. Lord Stanhope does not pledge himself to these being "the exact words of this commission, but as to its purport and meaning there is no doubt." They are, however, the exact words quoted by Fox in his speech in support of Mr. Baker's resolutions on the 17th.—*Parliamentary History*, xxiv., 207.]

[Footnote 87:] "Parliamentary History," xxiv., 151-154.]

[Footnote 88:] 95 to 76. "Strange to say, one of the cabinet ministers, Lord Stormont, president of the council, formed part of the final majority against the bill." —*Life of Pitt*, ii., 154.]

[Footnote 89:] "Life of Pitt," i., 155.]

[Footnote 90:] "Lives of the Chancellors," c. clix. Lord Thurlow.]

[Footnote 91:] "The Grenville Papers," iii., 374. It may, however, be remarked, as tending to throw some doubt on Mr. Grenville's statement, that Lord Campbell asserts that "Lord Mansfield, without entering into systematic opposition, had been much alienated from the court during Lord Rockingham's first administration." —*Lives of the Chief-justices*, ii., 468.]

[Footnote 92:] Vol. ii., pp. 229-232.]

[Footnote 93:] It will be seen hereafter that this doctrine was admitted in the fullest degree by Sir Robert Peel in the winter of 1884, when he admitted that his acceptance of office made him alone responsible for the dismissal of Lord Melbourne, though, in fact, he was taken entirely by surprise by the King's act, being in Italy at the time.]

[Footnote 94:] Lord John Russell, in his "Memorials of Fox" (ii., 253), affirms that "Lord Temple's act was probably known to Pitt;" but Lord Macaulay, in his "Essay on Pitt" (p. 326), fully acquits Pitt of such knowledge, saying that "he could declare, with perfect truth, that, if unconstitutional machinations had been employed, he was no party to them."]

[Footnote 95:] On Lord Effingham's motion, in condemnation of some of the proceedings of the Commons, which was carried February 4, 1784, by 100 to 53.]

[Footnote 96:] "Parliamentary History," xxiv., 383-385—debate of January 20, 1784.]

[Footnote 97:] *Ibid*, p. 283—January 12.]

[Footnote 98:] *Ibid*., pp. 251-257.]

[Footnote 99:] "Parliamentary History," xxiv., 478—February 2.]

[Footnote 100:] *Ibid*., p. 663.]

[Footnote 101:] "Parliamentary History," xxiv., 687, 695, 699.]

[Footnote 102:] The numbers were 201 to 189. The week before, on Mr. Powys's motion for a united and efficient administration, the majority had been 20—197 to 177. On a motion made by Mr. Coke, February 3, the majority had been 24—211 to 187. At the beginning of the struggle the majorities had been far larger—232 to 143 on Fox's motion for a committee on the state of the nation, January 12.]

[Footnote 103:] 191 to 190.]

[Footnote 104:] From December 19, when Pitt accepted office, to March 24, when the Parliament was dissolved.]

[Footnote 105:] "Memorials and Correspondence of C.J. Fox," by Earl Russell, ii., 229, 248.]

[Footnote 106:] *Ibid.*, p. 280.]

[Footnote 107:] That of April, 1831, after the defeat of the Government on General Gascoyne's amendment]

[Footnote 108:] Lord Macaulay, "Miscellaneous Essays," ii., 330.]

[Footnote 109:] Lord Macaulay, essay on William Pitt.]

[Footnote 110:] Alison ("History of Europe," xiii., 971) states the English force in the Netherlands in 1794 at 85,000 men. Lord Stanhope calls the English at Minden 10,000 or 12,000.]

[Footnote 111:] An eminent living writer (Mr. Leeky, "History of England," ii., 474) quotes with apparent approval another comparison between the father and son, made by Grattan, in the following words: "The father was not, perhaps, so good a debater as his son, but was a much better orator, a greater scholar, and a far greater man." The first two phrases in this eulogy may, perhaps, balance one another; though, when Mr. Lecky admits that "Lord Chatham's taste was far from pure, and that there was much in his speeches that was florid and meretricious, and not a little that would have appeared absurd bombast but for the amazing power of his delivery," he makes a serious deduction from his claim to the best style of eloquence which no one ever made from the speeches of his son. But Grattan's assertion that the man who, as his sister said of him, knew but two books, the "Æneid" and the "Faerie Queene," was superior in scholarship to one who, with the exception of his rival, Fox, had probably no equal for knowledge of the great authors of antiquity in either House of Parliament, is little short of a palpable absurdity. We may, however, suspect that Grattan's estimate of the two men was in some degree colored by his personal feelings.

With Lord Chatham he had never been in antagonism. On one great subject, the dispute with America, he had been his follower and ally, advocating in the Irish House of Commons the same course which Chatham upheld in the English House of Peers. But to Pitt he had been almost constantly opposed. By Pitt he and his party, whether in the English, or, so long as it lasted, in the Irish Parliament, had been repeatedly defeated. The Union, of which he had been the indefatigable opponent, and to which he was never entirely reconciled, had been carried in his despite; and it was hardly unnatural that the recollection of his long and unsuccessful warfare should in some degree bias his judgment, and prompt him to an undeserved disparagement of the minister by whose wisdom and firmness he had been so often overborne.]

[Footnote 112:] Massey's "History of England," iii., 447; *confer* also Green's "History of the English People," vol. iv.]

[Footnote 113:] Hallam ("Middle Ages," ii., 386, 481), extolling the condition of "the free socage tenants, or English yeomanry, as the class whose independence has stamped with peculiar features both our constitution and our national character," gives two derivations for the name; one "the Saxon *soe*, which signifies a franchise, especially one of jurisdiction;" and the other, that adopted by Bracton, and which he himself prefers, "the French word *soc*, a ploughshare."]

[Footnote 114:] Lord Colchester's "Diary," i., 68, mentions that the officiating clergyman was Mr. Burt, of Twickenham, who received £500 for his services. Lord John Russell ("Memorials and Correspondence of Fox," ii., 284-389) agrees in stating that the marriage was performed in the manner prescribed by the Common Prayer-book. Mr. Jesse, in his "Life of George III.," ii., 506, gathering, as the present writer can say from personal knowledge, his information from some papers left behind him by the late J.W. Croker, says: "The ceremony was performed by a Protestant clergyman, though in part, apparently, according to the rites of the Roman Catholic Church." Lord John Russell avoids discussing the question whether the marriage involved the forfeiture of the inheritance of the crown, an avoidance which many will interpret as a proof that in his opinion it did. Mr. Massey's language ("History of England," iii., 327) clearly intimates that he holds the same opinion.]

[Footnote 115:] Russell's "Life of Fox," ii., 187.]

[Footnote 116:] Fox's private correspondence is full of anticipations that the Regent's first act will be to dismiss Pitt, and to make him minister. In a letter of December 15 he even fixes a fortnight as the time by which he expects to be installed; while Lord Loughborough, who was eager to possess himself of the Great Seal—an expectation in which, though well-founded, he would, as it proved, have found himself disappointed—was led by his hopes to give the Prince counsel of so extraordinary a nature that it is said that the ministers, to whose knowledge it had come, were prepared, if any attempt had been made to act upon it, or even openly to avow it, to send the learned lord to the Tower. ("Diary of Lord Colchester," i., 28.) In an elaborate paper which he drew up and read to the Prince at Windsor, he assured his Royal Highness, speaking as a lawyer, that "the administration of government devolved to him of right. He was bound by every duty to assume it, and his character would be lessened in the public estimation, if he took it on any other ground but right, or on any sort of compromise. The authority of Parliament, as the great council of the nation, would be interposed, not to confer but to declare the right. The mode of proceeding should be that in a short time his Royal Highness should signify his intention to act by directing a meeting of the Privy Council, when he should declare his intention to take upon himself the care of the state, and should at the same time signify his desire to have the advice of Parliament, and order it by proclamation to meet early for the despatch of business.... It is of vast importance in the outset that he should appear to act entirely of himself, and, in the conferences he must necessarily have, not to consult, but to listen and direct." The entire paper is given by Lord Campbell ("Lives of the Chancellors," c. clxx.).]

[Footnote 117:] Hume's account of this transaction is, that the Duke "desired that it might be recorded in Parliament that this authority was conferred on him from their own free motion, without any application on his part; ... and he required that all the powers of his office should be specified and defined by Parliament."]

[Footnote 118:] "Parliamentary History," xxvii., 803—speech of Mr. Hardinge, one of the Welsh judges, and M.P. for Old Sarum.]

[Footnote 119:] I take this report, or abstract, of Lord Camden's speech from the "Lives of the Chancellors," c. cxlvii.]

[Footnote 120:] "Memorials of Fox," ii., 292.]

[Footnote 121:] The proceedings of the Irish Parliament on this occasion will be mentioned in the next chapter.]

[Footnote 122:] Mr. Hallam (iii., 144, ed. 1832) gives a definition of the term "unconstitutional" which seems rather singular: "By unconstitutional, as distinguished from 'illegal,' I mean a novelty of much importance, tending to endanger the established laws." May not the term rather be regarded as referring to a distinct class of acts—to those at variance with the recognized *spirit* of the constitution or principles of government, with the preservation of the liberties of the people, as expressed or implied in the various charters, etc., but not forbidden by the express terms of any statute?]

[Footnote 123:] The entry in the "Parliamentary History," November 20, 1788, is: "Both Houses met pursuant to the last prorogation. Later meetings were in consequence of successive adjournments."]

[Footnote 124:] In the Commons by 183 to 33; in the Lords by 119 to 11.]

CHAPTER V

The Affairs of Ireland.—Condition of the Irish Parliament.—The Octennial Bill.—The Penal Laws.—Non-residence of the Lord-lieutenant.—Influence of the American War on Ireland.—Enrolment of the Volunteers.—Concession of all the Demands of Ireland.—Violence of the Volunteers.—Their Convention.—Violence of the Opposition in Parliament: Mr. Brownlow, Mr. Grattan, Mr. Flood.—Pitt's Propositions Fail.—Fitzgibbon's Conspiracy Bill.—Regency Question.—Recovery of the King.—Question of a Legislative Union.—Establishment of Maynooth College.—Lord Edward Fitzgerald.—Arguments for and against the Union.—It passes the Irish Parliament.—Details of the Measure.—General Character of the Union.—Circumstances which Prevented its Completeness.

In describing the condition of Ireland and the feelings of its people, in the latter years of the reign of George II., Mr. Hallam has fixed on the year 1753 as that in which the Irish Parliament first began to give vent to aspirations for equality with the English Parliament in audible complaints; and the Irish House of Commons, finding the kingdom in the almost unprecedented condition of having "a surplus revenue after the payment of all charges," took steps to vindicate that equality by a sort of appropriation bill.

There were, however, three fundamental differences between the Parliaments of the two countries, which, above all others, stood in the way of such equality as the Irish patriots desired: the first, that by a law as old as the time of Henry VII., and called sometimes the Statute of Drogheda, from the name of the town in which it was first promulgated, and sometimes Poynings' Act, from the name of Sir Henry Poynings, the Lord-deputy at the time, no bill could be introduced into the Irish Parliament till it had received the sanction of the King and Privy Council in England; the second, that the Parliament lasted for the entire life of the King who had summoned it—a regulation which caused a seat in the House of Commons to be regarded almost as a possession for life, and consequently enormously increased the influence of the patrons of boroughs, some of whom could return a number of members such as the mightiest borough monger in England could never aspire to equal.[125] The third difference, of scarcely inferior importance, was, that the Parliament only sat in alternate years. But, though these arrangements suited the patrons and the members of the House of Commons, it was not strange that the constituencies, whose power over their representatives was almost extinguished by them, regarded them with less complacency, and, at the general election which was the consequence of the accession of George III., pledges were very generally exacted from the candidates that, if elected, they would endeavor to procure the passing of a septennial act like that which had been the law in England ever since the early years of George I. A bill with that object was introduced in 1761, and reported on not unfavorably as to its principle by the English law advisers to whom the Privy Council referred it. But, as if it had been designed to exemplify in the strongest possible manner the national propensity for making blunders, it contained one clause which rendered it not only impracticable but ridiculous. The clause provided that no member should take his seat or vote till his qualification had been proved before the Speaker in a full house. But the Speaker could not be chosen till the members had established their right of voting, so that the whole was brought to a deadlock, and the bill, if passed, could never have been carried out.

In the ministry of 1767, however—that of the Duke of Grafton and Lord Chatham—Lord Halifax was replaced at Dublin Castle by Lord Townsend, who, among his other good qualities, deserves specially honorable mention as the first Lord-lieutenant who made residence in Dublin his rule on principle; for till very lately non-residence had been the rule and residence the exception, a fact which is of itself a melancholy but all-sufficient proof of the absolute indifference to Irish interests shown by all classes of English statesmen. And under his government a bill for shortening Parliaments was passed, though it fixed the possible duration of each Parliament at eight years instead of seven, the variation being made to prevent a general election from being held at the same time in both countries, but, according to common belief, solely in order to keep up a mark of difference between the Irish and English Parliaments. And those who entertained this suspicion fancied they saw a confirmation of it in the retention of the regulation that the Irish Parliament should only sit in alternate years, a practice wholly inconsistent with any proper idea of the duties and privileges of a Parliament such as prevailed on this side of the Channel; since a Parliament whose sessions were thus intermittent could not possibly exercise that degree of supervision over the revenue, either in its collection or its expenditure, which is among its most important duties. And the continued maintenance of this practice must be regarded farther as a proof that the English legislators had not yet learned to consider Ireland as an integral part of the kingdom, entitled in every particular to equal rights with England and Scotland. Indeed, it is impossible for any Englishman to contemplate the history of the treatment of Ireland by the English legislators, whether Kings, ministers, or Parliaments, for more than a century and a half, without equal feelings of shame at the injustice and wonder at the folly of their conduct. Not only was Ireland denied freedom of trade with England (a denial as inconsistent not only with equity but also with common-sense as if Windsor had been refused free trade with London),[126] but Irish manufactures were deliberately checked and suppressed to gratify the jealous selfishness of the English manufacturers. Macaulay, in his zeal for the memory of William III., has not scrupled to apologize for, if not to justify, the measures deliberately sanctioned by that sovereign for the extinction of the Irish woollen manufactures, on the ground that Ireland was not a sister kingdom, but a colony; that "the general rule is, that the English Parliament is competent to legislate for all colonies planted by English subjects, and that no reason existed for considering the case of the colony in Ireland as an exception."[127] There is, perhaps, no passage in his whole work less to his credit. But, if such was the spirit in which an English historian could write of Ireland in the latter half of this present century, it may, perhaps, diminish our wonder at the conduct of our legislators in an earlier generation.

The penal laws on the subject of religion were also conceived and carried out in a spirit of extraordinary rigor and injustice. By far the larger portion of the Irish population still adhered to the Roman Catholic faith; but, as far as the negative punishment of restrictions and disabilities could go, its profession was visited as one of the most unpardonable of offences. No Roman Catholic could hold a commission in the army, nor be called to the Bar, nor practise as an attorney; and when it was found that a desire to devote themselves to the study of the law had led many gentlemen to acknowledge a conversion to Protestantism, a statute was actually passed to require them to prove their sincerity by five years' adherence to their new form of religion before they could be regarded as having washed off the defilement of their old heresy sufficiently to be thought worthy to wear a gown in the Four Courts. No Roman Catholic might keep a school; while a strange refinement of intolerance had added a statute prohibiting parents from sending their children to Roman Catholic Schools in a foreign country.

And the manner in which the government was carried on was, if possible, worse even than the principle. The almost continual absence of the Lord-lieutenant inevitably left the chief management of the details in the hands of underlings, and the favor of the Castle was only to be acquired by the lowest time-serving, of which those who could influence elections, wealthy and high-born as they for the most part were, were not more innocent than the representatives. No support to government could be looked for from either peer or commoner unless it were purchased by bribes more or less open, which it was equally discreditable to ask and to grant; for one of the worst fruits of the system which had so long reigned throughout the island was the general demoralization of all classes. Mr. Fronde gives George III. himself the credit of being the first person who resolutely desired to see a change of the system, and to "try the experiment whether Ireland might not be managed by open rectitude and real integrity."[128] But his first efforts were baffled by the carelessness or incompetency of the Viceroys, since it was difficult to find any man of ability who would undertake the office. And for some years things went on with very little change, great lords of different ranks having equally no object but that of controlling the Castle and engrossing the patronage of the government, and in not a few instances of also procuring large grants or pensions for themselves, each seeking to build up an individual influence which no Viceroy could ever have withstood, had they been united instead of being separated by mutual jealousies, which enabled him from time to time to play off one against the other.

But the war with the North American Colonies, which broke out in 1774, by some of its indirect consequences brought about a great change in the affairs of Ireland. The demand for re-enforcements to the armies engaged in America could only be met by denuding the British islands themselves of their necessary garrisons. No part of them was left so undefended as the Irish coast; and, after a time, the captains of some of the American privateers, learning how little resistance they had to fear, ventured into St. George's Channel, penetrated even into the inland waters, and threatened Carrickfergus and Belfast. In matters of domestic policy it was possible to procrastinate, to defer deciding on relaxations of the penal laws or the removal of trade restrictions, but to delay putting the country into a state of defence against an armed enemy for a single moment was not to be thought of; yet the government was powerless. Of the regular army almost every available man was in, or on his way to, America, and the most absolute necessity, therefore, compelled the Irish to consider themselves as left to their own resources for defence. It was as impossible to levy a force of militia as one of regular troops, for the militia could not be embodied without great expense; and the finances of the whole kingdom had been so mismanaged that money was as hard to procure as men. In this emergency several gentlemen proposed to the Lord-lieutenant to raise bodies of volunteers. The government, though reluctant to sanction the movement, could see no alternative, since the presence of an armed force of some kind was indispensable for the safety of the island. The movement grew rapidly; by the summer of 1779 several thousand men were not only under arms, but were being rapidly drilled into a state of efficiency, and had even established such a reputation for strength, that, when in the autumn the same privateers that had been so bold in Belfast Lough the year before reached the Irish coast, in the hope of plundering Limerick or Galway, they found the inhabitants of the district well prepared to receive them, and did not venture to attempt a descent on any part of the island. And, when the Parliament met in October, some of the members, who saw in the success that could not be denied to have attended their exertions an irresistible means of strengthening the rising pretensions of Ireland to an equality of laws and freedom with England, moved votes of thanks in both Houses to the whole body of Volunteers. They were carried by acclamation, and the Volunteers of the metropolis lined the streets between the Parliament House and the Castle when, according to custom, the members of the two Houses marched in procession to present their addresses to the Lord-lieutenant. Such a recognition of the power of this new force stimulated those members who claimed in a special degree the title of Friends of Ireland to greater exertion. A wiser government than that of Lord North would have avoided giving occasion for the existence of a force which the utter absence of any other had made masters of the situation. The Volunteers even boasted that they had been called into existence by English misgovernment. In the words of one of their most eloquent advocates, "England had sown her laws like dragons' teeth, and they had sprung up as armed men."

Ireland began to feel that she was strong, and, not unnaturally desired to avail herself of that strength, which England now could not question, to put forward demands for concessions which in common fairness could not well be denied. In 1778, when Lord North, in the hope of recovering the allegiance of the North American Colonies, brought forward what he termed his conciliatory propositions, the Irish members began to press their demand that the advantages thus offered to the Americans should be extended to their own countrymen also; that the fact of the Irish not having rebelled should not be made a plea for treating them worse than those who had; and in the front of all their requests was one for the abolition of those unjust and vexatious duties which shackled their trade and manufactures. But the jealousy of the English and Scotch manufacturers was still as bitter, and, unhappily, still as influential, as it had proved in the time of William III. And, to humor the grasping selfishness of Manchester and Glasgow, Lord North met the demands of the Irish with a refusal of which every word of his speech on the propositions to America was the severest condemnation, and which he sought to mitigate by some new regulations in favor of the linen trade, to which the English and Scotch manufacturers made no objection, since they had no linen factories. The Irish, in despair, had recourse to non-importation agreements, of which the Americans had set the example, binding themselves not to import nor to use any articles of English or Scotch manufacture with which they could possibly dispense. And the result was, that Lord North yielded to fear what he had refused to justice, and the next year brought in bills to grant the Irish the commercial equality which they demanded. Some of the most oppressive and vexatious of the penal laws were also relaxed; and some restrictions which the Navigation Act imposed on commerce with the West Indies were repealed. But, strange to say, the English ministers still clung to one grievance of monstrous injustice, and steadily refused to allow judicial appointments to be placed on the same footing as in England, and to make the seat of a judge on the bench depend on his own good conduct, instead of on the caprice of a king or a minister.

But the manifest reluctance with which the English government had granted this partial relief encouraged the demand for farther concessions. The Irish members, rarely deficient in eloquence or fertility of resource, had been lately re-enforced by a recruit of pre-eminent powers, whom Lord Charlemont had returned for his borough of Moy, Henry Grattan; and, led by him, began to insist that the remaining grievances, to the removal of which the nation had a right, would never be extinguished so long as the supreme power of legislation for the country rested with the English and Scotch Parliament; and that the true remedy was only to be found in the restoration to the Irish Parliament of that independence of which it had been deprived ever since the time of Henry VII. They were encouraged by the visibly increasing weakness of Lord North's administration. Throughout the year 1781 it was evidently tottering to its fall. And on the 22d of February, 1782, Grattan brought forward in the Irish House of Commons a resolution, intended, if carried, to lay the foundation of a bill, "that a claim of any body of men other than the King, Lords, and Commons of Ireland to bind this kingdom is unconstitutional, illegal, and a grievance." This resolution aimed at the abolition of Poynings' Act. Other resolutions demanded the abolition of the "powers exercised by the Privy Council under color of Poynings' Act," and a farther relaxation of the penal laws. So helpless did the government by this time feel itself, that the Attorney-general, who was its spokesman on this occasion, could not venture to resist the principle of these resolutions, but was contented to elude them for the time by objections taken to some of the details; and Grattan gave notice of another motion to bring the question to a more definite decision, which he fixed for the 16th of April.

Before that day came Lord North's government had ceased to exist, and had been replaced by Lord Rockingham's, one most influential member of which was the most distinguished of living Irishmen, Mr. Burke, who, while in opposition, had always shown himself a warm supporter of the claims of his countrymen, and was not likely to have his ardor in the cause damped by being placed in a situation where he could procure a friendly hearing to his counsels. Once more they had increased their demands, requiring, besides the removal of the purely political grievances, a surrender of the right of appeal from the Irish to the English courts of law. But their new masters were inclined to grant everything which seemed requisite to the establishment of complete equality between the two kingdoms; and though the new ministry was dissolved in a few months by the premature death of its chief, he lived long enough to carry the repeal of Poynings' Act, the retention of which was now admitted to be not only senseless but mischievous, since the existence of a body invested with nominal dignity, but practically powerless, was calculated not only to provoke discontent, but to furnish a lever for agitation.

The repeal was, however, nothing less than the establishment of an entirely new constitution in Ireland. The Irish Parliament, the meetings of which had hitherto been a mere form and farce, was installed in a position of absolute independence, to grant money or to make laws, subject to no other condition than that their legislation should be of a character to entitle it to the royal assent, a condition to which every act of the British Parliament was likewise and equally liable. "Unhappily, as an Irish patriotic writer exclaims on this occasion, it was written in the book of fate that the felicity of Ireland should be short-lived."[129] And a similar shortness of existence was to be the lot of the separate independence of her Parliament. Even while framing instructions for the Lord-lieutenant, in his honest desire to inaugurate a system of just government for Ireland, George III. had warned him on no account to "summon a Parliament without his special command."[130] And, regarded by the light of subsequent events, it can hardly be denied that the prohibition displayed an accurate insight into the real difficulties of the country, and also into the character of the people themselves as the source of at least some of those difficulties. We ought not to judge its leaders too severely. A nation which has been long kept in bondage, and is suddenly presented with liberty, is hardly more able to bear the change than a man immured for years in a dark dungeon can at once endure the unveiled light of the sun; and independence had been granted to the Irish too suddenly for it to be probable that they would at once and in every instance exercise it wisely.

All parties were to blame in different degrees. The first danger came from the Volunteers, who, flushed with self-importance, from the belief that it was the imposing show of their strength which had enabled the Parliament to extort Lord Rockingham's concession from the English Houses, now claimed to be masters of the Parliament itself. With the termination of the American war, and the consequent return of the English army to Europe, the reason for their existence had passed away. But they refused to be disbanded, and established a convention of armed delegates, to sit in Dublin during the session of Parliament, and to overawe the Houses into passing a series of measures which they prescribed, and which included a Parliamentary Reform Bill of a most sweeping character. On this occasion, however, the House of Commons acted with laudable firmness. Led by Mr. Fitzgibbon, a man of great powers, and above all suspicion of corruptibility, it spurned the dictation of an unauthorized body, and rejected the Reform Bill, avowedly on the ground of its being presented to it "under the mandate of a military congress;" and the Convention, finding itself powerless to enforce its mandates, dissolved.

But the difficulties of the government were not over with the suppression of the Volunteer Convention. The Lord-lieutenant had a harder, because a more enduring, contest to encounter with the Parliament and the patrons of the boroughs. A single act of Parliament may substitute a new law for an old one; but no one resolution or bill has a magical power to extinguish long habits of jobbery and corruption. Members and patrons alike seemed to regard the late concessions as chiefly valuable on account of the increased value which it enabled them to place on their services to the government; and one cannot read without a feeling of shame that one or two of the bishops who were wont to be regarded as the proprietors of the seats for their diocesan cities, were not behind the most nameless lay boroughmongers in the resolution they evinced make a market of their support of the government. The consequence was that the government was unable to feel confident of its power to carry any measure except at a price that it was degrading to pay; while of those few members who were above all suspicion of personal corruption, many were so utterly wrong-headed, and had their minds so filled with unreasonable jealousy for what they called the honor and dignity of Ireland, and with a consequent distrust of England and of all Englishmen, that their honest folly was even a greater obstacle to wise and good government than the mean cunning of the others. There can hardly be a more striking proof of the difficulties to be overcome by a minister than is furnished by a speech made by a gentleman of the highest character, and of deservedly wide influence in the Northern counties, Mr. Brownlow, of Lurgan, one of the members for Armagh, which is quoted by Mr. Froude.[131]

Pitt was painfully conscious of the commercial injustice with which hitherto Ireland had always been treated, and in the very first year of his administration he applied himself to the removal of the most mischievous of the grievances of which the Irish merchants complained, adopting to a great extent a scheme which had been put before him by one of the most considerable gentlemen of that body, which was based on the principle of equalization of duties in both countries. It is unnecessary here to enter into the details of the measure which he introduced into the House of Commons. He avowed it to be the commencement of a new system of government for Ireland, "a system of a participation and community of benefits, a system of equality and fairness, which, without tending to aggrandize one portion of the empire or to depress the other, should seek the aggregate interest of the whole; it was a substitute for the system which had hitherto been adopted of making the smaller country completely subordinate to and subservient to the greater, of making the smaller and poorer country a mere instrument for the advantage of the greater and wealthier one. He, therefore, proposed now to create a situation of perfect commercial equality, in which there was to be a community of benefits, and also to some extent a community of burdens." And he urged the House to "adopt that system of trade with Ireland that would tend to enrich one part of the empire without impoverishing the other, while it would give strength to both; that, like mercy, the favorite attribute of Heaven,

"'Is twice blessed—
It blesseth him that gives and him that takes.'"

It might, he said, be regarded as "a treaty with Ireland by which that country would be put on a fair, equal, and impartial footing with Great Britain, in point of commerce, with respect to foreign countries and our colonies." The community of burdens which his measure would impose on Ireland was this: that whenever the gross hereditary revenue of Ireland should exceed £650,000 (an amount considerably in excess of anything it had ever yet reached), the excess should be applied to the support of the fleet of the United Kingdom. It was, in fact, a burden that could have no existence at all until the Irish trade had become far more flourishing and productive than as yet it had ever been. Yet a measure conceived in such a spirit of liberality, and framed with such careful attention to the minutest interests of Irish trade, Mr. Brownlow did not hesitate to denounce as one "tending to make Ireland a tributary nation to Great Britain. The same terms," he declared, "had been held out to America, and Ireland had equal spirit with America to reject them." He even declared that "it was happy for Mr. Orde" (the Chief Secretary, who had introduced the measure into the Irish House of Commons) "that he was in a country remarkable for humanity. Had he proposed such a measure in a Polish Diet, he would not have lived to carry back an answer to his master. If," he concluded, "the gifts of Britain are to be accompanied with the slavery of Ireland, I will never be a slave to pay tribute; I will hurl back her gifts with scorn." Baffled by such frantic and senseless opposition, Pitt condescended to remodel his measure. In its new form it was not so greatly for the advantage of Ireland. He had been constrained to admit some limitation of his original liberality by the opposition which, it had met with in England also where Fox, at all times an avowed enemy of freedom of trade, had made himself the mouth-piece of the London and Liverpool merchants, who could not see, without the most narrow-minded apprehension, the monopoly of the trade with India and the West Indies, which they had hitherto enjoyed, threatened by the admission of Ireland to its benefits. And now a clause in the second bill, binding the Irish Parliament to reenact the Navigation Laws existing in England, called up an opposition from Grattan[132] as furious as that with which Mr. Brownlow had denounced the original measure. To demand the enactment of the English Navigation Law, he declared, was "a revocation of the constitution;" and his rival, Flood, in his zeal to emulate his popularity with the mob, surpassing him in vehemence, inveighed against the clause, as one intended to make the Irish Parliament a mere register of the English Parliament, "which it should never become". All the arguments brought forward in favor of the measure by the supporters of the government— arguments which, probably, no one would now be found to deny to have been unanswerable—failed to make the slightest impression on a House in which the chief object of each opponent of the ministry seemed to be to outrun his fellows in violence; and eventually the measure fell to the ground, and for fifteen years more Ireland was deprived of the advantages which had been intended for her.

And even yet the danger from the Volunteers was not wholly extinguished. Though their Convention had been suppressed, its leaders had only changed their tactics. Under the guidance of a Dublin ironmonger, named Napper Tandy, they now proposed to convene a Congress, to consist, not, as before, of delegates from the Volunteer body, but of persons who should be representatives of the entire nation; and Tandy had even the audacity to issue circulars to the sheriffs of the different counties, to require them, in their official capacity, to summon the people to return representatives to this Congress. The Sheriff of Dublin, a man of the name of O'Reilly, obeyed the requisition; but Fitzgibbon, who, luckily, was now Attorney-general, instantly prosecuted him for abuse of his office. He was convicted, fined, and imprisoned, and his punishment deterred others from following his example. And a rigorous example had become indispensable, since it was known to the government that Tandy and some of his followers were acting in connection with French emissaries, and that their object was the separation of Ireland from England, and, in the minds of some of them, certainly the annexation of the country to France; indeed, on one occasion Fitzgibbon asserted in the House of Commons that he had seen resolutions inviting the French into the country. The government would gladly have established a militia to supersede the Volunteers, but the temper of the Irish Parliament, in its newly-acquired independence, rendered any such attempt hopeless; and Mr. Grattan, with a perversity of judgment which his warmest admirers must find it difficult to reconcile with statesmanship, if not with patriotism, even opposed with extreme bitterness a bill for the establishment of a police for Dublin, though he could not deny that there existed in the city an organized body of ruffians, who made not only the streets but even the dwelling-houses of the more orderly citizens unsafe, by outrages of the worst kind, committed on the largest scale—assaults, plunderings, ravishments, and murders. In the rural districts of the South the disturbances were so criminally violent, and so incessant, that the Lord-lieutenant was compelled to request the presence of some additional regiments from England, as the sole means of preserving any kind of respect for the law; and more than once the mobs of rioters showed themselves so bold and formidable, that the soldiers were compelled to fire in self-defence, and order was not restored but at the cost of many lives.

Presently a Conspiracy Bill was passed, and gradually the firmness of the government re-established a certain amount of internal tranquillity. But shortly afterward a crisis arose which, more than the debates on the commercial propositions, or on the Volunteers, or on the police, showed how over-liberal had been the confidence of the English minister who had repealed Poynings' Act, and had bestowed independent authority on the Irish Parliament before the members had learned how to use it. We have seen how keen a contest was excited in the English Parliament by the deranged condition of the King's health in 1788, and the necessity which consequently arose for the appointment of a Regency. Grattan was in London at the time, where he had contracted a personal intimacy with Fox, and had been presented by him to the Prince of Wales, whose graciousness of manner, and profession of adherence to the Whig system of politics, secured his attachment to that party. Grattan was easily indoctrinated by Fox with his theory of the indefeasible claim of the Prince to the Regency as his birthright, and is understood to have promised that the Irish Parliament should adopt that view. The case was one which seemed unprovided for. There was no question but that the law enacted that the sovereign of England should also be the sovereign of Ireland. But no express law of either country contained any such stipulation respecting a Regent; and Grattan conceived that, in the absence of any pre-existing ordinance, it would be easy to contend that the

Irish Parliament was the sole judge who the Regent should be, and on what terms he should exercise the royal authority.

The Irish Parliament had been prorogued in 1787 to the 5th of February, 1789, the same day on which, after numerous examinations of the physicians in attendance on the royal patient, and after the passing of a series of resolutions enunciating the principles on which the government was proceeding, Pitt introduced the Regency Bill into the English House of Commons, being prepared to conduct it through both Houses with all the despatch that might be consistent with a due observance of all the forms of deliberation. Grattan's object was to anticipate the decision of the English Parliament, so as to avoid every appearance that the Irish Parliament was only following it; and he therefore proposed that the House of Commons should instantly vote an address to the Prince, requesting him to take upon himself the Regency of the kingdom of Ireland, by his own natural right as the heir of the crown; making sure not only that his advice would be taken by those whom he was addressing, but that the House of Lords would not venture to dissent from it.

Fitzgibbon, as Attorney-general and spokesman of the government in the Commons, as a matter of course opposed such precipitate action, not only warning his hearers of the folly and danger of taking a step "which might dissolve the single tie which now connected Ireland with Great Britain," but explaining also the whole principle of the constitution of the two kingdoms, so far as it was a joint constitution, in terms which give his speech a permanent value as a summary of its principle and its character. He recalled to the recollection of the House the act of William and Mary, which declares "the kingdom of Ireland to be annexed to the imperial crown of England, and the sovereign of England to be by undoubted right sovereign of Ireland also;" and argued from this that Mr. Grattan's proposal was contrary to the laws of the realm and criminal in the extreme. "The crown of Ireland," as he told his hearers, "and the crown of England are inseparably united, and the Irish Parliament is totally independent of the British Parliament. The first of these positions is your security, the second your freedom, and any other language tends to the separation of the crowns or the subjection of your Parliament. The only security of your liberty is the connection with Great Britain; and gentlemen who risk breaking the connection must make up their minds to a union. God forbid I should ever see that day; but, if the day comes on which a separation shall be attempted, I shall not hesitate to embrace a union rather than a separation."

He proceeded to show that, as the Irish Parliament had itself enacted that all bills which passed their two Houses should require the sanction of the Great Seal of England, they actually had no legal power to confer on the

Prince of Wales such authority as Grattan advised his being invested with, whatever might be the form of words in which their resolution was couched. He pointed out, also, that if the Irish Parliament should insist on appointing the Prince of Wales Regent before it was known whether he would accept the Regency of England, it was manifestly not impossible "that they might be appointing a Regent for Ireland being a different person from the Regent of England; and in that case the moment a Regent was appointed in Great Britain, he might send a commission under the Great Seal appointing a Lord-lieutenant of Ireland, and to that commission the Regent of Ireland would be bound to pay obedience. Another objection of great force to his mind was, that the course recommended by Grattan would be a formal appeal from the Parliament of England to that of Ireland. It would sow the seeds of dissension between the Parliaments of the two countries. And, indeed, those who were professing themselves advocates for the independence of the Irish crown were advocates for its separation from England."

But the House was too entirely under the influence of Grattan's impassioned eloquence for Fitzgibbon's more sober arguments to be listened to. The address proposed by Grattan was carried by acclamation; and the peers were scarcely less unanimous in its favor, one of the archbishops even dilating on "the duty of availing themselves of the opportunity of asserting the total independence of Ireland." Even when, on a second discussion as to the mode in which the address was to be presented to the Prince, Fitzgibbon reported that he had consulted the Chancellor and all the judges, and that they were unanimously of opinion that, till the Regency Bill should be passed in England, the address was not only improper but treasonable, he found his warning equally disregarded. And when the Lord-lieutenant refused to transmit the address to England, on the avowed ground of its illegality, Grattan proposed and carried three resolutions: the first, that the address was not illegal, but that, in addressing the Prince to take on himself the Regency, the Parliament of Ireland had exercised an undoubted right; the second, that the Lord-lieutenant's refusal to transmit the address to his Royal Highness was ill-advised and unconstitutional; the third, that a deputation from the two Houses should go to London, to present the address to the Prince. Mr. Fronde affirms that the deputation, even when preparing to sail for England, was very irresolute and undecided whether to present the address or not, from a reasonable fear of incurring the penalties of treason, to which the lawyers pronounced those who should present it liable. But their courage was not put to the test. As has been already seen, before the end of the month the King's recovery was announced, and the question of a Regency did not occur again till the Irish Parliament had been united to the English.

Since Lord Rockingham's concessions, in 1782, the project of a legislative union between the two countries, resembling that which united Scotland to England, had more than once been broached. We have seen it alluded to by Fitzgibbon in the course of these discussions, and it was no new idea. It had been discussed even before the union with Scotland was completed, and had then been regarded in Ireland with feelings very different from those which prevailed at a later period. Ten years after the time of which we are speaking, Grattan denounced the scheme with almost frantic violence. Fitzgibbon (though after the Rebellion he recommended it as indispensable) as yet regarded it only as an alternative which, though he might eventually embrace it, he should not accept without extreme reluctance. But at the beginning of the century all parties among the Protestant Irish had been eager for it, and even the leading Roman Catholics had been not unwilling to acquiesce in it. Unluckily, the English ministers were unable to shake off the influence of the English manufacturers; and they, in another development of the selfish and wicked jealousy which had led them in William's reign to require the suppression of the Irish woollen manufacture, now, in Anne's, rose against the proposal of a legislative union.[133] In blindness which was not only fatal but suicidal also, "they persuaded themselves that the union would make Ireland rich, and that England's interest was to keep her poor;" as if it had been possible for one portion of the kingdom to increase in prosperity without every other portion benefiting also by the improvement.

However, in the reign of Anne the union was a question only of expediency or of wisdom. The wide divergence of the two Parliaments on this question of the Regency transformed it into a question of necessity. The King might have a relapse; the Irish Parliament, on a recurrence of the crisis, might re-affirm its late resolutions; might frame another address to the Prince of Wales; and there might be no alternative between seeing two different persons Regents of England and Ireland, or, what would be nearly the same thing, seeing the same person Regent of the two countries on different grounds, and exercising a different authority.

And if these proceedings of the Irish Parliament had wrought in the mind of the great English minister a conviction of the absolute necessity of preventing a recurrence of such dangers by the only practicable means open to him—the fusion of it into one body with the English Parliament by a legislative union—the occurrences of the ensuing ten years enforced that conviction with a weight still more irresistible. It has been seen how stirring an influence the revolutionary fever engendered by the overthrow of the French monarchy for a time exerted even over the calmer temper of Englishmen. In Ireland, where, ever since Sarsfield and his brave garrison enlisted under the banner of Louis XIV., a connection more or less intimate with France had been constantly kept up, the events in Paris had produced a far deeper and wider effect. More than one demagogue among the Volunteers had avowed a desire to see the whole country transfer its allegiance from the English to the French sovereign; and this preference was more pronounced after the triumph of democracy in the French capital. For the leaders of the movement, themselves nearly all men of the lowest degree, denounced the Irish nobles with almost as much vehemence as the English connection.

Yet Pitt's policy, dictated partly by a spirit of conciliation, and still more by feelings of justice, was gradually removing many of the grievances of which the Irish had real reason to complain. Next to the restrictions on trade, nothing had made such an impression on his mind as the iniquity of the penal laws; and those he proceeded to repeal, encouraging the introduction of bills to throw open the profession of the law to Roman Catholics, to allow them seats on the magistrates' bench and commissions in the army, and to grant them the electoral franchise, a concession which he himself would willingly have extended by admitting them to Parliament itself. But these relaxations of the old Penal Code, important as they were, only conciliated the higher classes of the Roman Catholics. Most of the Roman Catholic prelates, and most of the Roman Catholic lay nobles, proclaimed their satisfaction at what had been done, and their good-will toward the minister who had done it; but the professional agitators were exasperated rather than conciliated at finding so much of the ground on which they had rested cut from beneath their feet. So desirous was Pitt to carry conciliation to the greatest length that could be consistent with safety, that he held more than one conference with Grattan himself; but he found that great orator not very manageable, partly, as it may seem from some of Mr. Windham's letters, through jealousy of Fitzgibbon, who was now the Irish Chancellor,[134] and still more from a desire to propitiate the Roman Catholics, for whom he demanded complete and immediate Emancipation; while Pitt, who was, probably, already resolved on accomplishing a legislative Union, thought, as far as we can judge, that Emancipation should follow, not precede, the Union, lest, if it should precede it, it might prove rather a stumbling-block in the way than a stepping-stone to the still more important measure.

It is not very easy to determine what influence the "Emancipation," as it was rather absurdly called,[135] if it had been granted at that time, might have had in quieting the prevailing discontent. With one large party it would probably have increased it, for there was quite as great an inclination to insurrection in Ulster as in Leinster or Munster; and with the Northern Presbyterians animosity to Popery was at least as powerful a feeling as sympathy with the French Republicans. A subsequent chapter, however, will afford a more fitting opportunity for discussing the arguments in favor of or against Emancipation. What seems certain is, that a large party among the Roman Catholics of the lower class valued Emancipation itself principally as a measure to another end—a separation from England. Pitt, meanwhile, hopeless of reconciling the leaders of the different parties—the impulsive enthusiasm of Grattan with the sober, practical wisdom of Fitzgibbon—pursued his own policy of conciliation united with vigor; and one of the measures which he now carried subsists, unaltered in its principle, to the present day.

There was no part of the penal laws of which the folly and iniquity were more intolerable than the restrictions which they imposed on education. To a certain extent, they defeated themselves. The clause which subjected to severe penalties a Roman Catholic parent who sent his child abroad to enjoy the benefits of an education which he was not allowed to receive at home, was manifestly almost incapable of enforcement, and the youths designed for orders in the Romish Church had been invariably sent to foreign colleges—some to Douai or St. Omer, in France; some to the renowned Spanish University of Salamanca. But the French colleges had been swept away by the Revolution, which also made a passage to Spain (the greater expense of which had at all times confined that resource to a small number of students) more difficult; and the consequence was, that in 1794 the Roman Catholic Primate, Dr. Troy, petitioned the government to grant a royal license for the endowment of a college in Ireland. Justice and policy were equally in favor of the grant of such a request. For the sake of the whole kingdom, and even for that of Protestantism itself, it was better that the Roman Catholic priesthood should be an educated rather than an ignorant body of men; and, in the temper which at that time prevailed over the western countries of the Continent, it was at least equally desirable that the rising generation should be preserved from the contagion of the revolutionary principles which the present rulers of France were so industrious to propagate. Pitt at once embraced the idea, and in the spring of the next year a bill was introduced into the Irish Parliament by the Chief Secretary, authorizing the foundation and endowment of a college at Maynooth, in the neighborhood of Dublin, for the education of Roman Catholics generally, whether destined for the Church or for lay professions. It is a singular circumstance that the only opposition to the measure came from Grattan and his party, who urged that, as the Roman Catholics had recently been allowed to matriculate and take degrees at Trinity College, though not to share in the endowments of that wealthy institution, the endowment of another college, to be exclusively confined to Roman Catholics, would be a retrograde step, undoing the benefits of the recent concession of the authorities of Trinity;

would be "a revival and re-enactment of the principles of separation and exclusion," and an injury to the whole community. For, as he wisely contended, nothing was so important to the well-doing of the entire people as the extinction of the religious animosities which had hitherto embittered the feelings of each Church toward the other, and nothing could so surely tend to that extinction as the uniting the members of both from their earliest youth, in the pursuit both of knowledge and amusement, as school-fellows and playmates. If Mr. Froude's interpretation of the motives of those who influenced Grattan on this occasion be correct, he was unconsciously made a tool of by those whose real object was a separation from England, of the attainment of which they despaired, unless they could unite Protestants and Roman Catholics in its prosecution. The bill, however, was passed by a very large majority, and £9000 a year was appropriated to the endowment of the college. Half a century afterward, as will be seen, that endowment was enlarged, and placed on a more solid and permanent footing, by one of the ablest of Pitt's successors. It was a wise and just measure; and if its success has not entirely answered the expectations of the minister who granted it, its comparative failure has been owing to circumstances which the acutest judgment could not have foreseen.

But it seems certain that neither the concession nor the refusal of any demands put forward by any party in Ireland could have prevented the insurrection which broke out shortly afterward. There were two parties among the disaffected Irish—or it should, perhaps, rather be said that two different objects were kept in view by them—one of which, the establishment of a republic, was dearer to one section of the malcontents; separation from England, with the contingency of annexation to France, was the more immediate aim of the other, though the present existence of a republican form of government in France to a great extent united the two. As has been mentioned before, the original movers in the conspiracy were of low extraction, Dublin tradesmen in a small way of business. Napper Tandy was an ironmonger, Wolfe Tone was the son of a coach-maker. But they had obtained a recruit of a very different class, a younger son of the Duke of Leinster, Lord Edward Fitzgerald, a man of very slender capacity, who, at his first entrance into Parliament, when scarcely more than of age, had made himself remarkable by a furious denunciation of Pitt's Irish propositions; had married a natural daughter of the Duke of Orleans, a prince, in spite of his royal birth, one of the most profligate and ferocious of the French Jacobins; and had caught the revolutionary mania to such a degree that he abjured his nobility, and substituted for the appellation which marked his rank the title of "Citizen Fitzgerald." He had enrolled himself in a society known as the United Irishmen, and had gone to France, as its plenipotentiary, to arrange with Hoche, one of the most brilliant and popular of the French generals, a scheme for the invasion of Ireland, in which he promised him that, on his landing, he should be joined by tens of thousands of armed Irishmen. Hoche entered warmly into the plan, was furnished with a splendid army by the Directors, and in December, 1796, set sail for Ireland; but the fleet which carried him was dispersed in a storm; many of the ships were wrecked, others were captured by the British cruisers, and the remnant of the fleet, sadly crippled, was glad to regain its harbors. Two years afterward another invading expedition had still worse fortune. General Humbert, who in 1796 had been one of Hoche's officers, did succeed in effecting a landing at Killala Bay, in Mayo; but he and the whole of his force was speedily surrounded, and compelled to surrender; and a month afterward a large squadron, with a more powerful division of troops, under General Hardy, on board, found itself unable to effect a landing, but fell in with a squadron under Sir John Warren, who captured every ship but two; Wolfe Tone, who was on board one of them, being taken prisoner, and only escaping the gallows by suicide.

This happened in October, 1798. But it is difficult to conceive with what object these last expeditions had been despatched from France at all; for in the preceding summer the rebellion of the Irish had broken out, and had been totally crushed in a few weeks;[136] not without terrible loss of life on both sides, nor without the insurgent leaders—though many of them were gentlemen of good birth, fortune, and education, and still more were clergy—showing a ferocity and ingenuity in cruelty which the worst of the French Jacobins had scarcely exceeded; one of the saddest circumstances of the whole rebellion being, that the insurgents, who had burnt men, women, and children alive, who had deliberately hacked others to pieces against whom they did not profess to have a single ground of complaint beyond the fact that they were English and Protestant, found advocates in both Houses of the English Parliament, who declared that the rebellion was owing to the severity of the Irish Viceroy and his chief councillors, who denied that the rebels had solicited French aid, and who even voted against granting to the government the re-enforcements necessary to prevent a revival of the treason.

The rebellion was crushed with such celerity as might have convinced the most disaffected of the insanity of defying the power of Great Britain; but it was certain that the spirit which prompted the rebellion was not extinguished, and that, as it had been fed before, so it would continue to be fed by the factious spirit of members of the Irish House of Commons, and of those who could return members,[137] so long as Ireland had a separate Parliament. Not, indeed, that Pitt required the argument in favor of a Union which was thus furnished. The course adopted by the Irish Parliament on the Regency question was quite sufficient to show how great a mistake had been made by the repeal of Poynings' Act. But what the rebellion proved was, that the Union would not admit of an instant's delay; and Pitt at once applied himself to the task of framing a measure which, while it should strengthen England, by the removal of the necessity for a constant watchfulness over every transaction and movement in Ireland, should at the same time confer on and secure to Ireland substantial advantages, such as, without a Union, the English Parliament could scarcely be induced to contemplate.

Mr. Hallam, in one of the last chapters of his work,[138] while showing by unanswerable arguments the advantages which Scotland has derived from her Union with England, has also enumerated some of the causes which impeded the minister of the day in his endeavors to render it acceptable to the Scotch members to whom it was proposed. The most apparently substantial of these was the unprecedented character of the measure. No past "experience of history was favorable to the absorption of a lesser state, at least where the government partook so much of the republican form, in one of superior power and ancient rivalry." But, in the case of the present measure, what had thus been a difficulty in the Scotch Union might have been expected to be regarded as an argument in its favor, since the keenest patriots among the Scotch had long been convinced that the Union had brought a vast increase of prosperity and importance to their country, and what was now confessed to have proved advantageous to Scotland might naturally be expected to be equally beneficial to Ireland. Another obstacle had been the fear of the danger to which the Presbyterian Church might be "exposed, when brought thus within the power of a Legislature so frequently influenced by one which held her, not as a sister, but rather a bastard usurper to a sister's inheritance." But here again experience might give her testimony in favor of an Irish Union, since it was incontestable that those apprehensions—which, no doubt, many earnest Scotchmen had sincerely entertained—had not been realized, but that since the Union the Presbyterian Church had enjoyed as great security, as complete independence, and as absolute an authority over its members as in the preceding century; that the Parliament had never attempted the slightest interference with its exercise of its privileges, and that the Church of England had been equally free from the exhibition of any desire to stimulate the Parliament to such action; while the Roman Catholic Church, which had many more adherents in England than the Presbyterian Church had ever had, was quite powerful enough to exact for itself the maintenance of its rights, and the minister was quite willing to grant equal securities to those which, at the beginning of the century, had been thought sufficient for the Church of Scotland. A third reason which our great historical critic puts forward for the disfavor with which the Union was at the time regarded by many high-minded Scotchmen, he finds in "the gross prostitution with which a majority sold themselves to the surrender of their own legislative existence." That similar means were to some extent employed to win over opponents of the government in Ireland cannot, it must be confessed, be denied, though the temptations held out to converts oftener took the shape of titles, promotions, appointments, and court favors than of actual money. The most recent historian of this period — who, to say the least, is not biassed in favor of either the English or Irish government of the period — pronounces as his opinion, formed after the most careful research, that the bribery was on the other side. "Cornwallis and Castlereagh" (the Lord-lieutenant and the Chief Secretary) "both declared it to be within their knowledge that the Opposition offered four thousand pounds, ready money, for a vote. But they name only one man who was purchased, and his vote was obtained for four thousand pounds. From the language of Lord Cornwallis, it is certain that if money was spent by the government in this way it was without his knowledge; but many things may have been done by the inferior agents of the government, and possibly by Castlereagh himself, which they would not venture to lay before the Lord-lieutenant. It appears, however, from the papers which have recently come to light, that the prevalent belief of the Union having been mainly effected by a lavish expenditure of money is not well-founded; still it is certain that some money was expended in this way." Besides actual payment for votes, he adds that a very large sum — a hundred thousand pounds — is said to have been expended in the purchase of seats, the holders of which were, of course, to vote against the measure; and names Lord Downshire as subscribing £5000, Lord Lismore and Mr. White £3000 each, while the government funds were chiefly expended "in engaging[139] young barristers of the Four Courts to write for the Union." But, even if it were true that corruption was employed to the very utmost extent that was ever alleged by the most vehement opponent of the measure and of the government, it may be feared that very few of the last century Irishmen would have been so shocked at it as to consider that fact an objection to the Union, especially, it is sad and shameful to say, among the upper classes. The poorer classes, those who could render no political service to a minister, as being consequently beneath official notice, were unassailed by his temptations; but the demoralization of the men of rank and property was almost universal, and few seats were disposed of, few votes were given, except in return for favors granted, or out of discontent at favors refused. And it cannot be denied that the tendency to political jobbery had not been diminished by the concessions of 1782, if, indeed, it may not be said that the increased importance which those concessions had given to the Irish Parliament had led the members of both Houses to place an increased value on their services. Certainly no previous Lord-lieutenant had given such descriptions of the universality of the demands made on him as were forwarded to the English government by those who held that office in the sixteen years preceding the outbreak of the Rebellion.

It is remarkable that the transaction which, as has been said before, may be conceived to have first forced on Pitt's mind the conviction of the absolute necessity of the Union—namely, the course pursued by the Irish Parliament on the Regency Bill—bore a close resemblance to that which, above all other considerations, had made the Scotch Union indispensable, namely, the Act of Security passed by the Scottish Estates in 1703, which actually provided that, on the decease of Queen Anne without issue, the Estates "should name her successor, but should be debarred from choosing the admitted successor to the crown of England, unless such forms of government were settled as should fully secure the religion, freedom, and trade of the Scottish nation."[140] The Scotch Estates, therefore, had absolutely regarded the possible separation of the two kingdoms as a contingency which might become not undesirable; and, though it was too ticklish an argument to bring forward, it may very possibly have occurred to Pitt that a similar vote of the Irish Parliament was not impossible. The claim which Grattan, following Fox, had set up on behalf of the Prince of Wales, was one of an indefeasible right to the Regency; and, as far as right by inheritance went, his claim to the crown, if, or whenever, a vacancy should occur, was far less disputable. But, as has been mentioned in the last chapter, a question had already been raised whether his Royal Highness had not forfeited his right to the succession, and it was quite possible that that question might be renewed. The fact of the Prince's marriage to a Roman Catholic was by this time generally accepted as certain; the birth of the Princess Charlotte gave greater importance to the circumstance than it seemed to have while the Prince remained childless; and, if the performance of the marriage ceremony should be legally proved, and the English law courts should pronounce that the legal invalidity of the marriage did not protect the Prince from the penalty of forfeiture, it was highly probable that the Irish Parliament would take a different view— would refuse, in spite of the Bill of Rights, to regard marriage with a Roman Catholic as a disqualification, but would recognize the Prince of Wales as King of Ireland.

Several minor considerations, such as the desirableness of uniformity in the proceedings of the two countries with respect to Money Bills, the Mutiny Act, and other arrangements of parliamentary detail, all pointed the same way; and, on the whole, it may be said that scarcely any of the opponents of the government measure were found to deny its expediency, especially as regarded the interests of Great Britain. The objections which were made were urged on different grounds. In the Irish House of Commons, a member who, though a young man, had already established a very high reputation for professional skill as a barrister, for eloquence equally suited to the Bar and to the Senate, and for sincere and incorruptible patriotism, Mr. Plunkett, took upon himself to deny the competency of the Irish Parliament to pass a bill not only to extinguish its own existence, but to prevent the birth of any future Parliament, and to declare that the act, if it "should be passed," would be a mere nullity, and that no man in "Ireland would be bound to obey it." And, in the English House of Commons, Mr. Grey may be thought to have adopted something of the same view, when he proposed an amendment "to suspend all proceedings on the subject till the sentiments of the people of Ireland respecting that measure could be ascertained." He did not, of course, deny (he was speaking on the 21st of April, 1800) that the bill had been passed by both Houses of the Irish Parliament by considerable majorities.[141] But he contended that that Parliament did not speak the sentiments of the people; and, that being the case, that its voice was of no authority. It is evident that all arguments founded on a denial of the omnipotence of a Parliament, whether English or Irish, are invalid. The question of that omnipotence, as has been seen in a former chapter, had been fully discussed when Mr. Pitt's father denied the power of Parliament to tax the American Colonies; and that question may fairly be regarded as having been settled at that time. It is equally clear that the denial that, on any question whatever, the House of Commons must be taken to speak the sentiments of the constituencies, whether the proposal of such question had been contemplated at the time of their election or not, is the advancement of a doctrine wholly inconsistent with our parliamentary constitution, and one which would practically be the parent of endless agitation and mischief. To expect that the members could pronounce on no new question without a fresh reference to their constituents, would be to reduce them from the position of representatives to that of delegates; such as that of the members of the old States-general, in France, whose early decay is attributed by the ablest political writers in no small degree to the dependence of the members on their constituents for precise instructions. Another argument on which Mr. Grey insisted with great earnestness is worth preserving, though subsequent inventions have destroyed its force; he contended that the example of the Scotch Union did not, when properly considered, afford any argument in favor of an Irish Union, from the difference of situation of the two countries. Scotland was a part of the same island as England; "there was no physical impediment to rapid and constant communication; the relative situation of the two countries was such that the King himself could administer the executive government in both, and there was no occasion for a separate establishment being kept up in each." But the sea lay between England and Ireland, and the delays and sometimes difficulties which were thus interposed rendered it "necessary that Ireland should have a separate government;" and he affirmed that "this was an insuperable bar to a beneficial Union," quoting a saying of Lord Somers, that "if it were necessary to preserve a separate executive government at Edinburgh after the Union, he would abandon the measure." Mr. Grey even denied that the prosperity of Scotland since the Union was mainly attributable to that measure. "It was not the Union; it was the adoption of a liberal policy, the application of a proper remedy to the particular evils under which the country labored, that removed the causes which had impeded the prosperity of Scotland." But this argument was clearly open to the reply that the adoption of that liberal policy had been a direct effect of the Union, and would have been impracticable without it, and was, therefore, a strong inducement to the adoption of a similar Union with Ireland, where the existing evils were at least as great as those which, a century before, had kept down Scotland. Another of his arguments has been remarkably falsified by the event. With a boldness in putting forward what was manifestly, indeed avowedly, a party objection, and which, as such, must be looked upon as somewhat singular, he found a reason for resisting the addition of a hundred Irish members to the British House of Commons in the probability that they would, as a general rule, be subservient to the minister. He instanced "the uniform support which the members for Scotland had given to every act of ministers," and saw in that example "reason to apprehend that the Irish members would become a no less regular band of ministerial adherents." It would be superfluous to point out how entirely contrary the result has been to the prediction.

It is, however, beside the purpose of this work to dwell on the arguments by which the minister supported his proposal, or on those with which the Opposition resisted it, whether apparently founded on practical considerations, such as those brought forward by Mr. Grey, or those of a more sentimental character, which rested on the loss of national "dignity and honor," which, it was assumed, would be the consequence of the measure. It seems desirable rather to explain the principal conditions on which the Union was to be effected, as Pitt explained it to the House of Commons in April, 1800. In the preceding year he had confined himself to moving a series of resolutions in favor of the principle, which, though they were adopted by both Houses in England, he did not at that time endeavor to carry farther, since in the Irish House of Commons the utmost exertions of the government could only prevail by a single vote;[142] and he naturally thought such a majority far too slender to justify his relying on it so far as to proceed farther with a measure of such vast importance. But, during the recess, he had introduced some modifications into his original draft of the measure, which, though slight, were sufficient to conciliate much additional support; and the consequence was, that in February of this year both the Irish Houses accepted it by sufficient majorities;[143] and, therefore, he now felt able to lay the details of the measure before the English Parliament. To take them in the order in which he enumerated them, that which had appeared to the Irish Parliament "the first and most important, was the share which the Irish constituencies ought to have in the representation of the House of Commons." On this point, "the Parliament of Ireland was of opinion that the number of representatives for Ireland ought to be one hundred." And he was not disposed to differ from the conclusion to which it had come. He regarded it, indeed, as "a matter of but small importance whether the number of representatives from one part of the united empire were greater or less. If they were enough to make known the local wants, to state the interests and convey the sentiments of the part of the empire they represented, it would produce that degree of general security which would be wanting in any vain attempt to obtain that degree of theoretical perfection about which in modern times they had heard so much." He approved of "the principle which had been laid down upon this part of the subject in the Parliament of Ireland—a reference to the supposed population of the two countries, and to the proposed rate of contribution. The proportion of contribution proposed to be established was seven and a half for Great Britain, and one for Ireland; while in the proportion of population Great Britain was to Ireland as two and a half or three to one;[144] so that the result, on a combination of these two calculations, would be something more than five to one in favor of Great Britain, which was about the proportion which it was proposed to establish between the representation of the two countries." The principle of selection of the constituencies which had been adopted he likewise considered most "equitable and satisfactory for Ireland. The plan proposed was, that the members of the counties and the principal commercial cities should remain entire.... The remaining members were to be selected from those places which were the most considerable in point of population and wealth.... This was the only plan which could be adopted without trenching on the constitution; it introduced no theoretical reforms in the constitution or in the representation of this country; it made no distinction between different parliamentary rights, nor any alteration, even the slightest, in the internal forms of Parliament."

Another consideration which he had kept in mind in framing this measure was this: "By the laws of England care had been taken to prevent the influence of the crown from becoming too great by too many offices being held by members of Parliament." And Pitt had no doubt that there would be a general feeling "that some provision ought to be made on this subject" in the arrangements for the new Parliament. At present, among the representatives of the counties and great commercial towns, whose seats were to be preserved in the new united Parliament, there were not above five or six who held offices; and, though it was impossible to estimate the possible number of place-holders with precision, he thought what would he most fair for him to propose would be, that "no more than twenty of the Irish members should hold places, and that if it should happen that a greater number did hold places during pleasure, then those who had last accepted them should vacate their seats."

In the House of Peers he proposed that twenty-eight lords temporal of Ireland should have seats in the united Parliament, who should be elected for life by the Peers of Ireland—an arrangement which differed from that which, at the beginning of the century, had been adopted for the representative Peers of Scotland; but he argued, and surely with great reason, that "the choice of Peers to represent the Irish nobility for life was a mode that was more congenial to the general spirit and system of a Peerage than that of their being septennially elected, as the nobility of Scotland were." Of the spiritual Peers, four were to sit in rotation; to the lay Peers a farther privilege was given, which the minister regarded as of considerable, and even constitutional importance. By the articles of the Scotch Union, a Peer, if not chosen as a representative of the Peerage, was not eligible as a candidate for the House of Commons in either England or Scotland. But this bill "reserved a right to the Peers of Ireland who should not be elected to represent their own Peerage, to be elected members of the House of Commons of the united Parliament of Great Britain;" and Pitt urged that this was "a far better mode of treatment than had been adopted for the nobility of Scotland; so that a nobleman of Ireland, if not representing his own order, might be chosen as a legislator by a class of inferior rank, which he was so far from regarding as improper, that he deemed it in a high degree advantageous to the empire, analogous to the practice as well as friendly to the spirit of the British constitution." And he enforced his argument by pointing out with honest pride the advantage which in that respect the spirit and practice of our constitution gave to our nobility over the nobles of other countries. "We know full well," he continued, "the advantage we have experienced from having in this House those who, in the course of descent, as well as in hopes of merit, have had a prospect of sitting in our House of Peers. Those, therefore, who object to this part of the arrangement" (for, as he had previously mentioned, it had been made a subject not only of objection, but of ridicule) "can only do so from the want of due attention to the true character of our constitution, one of the great leading advantages of which is, that a person may for a long time be a member of one branch of the Legislature, and have it in view to become a member of another branch of it. This it is which constitutes the leading difference between the nobility of Great Britain and those of other countries. With us they are permitted to have legislative power before they arrive at their higher stations; and as they are, like all the rest of mankind, to be improved by experience in the science of legislation as well as in every other science, our constitution affords them that opportunity by their being eligible to seats in this House from the time of their majority. This is one of those circumstances which arise frequently in practice, but the advantages of which do not appear in theory till chance happens to cast them before us, and makes them subjects of discussion. These are the shades of the British constitution in which its latent beauties consist;" and he affirmed his conviction that this privilege would prove "an advantage to the nobility of Ireland, and an improvement in the system of representation in the House."

It will hardly be denied that the arrangement that the representative Peers of Ireland should enjoy their seats for life did make it desirable that those who were not so elected to the Upper House should be eligible as candidates for a place in the Lower House. Otherwise, those who were not chosen as representatives of the peerage would have been placed in the anomalous and unfair position of being the only persons in the kingdom possessed of the requisite property qualification, and not disqualified by sex or profession, who were absolutely excluded from the opportunity of distinguishing themselves and serving their country in Parliament. How great the practical benefit to the House of Commons and the country the clause he was recommending was calculated to confer, was shown in a remarkable manner the very year of his death, when an Irish Peer was returned to the House of Commons, who, retaining his seat for nearly sixty years as the representative of different constituencies, the University of Cambridge being among the number, during the course of that period rose through a variety of offices to that of Prime-minister, and, as is admitted even by those who dissented most widely from some of his opinions and actions, earned for himself an honorable reputation, as one who had rendered faithful services to the crown, and on more than one occasion had conferred substantial benefits on the country.

The arrangements proposed with respect to the Peers were not opposed. But Mr. Grey—generally acting as the spokesman of the Opposition on this question—raised an objection to making so large an addition as that of one hundred new members to the British House of Commons. He repeated his prophecy, made on a previous occasion, of the subserviency to the minister which the Irish members might be expected to exhibit, and therefore moved an amendment to reduce the number of Irish representatives to eighty-five; but, to obviate the discontent which such a reduction might be expected to excite in Ireland, he proposed to diminish the number of English members also, by disfranchising forty "of the most decayed boroughs," a step which would leave the number of members in the new united Parliament as nearly as possible the same as it was before. He found, however, very few to agree with him; his amendment was rejected by 176 to 34; and the minister's proposal was adopted in all its details.

Mr. Pitt touched lightly on the next article, which limited the royal prerogative of creating Peers by a provision that the King should never confer any fresh Irish peerage till three peerages should have become extinct. This, again, was a point of difference between the conditions of the Scotch and Irish Unions; since by the terms of the Scotch Union the King was forever debarred from creating any new Scotch peerages. But it was pointed out that the greater antiquity of the Scotch peerages, and the circumstance that in Scotland the titles descended to collateral branches, were calculated to make the extinction of a Scotch peerage an event of very rare occurrence; while the comparative newness (with very few exceptions) of Irish peerages, and the rule by which they are "confined to immediate male descendants," rendered the entire extinction of the Irish peerage probable, "if the power of adding to or making up the number were not given to the crown."

Recent legislation has given such importance to the next resolution, that it will be well to quote his precise words:

"5. That it would be fit to propose, as the fifth article of union, that the Churches of that part of Great Britain called England and of Ireland shall be united into one Church; and that when his Majesty shall summon a Convocation, the archbishops, bishops, and clergy of the several provinces in Ireland shall be respectively summoned to and sit in the Convocation of the united Church, in the like manner and subject to the same regulations as to election and qualification as are at present by law established with respect to the like orders of the Church of England; and that the doctrine, worship, discipline, and government of the said united Church shall be preserved as now by law established for the Church of England, saving to the Church of Ireland all the rights, privileges, and jurisdictions now thereunto belonging; and that the doctrine, worship, discipline, and government of the Church of Scotland shall likewise be preserved as now by law, and by the Act of Union established for the Church of Scotland; and that the continuance and preservation forever of the said united Church, as the Established Church, of that part of the said United Kingdom called England and Ireland, shall be deemed and taken to be an essential and fundamental article and condition of the Union."

Pitt's comment on this article was so brief as to show that he regarded its justice as well as its importance too obvious to need any elaborate justification. He pointed out that that portion of it which related to Convocation had been added by the Irish Parliament, and "would only say on so interesting a subject that the prosperity of the Irish Church could never be permanent, unless it were a part of the Union, to leave as a guard a power to the United Parliament to make some provision in this respect as a fence beyond any act of their own that could at present be agreed on." But, while he thus showed his conviction that the permanent prosperity of the Irish Church was essential to the welfare of the kingdom, he was by no means insensible to the claims of the Roman Catholic Church (as founded not more in policy than in justice) to be placed in some degree on a footing of equality with it; not only by a recognition of the dignity of its ministers, but also by an endowment which should be proportioned to their requirements, and should place them in a position of worldly competence and comfort for which hitherto they had been dependent on their flocks.[145] To use the expression of a modern statesman, he contemplated "levelling up," not "levelling down." Perhaps it may be said that he contemplated levelling up, as the surest and most permanent obstacle to any proposal of levelling down.

At the same time it is fair to remark, that the argument which on a recent occasion was so strongly pressed by the champions of the Church, that it was beyond the power of Parliament to repeal what was here declared to be "an essential and fundamental article and condition of the Union," is untenable, on every consideration of the power of Parliament, and, indeed, of common-sense; since it would be an intolerable evil, and one productive of the worst consequences, if the doctrine were admitted that any Parliament could make an unchangeable law and bind its successors forever; and, moreover, since the very words of this article do clearly imply the power of Parliament over the Church, the power asserted, to "make some provision for the permanence of its prosperity," clearly involving a power to make provisions of an opposite character. The expediency or impolicy, the propriety or unrighteousness, of a measure must always depend on the merits of the question itself at the time, and not on the judgment or intentions of legislators of an earlier generation. And advocates weaken instead of strengthening their case when they put forward arguments which, however plausible or acceptable to their own partisans, are, nevertheless, capable of refutation.

The next article related to a question of paramount practical importance, and of special interest, since, as has been seen before, there was no subject on which the past legislation of the English Parliament had been so discreditable. But the jealousy of English manufacturers, though it had prevailed over the indifference of William III., who reserved all his solicitude for matters of foreign diplomacy, could find no echo in the large mind and sound commercial and financial knowledge of the modern statesman. He laid it down as the principle of his legislation on this subject—a principle which "he was sure that every gentleman in the House was ready to admit—that the consequence of the Union ought to be a perfect freedom of trade, whether of produce or manufacture, without exception, if possible; that a deviation from that principle ought to be made only when adhering to it might possibly shake some large capital, or materially diminish the effect of the labor of the inhabitants, or suddenly and violently shock the received opinion or popular prejudices of a large portion of the people; but that, on the whole, the communication between the two kingdoms should in spirit be free; that no jealousy should be attempted to be created between the manufacturers of one place or the other upon the subject of 'raw materials' or any other article; for it would surely be considered very narrow policy, and as such would be treated with derision, were an attempt made to create a jealousy between Devonshire and Cornwall, between Lancashire and Durham.... He said, then, that the principle of the Union on this head should be liberal and free, and that no departure from it should ever take place but upon some point of present unavoidable necessity." He was even able to add (and he must have felt peculiar satisfaction in making the statement, since the change in the feelings of the English manufacturers on the subject must have been mainly the fruit of his own teaching, and was a practical recognition of the benefits which they had derived from his commercial policy taken as a whole), that "the English manufacturers did not wish for any protective duties; all they desired was free intercourse with all the world; and, though the want of protective duties might occasion them partial loss, they thought it amply compensated by the general advantage." He even thought the arrangements now to be made "would encourage the growth of wool in Ireland, and that England would be able to draw supplies of it from thence; and he did not fear that there would be trade enough for both countries in the markets of the world, and in the market which each country would afford to the other." The English manufacturers did not, however, acquiesce very cheerfully in every part of his commercial arrangements. On the contrary, against the clause which repealed all prohibitions of or bounties on exportation of different articles grown or manufactured in either country, they petitioned, and even set up a claim, which was granted, to be heard by counsel and to produce witnesses. But Pitt steadily refused the least modification of this part of his measure, not merely on account of its intrinsic reasonableness and justice, but because there was scarcely any condition to which the Irish themselves attached greater importance.

An equally important and more difficult matter to adjust to the satisfaction of both Parliaments was the apportionment of the financial burdens between the two nations. It would be tiresome as well as superfluous to enter into minute details; the more so as the arrangement proposed was of a temporary character. After a long and minute discussion, Pitt's appraisement was admitted to come as near to strict fairness and equity as any that could be made; the separate discharge of its public debt already incurred was left to each kingdom; and it was farther settled that for twenty years fifteen parts of the expense of the nation out of seventeen should be borne by Great Britain and two by Ireland.

Other articles provided that the laws and courts of both kingdoms, civil and ecclesiastical, should remain in their existing condition, subject, of course, to such alterations as the united Legislature might hereafter deem desirable.

The resolutions, when adopted—as they speedily were—were embodied in a bill, which passed through the last stage by receiving the royal assent at the beginning of July. The state of public feeling in Ireland was not yet sufficiently calmed down after the Rebellion for it to be prudent to venture on a general election, and it was, consequently, ordained that the members for the Irish counties and for those Irish boroughs which had been selected for the retention of representation should take their seats in the united Parliament on its next meeting. On the 22d of January, 1801, the united, or, to give it its more proper designation, the Imperial Parliament held its first meeting, being, although in its sixth session, so far regarded as a new Parliament, that the King directed a fresh election of a Speaker.

The Union, as thus effected, was so far a vital change in the constitution of both Great Britain and Ireland, that it greatly altered the situation in which each kingdom had previously stood to the other. Till 1782 the position of Ireland toward England had been one of entire political subordination; and, though that had in appearance been modified by the repeal of Poynings' Act, yet no one doubted or could doubt that, whenever the resolutions of the two Parliaments came into conflict, the Irish Parliament would find submission unavoidable. But by the Union that subordination was terminated forever. The character of the Union—of the conditions, that is, on which the two countries were united—was one of perfect and complete equality on all important points, indeed, in all matters whatever, except one or two of minor consequence, where some irremovable difference between them compelled some trifling variations. It was not a connection of domination on the one side and subordination on the other, where every concomitant circumstance might tempt the one to overbearing arrogance, while the other could not escape a feeling of humiliation. It was rather—to quote the eloquent peroration of Pitt, when, in the preceding year, he first introduced the subject to the consideration of the House of Commons—"a free and voluntary association of two great countries, joining for their common benefit in one empire, where each retained its proportionate weight and importance, under the security of equal laws, reciprocal affection, and inseparable interests; and which wanted nothing but that indissoluble connection to render both invincible."

On that occasion Pitt had argued, from the great subsequent increase in the population and wealth of Edinburgh and Glasgow, and in the prosperity of the whole country of Scotland, that a similar result might be looked for in Ireland. And the general trade of Ireland, and especially the linen manufacture, within a very few years began to realize his prediction. So that it is strange to find Fox, on the great minister's death, five years afterward, reiterating his disapproval of the Union as a plea for refusing him the appellation of a great statesman.[146] In one point alone the intrigues of a colleague prevented Pitt from carrying out to the full his liberal and enlightened views, and compelled him to leave the Union incomplete in a matter of such pre-eminent importance, that it may be said that all the subsequent disquietudes which have prevented Ireland from reaping the full benefit he desired from the Union are traceable to his disappointment on that subject.[147] We have seen that he contemplated, as a natural and necessary consequence or even part of the Union, an extensive reform of the laws affecting the Roman Catholics. Indeed, the understanding that he was prepared to introduce a measure with that object had no small weight in conciliating in some quarters support to the Act of Union. Accordingly, when describing the arrangements which he had in view for the Church of Ireland, he indicated his intention with sufficient plainness by the statement, that "it might be proper to leave to Parliament an opportunity of considering what might be fit to be done for his Majesty's Catholic subjects;" words which were generally understood to express his feeling, that both justice and policy required the removal of the restrictions which debarred the Roman Catholics from the complete enjoyment of political privileges. But the history and different bearings of that question it will be more convenient to discuss in a subsequent chapter, when we shall have arrived at the time when it was partially dealt with by the ministry of the Duke of Wellington.

Notes:

[Footnote 125:] Mr. Froude says four great families—the Fitzgeralds of Kildare, the Boyles, the Ponsonbys, and the Beresfords—returned a majority of the House of Commons ("English in Ireland," ii., 5); and besides those peers, the arrangement for the Union proved that the influence of the Loftuses and the Hills fell little short of them.]

[Footnote 126:] Such a system actually had existed in France, where articles of ordinary trade could not be transported from one province to another without payment of a heavy duty; but Colbert had abolished that system in France above one hundred years before the time of which we are speaking.]

[Footnote 127:] "History of England," vol. v., c. xxiii., p. 57.]

[Footnote 128:] "The English in Ireland," ii., 39.]

[Footnote 129:] Fronde's "English in Ireland," ii., 345. He does not name the author whom he quotes.]

[Footnote 130:] *Ibid.*, ii, 42.]

[Footnote 132:] Mr. Froude imputes to Grattan a singularly base object. "Far from Grattan was a desire to heal the real sores of the country for which he was so zealous. These wild, disordered elements suited better for the campaign in which he engaged of renovating an Irish nationality." — *English in Ireland*, ii., 448. But, however on many points we may see reason to agree with Mr. Froude's estimate of the superior wisdom of Fitzgibbon, we conceive that this opinion is quite consistent with our acquittal of the other of the meanness of deliberately aiming at a continuance of evils, in order to find in them food for a continuance of agitation.]

[Footnote 133:] Froude, "English in Ireland," i., 304.]

[Footnote 134:] See especially a letter of Mr. Windham's. quoted by Lord Stanhope ("Life of Pitt," ii., 288).]

[Footnote 135:] Mr. Archdall, in his place in Parliament, denounced the term as utterly inapplicable. "Emancipation meant that a slave was set free. The Catholics were not slaves. Nothing more absurd had ever been said since language was first abused for the delusion of mankind."]

[Footnote 136:] The first beginning of the insurrection was at Prosperous, County Kildare, May 24. General Lake dealt it the final blow on Vinegar Hill, June 21.]

[Footnote 137:] Mr. Sheridan, Mr. Tierney, and Lord William Russell led the denunciations of the government in the English House of Commons. A protest against Pitt's refusal to dismiss the Lord-lieutenant, Lord Camden, the Chancellor Fitzgibbon, and the Commander-in-chief, Lord Carhampton, was signed by the Dukes of Norfolk,

Devonshire, and Leinster; Lords Fitzwilliam, Moira, and Ponsonby, "two of them Irish absentees, who were discharging thus their duties to the poor country which supported their idle magnificence." — *The English in Ireland*, iii., 454.]

[Footnote 138:] "Constitutional History," iii., 451 seq.]

[Footnote 139:] Massey's "History of England," iv., 397 (quoting the Cornwallis correspondence).]

[Footnote 140:] Lord Stanhope's "Reign of Queen Anne," p. 89.]

[Footnote 141:] In the House of Commons by 158 to 115; in the House of Lords, February 10, by 75 to 26.]

[Footnote 142:] An amendment pledging the House to maintain "an independent Legislature, as established in 1782," was only defeated by 106 to 105.]

[Footnote 143:] In the House of Commons the majority was 158 to 115; in the House of Lords, 75 to 26.]

[Footnote 144:] This estimate, which was but a guess, proved very inaccurate. The first census for the United Kingdom, which was taken the next year (1801), showed that Ireland was considerably more populous than its own representatives had imagined. The numbers returned (as given by Alison, "History of Europe," ii., 335, c. ix., sec. 8) were:

England.............................. 8,382,484
Wales................................. 547,346
Scotland........................... 1,599,068
Army, Navy, etc............... 470,586

Total................................. 10,999,434
Ireland.............................. 5,396,436

So that the proportion of population in Great Britain, as compared with that of Ireland, only exceeded two to one by an insignificant fraction.]

[Footnote 145:] See his letter to the King, dated January 31, 1801, quoted by Lord Stanhope in the appendix to vol. iii. of his "Life of Pitt," p. 25.]

[Footnote 146:] Mr. Fox, called on by Mr. Alexander to explain his expressions (in the debate relative to Mr. Pitt's funeral), by which he had declared his disapprobation of the Union, and his concurrence in opinion with Mr.

O'Hara that it ought to be rescinded. Mr. Fox repeated his disapprobation, but disclaimed ever having expressed an opinion or entertained a thought of proposing its repeal, that being now impracticable, though he regretted its ever having been effected.—*Diary of Lord Colchester*, February 17, 1806, ii., 39.]

[Footnote 147:] It may be remarked that in another respect also political critics have pronounced the Union defective. Archbishop Whately, whose long tenure of office in Ireland, as well as the acuteness and candor which he brought to bear on every subject he discussed, entitle his opinions to most respectful consideration, held this view very strongly. In several conversations which he held with Mr. W.N. Senior, in 1858 and 1862, he condemned the retention of the Lord-lieutenancy as "a half measure," which, however unavoidable at the time when "no ship could be certain of getting from Holyhead to Dublin in less than three weeks," he pronounced "inconsistent with the fusion of the two peoples, which was the object of the Union," and wholly indefeasible "in an age of steam-vessels and telegraphs." And, besides its theoretical inconsistency, he insisted that it produced many great and practical mischiefs, among which he placed in the front "the keeping up in people's minds the notion of a separate kingdom; the affording a hotbed of faction and intrigue; the presenting an image of Majesty so faint and so feeble as to be laughed at and scorned. Disaffection to the English Lieutenancy is cheaply shown, and it paves the way toward disaffection to the English crown." And he imputed its continued retention to "the ignorance which prevails in England of the state of feeling in Ireland."—*Journals and Conversations Relating to Ireland*, by W.N. Senior, ii., 130, 251, and *passim*. And it is worthy of observation that a similar view is expressed by a Scotch writer of great ability, who, contrasting the mode in which Scotland is governed with that which prevails In Ireland, farther denounces the Viceroyalty "as a distinct mark that Ireland is not directly under the sovereignty of Great Britain, but rather a dependency, like India or the Isle of Man."—*Ireland*, by J.B. Kinnear, quoted in the *Fortnightly Review*, April 1, 1881. It is remarkable that in 1850 a bill for the abolition of the office was passed in the House of Commons by a large majority (295 to 70), but was dropped in the House of Lords, chiefly on account of the opposition of the Duke of Wellington. But it is, at all events, plain that the reasons, arising from the difficulty and uncertainty of communication, which made its abolition impossible at the beginning of the century, have passed away with the introduction of steam-vessels and telegraphs. Communication of London with Dublin is now as rapid as communication with Edinburgh, and, that being the case, it is not easy to see how an establishment which has never been thought of for Scotland can be desirable for Ireland.]

CHAPTER VI

A Census is Ordered.—Dissolution of Pitt's Administration.—Impeachment of Lord Melville.—Introduction of Lord Ellenborough into the Cabinet.—Abolition of the Slave-trade.—Mr. Windham's Compulsory Training Bill.—Illness of the King, and Regency.—Recurrence to the Precedent of 1788-'89.—Death of Mr. Perceval.—Lord Liverpool becomes Prime-minister.—Question of Appointments in the Household.—Appointment of a Prime-minister.

The Union with Ireland was the last great work of Pitt's first administration, and a noble close to the legislation of the eighteenth century. But the last months of the year were also signalized by another enactment, which, though it cannot be said to have anything of a character strictly entitled to the name of constitutional, nevertheless established a practice so valuable as the foundation of a great part of our domestic legislation, that it will, perhaps, hardly be considered foreign to the scope and purpose of this volume to record its commencement. In November, 1800, Mr. Abbott, the member for Helstone, brought in a bill to take a census of the people of the United Kingdom, pointing out not only the general importance of a knowledge of the population of a country in its entire amount and its different classes to every government, but also its special bearing on agriculture and on the means requisite to provide subsistence for the people, on trade and manufactures, and on our resources for war. Such a census as he proposed had been more than once taken in Holland, Sweden, Spain, and even in the United States, young as was their separate national existence; it had been taken once—nearly fifty years previous—in Scotland; and something like one had been furnished in England in the reign of Edward III. by a subsidy roll, and in that of Elizabeth by diocesan returns furnished by the Bishops to the Privy Council.[148] He farther argued for the necessity of such a proceeding from the different notions entertained by men of sanguine or desponding tempers as to the increase or diminution of the population. "Some desponding men had asserted that the population had decreased by a million and a half between the Revolution and Peace of Paris, in 1763; others (of whom the speaker himself was one) believed that, on the contrary, it had increased in that interval by two millions." His motion was unanimously adopted by both Houses; and when the census was taken, its real result furnished as strong a proof of its usefulness as any of the mover's arguments, by the extent of the prevailing miscalculations which it detected. For Mr. Abbott, who had spared no pains to arrive at a correct estimate, while he mentioned that some persons reckoned the population of England and Wales at 8,000,000, pronounced that, according to other statements, formed on a more extensive investigation, and, as it seemed to him, on a more correct train of reasoning, the total number could not be less than 11,000,000. In point of fact, excluding those employed in the army and navy, who were nearly half a million, the number for England and Wales fell short of nine millions.[149] It would be quite superfluous to dilate on the value of the information thus supplied, without which, indeed, much of our subsequent legislation on poor-laws, corn-laws, and all matters relating to rating and taxation, would have been impracticable or the merest guesswork.

As was mentioned in the preceding chapter, Pitt found himself unable to fulfil the hopes which, in his negotiations with different parties in Ireland, he had led the Roman Catholics to entertain of the removal of their civil and political disabilities. So rigorous were those restrictions, both in England and Ireland, that a Roman Catholic could not serve even as a private in the militia; and a motion made in 1797 by Mr. Wilberforce—a man who could certainly not be suspected of any leaning to Roman Catholic doctrine— to render them admissible to that service, though it was adopted in the House of Commons, was rejected by the House of Lords. But Pitt, who on that occasion had supported Wilberforce, did not confine his views to the removal of a single petty disability, but proposed to put the whole body of Roman Catholics on a footing of perfect equality with Protestants in respect of their eligibility to every kind of office, with one or two exceptions. And during the autumn of 1800 he was busily engaged in framing the details of his measure, in order to submit it to his royal master in its entirety, and so to avoid disquieting him with a repetition of discussions on the subject, which he knew to be distasteful to him. For, five years before, George III. had consulted the Chief-justice, Lord Kenyon, and the Attorney-general, Sir John Scott (afterward Lord Eldon), on the question whether some proposed concessions to Dissenters, Protestant as well as Roman Catholic, did not "militate against the coronation oath and many existing statutes;" and had received their legal opinion that the tests enacted in the reign of Charles II., "though wise laws, and in policy not to be departed from, might be repealed or altered without any breach of the coronation oath or Act of Union" (with Scotland).[150] Their opinions on the point were the more valuable, since they were notoriously opposed to their political convictions, and might be supposed to have carried sufficient conviction to the royal mind. But his Majesty's scruples were now, unfortunately, revived by the Lord Chancellor, who, strange to say, was himself a Presbyterian; and who treacherously availed himself of his knowledge of what was in contemplation to anticipate the Prime-minister's intended explanations to the King. He fully succeeded in his object of fixing the King's resolution to refuse his assent to the contemplated concessions (which, by a curious confusion of ideas, his Majesty even characterized as "Jacobinical"[151]), though not in the object which he had still more at heart, of inducing the King to regard him as the statesman in the whole kingdom the most deserving of his confidence. The merits of the question will be more appropriately examined hereafter. It is sufficient to say here that Pitt, conceiving himself bound by personal honor as well as by statesman-like duty to persevere in his intended measure, or to retire from an office which no man is justified in holding unless he can discharge its functions in accordance with his own judgment of what is required by the best interests of the state, resigned his post, and was succeeded by Mr. Addington.

Addington's ministry was made memorable by the formation of the Northern Confederacy against us, and its immediate and total overthrow by Nelson's cannon; and for the Peace of Amiens, severely criticised in Parliament, as that of Utrecht and every subsequent treaty with a similar object had been, but defensible both on grounds of domestic policy, as well as on that of affording us a much-needed respite from the strain of war; though it proved to be only a respite, and a feverish one, since at the end of two years the war was renewed, to be waged with greater fury than ever. But it was too short-lived for any constitutional questions to arise in it. And when, in 1804, Pitt resumed the government, his attention was too completely engrossed by the diplomatic arrangements by which he hoped to unite all the nations east of the Rhine in resistance to a power whose ever aggressive ambition was a standing menace to every Continental kingdom, for him to be able to spare time for the consideration of measures of domestic policy, except such as were of a financial character. But, though his premature death rendered his second administration shorter than even Addington's, it was not wholly unproductive of questions of constitutional interest. It witnessed a recurrence to that which cannot but be regarded as among the most important privileges of the House of Commons, the right of impeaching a minister for maladministration. A report of a commission appointed for the investigation of the naval affairs of the kingdom had revealed to Parliament a gross misapplication of the public money committed by the Paymaster of the Navy. And, as that officer could not have offended as he had done without either gross carelessness or culpable connivance on the part of the Treasurer of the Navy, Lord Melville, who had since been promoted to the post of First Lord of the Admiralty, the House of Commons ordered his impeachment at the Bar of the House of Lords; the vote being passed in 1805, during Pitt's administration, though the trial did not take place till the year following. In reality, the charge did not impugn Lord Melville's personal honor, on which at first sight it appeared to press hardly, Mr. Whitbread himself, the member for Bedford, who was the chief promoter and manager of the impeachment, admitting that he never imputed to Lord Melville "any participation in the plunder of the public;" and, as Lord Melville was acquitted on every one of the charges brought against him, the case might have been passed over here with the barest mention of it, were it not that Lord Campbell has pointed out the mode of procedure as differing from that adopted in the great trial of Warren Hastings, twenty years before; and, by reason of that difference, forming a model for future proceedings of the same kind, if, unhappily, there should ever be occasion given for a similar prosecution. The credit of the difference Lord Campbell gives to the Chancellor, Lord Erskine, who, "instead of allowing the House of Lords to sit to hear the case a few days in a year, and, when sitting, being converted from a court of justice into a theatre for rhetorical display, insisted that it should sit, like every other criminal tribunal, *de die in diem*, till the verdict was delivered. And he enforced both upon the managers of the House of Commons and on the counsel for the defendant the wholesome rules of procedure established for the detection of crime and the protection of innocence."[152] It is well known that on the trial of Hastings the managers of that impeachment, and most especially Burke, claimed a right of giving evidence such as no court of law would have admitted, and set up what they entitled "a usage of Parliament independent of and contradistinguished from the common law."[153] But on that occasion Lord Thurlow, then Chancellor, utterly denied the existence of any such usage—a usage which, "in times of barbarism, when to impeach a man was to ruin him by the strong hand of power, was quoted in order to justify the most arbitrary proceedings." He instanced the trial of Lord Stafford, as one which "was from beginning to end marked by violence and injustice," and expressed a "hope that in these enlightened days no man would be tried but by the law of the land." We may fairly agree with Lord Campbell, that it is to be hoped that the course adopted by Lord Erskine in this case has settled the principle and mode of procedure for all future time; since certainly the importance of an impeachment, both as to the state interests involved in it, and the high position and authority of the defendant, ought to be considered as reasons for adhering with the greatest closeness to the strict rules of law, rather than for relaxing them in any particular.

But, as was natural, the public could spare little attention for anything except the war, and the arrangements made by the minister for engaging in it with effect; the interest which such a state of things always kindles being in this instance greatly inflamed by Napoleon's avowal of a design to invade the kingdom, though it is now known that the preparations of which he made such a parade were merely a feint to throw Austria off her guard.[154] During Addington's administration Pitt had spoken warmly in favor of giving every possible encouragement to the Volunteer movement, and also in support of a proposal made by an independent member, Colonel Crawford, to fortify London; and one of his first measures after his resumption of office was a measure, known as the Additional Force Bill, to transfer a large portion of the militia to the regular army. It was so purely a measure of detail, that it would hardly have been necessary to mention it, had it not been for an objection made to it by the Prime-minister's former colleague, Lord Grenville, and for the reply with which that objection was encountered by the Chief-justice, Lord Ellenborough; the former denouncing it as unconstitutional, since, he declared, it tended to establish a large standing army in time of peace; and Lord Ellenborough, on the other hand, declaring the right of the crown to call out the whole population in arms for the defence of the realm to be so "radical, essential, and hitherto never questioned part of the royal prerogative, that, even in such an age of adventurous propositions, he had not expected that any lord would have ventured to question it."[155]

Pitt died in the beginning of 1806, and was succeeded by an administration of which his great rival, Fox, was the guiding spirit while he lived, though Lord Grenville was First Lord of the Treasury, and, after Fox's death, which took place in September, the undisputed Prime-minister. But the formation of the administration was not completed without a step which was at once strongly denounced, not only by the regular Opposition, but by several members of political moderation, as a violation, if not of the letter, at least of the spirit, of the constitution, the introduction of the Lord Chief-justice, Lord Ellenborough, into the cabinet. It was notorious that he was invited to a seat among that body as the representative of a small party, the personal friends of Lord Sidmouth. For the ministry was formed in some degree on the principle of a coalition; Lord Grenville himself having been a colleague of Pitt throughout the greater part of that statesman's first ministry, and as such having been always opposed to Fox; while Lord Ellenborough had been Attorney-general in Addington's administration, which avowedly only differed from Pitt on the single subject of the Catholic question.

The appointment was at once made the subject of motions in both Houses of Parliament. In the House of Lords, Lord Bristol, who brought the question forward, denounced "this identification of a judge with the executive government as injurious to the judicial character, subversive of the liberty of the people, and having a direct and alarming tendency to blend and amalgamate those great elementary principles of political power which it is the very object of a free constitution to keep separate and distinct." In the House of Commons, Mr. Canning took a similar objection; and, though he admitted that a precedent for the act might be found in the case of Lord Mansfield who, while Chief-justice, had also been a cabinet minister in the administration of 1757, he argued forcibly that that precedent turned against the ministry and the present appointment, because Lord Mansfield himself had subsequently admitted that "he had infringed the principles of the constitution by acting as a cabinet minister and Chief-justice at the same time." Fox, in reply, relied principally on two arguments. The first was, that "he had never heard of such a thing as the cabinet council becoming the subject of a debate in that House. He had never known of the exercise of the King's prerogative in the appointment of his ministers being brought into question on such grounds as had now been alleged." The second, that "in point of fact there is nothing in the constitution that recognizes any such institution as a cabinet council; that it is a body unknown to the law, and one which has in no instance whatever been recognized by Parliament." He farther urged that as Lord Ellenborough was a privy councillor, and as the cabinet is only a select committee of the Privy Council, he was, "in fact, as liable to be summoned to attend the cabinet, as a privy councillor, as he was in his present situation."

The last argument was beneath the speaker to use, since not one of his hearers was ignorant that no member of the Privy Council unconnected with the government ever is summoned to the deliberations of the cabinet; and though, as he correctly stated, "there is no legal record of the members comprising any cabinet," it may safely be affirmed that since July, 1714, when the Duke of Argyll and the Duke of Somerset claimed admission to the deliberations of the ministers, on account of the danger in which the Queen lay, though they admitted that they had received no summons to attend,[156] there has been no instance of any privy councillor attending without a summons; nor, except at the accession of a new sovereign, of summonses being sent to any members of the council except the actual ministers. The second argument was even worse, as being still more sophistical. It might be true that no law nor statute recognized the cabinet as a body distinct from the Privy Council, but it was at least equally true that there was no one who was ignorant of the distinction; that it was, in truth, one without which it would be difficult to understand the organization or working of any ministry. The indispensable function and privilege of a ministry is, to deliberate in concert and in private on the measures to be taken for the welfare of the state; but there could be little chance of concert, and certainly none of privacy, if every one who has ever been sworn a member of the Privy Council had a right to attend all its deliberations. Again, to say that the King's prerogative, as exercised in the choice of his advisers, is a thing so sacred that no abuse of it, or want of judgment shown in its exercise, can warrant a complaint, is inconsistent with every principle of constitutional government, and with every conceivable idea of the privileges of Parliament. In fact, Parliament has claimed a right to interfere in matters apparently touching more nearly the royal prerogative, and it is only in the reign preceding the present reign that hostile comments have been made in Parliament on the appointment of a particular person as ambassador to a foreign power. Yet the post of ambassador is one which might have been supposed to have been farther removed from the supervision of Parliament than that of a minister, an ambassador being in a special degree the personal representative of the sovereign, and the sovereign therefore, having, it might be supposed, a right to a most unfettered choice in such a matter.

Stripped of all technicalities, and even of all reference to the manifest possibility of such a circumstance arising as that the Chief-justice, if a member of a cabinet, may have a share in ordering the institution of a prosecution which, as a judge, it may be his lot to try, one consideration which is undeniable is, that a member of a cabinet is of necessity, and by the very nature of his position in it, a party man, and that it is of preeminent importance to the impartiality of the judicial bench, and to the confidence of the people in the purity, integrity, and freedom from political bias of their decisions, that the judges should be exempt from all suspicion of party connection. Lord Campbell even goes the length of saying, what was not urged on either side of either House in these debates, that it was alleged by at least one contemporary writer that Lord Mansfield's position in the cabinet did perceptibly influence some of his views and measures respecting the Press;[157] and, though in both Houses the ministry had a majority on the question of the propriety of the appointment, he records his own opinion[158] that "the argument was all on the losing side;" and that Mr. Fox showed his consciousness that it was so by his "concession that the Chief-justice should absent himself from the cabinet when the expediency of commencing prosecutions for treason or sedition was to be discussed." He adds, also, that "it is said that Lord Ellenborough himself ere long changed his opinion, and, to his intimate friends, expressed deep regret that he had ever been prevailed upon to enter the cabinet."

But, if the composition of the cabinet of 1806 has in this respect been generally condemned, on the other hand the annals of that ministry, short-lived as it was, are marked by the enactment of one great measure which has been stamped with universal approbation. It may, perhaps, be said that the existence, promotion, discouragement, or suppression of a branch of trade has no title to be regarded as a constitutional question. But the course which the British Parliament, after a long period of hesitation, has adopted respecting, not only the slave-trade, but the employment of slave-labor in any part of the British dominions, is so intimately connected with the great constitutional principle, that every man, whatever be his race or nation or previous condition, whose foot is once planted on British soil, is free from that moment, that it cannot be accounted a digression to mention the subject here. To our statesmen of Queen Anne's time traffic in slaves was so far from being considered discreditable, that the ministry of that reign prided themselves greatly on what was called the Assiento Treaty with Spain, by which they secured for the British merchants and ship-owners the privilege of supplying the West India Islands with several thousand slaves a year. In 1748 the ministers of George II were equally jealous of the credit of renewing it. It had even on one occasion been decided in the Court of Common Pleas that an action of trover could be maintained for a negro, "because negroes are heathens;" though Chief-justice Holt scouted the idea of being bound by a precedent which would put "a human being on the same footing as an ox or an ass," and declared that "in England there was no such thing as a slave." Subsequent decisions, however, of two Lord Chancellors—Lord Talbot and Lord Hardwicke—were not wholly consistent with the doctrine thus laid down by Holt; and the question could not be regarded as finally settled till 1772, when a slave named Somersett was brought over to England from Jamaica by his master, and on his arrival in the Thames claimed his freedom, and under a writ of *habeas corpus* had his claim allowed by Lord Mansfield. The master's counsel contended that slavery was not a condition unsanctioned by English law, for villeinage was slavery, and no statute had ever abolished villeinage. But the Chief-justice, in the first place, denied that villeinage had ever been slavery such as existed in the West Indies; and, in the second place, he pronounced that, whether it had been or not, it had, at all events, long ceased in England, and could not be revived. "The air of England has long been too pure for a slave, and every man is free who breathes it. Every man who comes into England is entitled to the protection of English law."[159] But this freedom was as yet held to be only co-extensive with these islands. And for sixty years more our West India Islands continued to be cultivated by the labor of slaves, some of whom were the offspring of slaves previously employed, though by far the greater part were imported yearly from the western coast of Africa. The supply from that country seemed inexhaustible. The native chiefs in time of war gladly sold their prisoners to the captains of British vessels; in time of peace they sold them their own subjects; and, if at any time these modes of obtaining slaves slackened, the captains would land at night, and, attacking the villages on the coast sweep off the inhabitants on board their ships, and at once set sail with their booty. The sufferings of these unhappy captives in what was called the "middle passage"—the passage between their native land and the West India Islands—were for a long time unknown or disregarded, till, early in Pitt's first ministry, they attracted the notice of some of our naval officers who were stationed in the West Indies, and who, on their return to England, related the horrors which they had witnessed or heard of—how, between decks too low to admit of a full-grown man standing upright, the wretched victims, chained to the sides of the ships, lay squeezed together in such numbers, though the whole voyage was within the tropics, that, from the overpowering heat and scantiness of food, it was estimated that two-thirds of each cargo died on the passage. Most fortunately for the credit of England, the fearful trade was brought under the notice of a young member of Parliament singularly zealous in the cause of humanity and religion, endowed with untiring industry and powerful eloquence, and connected by the closest ties of personal intimacy with Mr. Pitt. To hear of such a system of organized murder, as the British officers described the slave-trade to be, was quite sufficient to induce Mr. Wilberforce to resolve to devote himself to its suppression. He laid the case in all its horrors before his friend the Prime-minister, a man as ready as himself to grapple with and extinguish all proved abuses; and Pitt at once promised him all the support which he could give. It was no easy task that he had taken on himself. A year or two before, Burke had applied himself to frame some regulations which he hoped might gradually remove the evil; but, little as he was moved by considerations of popularity or daunted by difficulty, he had abandoned the attempt, as one which would meet with a resistance too powerful to be overcome. Wilberforce was not a bolder man than Burke, but he had no other object to divide his attention, and, therefore, to this one he devoted all his faculties and energies, enlisting supporters in every quarter, seeking even the co-operation of the French government, and opening a correspondence with the French Secretary of State, M. Montmorin, a statesman of great capacity, and, what was far rarer in France, of incorruptible honesty. M. Montmorin, however, though alive to the cruelty of the traffic, was unable to promise him any aid, alleging the fears of the French planters that its abolition "would ruin the French islands. He said that it was one of those subjects upon which the interests of men and their sentiments were so much at variance, that it was difficult to learn what was practicable."[160]

Wilberforce had already found that the English merchants were still less manageable. Pitt had entered so fully into his views, that in 1788 he himself moved and carried a resolution pledging the House of Commons to take the slave-trade into consideration in the next session. And another friend of the cause, Sir W. Dobben, brought in a bill to diminish the horrors of the middle passage by proportioning the number of slaves who might be conveyed in one ship to the tonnage of the vessel. But those concerned in the West India trade rose up in arms against even so moderate a measure, and one so clearly demanded by the most ordinary humanity as this. The Liverpool merchants declared that the absence of restrictions on the slave-trade had been the chief cause of the prosperity and opulence of their town, and obtained leave to be heard by counsel against the bill. But Fox united with Pitt on this subject, and the bill was carried. But this was all the practical success which the efforts of the "Abolitionists," as they began to be called, achieved for many years. And even that was not won without extreme difficulty; Lord Chancellor Thurlow opposing it with great vehemence in the House of Lords, as the fruit of a "five days' fit of philanthropy which had just sprung up," and pointing to the conduct of the French government, which, as he asserted, had offered premiums to encourage the trade, as an example that we should do well to follow. It was even said that he had contrived to incline the King himself to the same view; to have persuaded him that the trade was indispensable to the prosperity of our manufacturers, and, in the Chancellor's words, "that it was his royal duty to show some humanity to the whites as well as to the negroes." And more than once, when bills to limit or wholly suppress the trade had been passed by the Commons, the same mischievous influence defeated them in the Lords. The last years of Pitt's first administration were too fully occupied with the affairs of Ireland, negotiations with foreign powers, and the great war with France, to enable him to keep pace with his friend's zeal on the subject. But in his second administration, occupied though he was with a recurrence of the same causes, he found time to prepare and issue an Order in Council prohibiting the importation of slaves into our fresh colonial acquisitions, and the employment of British ships to supply the Dutch, French, and Spanish islands.

And this Order in Council paved the way for the total abolition. One of the earliest proceedings of the new ministry was the introduction by the Attorney-general, Sir Arthur Pigott, of a bill to extend and make it perpetual; to forbid "the importation of African negroes by British ships into the colonies conquered by or ceded to us in war; or into the colonies of any neutral state in the West Indies. For at present every state that had colonies in America or the West Indies, and that was not actually at war with us, availed itself of the opportunity of British shipping to carry on the trade." It was resisted as vehemently as any former measure with the same object, and partly on the new ground that it would in no degree stop the trade or diminish the sufferings of the Africans, but would merely rob our ship-owners of their profits to enrich the Americans. Mr. Rose, the member for Christchurch, who advanced this argument, had been a friend of Pitt; yet, though he quoted an instance of a single vessel having buried one hundred and fifty-two slaves on one voyage, he was not ashamed to deprecate the bill, on the plea that "the manufacturers of Manchester, Stockport, and Paisley would be going about naked and starving, and thus, by attending to a supposed claim for relief from a distant quarter, we should give existence to much more severe distress at home." The bill, however, was carried in both Houses, and received the royal assent. And Fox, who supported it warmly in his speech on the third reading (one of the last speeches which he ever addressed to the House), invited Wilberforce to regard it as a stepping-stone to the total abolition of the trade, and as an encouragement to renew his motion for that object; and, though he could not promise him the support of the government as a government, he "could answer for himself and many of his friends who held the highest and most dignified stations in the other House of Parliament. They still felt the question of the total abolition as one involving the dearest interests of humanity, and as one which, should they be successful in effecting it, would entail more true glory upon their administration, and more honor upon their country, than any other transaction in which they could be engaged."

Mr. Fox did not live to see the opening of another session; but, when that time came, the position which he had taken up, that the measure of which he had thus promoted the passing was an encouragement to do more, was adopted to its full extent by the chief of his colleagues, Lord Grenville, who, in February, 1807, himself brought forward a motion for the entire abolition of the trade. Though he was Prime-minister, he could not introduce it as a government measure, since two of his colleagues—Lord Sidmouth, the President of the Council, and Mr. Windham, the Secretary of State for the Colonies—opposed it; though the former professed a desire to see the trade abolished, but would have preferred to attain that end by imposing such a tax on every slave imported as should render the trade unprofitable. He had another obstacle also to encounter, in the vehement opposition of some of the princes of the royal family, the Dukes of Clarence and Sussex more especially, who were known to be canvassing against the bill, and were generally understood, in so doing, to be acting in accordance with the views of their elder brothers. But he was confident that by this time the feeling of the whole country was with him on the subject. He was resolved to rest his case on its justice, and therefore consented that the House should hear counsel on the subject, though he resisted their demand to be allowed to call witnesses. Accordingly, counsel were heard for the whole body of West India planters, and for those of one or two separate islands, such as Jamaica and Trinidad; for the Liverpool merchants, and even for the trustees of the Liverpool Docks. But some of their reasonings he even turned against themselves, refusing for a moment to admit "that the profits obtained by robbery could be urged as an argument for the continuance of robbery." He denounced the trade as "the most criminal that any country could be engaged in," and as one that led to other crimes in the treatment of the slaves after they reached the West Indies. He instanced "three most horrible and dreadful murders of slaves" that had been committed in Barbadoes, and quoted the report of Lord Seaforth, governor of the island, who, on investigation, had found that by the law of the colony the punishment affixed to such murders was a fine of eleven pounds. He was opposed by the Duke of Clarence, who directed his remarks chiefly to a defence of the general humanity of the planters; and by Lord Westmoreland, who, in a speech of singular intemperance, denounced the principle of the measure, as one after the passing of which "no property could be rendered safe which could fall within the power of the Legislature." He even made it an argument against the bill that its principle, if carried to its legitimate logical end, must tend to the abolition of slavery as well as of the slave-trade. He objected especially to the assertion in the preamble that the trade was "contrary to justice and humanity," declaring that those words were only inserted in the hope that by them "foreign powers might be humbugged into a concurrence with the abolition," and wound up his harangue by a declaration that, though he should "see the Presbyterian and the prelate, the Methodist and pew-preacher, the Jacobin and the murderer, unite in support of it, he would still raise his voice against it." It must have been more painful to the minister to be opposed by so distinguished an officer as Lord St. Vincent, who resisted the bill chiefly on the ground that "its effect would be to transfer British capital to other countries, which would not be disposed to abandon so productive a trade," and declared that he could only account for Lord Grenville's advocacy of it "by supposing that some Obi man had cast his spell upon him." But the case was too strong for any arguments to prevail which were based solely on the profits of a trade which no one pretended to justify. The bill passed the Lords by a majority of nearly three to one; in the House of Commons, where the opposition was much feebler, by one infinitely larger;[161] and, by a somewhat remarkable coincidence, it received the royal assent on the same day on which Lord Grenville announced to his brother peers that his administration was at an end.

Even before the abolition had thus become law, the member for Northumberland, Earl Percy, endeavored to give practical effect to Lord Westmoreland's view, that emancipation of the slaves was its inevitable corollary, by moving for leave to bring in a bill for the gradual abolition of slavery in the British settlements of the West Indies. But he was opposed by Lord Howick,[162] though he had been among the earnest advocates of abolition, partly for the sake of the negroes themselves, and partly on the ground that the Legislature had no "right to interfere with the property of the colonists;" little foreseeing that the measure which he now opposed was reserved for his own administration, and that its accomplishment would be one of its chief titles to the respectful recollection of posterity. And, as the House was presently counted out, the discussion would not have been worth recording, were it not for the opportunity which it gave of displaying the practical and moderate wisdom of Wilberforce himself, who joined in the opposition to Lord Percy's motion. "The enemies of abolition had," he said, "always confounded abolition with emancipation. He and his friends had always distinguished between them; and not only abstained from proposing emancipation, but were ready to reject it when proposed by others. How much soever he looked forward with anxious expectation to the period when the negroes might with safety be liberated, he knew too well the effect which the long continuance of abject slavery produced upon the human mind to think of their immediate emancipation, a measure which at the present moment would be injurious both to them and to the colonies. He and those who acted with him were satisfied with having gained an object which was safely attainable."

And they had reason to be satisfied. For the good work thus done was not limited by the extent of the British dominions, vast as they are. The example of the homage thus paid by the Parliament and the nation to justice and humanity was contagious; the principle on which the bill was founded and was carried being such that, for mere shame, foreign countries could hardly persist in maintaining a traffic which those who had derived the greatest profit from it had on such grounds renounced; though our ministers did not trust to their spontaneous sympathies, but made the abolition of the traffic by our various allies, or those who wished to become so, a constant object of diplomatic negotiations, even purchasing the co-operation of some by important concessions, in one instance by the payment of a large sum of money. The conferences and congresses which took place on the re-establishment of peace gave them great facilities for pressing their views on the different governments. And Lord Liverpool's instructions to Lord Castlereagh and the Duke of Wellington, as plenipotentiaries of our government,[163] show the keen interest which he took in the matter, and the skilful manner in which he sought to avail himself of the predominant influence which the exertions and triumphs of this country had given her with every foreign cabinet. Though Portugal was an ally to whom we regarded ourselves as bound by special ties, as well as by the great benefits we had conferred on her, yet, as she clung with the greatest pertinacity to the trade, he did not scruple to endeavor to put a constraint upon her which should compel her submission, and instructed Lord Castlereagh "to induce the Congress to take the best means in their power to enforce it by the adoption of a law, on the part of the several states, to exclude the colonial produce of those countries who should refuse to comply with this system of abolition."

And exertions so resolutely put forward were so successful, that the trade was avowedly proscribed by every European nation, though unquestionably it was still carried on by stealth by merchants and ship-owners of more than one country—not, if the suspicions of our statesmen were well founded, without some connivance on the part of their governments. Nor were our efforts in the cause the fitful display of impulsive excitement. We have continued them and widened their sphere as occasions have presented themselves, exerting a successful influence even over unchristian and semi-civilized governments, of which an instance has very recently been furnished, in the assurances given by the Khedive of Egypt to our minister residing at his court, that he is taking vigorous measures to suppress the slave-trade, which is still carried on in the interior of Africa; and that we may believe his promise that he will not relax his exertions till it is extinguished, at least in the region on the north of the equator.

Individuals, as a rule, are slow to take warning from the experience of others; slower, perhaps, to follow their example in well-doing. Nations are slower still. When such an example is followed, still more when it is adopted by a general imitation, it will usually be found not only that the good is of a very unusual standard of excellence, but that he or they who have set the example are endowed with a force of character that predisposes others to submit to their influence. And credit of this kind England may fairly claim for the general abolition of the slave-trade; for the condemnation and abolition of the slave-trade had this distinguishing feature, that the idea of such a policy was of exclusively British origin. No nation had ever before conceived the notion that to make a man a slave was a crime. On the contrary, there were not wanting those who, from the recognition of such a condition in the Bible, argued that it was a divine institution. And they who denounced it, and labored for its suppression, had not only inveterate prejudice and long custom to contend with, but found arrayed against them many of the strongest passions that animate mankind. The natural desire for gain united merchants, ship-owners, and planters in unanimous resistance to a measure calculated to cut off from them one large source of profit. Patriotism, which, however misguided, was sincere and free from all taint of personal covetousness, induced many, who wore wholly unconnected either with commerce or with the West Indies, to look with disfavor on a change which not only imperilled the interests of such important bodies of men, but which they were assured by those concerned, must render the future cultivation of estates in the West Indies impracticable; while such a result would not only ruin those valuable colonies, but would also extinguish that great nursery for our navy which was furnished by the vessels at present engaged in the West India trade. To disregard such substantial considerations to risk a loss of revenue, a diminution of our colonial greatness, and a weakening of our maritime power, even while engaged in a formidable war, under no other pressure but that of a respect for humanity and justice, was certainly a homage to those virtues, and also an act of self-denying courage, of which the previous history of the world had furnished no similar example; and it is one of which, in one point of view, the nation may be more justly proud than of the achievements of its wisest statesmen, or the exploits of its most invincible warriors. For it was the act of the nation itself. No previous sentiment of the people paved the way for Pitt's triumphs in finance, for Nelson's or Wellington's victories by sea and land; but the slave-trade could never have been abolished by any parliamentary leader, had not the nation as a whole become convinced of its wickedness, and, when once so convinced, resolved to brave everything rather than persist in it. The merit of having impressed it with this conviction belongs to Mr. Wilberforce, whose untiring, unswerving devotion of brilliant eloquence and practical ability to the one holy object, and whose ultimate success, give him a just claim to be reckoned among the great men of a generation than which the world has seen none more prolific of every kind of greatness. But the nation itself is also entitled to no slight credit for having so rapidly appreciated the force of his teaching, and for having encouraged its representatives to listen to his voice, by the knowledge that by adopting his measures they would be carrying out the wish and determination of the whole people.

    A measure for the strengthening of the army, introduced by the Secretary of State for War, Mr. Windham, though not one of perpetual force, since it required to be renewed every year, claims a brief mention, from the extent to which one of its clauses trenched on the freedom of the subject, by making every man of military age (from sixteen years old[164] to forty) liable to be compelled to submit to military training for a certain period of each year. "Nothing," to quote the Secretary's words, "was to exempt any man from the general training but his becoming a volunteer at his own expense, the advantage of which would be that he could train himself if he chose, and fight, if occasion required it, in the corps to which he should belong, instead of being liable to fall in among the regulars.... As out of the immense mass of the population some selection must be made, those called on to be trained were to be selected by lot, and he would have the people divided into three classes, between the ages of sixteen and forty: the first class to comprehend all from sixteen to twenty-four; the second, those between twenty-four and thirty-two; and the third, all from thirty-two to forty. The number of days for training he proposed to limit to twenty-six, with an allowance of a shilling a day for each man." The result aimed at by this part of his measure was the creation of a force different from and unconnected with the militia; and he did not conceal his hope that the military habits which it would implant in a large portion of the population would lead many of those thus about to be trained to enlist in the regular army. To the militia itself he paid a high but not undeserved compliment, declaring it "for home service certainly equal to any part of our regular forces, with the single exception that it had never seen actual service." But the militia could not be called on to serve out of the kingdom; and his object was to increase the force available for foreign service—"to see the great mass of the population of the country so far trained as to be able to recruit immediately whatever losses the regular army might sustain in action." As yet, the number of men yearly obtained by recruiting fell far short of the requirements of the service. Wellington had not yet begun that career of victory which created a national enthusiasm for war, and filled our ranks with willing soldiers. And another clause of the same bill was framed in the hope of making the service more acceptable to the peasantry, by limiting the time for which recruits were to be enlisted, and entering men, at first, in the infantry for seven years, or in the cavalry (as that branch of the service required a longer apprenticeship) for ten; then allowing them the option of renewing their engagement for two periods—in the infantry of seven years each, in the cavalry of six and five, with increased pay during each of the two periods, and a small pension for life, if the soldier retired after the second period; and "the full allowance of Chelsea," which was to be farther raised to a shilling a day, for those who elected to serve the whole twenty-one years. This principle the present reign has seen carried to a much greater extent, but the change is too recent for even the most experienced officers to be agreed on its effects. And it is only because of this recent extension of it that this clause is mentioned here. But the enactment of a law of compulsory service was clearly an inroad on the great constitutional right of every man to choose his own employment. At the same time, it is equally clear that it was only such an inroad as under the circumstances, was fully justifiable. It is true that all danger of French invasion had passed away with Trafalgar;

but the kingdom was still engaged in a gigantic war, and the necessity of the case—always the supreme law—was so little denied by the Opposition, that their objections to the bill were directed entirely against the clause for limited enlistment, and not against that which abridged the subject's liberty, by compelling him to learn to serve his country in war.

The reign of George III., which had now lasted fifty years, was drawing practically to a close. The excitement caused by the ministerial changes in 1801 had already brought on one relapse, though fortunately a very brief one, of the King's malady of 1788; and in the autumn of 1810 the death of the daughter who was supposed to be his especial favorite, the Princess Amelia, produced a recurrence of it, which, though at first the physicians entertained more sanguine hopes of his speedy recovery than on any former occasion, he never shook off. More than one change of ministry had recently taken place. In 1807 Lord Grenville had been compelled, as Pitt had been in 1801, to choose between yielding his opinions on the Catholic question or resigning his office, and had chosen the latter alternative. He had been succeeded for two years by the Duke of Portland; but in 1809 that nobleman had also retired, and had been succeeded by his Attorney-general, Mr. Perceval, the only practising barrister who had ever been so promoted. And he now being Prime-minister, and, as such, forced to make arrangements for carrying on the government during the illness of his sovereign, naturally regarded the course pursued in 1789 as the precedent to be followed. Accordingly, on the 20th of December he proposed for the adoption of the House of Commons the same resolutions which Pitt had carried twenty-two years before—that the King was prevented by indisposition from attending to public business; that it was the duty of Parliament to provide means for supplying the defect of the personal exercise of the royal authority, and its duty also to determine the mode in which the royal assent to the measures necessary could be signified. And he also followed Pitt's example in expressing by letter to the Prince of Wales his conviction that his Royal Highness was a person most proper to be appointed Regent, and explaining at the same time the restrictions which seemed proper to be imposed on his immediate exercise of the complete sovereign authority; though the advanced age at which the King had now arrived made it reasonable that those restrictions should now be limited to a single year. The Prince, on his part, showed that time had in no degree abated his repugnance to those restrictions, and he answered the minister's letter by referring him to that which he had addressed to Pitt on the same subject in 1788. And he induced all his brothers to address to Perceval a formal protest against "the establishment of a restricted Regency," which they proceeded to describe as perfectly unconstitutional, as being contrary to and subversive of the principles which seated their family upon the throne of this realm.[165]

Perceval, however, with Pitt's example before him, had no doubt of the course which it was his duty to pursue; and the Opposition also, for the most part, followed the tactics of 1789; the line of argument now adopted by each party being so nearly identical with that employed on the former occasion, that it is needless to recapitulate the topics on which the different speakers insisted; though it is worth remarking that Lord Holland, who, as the nephew of Fox, thought it incumbent on him to follow his uncle's guidance, did on one point practically depart from it. As his uncle had done, he denied the right of the Houses to impose any restrictions on the Prince's exercise of the royal authority; but, at the same time, he consented to put what may be called a moral limitation on that exercise, by adding to an amendment which he proposed to the resolution proposed by the minister an expression of "the farther opinion of the House that it will be expedient to abstain from the exercise of all such powers as the immediate exigencies of the state shall not call into action, until Parliament shall have passed a bill or bills for the future care of his Majesty's royal person during his Majesty's present indisposition."

It is remarkable that the leaders of the Opposition were in a great degree stimulated in the line they took by the very same hopes which had animated Fox and his followers in 1789—the expectation that the Regent's first act would be to discard the existing ministry, and to place them in office. But again they were disappointed in their anticipations, of the realization of which they had made so sure that they had taken no pains to keep them secret. They even betrayed their mortification to the world when the Prince's intentions on the subject of the administration became known by the violence of their language in Parliament, some of their party denouncing the employment of the Great Seal to give the royal assent to the bill as "fraud and forgery." Nor, indeed, could the Regent himself, even while expressing his intention to make no change in the administration, lest "any act of his might in the smallest degree have the effect of interfering with the progress of his sovereign's recovery," suppress an expression of dissatisfaction at the recent arrangements, which he considered had placed him in "a situation of unexampled embarrassment," and had created "a state of affairs ill calculated, as he feared, to sustain the interests of the United Kingdom in this awful and perilous crisis, and most difficult to be reconciled to the general principles of the British constitution."[166] There were at this time general and apparently well-founded hopes of the King's recovery. For at intervals during the whole of January the Prime-minister had interviews with his Majesty; and, on the very day on which the bill became law, the King himself mentioned it to Lord Eldon, the Chancellor, and said that he acquiesced in it from perfect confidence in the advice of his physicians, and on the sound judgment and personal attachment of his ministers.

For the present, therefore, no change was made in the administration; but when, in the spring of the following year, Mr. Perceval was murdered, the necessity for a new arrangement which this strange and calamitous atrocity forced upon the Regent—who by this time had come into possession of his full authority—led to his making offers of the conduct of affairs to more than one prominent statesman, all of them, as is somewhat remarkable, being peers. And, though the proposals eventually came to nothing, and the negotiations terminated in the re-establishment of the former ministry, with Lord Liverpool at its head, yet some of the causes to which their failure was publicly or generally attributed seem desirable to be recorded, because the first, and that most openly avowed, bears a not very distant resemblance to the complication which baffled Sir Robert Peel's endeavors to form an administration in 1839; and another corresponds precisely to a proposal which, in 1827, the Regent—then King George IV.—did himself make to the Duke of Wellington. It is unnecessary to dwell on the singular manner in which the Regent first professed to give his confidence to Lord Wellesley, then transferred it to Lord Moira,[167] and then to a certain extent included Lord Grey and Lord Grenville in it. Nor would it be profitable to discuss the correctness or incorrectness of the suspicion expressed by Mr. Moore, in his "Life of Sheridan"—who was evidently at this time as fully in the Regent's confidence as any one else—that "at the bottom of all these evolutions of negotiation there was anything but a sincere wish, that the object to which they related should be accomplished."[168] The reason avowed by Lord Grey and Lord Grenville for refusing a share in the projected administration was the refusal of Lord Moira, who had been employed by the Prince to treat with them on the subject, to allow them to make a power of removing the officers at present filling "the great offices of the household"[169] an express condition of their acceptance of ministerial office. They affirmed that a "liberty to make new appointments" to these offices had usually been given on every change of administration. But Lord Moira, while admitting that "the Prince had laid no restriction on him in that respect," declared that "it would be impossible for him to concur in making the exercise of this power positive and indispensable in the formation of the administration, because he should deem it on public grounds peculiarly objectionable." Such an answer certainly gives a great color to Moore's suspicion, since it is hardly possible to conceive that Lord Moira took on himself the responsibility of giving it without a previous knowledge that it would be approved by his royal master. In a constitutional point of view, there can, it will probably be felt, be no doubt that the two lords had a right to the liberty they required. And the very men concerned, the great officers of the household, were evidently of the same opinion, since the chief, Lord Yarmouth, informed Sheridan that they intended to resign, in order that he might communicate that intention to Lord Grey; and Sheridan, who concealed the intelligence from Lord Grey, can hardly be supposed, any more than Lord Moira, to have acted in a manner which he did not expect to be agreeable to the Prince. But, in Canning's opinion, this question of the household was only the ostensible pretext, and not the real cause, of those two lords rejecting the Regent's offers; the real cause being, as he believed, that the Prince himself had already named Lord Wellesley as Prime-minister, and that they were resolved to insist on the right of the Whig party to dictate on that point to the Regent,[170] just as, in 1782, Fox had endeavored to force the Duke of Portland on the King, when his Majesty preferred Lord Shelburne. As has been intimated in a former page, it will be seen hereafter that in 1839 a similar claim to be allowed to remove some of the ladies of the royal household, and the rejection of that claim by the sovereign, prevented Sir R. Peel from forming an administration. And, as that transaction was discussed at some length in Parliament, it will afford a better opportunity for examining the principle on which the claim and practice (for of the practice there is no doubt) rest. For the present it is sufficient to point out the resemblance between the cases.

But it is remarkable that, unwarrantable as the pretension of the Whig leaders was to dictate to the Regent to whom he should confide the lead of the government (if, indeed, Canning be correct in his opinion), yet it was not one to which the Regent felt any repugnance, since, in 1827, when Lord Liverpool's illness again left the Treasury vacant, he, being then on the throne as George IV., proposed to the Duke of Wellington to desire the remaining members of the administration themselves to select a chief under whom they would be willing to continue in his service; but the Duke told him that the plan of allowing them to choose their own leader would be most derogatory to his position; that the choice of the Prime-minister was an act which ought to be entirely his own, for that, in fact under the British constitution, it was the only personal act of government which the King of Great Britain had to perform.[171] Though not generally a great authority on constitutional points, we apprehend that the Duke was clearly correct in this view, which, indeed, has been so invariably carried out in practice, that the King's suggestion would not have deserved mention had it not been a king's. So far from it belonging to any individual subject or to any party to name the Prime-minister, to do so is even beyond the province of the Parliament. Parliament decides whether it will give its confidence to an administration of one party or the other; but not only has no vote ever been given on the question whether one member of the dominant party be fitter or not than another to be its head, but we do not remember a single instance of any member of either House expressing an opinion on the subject in his place in Parliament. To do so would be felt by every member of experience to be an infringement on the prerogative of his sovereign; and it may be added that a contrary practice would certainly open the door to intrigue, or, what would be equally bad, a suspicion of intrigue, and would thus inevitably diminish the weight which even the Opposition desire to see a Prime-minister possess both in Parliament and in the country.

Notes:

[Footnote 148:] It is somewhat remarkable that Lord Macaulay, in his endeavors to estimate the population in 1685, takes no notice of any of these details mentioned by Mr. Abbott.]

[Footnote 149:] The details of this census of 1801 are given in a note in the preceding chapter (see page 185), from which it appears that the entire population of the United Kingdom was in that year 16,395,870. Sir A. Alison, in different chapters of the second part of his "History of Europe," gives returns of subsequent censuses, from the last of which (c. lvi., s. 34, note), it appears that in 1851 the population amounted to 27,511,862. an increase of 11,116,792 in half a century.]

[Footnote 150:] "Lives of the Chief-justices," by Lord Campbell, iii., 87, life of Lord Kenyon.]

[Footnote 151:] "What is this," said George III. to Mr. Dundas, "which this young lord (Castlereagh) has brought over, which they are going to throw at my head? The most Jacobinical thing I ever heard of! I shall reckon any man my personal enemy who proposes any such measure." —*Life of Pitt*, iii., 274.]

[Footnote 152:] "Lives of the Chancellors," c. clxxxiv., life of Lord Erskine.]

[Footnote 153:] "Lives of the Chancellors," c. clix., life of Lord Thurlow.]

[Footnote 154:] See "Memoires de M. de Metternich," ii., 156.]

[Footnote 155:] "Lives of the Chief-justices," iii., 175.]

[Footnote 156:] Lord Stanhope, "History of England," i., 133.]
[Footnote 157:] "Lives of the Chief-justices," ii., 451. He is quoting H. Walpole.]
[Footnote 158:] Ibid., iii., 187.]
[Footnote 159:] Campbell's "Lives of the Chief-justices," II., 139, life of Chief-justice Holt; and p. 418, life of Lord Mansfield.]
[Footnote 160:] "Life of Wilberforce," i., 158.]
[Footnote 161:] The division in the Lords was 100 to 36; in the Commons, 283 to 16.]
[Footnote 162:] Afterward the Earl Grey of 1831.]
[Footnote 163:] See especially his "Letters to Lord Castlereagh," p. 814; and "Life of Lord Liverpool," i., 512; ii., 35, 49, 127.]
[Footnote 164:] Lord Colchester's "Diary," ii., 49, dated April 3, 1806, says eighteen years. But Mr. Windham's speech, as reported in the "Parliamentary History," second series, vi., 685, says sixteen years; and as he divides the ages into three classes, the two latter of which, from twenty-four to thirty-two, and from thirty-two to forty, are of eight years each, it is probable that the younger class was of the same duration, i.e., from sixteen to twenty-four.]
[Footnote 165:] Lord Colchester's "Diary," ii., 300.]
[Footnote 166:] See "Diary of Lord Colchester" (Speaker at the time), c. xxxvi., p. 316. He gives the whole of the Prince's letter to Perceval (which had been composed by Sheridan), and of Perceval's reply. The Regency Bill became law February 5, 1811.]
[Footnote 167:] A letter of Lord Wellesley to Lord Grey, June 4 (given by Pearce, "Life of Lord Wellesley," iii., 270), shows that Lord Moira had been in communication with Lord Grey and Lord Grenville before Lord Wellesley had given up the idea of forming a ministry. And though Lord Grey in his reply (p. 272) expresses his conviction that Lord Moira's letter was not "an authorized communication," but only "a private communication," it is clear that it could not have been written without the privity of the Regent.]
[Footnote 168:] "Life of Sheridan," ii., 425.]
[Footnote 169:] Pearce's "Life of Lord Wellesley," iii., 276. All the letters which passed between Lord Grey, Lord

Grenville, Lord Moira, and Lord Wellesley himself are given at full length by Mr. Pearce in that chapter.]

[Footnote 170:] Stapleton's "George Canning and his Times," p. 202.]

[Footnote 171:] Mr. Stapleton affirms that his Royal Highness actually did adopt this plan on this occasion: "His Royal Highness adopted the unprecedented course of commanding his servants to elect the First-minister. Their choice fell on Lord Liverpool." —*George Canning and his Times*, p. 208. Mr. Stapleton, however, gives no authority for this assertion, and he was probably mistaken, since Lord Liverpool's papers afford no corroboration of it, but rather tend to disprove it.]

CHAPTER VII

The Toleration Act.—Impropriety of making Catholic Emancipation (or any other Important Matter) an Open Question.—Joint Responsibility of all the Ministers.—Detention of Napoleon at St. Helena.—Question whether the Regent could Give Evidence in a Court of Law in a Civil Action.—Agitation for Reform.—Public Meetings.—The Manchester Meeting.—The Seditious Meetings Prevention Bill.—Lord Sidmouth's Six Acts.

The war was daily becoming of more exciting interest, and, so far as our armies were concerned, was rapidly assuming greater proportions. While the Duke of Portland was still at the head of affairs, Napoleon, by his unprovoked attacks on both the Peninsular kingdoms, had at last opened a field of action to our armies, in which even the most sanguine of those who placed a loyal confidence in the old invincibility of English prowess could not have anticipated the unbroken series of glories which were to reward their efforts. For four years Lord Wellington had contended against all the most renowned marshals of the Empire,[172] driving them back from impregnable lines of defence, defeating them in pitched battles, storming their strongest fortresses, without ever giving them room to boast of even the most momentary advantage obtained over himself; and he was now on the eve of achieving still more brilliant and decisive triumphs, which were never to cease till he had carried his victorious march far into the heart of France itself.

At such a time it may well be supposed that the attention of the new ministry was too fully occupied with measures necessary for the conduct of the war to leave it much time for domestic legislation. Yet even its first session was not entirely barren.

In the first excitement of the Restoration, when the nation was still exasperated at the recollection of what it had suffered under the triumphant domination of the Puritans, two laws had been framed to chastise them, conceived in a spirit as intolerant and persecuting as had dictated the very worst of their own. One, which was called the Conventicle Act, inflicted on all persons above the age of sixteen, who should be present at any religious service performed in any manner differently from the service of the Church of England, in any meeting-house, where more than five persons besides the occupiers of the house should be present, severe penalties, rising gradually to transportation; and gave a single magistrate authority to convict and to pass sentence on the offenders. The other, commonly known as the Five Mile Act, forbade all ministers, of any sect, who did not subscribe to the Act of Uniformity, and who refused to swear to their belief in the doctrine of passive obedience, from teaching in any school, and from coming within five miles of any city, corporate town, or borough sending members to Parliament, or any town or village in which they themselves had resided as ministers. The latter statute had fallen into complete disuse, and many of the provisions of the former had been relaxed, though magistrates in general construed the relaxing enactments as leaving the relaxations wholly at their discretion to grant or to withhold, and were very much in the habit of withholding or abridging them. Other statutes, such as the Test Act, had subsequently been passed against every sect of Dissenters, though they had only imposed civil disabilities, and had not inflicted penalties. But the new Prime-minister was a man to whose disposition anything resembling persecution was foreign and repugnant. Before his predecessor's unhappy death he had already discussed with him the propriety of abolishing laws conceived in such a spirit; and he no sooner found himself at the head of the government than he prepared a bill to carry out his views. He drew a distinction between the acts inflicting penalties and those which only imposed disabilities. With these latter he did not propose to interfere; but, in July, his colleague, Lord Castlereagh, introduced into the House of Commons a bill to repeal the Conventicle Act and the Five Mile Act altogether, and, when it had passed the Commons, he himself moved its adoption by the Lords, enforcing his recommendation by the argument, that "an enlarged and liberal toleration was the best security to the Established Church, a Church not founded on the exclusion of religious discussion, but, in its homilies, its canons, and all the principles on which it rested, courting the investigation of the Scriptures, upon which it founded its doctrines." At the same time, while urging the repeal of acts which he truly branded as a disgrace to the statute-book, he was not blind to the duty imposed on him, as responsible for the public tranquillity, of taking care that meetings held ostensibly for purposes of devotion should not be perverted to the designs of political agitators; and therefore he provided in the bill for the registration of all places appropriated to religious worship, and for the exaction from "the preachers and teachers in those meetings of some test or security in the oaths to be taken by them." He had already secured the acquiescence of the bishops, and he was equally successful now in winning the assent of the House. The conditions, such as they were, did not prevent the bill from being entirely acceptable to the Non-conformists; and though their spokesman in the House of Commons, Mr. W. Smith, member for Norwich, confessed a wish "that it had gone a little farther, and had granted complete religious liberty," he at the same time expressed sincere gratitude on the part of the Non-conformists for what was thus done for them; and declared that, "as an act of toleration, it certainly was the most complete which had hitherto been passed in this country." It was, in fact, the beginning of the abandonment of that system of discouragement of and hostility to all sects except the Established Church, which had hitherto been regarded by a large party as one of the most essential principles of the constitution. And as such it makes the year 1812 in some respects a landmark in our constitutional history.

Mr. Smith had referred to an omission which prevented him from speaking of the bill as complete. He was alluding to the Test and Corporation Acts, which had been passed ten years later than the Conventicle Act, in the same reign of Charles II., and which many of the Non-conformists, and especially the Unitarians, had urged Lord Liverpool to include in this measure of repeal, but which he decided on retaining. As has been said above, he drew a distinction between acts inflicting penalties and those which went no farther than imposing political disabilities, feeling that any relief of Protestant Dissenters from such disabilities must inevitably lead to the concession of a similar indulgence to Roman Catholics, and not being as yet prepared to admit to Parliament the members of a Church which recognized the duty of obedience in any matter to a foreign sovereign; for, as the disabilities had been originally imposed on the Roman Catholics, so they were now maintained on political, not religious, grounds; and even those most opposed to a relaxation of them were careful to explain their resistance to be one which time and a change of circumstances might mitigate.[173]

As a fitter opportunity for discussing the question will be afforded by the Duke of Wellington's bill, in 1829, we should not have mentioned it at all in this place, had not Lord Liverpool, in arranging his administration, adopted a mode of dealing with it which, though rather a parliamentary or departmental than a constitutional innovation, was, nevertheless, one of so strange a character as to seem to call for examination. Ever since the formation of Walpole's ministry it had been the invariable rule and practice for all the members of the cabinet to act in concert on all measures of importance, or, indeed it may be said, on all measures on which a Parliamentary vote was taken. But, in arranging his administration after Mr. Perceval's death, Lord Liverpool found it absolutely impossible to form one satisfactory either to the nation or to himself if it were to be confined to members in perfect agreement with himself on the subject of the retention of the disabilities affecting the Roman Catholics; and therefore, in order to be able to form a ministry generally strong and respected, he adopted the strange expedient of allowing every member of it to act independently on this one question. He made it what was called an open question. The arrangement, as explained to the House of Commons by Lord Castlereagh, the ministerial leader of that assembly, was that, "in submission to the growing change of public opinion in favor of those claims (the Roman Catholic claims), and the real sentiments of certain members of the government, it had been resolved upon, as a principle, that the discussion of this question should be left free from all interference on the part of the government, and that every member of that government should in it be left to the free and unbiassed suggestions of his own conscientious discretion."

It was an arrangement which secured the Prime-minister the co-operation of Lord Castlereagh himself, and eventually of Mr. Canning; but it failed to propitiate the Opposition, the leader of which in the House of Commons, Mr. Ponsonby, turned it into open ridicule, affirming that "nothing could be more absurd than a cabinet professing to have no opinion on such an important subject." And it must be confessed that Mr. Ponsonby's language on the subject seems the language of common-sense. So far from the importance of a question justifying such an arrangement, that importance appears rather to increase, if possible, the necessity for absolute unanimity in the administration than to diminish it; and on a grave and momentous subject to leave each member of a ministry free to pronounce a separate and different judgment, so that one may resist what his colleague advocates, is to abdicate the functions of government altogether. To permit such liberty was either a proof that the ministry was weak altogether—which it was not—or that its conduct on this question was weak. In either case, it was a mischievous precedent that was thus set;[174] and the fact that it has since been followed in more than one instance, is so far from being any justification of it, that it rather supplies an additional reason for condemning it, as being the cause of wider mischief than if it had been confined to one single question, or had influenced the conduct of one cabinet only. It has often been said that the name "cabinet" is unknown to the law, and that what we call the cabinet is, in fact, only a committee of the Privy Council. As a statement of law the assertion may be correct, but it is certain that for more than a century and a half the constitution has adopted the principle that the cabinet consists of the holders of a certain, to some extent a fluctuating, number of the principal state officers; and, recognizing the responsibility of all for the actions of each member of it, does by that recognition sanction an expectation that on all questions, or at all events on all but those of the most trivial character, they will speak and act with that unanimity which is indispensable, not only to the strength of the government itself, but to its being held in respect by the people; such respect being, indeed, among the most essential elements of its strength.

The incidents of the war itself do not belong to a work such as this; but, tantalizing as it must be to an historian of any class to pass over the brilliant series of achievements which gave Britain the glory of being twice[175] the principal agent in the deliverance of Continental Europe, the glories of Salamanca, Victoria, Orthes, and Waterloo must be left to other writers, who, it is not unpatriotic to hope, may never again have similar cause for exulting descriptions. But out of the crowning triumph of Waterloo a difficulty arose which, though it may be difficult to characterize the principle on which it was settled, since it was not strictly a question of constitutional, international, or military law; and though the circumstances were so peculiar that the conclusion adopted is never likely to be referred to as a precedent, seems still deserving of a brief mention, especially as an act of Parliament was passed to sanction the decision of the cabinet. Baffled by the vigilance of our cruisers in every attempt to escape from one of the western ports of France to America, Napoleon was at last compelled to surrender himself to a British squadron. But, though he was our prisoner, the Prime-minister considered us, in all our dealings with him, as so bound by engagements to our allies, that he was to be regarded as "the common prisoner of all, so far that we should not give him up or release him without the joint consent of all." The question was full of difficulty. There were, probably, very few persons in this or any other country who did not coincide in the impropriety of releasing him, and so putting it in his power once more to rekindle a war in Europe. But it was a political view of the case, founded on a consideration of what was required by the tranquillity of Europe; and it was not easy to lay down any legal ground to justify the determination. Some regarded him as a French subject, and, if that view were correct, he could hardly be detained by us as a prisoner of war after we had concluded a treaty of peace with France. But, again, it seemed to some, the Lord Chancellor being among them, a questionable point whether in the last campaign we had been at war with France; whether, on the contrary, we had not assumed the character of an ally of France against him. And, on the supposition that we had been at war with France, a second question was raised by Lord Ellenborough, the Chief-justice, "what rights result on principle from a state of war, as against all the individuals of the belligerent nations—rights, whatever they may be, seldom, if ever, enforced against individuals, because individuals hardly ever make war but as part of an aggregate nation." The question—as, after consultation with Lord Ellenborough and his own brother, Sir William Scott, it finally appeared to Lord Eldon, on whom the Prime-minister naturally depended, as his chief legal counsellor, though in its political aspect he judged for himself—was, firstly, "whether it could possibly be inconsistent with justice or the law of nations that, till some peace were made by treaty with some person considered as Napoleon's sovereign, or till some peace were made with himself, we should keep him imprisoned in some part of our King's dominions." And, secondly, "whether there were any person who could possibly be considered his sovereign, after the treaty of 1814 had clothed him with the character of Emperor of Elba, with imperial dignity and imperial revenue." Lord Liverpool himself, however, raised another question: whether, by his invasion of France, he had not forfeited his right to be regarded as an independent sovereign; resting this doubt on a suggestion which, among others, he proposed to the Lord Chancellor, that "at Elba he enjoyed only a limited and conditional sovereignty, which ceased when the condition on which he held it was violated."

This last suggestion, it must be confessed, appears untenable, as totally inconsistent with the language of the Treaty of Fontainebleau, under the provisions of which Napoleon became sovereign of Elba, and which does not contain a single article which bears out the opinion that his sovereignty was limited or conditional. On the contrary, the words of the treaty expressly agree that "Elba should form during his life a separate principality, which should be possessed by him in full sovereignty and property."

There is no need to discuss the views of Blucher. On the news of Napoleon's landing at Frejus reaching the plenipotentiaries assembled at the Congress of Vienna, they at once issued a declaration that, "in breaking the convention which had established him at Elba, Buonaparte" (for they refused him his imperial appellation of Napoleon) "had destroyed the only legal title on which his existence depended.... He had placed himself out of the pale of civil and social relations, and, as the enemy and disturber of the peace of the world, he was delivered over to public justice." And the old Prussian, burning with a desire to avenge the indignities and injuries which he had inflicted on Prussia, avowed his determination to execute him as an outlaw, if he should fall into his hands. And it is still less worthwhile to inquire—though Lord Holland in his place in Parliament did desire the House to consult the judges on the point—whether, if Napoleon were a prisoner of war, he "were not entitled to his *habeas corpus*, if detained after the signature of a treaty of peace with all the powers, or any of which he could be considered as the subject."

On the whole, the simplest view of the position and of our detention of him, the view most reconcilable with the principles which regulate the waging and the relinquishing a state of war, seems to be to consider that

Napoleon was a sovereign with whom we were at war; that that war could only be terminated by a treaty of peace between ourselves and him; that it rested with us to conclude, or to abstain from concluding, any such treaty; and that, till we should conclude it, we had clearly a right to detain him as a prisoner of war. It must, at the same time, be admitted that modern history afforded no precedent for the detention of a prisoner for his whole life (unless, indeed, Elizabeth's imprisonment of the Queen of Scots may be considered as one), and that the most solid justification for it was necessity. To quote the language of Lord Eldon, "I believe it will turn out that, if you can't make this a *casus exceptionis* or *omissus* in the law of nations, founded upon necessity, you will not really know what to say upon it. *Salus Reipublicae suprema lex*, as to one state; *Salus omnium Rerumpublicarum* must be the *suprema lex* as to this case."[176]

In the course of the year 1818 a somewhat singular question as to the position of the Regent was raised by a claim advanced by Colonel Berkeley to produce his Royal Highness as a witness in a court of law. The Prince consulted the Prime-minister, and the Prime-minister referred it to the Attorney and Solicitor General, not concealing his own impression that it could not be consistent with his constitutional position and prerogative for the King to appear as a witness to be subjected to examination and cross-examination.[177] They, in their statement of opinion, assumed it to be an undeniable principle of the constitution that the sovereign, "by reason of his royal character, could not give testimony." And therefore they had no doubt that the Regent, exercising his authority, was equally prevented from so doing. Colonel Berkeley's counsel had urged that, even if he could not appear in open court and be sworn, he had the privilege of communicating his evidence in a peculiar mode, by certificate under the Sign Manual or Great Seal. But the Attorney and Solicitor General professed that they could not discover whence this last privilege was derived; they urged, as an insurmountable objection to such a contrivance, that "all instruments under the Sign Manual or Great Seal must, in point of form, be in the name of and on behalf of the King, which would manifestly be incongruous when the evidence certified was not that of the King, but of the Regent himself." And they quoted a case in which Lord Chief-justice Willes had said "that the certificate of the King, under his Sign Manual, of a fact (except in an old case in Chancery) had always been refused." As it had been urged also, on Colonel Berkeley's behalf, that the Prince had formerly "joined in proving the will of the Duke of Brunswick," his brother-in-law, they farther expressed an opinion that "he ought not to have done so, but should have left it to the other executors."

On the point whether "the King himself could give evidence orally or in any other manner," their opinion expressed very plainly the principle on which they maintained that he could not. "That he was not compellable to do so; that he could not be sworn (there being no power capable of administering an oath to him in a court of justice). That, whether his testimony be given *vivâ voce* or otherwise, no question in chief or on cross-examination could be proposed to him, was admitted by Colonel Berkeley's counsel. And that his testimony must be conclusive as to the facts stated by him, appeared necessarily to follow from the perfection ascribed by law to his royal character. For such remarkable exceptions, therefore, to the case of all other witnesses they could not but think that strong and decisive authority ought to be produced; while the silence of text-writers on the subject, so far from being favorable to the notion that the King can give evidence, appeared to afford a directly contrary inference." And they summed up their opinion in a few words: "that his Royal Highness the Prince Regent, while in the personal exercise of the royal authority, was in the situation of the King in this respect, and that the King could not by any mode give evidence as a witness in a civil suit."

It is very improbable that Colonel Berkeley should have made the application without previously ascertaining the willingness of the Prince to give evidence, could such a course be permitted. And as his Royal Highness, on receiving this opinion of the law-officers of the crown, did not come forward as a witness, that opinion may be held to have settled the question. And, apart from the constitutional objections relied on by those able lawyers, it is evident that there would be serious practical objections to the sovereign being made a witness. It would be derogatory to his royal character to put himself in a position where comments could be made, either by the opposing barrister or by the public outside, on his evidence. And, on the other hand, it would be perilously unfair to one litigant for his adversary to be able to produce a witness who was not subject to cross-examination, nor to remarks upon his testimony.

The reign of George III. was now drawing to its close, and, if it produced no legislation affecting the principles of the constitution (it will presently be seen that it did produce one measure which its opponents branded as a violation of these principles), yet in its last years it witnessed the revival of an agitation which was kept up with varying animation till it was temporarily quieted by the concession of its demands. We have seen that one of Pitt's earliest efforts at legislation had been directed to a reform in Parliament, an object which to the end of his life he considered of great importance, though the revolutionary spirit aroused by the troubles in France, and the open sympathy with the French Jacobins and Republicans avowed by a party among ourselves—which, if numerically weak, was sufficiently loud and active to be dangerous—prevented him from ever reopening the subject. But, though the French Revolution in this way proved for the time an insurmountable obstacle to the success of the reformers, in another way it insured the revival of the question, by the general spirit of inquiry which it awakened among the population at large, and which soon went beyond the investigation of any single abuse or anomaly. For even less far-sighted statesmen than Pitt confessed the existence of much that was not only theoretically indefensible, but practically mischievous. The period, little short of a century, which elapsed between the death of William III. and Pitt's accession to office had been one of almost complete stagnation and apathy. The Scotch Union, the Septennial Bill, the establishment of a militia, and the Place Bill of 1743 were the only instances of any legislation deserving the name of constitutional which made the reigns of Anne and the first two Georges memorable. And in the very nature of things it was impossible that, after so long a slumber, there should not be much to do, and many, whether capable or incapable, eager to bear a share in the work. The sudden cessation of the excitement of war had begotten a restless craving for some other excitement to take its place, and none seemed so creditable as energy and acuteness in the discovery and removal of abuses. Complaints were made, and not without reason, of the working of the poor-law; of the terrible severity of our criminal code; of the hardships and sufferings of the younger members of the working classes, especially in the factories; of the ignorance of a large portion of the people, in itself as prolific a cause of mischief and crime as any other. But, though committees and commissions were appointed by Parliament to investigate the condition of the kingdom in respect of these matters, a feeling was growing up that no effectual remedy would be applied till the constitution of the House of Commons itself were reformed, so as to make it a more real representation of the people than it could as yet be considered. And a farther stimulus to this wish for such a Parliamentary reform was supplied by the distress which a combination of circumstances spread among almost all classes in the years immediately following the conclusion of the second treaty of peace.[178] The harvests of the years 1816 and 1817 were unusually deficient, and this pressed heavily on the farmers and landed proprietors. The merchants and manufacturers, who, while every part of the Continent was disturbed or threatened by the operations of contending armies, had practically enjoyed almost a monopoly of the trade of the world, found their profits reduced, by the new competition to which the re-establishment of peace exposed them, to a point which compelled them to a severe reduction of expenditure. The uncertainty felt as to the results to be brought about by the inevitable repeal of the Bank Act of 1797, and the return to cash payments—results which it was impossible to estimate correctly beforehand—had a tendency to augment the distress, by the general feeling of uneasiness and distrust which it created. And the employers of labor could not suffer without those who depended on them for employment suffering still more severely. The consequence was, that there was a general stagnation of trade; numbers of artisans and laborers of every kind were thrown out of work, and their enforced idleness and poverty, which was its result, made them ready to become the tools of demagogues such as are never wanting in the hour of distress and perplexity. Meetings were convened, ostensibly to petition for reform, but in reality to afford opportunities for mob-orators, eager for notoriety, to denounce the government and those whom they styled the "ruling classes," as the causes of the present and past evils. From these meetings multitudes issued forth ripe for mischief. In some places they rose against the manufacturers, and destroyed their machines, to the recent introduction of which they attributed their want of employment. In others, still more senselessly, they even set fire to the stores of grain in the corn-dealers' warehouses, aggravating by their destruction the most painful of their own sufferings. On one occasion, a mob which had assembled in one of the eastern districts of London, on pretence of framing a petition to be presented to the Prince Regent, at the close of the meeting paraded the streets with a tricolor flag, the emblem of the French Revolutionists, and pillaged a number of shops, especially those of the gun-makers, spreading terror through all that side of the metropolis. In at least one instance the violence of the rioters rose to the height of treason. Assassins fired at the Regent in the Park as he was returning from the House of Lords, whither he had been to open Parliament; and when it was found that they had missed their aim, the mob attacked the royal carriage, pelting it with large stones, and breaking the windows; nor was it without some difficulty that the escort of troops cleared a path for him through the mob, and enabled him to reach Carlton House in safety.

The first effect of these outrages was to damage the cause of Reform itself, even such uncompromising reformers as Lord Grey denouncing "meetings at which extensive schemes of Reform were submitted to individuals incapable of judging of their propriety." The second consequence was to compel the ministers to take steps to prevent a recurrence of such tumults and crimes. At first they were contented with a temporary suspension of the *Habeas Corpus* Act; but, even while that suspension was in force, it did not entirely prevent meetings, at some of which the language of the speakers certainly bordered on sedition; and when the suspension was taken off, fresh meetings on a larger scale, and of a more tumultuous character than ever, were held in more than one rural district; finally, in July of 1819, the whole kingdom was thrown into a violent state of excitement by a meeting held at Birmingham, at which the leaders, assuming the newly-invented party name of Radicals, not only demanded the remodelling of the whole system of government, but, because Birmingham as yet sent no members to the House of Commons, took it upon themselves to elect Sir Charles Wolseley, a baronet of respectable family, as their representative to the Parliament, and charged him to claim a place in the House of Commons in the next session, by the side of those elected in obedience to the royal writs. Sir Charles was at once arrested on the charge of having at this meeting used seditious language calculated to lead to a breach of the peace; but the Radical leaders, far from being intimidated by this demonstration of vigor on the part of the government, immediately summoned a similar meeting in Manchester, announcing their intention to elect a representative of that great town likewise, which, though the largest of all the manufacturing towns, was also unrepresented in the Imperial Parliament. The magistrates prohibited the meeting. It was only postponed for a week, when the people assembled in such formidable numbers (no estimate reckoned them at fewer than 60,000), that the ordinary civil authorities deemed themselves unequal to dealing with it, and called in the aid first of the Yeomanry and then of a hussar regiment. The soldiers behaved with great forbearance, as soldiers always do behave on such occasions; but they were bound to execute the orders which were given them to arrest some of the leaders, and, in the tumult which was the inevitable consequence of their attempt to force a way through so dense a crowd, three or four lives were, unfortunately, lost.

So unusual a catastrophe called out the energies of both parties. The Radical leaders published manifestoes declaring the people had been "massacred" by the soldiers by the orders of the government. Meetings were held to denounce the conduct of the ministers, one being even promoted by Lord Fitzwilliam, as Lord-lieutenant of Yorkshire, a dignity of which he was instantly deprived; while, on the other hand, the grand-juries of Cheshire and Lancashire made reports of the condition of those counties to the Secretary of State, which showed that a most alarming spirit prevailed over the greater part of the district. "The most inflammatory publications had been issued in the principal towns, at a price which put them within the reach of the poorest classes of society. The training and military drilling of large bodies of men under regular leaders had been carried on to a great extent for some time, chiefly by night; and there was no doubt that an extensive manufacture of arms was going on." What was a hardly inferior symptom of danger was a system of intimidation which prevailed to a most serious degree. Many magistrates had received notices threatening their lives, and combinations had been formed to withhold custom from publicans and

shopkeepers who had come forward to support the civil power. In many parts of the two counties the grand-juries declared "that no warrant of arrest or other legal process could be executed; the payment of taxes had ceased, and the landlords were threatened with the discontinuance of their rents."
It was admitted that the spirit of disaffection was local, confined to three or four counties; but those counties were, next to Middlesex itself, the most populous and among the most important in the kingdom, and there was danger lest the feeling, if not checked, might spread. The crisis seemed so momentous, that some even of the Opposition leaders volunteered their counsels and aid to the ministers in dealing with it. And the ministers, after long deliberation, decided on calling Parliament together in November, and introducing some bills which they conceived necessary to enable them to restore and preserve tranquillity. They were six in number; and—perhaps, with some sarcastic reference to Gardiner's Six Acts in the sixteenth century— they were very commonly spoken of as Lord Sidmouth's Six Acts, that noble lord being the Home-secretary, to whose department they belonged. It is not necessary here to do more than mention the general purport of five of them. One prohibited military training without the sanction of the government; another empowered magistrates to search for arms which they had reason to believe were collected for illegal purposes; the third authorized the seizure of seditious and blasphemous libels; the fourth subjected publications below a certain size to the same stamp as that required for a newspaper; the fifth regulated the mode of proceeding in trials for misdemeanor of a political character. But these enactments were regarded as little more than arrangements of detail or procedure involving no principles, and some of them were admitted even by the most steadfast opponents of the ministers to be necessary. But the sixth, designed to restrain the practice of holding large open-air meetings—not, indeed, forever, but for a certain period, fixed at five years—was strongly resisted by the greater portion of the Whig party in both Houses, as a denial to the people of one of their most ancient and constitutional rights.[179]

Its principal clauses enacted that "no meeting exceeding the number of fifty persons (except a meeting of any county or division of any county, called by the Lord-lieutenant or sheriff of such county, etc., or by five or more acting justices of the peace for such county, or by the major part of the grand-jury; or any meeting of any city, borough, etc., called by the mayor or other head officer of such city, etc.) should be holden for the purpose or on the pretext of deliberating upon any public grievance, or upon any matter relating to any trade, manufacture, etc., or upon any matter of Church or State, or of considering, proposing, or agreeing to any petition, address, etc., etc., unless in the parish or township within which the persons calling any such meeting usually dwell;" and it required six days' notice of the intention to hold such meetings, with their time, place, and object, to be given to a magistrate. It empowered the magistrate to whom such notice was given to alter the time and place. It forbade adjournments intended to evade these prohibitions. It forbade any one to attend such meetings except freeholders of the county, or parishioners of the parish, or members of the corporation of the city or borough in which they were held, or members of the House of Commons for such places. It empowered magistrates to proceed to the places where such meetings were being held, and, if they thought it necessary, to require the aid of constables. It enacted that any meeting, the tendency of which should be "to incite or stir up the people to hatred and contempt of the person of his Majesty, his heirs and successors, or of the government or constitution of this country as by law established, should be deemed an unlawful assembly." It empowered one or more justices of the peace, in the event of any meeting being held contrary to the provisions of this act, to warn every one present, in the King's name, to depart; and made those who did not depart in obedience to such warning liable to prosecution for felony, and, if convicted, to seven years' transportation. It forbade the display of flags, banners, or ensigns at any meeting, and the employment of any drum, or military or other music; but it excepted from its operation "any meeting or assembly which should be wholly holden in any room."

There was one peculiarity in the line taken by the opponents of the bill, that they did not deny that the meetings which had induced the ministers to propose it were an evil, dangerous to the general tranquillity; but it was strongly urged by Lord Erskine and others that the existing laws were quite strong enough to deal with them, so that a new enactment was superfluous; and by others, in both Houses, that such meetings were "an ancient and constitutional mode of discussing abuses or petitioning Parliament," any interference with which was a greater evil than the meetings themselves, as being a violation of the constitution. Mr. Brougham in particular admitted, to the full extent of the assertions of the ministers themselves, "the wickedness and folly of many of the speeches" made at the recent meetings. He expressed with great force his entire disapproval of the system on which these meetings had been conducted, and admitted that the martial array which had been exhibited, and the vastness of the numbers of those who had attended, were of themselves calculated to excite alarm; but he declared that "he could not on that account acquiesce in a total subversion of a popular right." On the other hand, the ministers themselves did not deny "the general right of the people to petition the Legislature, or to carry their addresses to the foot of the throne. And therefore (as Lord Harrowby, the President of the Council, admitted) there could be no doubt of their right to assemble, so far as was necessary to agree to their petitions or addresses. It was a right that did not depend on the Bill of Rights, on which it was usually grounded, but had existed long before. But this bill," he contended, "imposed no restrictions on the legitimate enjoyment of that privilege; it only regulated the meetings at which it was to be exercised." And Lord Liverpool affirmed that the bill was not only "consistent with the existing laws and principles of the constitution, but was even proposed in furtherance of those principles, and for the purpose of protecting the people of this country against a series of evils which, if not checked, must subvert their laws and liberties."

In attempting to form a correct judgment on the question whether this bill were constitutional or unconstitutional, it must, I think, be admitted that, as has been remarked before, the terms "constitutional" and "unconstitutional" are somewhat vague and elastic. There is no one document—not Magna Charta, nor the Petition of Eight, nor the Bill of Rights—which can be said to contain the whole of the British constitution. Its spirit and principles are, indeed, to be found in all the laws, to which they give animation and life, but not in any one law. And among its leading principles are those which embrace the right of every individual to freedom of action and freedom of speech, so long as he does not commit any crime himself, nor tempt others to do so. Yet it does not follow that a new enactment which for a while abridges or suspends that freedom of action or speech is inconsistent with those constitutional principles.

Ministers, to whom the government of a country is intrusted, do wrong if they limit their operations to the punishment of offences which have been committed. It is at least equally their duty, as far as possible, to prevent their commission; to take precautionary measures, especially at times when there is notorious danger of offences being committed. At the same time they are bound not to legislate under the influence of panic; not to yield to fears having no substantial ground. And in their measures of precaution they are farther bound to depart from or overstep the ordinary law as little as is compatible with the attainment of their object. In all such cases each action of theirs must stand or fall by its own merits; by the greatness of the emergency which has caused it, and by its sufficiency for its end. For as no law, except such as forbids moral crimes, is invariable, so even the dearest privileges of each subject, being his for the common good, are liable to temporary suspension for that common good. But the burden of justification lies on those who propose that suspension.

Now, that this bill was such a suspension of the long-established rights of the subject, and so far an overstepping of the principles of the constitution, is admitted by the very fact of its framers only proposing for it a temporary authority. Had it not invaded a valuable and real right, it might have been made of perpetual obligation. But it is not easy to see how it can be denied that the dangers against which it was intended to guard were also real. It was certain that itinerant demagogues were visiting districts with which they had no connection, for the sole purpose of stirring up political agitation. It was clear that such meetings as they convened, where those assembled could only be counted by tens of thousands, were too large for deliberation, and were only meant for intimidation; and equally clear that, though the existing laws may have armed the magistrate with authority to disperse such meetings, they did not furnish him with the means of doing so without at least the risk of bloodshed (for such a risk must be involved in the act of putting soldiers in motion), and still less did they invest him with the desirable power of preventing such meetings. It was necessary, therefore, to go back to the original principles and objects of every constitution, the tranquillity, safety, and welfare of the nation at large. And it does not appear that this bill went beyond what was necessary for that object. Indeed, though party divisions are not always trustworthy tests of the wisdom or propriety of a measure, the unusual magnitude of the majorities by which on this occasion the minister was supported in both Houses may fairly be regarded as a testimony to the necessity of the bill,[180] while its sufficiency was proved by the abandonment of all such meetings, and the general freedom from agitation in every part Of the country which prevailed in the following year, though its most remarkable incident was one of which demagogues might well have taken advantage, if they had not had so convincing a proof of the power of government, and of the resolution of the ministers to exert it.[181]

Notes:

[Footnote 172:] Against Junot, at Vimiera and Rolica, in 1808; Soult, at Oporto, and Victor, at Talavera, in 1809; Massena and Ney, at Busaco and Torres Vedras, in 1810; Masséna and Bessiéres, at Fuentes d'Onor, in 1811. Ciudad Rodrigo and Badajoz had been taken in 1812, in spite of the neighborhood of Soult and Marmont. In July, 1813, a month after the formation of Lord Liverpool's ministry, he routed Marmont at Salamanca; in 1813 he took Madrid, and routed Jourdain at Vittoria; and, having subsequently defeated Soult at Sauroren, he crossed the French frontier in October.]

[Footnote 173:] A resolution, moved by Mr. Canning, to take the claims of the Roman Catholics into consideration in the next session had been carried in June by the large majority of 129; and when Lord Wellesley brought forward a similar motion in the House of Lords, not only did Lord Liverpool "protest against its being inferred from any declaration of his that it was, or ever had been, his opinion that under no circumstances would it be possible to make any alteration in the laws respecting the Roman Catholics," but the Chancellor, Lord Eldon, who was generally regarded as the stoutest champion of the existing law, rested his opposition entirely on political grounds, explaining carefully that he opposed the motion, "not because he quarrelled with the religion of the Roman Catholics, but because their religious opinions operated on their political principles in such a way as to render it necessary to adopt some defence against them," and met the motion by moving the previous question, avowedly because "he did not wish, at once and forever, to shut the door of conciliation;" and the previous question was only carried by a single vote—126 to 125.]

[Footnote 174:] "It (difference on the Catholic question) was an evil submitted to by the government, of which Mr. Fox, Lord Grenville, and Lord Grey were members, in the years 1806, 1807, as well as by the governments of Mr. Perceval, Lord Liverpool, and the Duke of Wellington." —*Peel's Memoirs*, i., 62. This passage would seem to imply that Peel believed the Catholic question to have been left "open" in 1806; but there is not, so far as the present writer is aware, any trace of such an arrangement on record, and Lord Liverpool's letter to the King, of November 10, 1826 ("Life," iii., 436), shows clearly that he was not aware of such a precedent for the arrangement which, in 1812, "he and others advised his Majesty" to consent to. Moreover, the condemnation passed on it by Mr. Ponsonby, who had been Chancellor of Ireland in 1806 and 1807, seems a clear proof that he knew nothing of it, though it is hardly possible that he should have been ignorant of it if it had existed.]

[Footnote 175:] To whom the chief glory of the Waterloo campaign belongs there can, of course, be no doubt; and though the Austrians and Prussians put forward a claim to an equal share, and Russia even to a preponderating one, in the first deposition of Napoleon, he himself constantly attributed his fall more to the Peninsular contest than to any of his wars east of the Rhine. And, indeed, it is superfluous to point out that almost to the last he gained occasional victories over the Continental armies, but that he never gained one advantage over the British force; and that Wellington invaded France the first week of October, 1813—nearly three months before a single Russian or German soldier crossed the Rhine.]

[Footnote 176:] Letter to Sir W. Scott, Twiss's "Life of Lord Eldon," ii., 272. It is remarkable that in his "Life of Lord Ellenborough" Lord Campbell takes no notice of this case.]

[Footnote 177:] The opinion of the Attorney and Solicitor General, Sir S. Shepperd and Sir R. Gifford, is given at length in the author's "Life of Lord Liverpool," ii., 373.]

[Footnote 178:] It is a shrewd observation of Sully, that it is never any abstract desire for theoretical reforms, or even for increased privileges, which excites in lower classes to discontent and outrage, but only impatience under actual suffering.]

[Footnote 179:] The bill (entitled "The Seditious Meetings Prevention Bill"), 60 George III., c. 6, is given at full length in Hansard's "Parliamentary Debates," series 1., vol. xli., p. 1655.]

[Footnote 180:] In the House of Lords the majority was 135 to 38; in the House of Commons, 851 to 128. And even of this minority, many would have supported the bill, if the ministers would have consented to adopt an amendment proposed by Lord Althorp, to limit its operation to a few of the northern and midland counties, in which alone, as he contended, any spirit of dangerous disaffection had been exhibited.]

[Footnote 181:] It may be as well to mention that these pages were written in the autumn of 1880.]

CHAPTER VIII

Survey of the Reign of George III.—The Cato Street Conspiracy.—The Queen's Return to England, and the Proceedings against her.—The King Visits Ireland and Scotland.—Reform of the Criminal Code.—Freedom of Trade.—Death of Lord Liverpool.—The Duke of Wellington becomes Prime-minister.—Repeal of the Test and Corporation Act.—O'Connell is Elected for Clare.—Peel Resigns his Seat for Oxford.—Catholic Emancipation.—Question of the Endowment of the Roman Catholic Clergy.—Constitutional Character of the Emancipation.—The Propriety of Mr. Peel's Resignation of his Seat for Oxford Questioned.

In the first month of 1820 George III. died. His had been an eventful reign, strangely checkered with disaster and glory; but, if we compare its close with its commencement, it was still more remarkably distinguished by a development of the resources and an increase in the wealth and power of the nation, to which the history of no other country in the same space of time affords any parallel.

Regarded from the first point of view, our successes greatly outweighed our disasters. The loss of our North American Colonies, the only event which can be so described, was far more than counterbalanced by our vast acquisitions in India, at the Cape of Good Hope, and Malta; while to our maritime supremacy, in the complete establishment of which Rodney and Nelson had crowned the work of Anson and Hawke, was now added a splendor of military renown far surpassing that achieved by any other of the nations which had borne their share in the overthrow of Napoleon.

The increase of our resources is sufficiently shown by a single fact. At his accession George III. found the kingdom engaged in the great seven years' war; one British army employed beyond the Rhine, another in India; fleets traversing the seas in every direction, capturing the Havana, in the West Indies; Manilla, in the East; and routing French squadrons in sight of their own harbors. While, to maintain these varied armaments, supplies were voted by Parliament in 1761 to what Lord Stanhope calls "the unprecedented amount of almost twenty millions." In 1813 the supplies reached nearly six times that amount,[182] and that prodigious sum was raised with greater ease than the revenue of 1761, the interest on the necessary loans being also lower than it had been on the former occasion.

The philosophical man of science will point with at least equal exultation to the great discoveries in art and science; to the achievements of the mechanic, the engineer, and the chemist; to the labors of Brindley and Arkwright and Watts, to which, indeed, this great expansion of the resources and growth of the wealth of the country is principally owing.

While, as the preceding chapters of this work have been designed to show, our political progress and advancement had been no less steady or valuable; yet, important from a constitutional point of view as were many of the labors of our legislators in these sixty years, they are surpassed in their influence on the future history of the nation, as well as in the reality and greatness of the changes which were produced by them in the constitution, by the transactions of the reigns of the next two sovereigns, though the two united scarcely equalled in their duration a quarter of that of their venerable father.

It has been seen how Pitt was baffled in his efforts to remodel the House of Commons, and to remove the disabilities under which the Roman Catholics labored, the reasons for which, even granting that they had been sufficient to justify their original imposition, had, in his judgment, long passed away. His pursuit of the other great object of his domestic policy, the emancipation of trade from the shackles which impeded its universal development, was rudely interrupted by the pressure of the war forced upon him by that very nation which he had desired to make the first partner, if one may use such an expression, in the prosperity which he hoped to diffuse by his commercial treaty with her. But, as in the case of other men in advance of their age, the principles which he had asserted were destined to bear fruit at a later period. And the mere fact of a change in the person of the sovereign seemed to make a change in the policy hitherto pursued less unnatural.

Yet, memorable as the reforms which it witnessed were destined to make it, no reign ever commenced with more sinister omens than that at which we have now arrived. The new King had not been on the throne a month, when a conspiracy was discovered, surpassing in its treasonable atrocity any that had been heard of in the kingdom since the days of the Gunpowder Plot; and, even before those concerned in that foul crime had been brought to punishment, the public mind was yet more generally and profoundly agitated by a scandal which, in one point of view, was still more painful, as in some degree involving the whole kingdom in its disgrace.

The marriage of the present sovereign to Mrs. Fitzherbert has already been mentioned. A few years afterward, in the year 1795, regarding that marriage as illegal, he had contracted a second with his cousin, the Princess Caroline of Brunswick. But, even in royal families, a more unfortunate alliance had never taken place. They had never met till she arrived in England for the wedding; and, as he had never professed any other motive for consenting to the match than a desire to obtain the payment of his debts, he did not think it necessary to disguise his feelings, or to change his habits, or even to treat her with decency for a single day. On his very first introduction to her he behaved to her with marked discourtesy.[183] Shortly after the marriage he formally separated himself from her, and, both before and after the separation, lived in undisguised licentiousness. She, on her part, indignant at his neglect and infidelity, and exasperated at the restrictions which he presently placed on her intercourse with their only child, made no secret of her feelings, and on many occasions displayed such disregard of the ordinary rules of prudence and propriety, that he had some color for charges of infidelity to her marriage vows which, after a few years, he brought against her. The King, her uncle, could not refuse to appoint a commission to investigate the truth of the accusation; but the commissioners unanimously acquitted her of any graver fault than imprudence. She was again received at court, from which she had been excluded while the inquiry was pending; but her husband's animosity toward her was not appeased. As time wore on, and as the King's derangement deprived her of her only protector, it even seemed as if he desired to give it all the notoriety possible, till at last, wearied out by his implacable persecution, she sought and obtained his permission to quit the country and take up her abode abroad. It was a most unfortunate resolution on her part. She fixed her residence in Italy, where she gradually learned to neglect the caution which she had observed in England, till, after a year or two, reports arose of her intimacy with a servant whom she had raised from a menial situation to that of the chief officer of her household, and whom she admitted to a familiarity of intercourse which others besides her husband thought quite incompatible with innocence. He sent agents into Italy to inquire into the truth of those rumors; and their report so greatly confirmed them that, even before the King's death, he laid it before the Prime-minister, with a demand that he should at once take steps to procure him a divorce, in which he professed to believe that the Princess herself would willingly acquiesce. He was so far correct, that her legal advisers were willing to advise her to consent to "a formal separation, to be ratified by an act of Parliament." But such an arrangement fell far short of the Prince's wishes. The Princess Charlotte, the heiress to his throne, had died in childbirth two years before, and he was anxious to be set free to marry again. The ministers were placed in a situation of painful embarrassment. There was an obvious difficulty in pointing out to one who already stood toward them in the character of their sovereign, and who must inevitably soon become so, that his own conduct made the prospect of obtaining a divorce from the Ecclesiastical Courts hopeless; and the only other expedients calculated to attain his end, "a direct application to Parliament for relief, founded upon the special circumstances of the case," or "a proceeding against the Princess for high-treason," were but little more promising. Indeed, it was afterward ascertained to be the unanimous opinion of the judges that the charge of high-treason could not be legally sustained, since the individual who was alleged to be the partner in the criminality imputed to her was a foreigner, and therefore, "owing no allegiance to the crown," could not be said to have violated it.[184]

He chafed under their resistance to his wish, and would have deprived them of their offices, could he have relied on any successors whom he might give them proving more complaisant; but, before he could make up his mind, the death of George III. forced upon both him and them the consideration of his and his wife's position, since it made it necessary to remodel the prayer for the royal family, and instantly to decide whether her name and title as Queen were to be inserted in it. He was determined that they should not be mentioned; and, as the practice of praying for a Queen Consort by name appeared not to have been invariable, they were willing to gratify him on this point, though it was evidently highly probable that she would consider this as a fresh insult, sufficient to justify her in carrying out a threat, which she had recently held out, of returning to England. Her ablest advisers did not, indeed, regard it in this light, since the prayer as now framed implored the Divine protection for "all the royal family" in general terms, in which she might be supposed to be included, and made no separate mention of any member of the family.[185] But, unfortunately, she was much more under the influence of counsellors who were neither lawyers nor statesmen, but who only desired to use her as a tool to obtain notoriety for themselves. A long negotiation ensued. It was inevitable that some application should be made to Parliament in connection with her affairs, since the annuity which had been settled upon her by Parliament in 1814, on the occasion of her departure from England, had expired with the life of the late King. And the ministers proposed that that annuity should now be raised from £35,000 to £50,000, on condition of her remaining abroad, having, by their positive refusal to concur in any proceedings against her while she remained abroad, extorted the King's acquiescence in this proposal, though he called it a "great and painful sacrifice of his personal feelings." They sought to conciliate her acceptance of it by mentioning her in it by her title of "Queen," and by coupling with it a sanction to her appointment of her law-officers, an Attorney and Solicitor General, an act which could only be exercised by a Queen. And, though a part of the condition of her residence abroad required that she should do so under some other title, that seemed only a conforming to an ordinary practice of royal princes on their travels. At the same time, the ministers stated frankly to Mr. Brougham, a lawyer of the highest reputation as an advocate, whom she had appointed her Attorney-general, that, if she should reject the offer, and come to England, as she had already announced her intention of doing, such a course would leave them no alternative, but would compel them to institute proceedings against her.

Eventually she preferred the advice of others to that of Mr. Brougham, or, as it may, perhaps, be more consistent with the real fact to say, she yielded to her own feelings of hatred of her husband, which, it must be confessed, were far from unnatural. She believed, or professed to believe, that he had more to dread from an exposure of his conduct than she had from any revelations of her actions; and, under this impression, in the spring she crossed the Channel and took up her residence in London. It was a step which seemed to Lord Liverpool to leave him no alternative, and, in consequence, he at once took the course which he had from the beginning conceived her arrival would render indispensable. He brought down to Parliament a royal message from the King, announcing that her return to England had made it necessary to communicate to the Houses documents relating to her conduct since her departure from the kingdom, which he recommended to their immediate and serious attention. He proposed the appointment by ballot of a committee of the House of Lords to examine those documents; and when the committee had reported that the documents containing "allegations deeply affecting the honor of the Queen, etc., ... appeared to the committee calculated to affect not only the honor of the Queen, but also the dignity of the crown and the moral feelings and honor of the country, so that in their opinion, they should become the subject of a solemn inquiry, which might be best effected in the course of a legislative proceeding," he introduced a "Bill of Pains and Penalties" to deprive her of her title of Queen, and to annul her marriage.

No one would willingly dwell on so melancholy and disgraceful a subject. As far as the Queen was concerned, a protracted investigation, during which a number of witnesses, favorable and unfavorable, were examined, left no doubt on the mind of almost all dispassionate people that the misconduct alleged against her had been abundantly proved. At the same time there was a feeling equally general that the King's treatment of her from the very beginning of their married life had disentitled him to any kind of relief; and this sentiment was so strongly shown by the gradual diminution of the majority in favor of the bill, as it proceeded through its several stages, that Lord Liverpool, who had already abandoned the clause annulling the marriage, eventually withdrew the whole bill, perceiving the impossibility of inducing the House of Commons to pass it when it should go down to that House.

No act of Lord Liverpool's ministry has been attacked with greater bitterness than that of allowing any proceedings whatever to be taken against the Queen, partly on the ground that, however profligate her conduct had been, it had certainly not been more gross than that of her husband, which had provoked and given opportunity for her errors; partly because a great scandal was thus published to the world, and a shock was given to the national decency and morality which the ministers, above all men, were bound to avoid; partly, also, because the mode of proceeding adopted was alleged to be wholly unprecedented; and because, as was contended, the power of Parliament ought not to be invoked to inflict penalties which, if deserved, should have been left to the courts of law. It cannot be denied that there is weight in these objections; but, in estimating their force, it must be considered that every part of the conduct of the ministers showed that their motive was not the gratification of the King's private feelings, whether directed to the object of indulging his enmity against his wife or to that of obtaining freedom to contract a second marriage; on the contrary, so long as the Queen remained abroad, no language could be more distinct, consistently with the respect due to his royal dignity, than that in which they expressed to him their insurmountable objection to every mode of proceeding against her which he had suggested, founded almost equally on considerations of "the interests of his Majesty and of the monarchy,"[186] and "the painful obligation" under which they conceived themselves to lie "of postponing their regard for his Majesty's feelings to great public interests."

But when the Queen came to England the case was greatly altered. The question now forced on the consideration of the cabinet was, not the mode of avoiding an intolerable scandal, but the choice between two scandals, both of the gravest character. The scandal to be dreaded from the revelations of the conduct of both King and Queen, that could not fail to result from the investigation which, in justice, must precede any attempt to legislate on the subject, was, indeed, as great as ever; but it had now to be compared with the alternative scandal of allowing a woman lying under such grievous imputations to preside over the British court, as, if resident in England, and in undisturbed possession of her royal rank, she of necessity must preside. The consequence would evidently have been that the court would have been deserted by all who could give lustre and dignity to it by their position and character; and, in the slights thus offered to her, royalty and the monarchy themselves would seem to be brought into contempt. The latter scandal, too, would be the more permanent. Grievous and shameful as might be the disclosures which must be anticipated from an investigation in which the person accused must be permitted the employment of every means of defence, including recrimination, the scandal was yet one which would, to a certain extent, pass away with the close of the inquiry. But, if she were left undisturbed in the enjoyment of her royal rank, and of privileges which could not be separated from it, that scandal would last as long as her life—longer, in all probability, than the reign. It is hardly too much to say that the monarchy itself might have been endangered by the spectacle of such a King and such a Queen; and the ministers might fairly contend that, of two great dangers and evils, they had, on the whole, chosen the least.

Lastly, if the Queen's conduct was to be investigated, though the mode adopted was denounced as unconstitutional by the Opposition (for, not greatly to their credit, the leading Whigs made her guilt or innocence a party question), it does not seem to deserve the epithet, though it may be confessed to have been unsupported by any direct precedent. Isabella, the faithless wife of Edward II., had, indeed, been condemned by "the Lords" to the forfeiture of many of the estates which she had illegally appropriated; but it does not appear that her violation of her marriage vows, or even her probable share or acquiescence in her husband's murder, formed any portion of the grounds of her deprivation. And the Parliament which attainted Catherine Howard proceeded solely on her confession of ante-nuptial licentiousness, without giving her any opportunity of answering or disproving the other charges which were brought against her. Unprecedented, therefore, the course now adopted may be admitted to have been. But it was the only practicable one. The different minutes of the cabinet, which the Prime-minister laid before the King, established most conclusively the correctness of their opinion that no impeachment for high-treason could lie against her. She could not be an accomplice in such an offence of one who, being a foreigner, could not have committed it. It was equally impossible for the King to sue for a divorce, as one of his subjects might have done; because it was the established practice of Parliament not to entertain a bill of divorce without the judgment of the Ecclesiastical Court being previously obtained and produced. And, under the circumstances, to obtain from the Ecclesiastical Court such a sentence as could alone lay the foundation for a bill of divorce was clearly out of the question.

The case was a new and extraordinary one, and, being such, could only be dealt with in some new and extraordinary manner. And in all such cases an appeal to Parliament seems the most, if not the only, constitutional mode of solving the difficulty. Where the existing laws are silent or inapplicable, the most natural resource clearly is, to go back to the fountain of all law; that is, to the Parliament, which alone is competent to make a new law. In one point of view the question may seem unimportant, since we may well hope that no similar case will ever arise to require the precedent now set to be appealed to; but not unimportant, if it in any way or degree contributes to establish the great principle, that the solution of all matters of moment to the state belongs to the Parliament alone: a principle which, in its legitimate completeness, carries with it a condemnation of many a modern association whose object, whether avowed or disguised, is clearly to supersede where it fails to intimidate the sole constitutional Legislature.

The abandonment of the bill was naturally hailed as a triumph by the Queen and her partisans; but with the excitement of the struggle against the government the interest taken in her case died away. The next year, when she demanded to be crowned with her husband, his refusal to admit her claim elicited scarcely any sympathy for her under this renewed grievance; in truth, it was one as to which precedent was unfavorable to her demand. And the mortification at finding herself already almost forgotten contributed to bring on an illness of which she died in less than a year after the termination of what was called her trial; and in a short time both she and it were forgotten.

For the next few years the history of the kingdom is one of progressive correction of abuses or defects. The King paid visits to Ireland and Scotland, parts of his dominions which his father had never once visited, and in both was received with the most exultant and apparently sincere acclamations. And, though one great calamity fell on the ministry in the loss of Lord Castlereagh—who, in a fit of derangement, brought on by the excitement of overwork, unhappily laid violent hands on himself—his death, sad as it was, could not be said to weaken or to affect the general policy of the cabinet. Indeed, as he was replaced at the Foreign Office by his old colleague and rival, Mr. Canning, in one point of view the administration may be said to have been strengthened by the change, since, as an orator, Canning had confessedly no equal in either House of Parliament. Another change was productive of still more practical advantage. Lord Sidmouth retired from the Home Office, and was succeeded by Mr. Peel, previously Secretary for Ireland; and the transfer of that statesman to an English office facilitated reforms, some of which were as yet little anticipated even by the new Secretary himself. The earliest of them, and one not the least important in its bearing on the well-doing of society, the mitigation of the severity of our Criminal Code, was, indeed, but the following up of a series of measures in the same direction which had been commenced in the time of the Duke of Portland's second administration, and, it must be added, in spite of its resistance. The influence of various trades, and of the owners of different kinds of property, pressing in turns upon our legislators, had rendered our code the most sanguinary that had, probably, ever existed in Christendom. Each class of proprietor regarded only the preservation of his own property, and had no belief in the efficacy of any kind of protection for it, except such as arose from the fear of death; nor any doubt that he was justified in procuring the infliction of that penalty to avert the slightest loss to himself. The consequence was that, at the beginning of the present century, there were above two hundred offences the perpetrators of which were liable to capital punishment, some of a very trivial character, such as cutting down a hop-vine in a Kentish hop-garden, robbing a rabbit-warren or a fish-pond, personating an out-pensioner of Greenwich Hospital, or even being found on a high-road with a blackened face, the intention to commit a crime being inferred from the disguise, even though no overt act had been committed. An act of Elizabeth made picking a pocket a capital offence; another, passed as late as the reign of William III., affixed the same penalty to shop-lifting, even when the article stolen might not exceed the value of five shillings. And the fault of these enactments was not confined to their unreasonable cruelty; they were as mischievous even to those whom they were designed to protect as they were absurd, as some owners began to perceive. In the list of capital offences was that of stealing linen from a bleaching-ground. And a large body of bleachers presented a petition to Parliament entreating the repeal of the statute which made it such on the ground that, practically, it had been found not to strike terror into the thieves, but almost to secure them impunity from the reluctance of juries to find a verdict which would sentence a fellow-creature to the gallows for such an offence.

Nor was this by any means the only instance in which the barbarity of the law defeated its object. And its combined impolicy and inhumanity had some years before attracted the notice of Sir Samuel Romilly, who had been Solicitor-general in the administration of 1806, and who, shortly after its dissolution, began to apply himself to the benevolent object of procuring the repeal of many of the statutes in question, and in the course of a few years did succeed in obtaining the substitution of milder penalties for several of the less flagitious offences. He died in 1818; but the work which he had begun was continued by Sir James Mackintosh, a man of even more conspicuous ability, and one who could adduce his own experience in favor of the changes which he recommended to the Parliament, since he had filled the office of Recorder of Bombay for eight years, and had discharged his duties with a most diligent and consistent avoidance of capital punishment, which he had never inflicted except for murder; his lenity, previously unexampled in that land, having been attended with a marked diminution of crime. He procured the substitution of milder penalties in several additional cases; and at last, in 1822, he carried a resolution engaging the House of Commons "the next session to take into its serious consideration the means of increasing the efficacy of the criminal law by abating its undue rigor." And this success had the effect of inducing the new minister to take the question into his own hands. Peel saw that it was one which, if it were to be dealt with at all, ought to be regulated by the government itself, and not be left to independent members, who could not settle it with satisfactory completeness; and therefore, in 1823, he introduced a series of bills to carry out the principle implied in Mackintosh's resolution of the preceding year, not only simplifying the law, but abolishing the infliction of capital punishment in above a hundred cases. He was unable to carry out his principle as fully as he could have desired. The prejudice in favor of still retaining death as a punishment for forgery was too strong for even his resolution as yet to overbear, though many private bankers supplied him with the same arguments against it in their case which had formerly been alleged by the bleachers. But the example which he now set, enforced as it was with all the authority of the government, was followed in many subsequent sessions, till at last our code, instead of the most severe, has become the most humane in Europe, and death is now never inflicted except for murder, or crimes intended or calculated to lead to murder. It is worth remarking, however, that neither Romilly, Mackintosh, nor Peel ever entertained the slightest doubt of the right of a government to inflict capital punishment. In the last address which Mackintosh delivered to the grand-jury at Bombay he had said: "I have no doubt of the right of society to inflict the punishment of death on enormous crimes, wherever an inferior punishment is not sufficient. I consider it as a mere modification of the right of self-defence, which may as justly be exercised in deterring from attack as in repelling it."[187] And in his diary, when speaking of a death-warrant which he had just signed, he says: "I never signed a paper with more perfect tranquillity of mind. I felt agitation in pronouncing the sentence, but none in subscribing the warrant; I had no scruple of conscience on either occasion."

And it seems that his position is unassailable. The party whose interest is to be kept in view by the Legislature in imposing punishments on offences is society, the people at large, not the offender. The main object of punishment is to deter rather than to reform; to prevent crime, not to take vengeance on the criminal. And, if crime be more effectually prevented by moderate than by severe punishments, society has a right to demand, for its own security (as a matter of policy, not of justice), that the moderate punishment shall, on that ground, be preferred. That punishments disproportioned in their severity to the magnitude of the offence often defeated their object was certain. Not only had jurymen been known to confess that they had preferred violating their oaths to doing still greater violence to their consciences, by sending a man to the gallows for a deed which, in their opinion, did not deserve it, but the very persons who had been injured by thefts or forgeries were often deterred from prosecution of the guilty by the knowledge that the forfeiture of their lives must follow their conviction. It was almost equally certain that criminals calculated beforehand on the chance of impunity which the known prevalence of these feelings afforded them. Wherever the sympathy of the public does not go along with the law, it must, to a great extent, fail; and that the terrible frequency of sanguinary punishment had failed in all its objects, was proved by the fact that, in spite of the numerous executions which took place, crimes increased in a still greater proportion than the population. Under the reformed system, now first inaugurated on an extensive scale, crimes have become rarer, detection and punishment more certain—a combination of results which must be the object equally of the law-giver and the philanthropist.

It is not quite foreign to this subject to relate that, a year or two before, a mode of trial had been abolished which, though long disused, by some curious oversight had still been allowed to remain on the statute-book. In the feudal times either the prosecutor or the prisoner, in cases of felony, had a right to claim that the cause should be decided by "wager of battle;" but it was an ordeal which, with one exception in the reign of George II., had not been mentioned for centuries. In 1817, however, the relatives of a woman who had been murdered, being dissatisfied with the acquittal of a man who had been indicted as her murderer, sued out "an appeal of murder" against him, on which he claimed to have the appeal decided by "wager of battle," and threw down a glove on the floor of the court to make good his challenge. The claim was protested against by the prosecutor; but Lord Ellenborough, the Chief-justice, pronounced judgment that, "trial by battle having been demanded, it was the legal and constitutional mode of trial, and must be awarded. It was the duty of the judges to pronounce the law as it was, and not as they might wish it to be."[188] He gave sentence accordingly; and, had the two parties been of equal stature and strength, the Judges of the Common Pleas might have been seen, in their robes, presiding from sunrise till sunset over a combat to be fought, as the law prescribed, with stout staves and leathern shields, till one should cry "Craven," and yield up the field. Fortunately for them, the alleged murderer was so superior in bodily strength to his adversary, that the latter declined the contest. But the public advancement of the claim for such a mode of decision was fatal to any subsequent exercise of it; and, in spite of the Common Council of London, who, confiding, perhaps, in the formidable appearance presented by some of the City Champions on Lord Mayor's Day, petitioned Parliament to preserve it, the next year the Attorney-general brought in a bill to abolish it, and the judges were no longer compelled to pronounce an absurd sentence in obedience to an obsolete law, framed at a time when personal prowess was a virtue to cover a multitude of sins, and might was the only right generally acknowledged.

The foundation, too, was laid for other reforms. Lord Liverpool was more thoroughly versed than any of his predecessors, except Pitt, in the soundest principles of political economy; and in one of the first speeches which he made in the new reign he expressed a decided condemnation, not only of any regulations which were designed to favor one trade or one interest at the expense of another, but generally of the whole system and theory of protection; and one of his last measures made an alteration in the manner of taxing corn imported from foreign countries, which was greatly to the advantage of the consumer. It was known as the "sliding-scale," the tax on imported corn varying with the price in the market, rising when the price fell, and falling when it rose; the design with which it was framed being to keep the price to the consumer at all times as nearly equal as possible. At first, however, it was vehemently denounced by the bulk of the agriculturists, who were re-enforced on this occasion by a large party from among the Whigs, and especially by some of those connected with Ireland. But a more suitable period for discussing the establishment of Free-trade as the ruling principle of our financial policy will occur hereafter.

The introduction of the sliding-scale was almost the last act of Lord Liverpool's ministry. At the beginning of 1827 he was preparing a fresh measure on the same subject, the effect of which was intended to diminish still farther the protection which the former act had given, and which was in consequence denounced by many landholders of great wealth and influence, led, on this subject, by the King's favorite brother, the Duke of York.[189] But, a few days after the meeting of Parliament, he was struck down by an attack of paralysis, from which he never recovered.

In his post as Prime-minister he was succeeded by Canning, not without great reluctance on the part of the King; not, probably, so much because he feared to find in him any desire to depart from the policy of Lord Liverpool, except on the Catholic question (for even on matters of foreign policy, on which Canning had always been supposed most to fix his attention, he had adopted the line which Lord Liverpool had laid down for the cabinet with evident sincerity),[190] as because his Majesty had never wholly forgiven him for the attitude which he had taken, differing on one or two points from that of his colleagues on the Queen's case. And, as has been mentioned in a former chapter, he even, with the object of evading the necessity of appointing him, suggested to the Duke of Wellington the singular scheme of allowing the remaining members of Lord Liverpool's cabinet to select their own chief,[191] which the Duke, though coinciding with him in his dislike of Canning, of whom he entertained a very causeless suspicion, rejected without hesitation, as an abandonment of the royal prerogative in one of its most essential duties or privileges. Another of his Majesty's notions, if it had been carried out, would have been one of the strangest violations of constitutional principle and practice which it is possible to conceive. The Duke of York, who had for many years been Commander-in-chief, died in January of the same year, and on his death the King actually proposed to take that office on himself. For the moment Lord Liverpool was able to induce him to abandon the idea, and to confer the post on the Duke of Wellington. But it had taken such possession of his mind that he recurred to it again when, on Canning becoming Prime-minister, the Duke resigned the office; and he pressed it on the Cabinet with singular pertinacity till, on Canning's death, the Duke was prevailed on to resume the command. It is evident that no arrangement could possibly be more inconsistent with every principle of the constitution. The very foundation of parliamentary government is, that every officer of every department is responsible to Parliament for the proper discharge of his duties. But the investiture of the sovereign with ministerial office of any kind must involve either the entire withdrawal of that department from parliamentary control, or the exposure of the sovereign to constant criticism, which, however essential to the efficiency of the department, and consequently to the public service, would be wholly inconsistent with the respect due to the crown. The first alternative it is certain that no Parliament would endure for a moment; the second, by impairing the dignity of the monarch, could scarcely fail in some degree to threaten the stability of the monarchy itself.

Canning's ministry was too brief to give time for any transaction of internal importance. That of Lord Goderich, who succeeded him, though longer by the almanac, was practically briefer still, since it never met Parliament at all, but was formed and fell to pieces between the prorogation and the next meeting of the Houses. But that which followed, under the presidency of the Duke of Wellington, though after a few months its composition became entirely Tory, is memorable for the first great departure from those maxims of the constitution which had been reckoned among its most essential principles ever since the Revolution. Of the measures which bear that character, one was carried against the resistance of the ministry, the other by the ministers themselves. And it may at first sight appear singular that the larger measure of the two was proposed by the Duke after those members of his cabinet who had originally been supposed to give it something of a Liberal complexion had quitted it. The Reform Bill of 1832—to which we shall come in the next chapter—has been often called a peaceful revolution. The Toleration Acts, as we may call the bills of 1828 and 1829, are scarcely less deserving of that character.

The constitution, as it had existed for the last hundred and forty years, had been not only a Protestant but a Church of England constitution. Not only all Roman Catholics, but all members of Protestant Non-conforming sects, all who refused to sign a declaration against the doctrine of Transubstantiation, and also to take the Sacrament according to the rites of the one Established Church, were disqualified for any appointment of trust. That the object with which the Test Act had been framed and supported was rather political than religious is notorious; indeed, it was supported by the Protestant Dissenters, though they themselves were to suffer by its operation, so greatly at that time did the dread of Popery and the French King overpower every other consideration.[192] On the Roman Catholics, after the reign of James II. had increased that apprehension, the restrictions were tightened. But those which inflicted disabilities on the Protestant Non-conformists had been gradually relaxed. The repeal of two, the Five Mile and the Conventicle Acts, had, as we have seen in the last chapter, been recent measures of Lord Liverpool. But the Test Act still remained, though it had long been practically a dead letter. The Union with Scotland, where the majority of the population was Presbyterian, had rendered it almost impossible to maintain the exclusion of Englishmen resembling the Scotch in their religious tenets from preferments, and even from seats in the House of Commons, to which Scotchmen were admissible. And though one Prime-minister (Stanhope) failed in his attempt to induce Parliament to repeal the Test Act, and his successor (Walpole) refused his countenance to any repetition of the proposal, even he did not reject such a compromise as was devised to evade it; and in the first year of George II.'s reign (by which time it was notorious that many Protestant Non-conformists had obtained seats in municipal corporations, and even in the House of Commons, who yet had never qualified themselves by compliance with the act of 1673) a bill of indemnity was introduced by the minister, with at least the tacit consent of the English bishops, to protect all such persons from the penalties which they had incurred. And the bill, which was only annual in its operation, was renewed almost every year, till, in respect of all such places or dignities (if a seat in the House of Commons can be described by either of those names), no one thought of inquiring whether a man, so long as he were a Protestant, adhered to the Established Church or not; members of the House of Commons even openly avowing their nonconformity, and at times founding arguments on the fact.

The practical nullification of the Test Act by these periodical bills of indemnity had been for some time used by two opposite parties—both that which regarded the maintenance of the exclusive connection of the constitution with the Church of England as of vital importance to both Church and constitution, and that which was opposed to all restrictions or disqualiflcations on religious grounds—as an argument in their favor. The one contended that there could be no sufficient reason for repealing a law from which no one suffered; the other, that it was a needless provocation of ill-feeling to retain a law which no one ever dreamed of enforcing. Hitherto the latter had been the weaker party. One or two motions for the repeal of the Test Act, which had been made in former years,[193] had been defeated without attracting any great notice; but in the spring of 1828 Lord John Russel, then a comparatively young member, but rapidly rising into influence with his party, carried a motion in the House of Commons for leave to bring in a bill to repeal the act, so far as it concerned the Protestant Non-conformists, by a very decisive majority,[194] in spite of all the efforts of Peel and his colleagues.

The ministry was placed in a difficult position by his success, since the usual practice for a cabinet defeated on a question of principle was to resign; and it is probable that they would not have departed from that rule now, had not this defeat occurred so early in their official life. But on this occasion it seemed to them that other questions had to be considered besides the constitutional doctrine of submission on the part of a ministry to the judgment of the Parliament.[195] Theirs was now the fourth administration that had held office within twelve months; and their resignation, which would compel the construction of a fifth, could hardly fail not only to embarrass the sovereign, but to shake public confidence in government generally. It was also certain that they could rely on a division in the House of Lords being favorable to them, if they chose to appeal from one House to the other. Under these circumstances, they had to consider what their line of conduct should be, and there never were two ministers better suited to deal with an embarrassment of that kind than the Duke of Wellington and Mr. Peel. The Duke's doctrine of government was that "the country was never governed in practice according to the extreme principles of any party whatever;"[196] while Peel's disposition at all times inclined him to compromise. He was quite aware that on this and similar questions public feeling had undergone great alteration since the beginning of the century. There was a large and increasing party, numbering in its ranks many men of deep religious feeling, and many firm supporters of the principle of an Established Church, being also sincere believers in the pre-eminent excellence of the Church of England, who had a conscientious repugnance to the employment of the most solemn ordinance of a religion as a mere political test of a person's qualifications for the discharge of civil duties. In the opinion of the Bishop of Oxford (Dr. Lloyd), this was the feeling of "a very large majority of the Church itself," and of the University.[197] Peel, therefore, came to the conclusion—to which he had no difficulty in bringing his colleague, the Prime-minister—that "it might be more for the real interests of the Church and of religion to consent to an alteration in the law" than to trust to the result of the debate in the House of Lords to maintain the existing state of things. Accordingly, after several conferences with the most influential members of the Episcopal Bench, he framed a declaration to be substituted for the Sacramental test, binding all who should be required to subscribe it—a description which included all who should be appointed to a civil or corporate office—never to exert any power or influence which they might thus acquire to subvert, or to endeavor to subvert, the Protestant Church of England, Scotland, or Ireland, as by law established. The declaration was amended in the House of Lords by the addition of the statement, that this declaration was subscribed "on the true faith of a Christian," introduced at the instigation of Lord Eldon, who had not held the Great Seal since the dissolution of Lord Liverpool's administration, but who was still looked up to by a numerous party as the foremost champion of sound Protestantism in either House.

Not that the addition of these words at all diminished the dissatisfaction with which the great lawyer regarded the bill. On the contrary, he believed it to be not only a weapon wilfully put into the hands of the enemies of the Established Church, but a violation of the constitution, of which, as he regarded it "the existing securities were a part." He pointed out that "the King himself was obliged to take the sacrament at his coronation;" and he argued from this and other grounds that "the Church of England, combined with the state, formed together the constitution of Great Britain; and that the acts now to be repealed were necessary to the preservation of that constitution."

With every respect for that great lawyer, his argument on this point does not appear sustainable. For the bill in question did not sweep away securities for the Established Church, but merely substituted, for one which long disuse and indemnity had rendered wholly inoperative, a fresh security, which, as it would be steadily put in force, might fairly be expected to prove far more efficacious. And it can hardly be contended that it was not within the province of the Legislature to modify an existing law in this spirit and with this object, however important might be the purpose for which that law had originally been framed. Nay, it might fairly be argued that the more important that object was, the more were they who strengthened the means of attaining that object entitled to be regarded as faithful servants and supporters of the principle of the constitution.

The measure, however, relieved the Protestant Dissenters alone. Not only did Lord Eldon's amendment preserve the Christian character of the Legislature, but the requirement to sign the declaration against Transubstantiation, which was unrepealed, left the Roman Catholics still under the same disqualifications as before. But the days of those disqualifications were manifestly numbered. Indeed, many of those who had followed the ministers in their original resistance to the repeal of the Test Act had been avowedly influenced by the conviction that it could not fail to draw after it the removal of the disabilities affecting the Roman Catholics. As has been said before, the disabilities in question had originally been imposed on the Roman Catholics on political rather than on religious grounds. And the political reasons for them had been greatly weakened, if not wholly swept away, by the extinction of the Stuart line of princes. Their retention or removal had, therefore, now become almost wholly a religious question; and the late bill had clearly established as a principle that, though the state had a right to require of members of other religious sects that they should not abuse the power which might arise from any positions or employments to which they might be admitted, to the subversion or injury of the Established Church of England, yet, when security for their innocuousness in this respect was provided, it was not justified in inquiring into the details of their faith. And if this were to be the rule of government for the future, the conclusion was irresistible that a similar security was all that the state was justified in demanding from Roman Catholics, and that it could have no warrant for investigating their opinion on Transubstantiation, or any other purely theological tenet. There could be no doubt that the feelings of the public had been gradually and steadily coming round to this view of the question. The last House of Commons had not only passed a bill to remove Roman Catholic disabilities (which was afterward thrown out in the House of Lords), but had also passed, by a still larger majority, a resolution, moved by Lord Francis Leveson Gower (who was now the Secretary for Ireland), in favor of endowing the Roman Catholic priests in Ireland. And at the late general election the opinions of the candidates on what was commonly called Catholic Emancipation had been the great cardinal question with a great number, probably a majority, of the constituencies.

It may be remarked that it was not the Test Act which excluded Roman Catholics from Parliament, but a bill which, fifteen years later, had been passed (probably under the influence of Lord Shaftesbury) at the time when the whole kingdom was excited by the daily expanding revelations of the

Popish Plot.[198] And this bill had a loop-hole which was never discovered till now but the discovery of which totally changed the whole aspect of the question. Even before the bill repealing the Test Act had passed through all its stages, Sir Francis Burdett had again induced the House of Commons to pass a resolution condemning the continuance of the Roman Catholic disabilities; to which, however, the peers, by a far larger majority, refused their concurrence.[199] But, within a month of this division, the aspect of the whole question was changed by the shrewdness of an Irish barrister, who had discovered the loop-hole or flaw in the bill of 1678 already alluded to, and by the energy and promptitude with which he availed himself of his discovery. Mr. O'Connell had a professional reputation scarcely surpassed by any member of the Irish Bar. He was also a man of ancient family in the county of Kerry. And, being a Roman Catholic, he had for several years been the spokesman of his brother Roman Catholics on most public occasions. He now, on examination of the bill of 1678, perceived that, though it forbade any Roman Catholic from taking a seat in either House of Parliament, it contained no prohibition to prevent any constituency from electing him its representative. And when, on the occasion of some changes which were made in the cabinet, the representation of the County Clare was vacated by its member, Mr. Vesey Fitzgerald, accepting the office of President of the Board of Trade, O'Connell instantly offered himself as a candidate in opposition to the new minister, who, of course, sought re-election.

Mr. Fitzgerald was a man who had always supported the demands of the Roman Catholics; he was also personally popular, and had the undivided support of nearly all the gentlemen and principal land-owners of the county, in which he himself had large property. But O'Connell's cause was taken up by the entire Roman Catholic priesthood; addresses in his favor were read at the altars of the different churches; and, after five days' polling, Mr. Fitzgerald withdrew from the contest. The Sheriff, in great perplexity, made a special return, reporting that "Mr. Fitzgerald was proposed, being a Protestant, as a fit person to represent the county in Parliament; that Mr. O'Connell, a Roman Catholic, was also proposed; that he, Mr. O'Connell, had declared before the Sheriff that he was a Roman Catholic, and intended to continue a Roman Catholic; and that a protest had been made by several electors against his return."

It was accepted as a return of O'Connell, who, however, made no attempt to take his seat, though when he first stood he had assured the electors that there was no law to prevent him from doing so; but the importance of his success was not to be measured by his actual presence or absence in the House of Commons for the remainder of a session. It had made it absolutely impossible to continue the maintenance of the disabilities; what one Irish constituency had done, other Irish constituencies might be depended on to do.[200] And it was quite certain that, as opportunity offered, almost every constituency in Munster and Connaught, and many in Leinster, would follow the example of Clare, and return Roman Catholic representatives; while to retain a law which prevented forty or fifty men duly elected by Irish constituencies from taking their seats must have appeared impossible to all but a few, whom respect for the undoubted sincerity of their attachment to their own religion and to the constitution, as they understood it, is the only consideration which can save them from being regarded as dangerous fanatics. At all events, the ministers were not among them. And the Duke of Wellington, though he had previously hoped, by postponing the farther consideration of the question for a year or two, to gain time for a calmer examination of it when the existing excitement had cooled down,[201] at once admitted the conviction that the result of the Clare election had rendered farther delay impossible. In his view, and that of those of his colleagues whose judgment he estimated most highly, the Irish constituencies and their probable action at future elections were not the only parties whose opinions or feelings must be regarded by a responsible statesman; but to them must be added the constituencies of the larger island also, since, while, to quote the language of Mr. Peel, "the general election of 1826 had taken place under circumstances especially calculated to call forth the manifestation of Protestant feeling throughout the country," they had returned a majority of members in favor of concession, as was proved by the recent division on Sir F. Burdett's motion. Moreover, apart from the merits or demerits of concession, taken by itself, there was a manifest danger that the keeping up of the excitement on the subject by a continued adherence to the policy of restriction might, especially among such a people as the Irish, so impulsive, and, in the lower classes, so absolutely under the dominion of the priests, kindle an excitement on other subjects also, still more difficult to deal with. It was even already certain that the Roman Catholic priests were endeavoring to tamper with the loyalty of the soldiers of their persuasion. Nor was it clerical influence alone that the government had to dread. A year or two before a Catholic Association had been formed, which included among its members all the wealthiest and ablest of the Roman Catholic laymen, noblemen, squires, and barristers. Its organization had been so skilfully conducted, and all its measures had been so carefully kept within the requirements of the law, that the crown lawyers, on being consulted, pronounced it impossible to interfere with it; and, by what may be called a peaceful agitation, it had attained such extraordinary power over the minds of the bulk of the Roman Catholics, that the Lord-lieutenant reported that "he was quite certain that they could lead on the people to open rebellion at a moment's notice, and that their organization was such that, in the hands of desperate and intelligent leaders, they would be extremely formidable[202]."

Under all these circumstances, the Duke had no hesitation in deciding that it had become absolutely necessary to concede the demands of the Roman Catholics and their supporters for a removal of their political disabilities. And it was equally obvious that, the more promptly the concession was made, the more gracious it would seem, and the greater was the probability of its having the conciliatory and tranquillizing effect the hope of which made it so desirable. He was not a man to lose time when he had once made up his mind. It was already too late in the session for anything to be done in 1828; but the Parliament had scarcely been prorogued before he put his views on the subject before the King, and began, in concert with the Home-secretary, to frame a bill such as he hoped might settle the long-agitated question, without doing more violence than was necessary to the feelings of those whose opposition or reluctance he was aware he should have to encounter: among whom was the King himself, who, though thirty years before he had, with an ostentation rather unbecoming, considering his position, put himself forward as an advocate of Emancipation, had subsequently changed his opinion, and had recently taken more than one occasion to declare that he had never doubted that, as the head and protector of the Protestant religion, he was bound to refuse his assent to any relaxation of the existing law.[203] The Duke, however, was too well acquainted with his royal master's character to apprehend any real firmness of resistance from him; but he knew that a great majority of the clergy, and no small portion of the country gentlemen, were conscientiously and immovably fixed in opposition to any concession at all, some refusing to regard the question in any but a purely religious light, and objecting to associate in the task of legislation for those whom they regarded as adherents of an idolatrous superstition; while those who mingled political reasoning with that founded on theology dwelt also on the danger to be apprehended to the state, if political power were given to those whose allegiance to the King was divided with another allegiance which they acknowledged to a foreign prelate. And he had presently an unmistakable proof afforded him how great was the strength of this party in the country. Peel was one of the representatives of the University of Oxford; and, as from his earliest enjoyment of a seat in Parliament he had been a prominent opponent of the Roman Catholic claims, he considered that it was to that maintenance of a policy identified in their eyes with that Protestant ascendency which his supporters took to be both the chief bulwark and one of the most essential parts of the constitution that he owed his position as their member. With a conscientiousness which was rather overstrained, and not quite consistent with the legitimate position of a member of the House of Commons as a representative, and not a delegate, he now conceived that his change of view on the subject made it proper for him to give his constituents an opportunity of making choice of some one else who should more faithfully represent them. He accordingly resigned his seat, offering himself at the same time for re-election. But he was defeated by a very large majority, though his competitor was one who could not possibly be put on a level with him either for university distinction or for parliamentary eminence.

Not the less, however, for all their difficulties and discouragements, did the ministers proceed in the course on which they had resolved. They inserted in the speech with which the King opened the session of 1829 a recommendation to the Houses "to take into consideration the whole condition of Ireland, and to review the laws which imposed civil disabilities on his Majesty's Roman Catholic subjects." And with as little delay as possible they introduced a bill to remove those disabilities. But there was another measure which they felt it to be indispensable should precede it. A previous sentence of the royal speech had described the Catholic Association as one "dangerous to the public peace, and inconsistent with the spirit of the constitution, keeping alive discord and ill-will among his Majesty's subjects, and one which must, if permitted to continue, effectually obstruct every effort permanently to improve the condition of Ireland." And the ministers naturally regarded it as their first duty to suppress a body which could deserve to be so described. They felt, too, that the large measure of concession and conciliation which they were about to announce would lose half its grace, and more than half its effect, if it could possibly be represented as a submission to an agitation and intimidation which they had not the power nor the courage to resist. They determined, therefore, to render such an imputation impossible, by previously suppressing the Association. It was evident that it could not be extinguished by any means short of an act of Parliament. And the course pursued, with the discussions which took place respecting it, show in a very clear and instructive manner the view taken by statesmen of the difference between what is loyal or illegal, constitutional or unconstitutional; their apprehension that conduct may be entirely legal, that is to say, within the letter of the law, but at the same time perfectly unconstitutional, outside of and adverse to the whole spirit of the constitution. The royal speech had not ventured to describe the Association as illegal. The Duke of Wellington expressly admitted that "in the original institution and formation of the society there was nothing strictly illegal."[204] And its founder and chief, Mr. O'Connell, had been at all times careful to inculcate on his followers the necessity of avoiding any violation of the law. But the speech had also declared the association to be "inconsistent with the spirit of the constitution." And its acts, as the Duke proceeded to describe them, certainly bore out that declaration. "Those acts consisted principally in levying a tax upon certain of his Majesty's subjects called Catholic rent, and this by means and acts of extreme violence; by appointing persons to collect these rents; and farther by adopting measures to organize the Catholic population; by appointing persons to superintend that organization; and by assuming to themselves the government of the country; and, still more, affecting to assume it. Besides, they expended this rent in a manner contrary to, and utterly inconsistent with, all law and order and the constitution of the country." No member of either House denied the accuracy of this description of the Association's proceedings. And if it were correct, it was incontrovertible that the denunciation of it as an utterly unconstitutional body was not too strong. Indeed, the fact of its "levying a tax" upon a portion of the King's subjects (to say nothing of the intimidation, amounting to compulsion, by which, as was notorious, it was in many instances exacted) was the assumption of one of the most important functions of the Imperial Parliament; it was the erection of an *imperium in imperio*, which no statesmen intrusted with the government of a country can be justified in tolerating. And this was felt by the Opposition as well as by the ministers; by the Whigs as fully as by the Tories. The most eloquent of the Whig party, Mr. Stanley, was as decided as Mr. Peel himself in affirming that the existence of the Association was "inconsistent with the spirit of the constitution," and that it was "dangerous that the people of a country should look up to any public body distinct from the government, opposed to the government, and monopolizing their attachment and obedience."[205]

It was, therefore, with the almost unanimous approval of both parties that the bill framed for the suppression of the Association was received. The framing of such a bill was not unattended by difficulties, as Peel acknowledged,[206] since "no one wished to declare that every political meeting was illegal;" while at the same time it was necessary to guard against "having its enactments evaded, since a more dangerous precedent than the successful evasion of acts of the Legislature could scarcely be conceived." But the measure, as it was proposed, skilfully steered clear of these difficulties. It met them by intrusting "the enforcement of the law to be enacted to one person alone." The bill proposed "to give to the Lord-lieutenant, and to him alone, the power of suppressing any association or meeting which he might think dangerous to the public peace, or inconsistent with the due administration of the law; together with power to interdict the assembly of any meeting of which previous notice should have been given, and which he should think likely to endanger the public peace, or to prove inconsistent with the due administration of the law." And farther, "to interdict any meeting or association which might be interdicted from assembling, or which might be suppressed under this act, from receiving and placing at their control any moneys by the name of rent, or any other name." But the act was not to be one of perpetual duration. It could not be concealed that such a prohibition or limitation of the general right of public meeting and public discussion was a suspension of a part of the constitution; and therefore the ministers were content to limit its operation "to one year and the end of the then next session of Parliament," feeling "satisfied that there would be no objection to continue it, if there should be any necessity for its continuance." And this limitation was a substantial mitigation of its severity. It made the bill, as Mr. Stanley correctly described it, "not a permanent infringement on the constitution, but a temporary deviation from it, giving those powers which were necessary at the moment," but not maintaining them an hour longer than they were necessary.

And this seems to be the course most in accordance with the spirit of the constitution, with former practice, with common-sense. Deeds which violate the letter of the law can be dealt with by the law. But actions or courses of action which, even if they may be thought to overstep the law, transgress it so narrowly as to elude conviction, can only be reached by enactments which also go in some degree beyond the ordinary law; and, so going beyond it, are to that extent encroachments on the ordinary privileges and rights of the subject, and suspensions of the constitution. But the very term "suspension" shows that the power conferred is but temporary, otherwise it would be synonymous with abrogation. And all parties may wisely agree, as they did in this instance, to a temporary suspension of the people's rights, though there would be none to whom their permanent abrogation would not be intolerable.

The bill, then, for the suppression of the Association passed with universal approval, and it may be regarded as furnishing a model for dealing with similar associations, if ever they should arise. And as soon as it was passed Mr. Peel introduced the greater measure, that for the repeal of the disabilities. In drawing the necessary bill the ministers had had two questions of special importance to consider: firstly, whether it should be unlimited concession which should be granted, such as would throw open to the Roman Catholics every kind of civil office; and, secondly, whether it should be accompanied by any other measure, which might render it more palatable to its adversaries, as diminishing a portion at least of the dangers which those who regarded the question in a purely political light most apprehended. On the first point it was determined that, with the exception of three civil offices, those of the Lord Chancellors of England and Ireland

and the Lord-lieutenant of Ireland,[207] and some of a purely ecclesiastical character, such as the Judge of the Court of Arches, every kind of preferment should be opened to the Roman Catholics.[208] The declaration against Transubstantiation and the oath of supremacy, certain expressions in which were the obstacles which had hitherto kept the Roman Catholics out of office and out of Parliament, were to be repealed, and another to be substituted for them which should merely bind him who took it to defend the King, to maintain the Protestant succession, and to declare that "it was not an article of his faith, and that he renounced, rejected, and abjured the opinion, that princes excommunicated or deposed by the Pope might be deposed and murdered; and that he disclaimed, disavowed, and solemnly abjured any intention to subvert the present Church Establishment as settled by law within this realm, and that he would never exercise any privilege to which he was or might become entitled to disturb or weaken the Protestant religion or Protestant government in this kingdom."[209]

The second question was, it will probably be confessed, even more important. Pitt, who had always contemplated, and had encouraged the Irish Roman Catholics to contemplate, the abolition of their political disabilities as an indispensable appendage to, or, it may be said, part of the Union, had designed, farther, not to confine his benefits to the laymen, but to endow the Roman Catholic clergy with adequate stipends, a proposal which was received with the greatest thankfulness, not only by the Irish prelates and clergy themselves, but also by the heads of their Church at Rome, who were willing, in return, to give the crown a veto on all the ecclesiastical appointments of their Church in the two islands.[210] The justice of granting such an endowment could hardly be contested. The Reformation in Ireland, if what had taken place there could be called a reformation at all, had been wholly different from the movement which had almost extinguished Popery in England. The great majority of the Irish people had never ceased to adhere to the Romish forms, and the Reformation there had been simply a transfer of the property of the Romish Church to the Church of England, unaccompanied by any corresponding change of belief in the people, who had an undeniable right to claim that the state, while making this transfer, should not deprive of all provision the clergy to whose ministrations they still clung with a zeal and steadiness augmented rather than diminished by the discouragements under which they adhered to them.

The policy of granting such endowment was equally conspicuous. No measure could so bind the clergy to the government; and no such security for the loyalty and peaceful, orderly behavior of the poorer classes could be provided, as might be expected from the attachment to the government of those who had over them an influence so powerful in its character and so unbounded in its strength as their priests. And the Duke of Wellington, who had at one time been himself the Irish Secretary, and, as an intimate friend of Lord Castlereagh, who held that office at the time of the Union, had a perfect knowledge of what had been intended at that time—and who was, of course, aware of the very decided favor which the House of Commons had so lately shown to the project—proposed to follow out Pitt's plan in that particular, and to connect a provision[211] for the Roman Catholic clergy with the removal of their political disabilities from the laymen. Unluckily, Peel, who, throughout the whole transaction, was, of all the cabinet, the counsellor on whose judgment he most relied, took a different view of the expediency of making such a provision, having, indeed, "no objection to it in point of principle." But he saw many practical difficulties, which he pressed on the Duke with great earnestness. He argued that for the government "to apply a sum of money to the payment of the ministers of the Church of Rome in Ireland, granting a license for the performance of their spiritual functions, would be a virtual and complete supersession, if not repeal, of the laws which prohibit intercourse with Rome;" and asked, "Could the state affect to be ignorant that the bishop whom it paid derived his right to be a bishop from the See of Rome?" Another difficulty he found in the apprehension that "the admission of the right of the Roman Catholic clergy to an endowment might produce similar claims on the part of the Dissenters in England, who contribute in like manner to the support of their own religion and of the established religion also." He suggested, farther, that, if the Roman Catholic priest were allowed, in addition to his stipend, "to receive dues, Easter offerings, etc., from his parishioners, his condition would then be better than that of the ministers of the Established Church in many of the parishes in Ireland." And, finally, he urged the practical objection, that the endowment would greatly strengthen the opposition to the whole measure, by the reluctance which, "on purely religious grounds," many would feel to the endowment of the Roman Catholic faith, who would yet be inclined to acquiesce in the removal of the disabilities, "on grounds rather political than religious." He was "not insensible to the importance of establishing some bond of connection between the Roman Catholic clergy and the state;" but he believed that the omission of a provision for their endowment "was important to the ultimate success of the government in proposing the measure before them."

    It is not probable that the Duke was greatly influenced by the first, or what may be called the constitutional, objection—that any concert with the Papal Court with respect to the appointments or endowments of its clergy would be a violation of the act which prohibited any intercourse with Rome. The removal of the disabilities required the repeal of one act of Parliament;

and, if the holding communications with Rome on the subject of clerical appointments should be so construed as to require the repeal of another, it would hardly seem that there could be any greater violation of or departure from the principles of the constitution in repealing two acts than in repealing one. As to the second of Peel's objections, the English Dissenters could not possibly be said to stand on the same ground as the Irish Roman Catholics, since their ministers had certainly never been deprived by any act of the state of any provision which they had previously enjoyed; but their position as unendowed ministers was clearly one of their own making. The possible inferiority in point of emolument of some of the Protestant cures in Ireland to that which might be enjoyed by some of the Roman Catholic clergy could hardly be regarded as the foundation of any argument at all, since no law had ever undertaken, or ever could undertake, to give at all times and under all circumstances equal remuneration to equal labors. But the consideration last suggested was exactly the one to influence such a mind as that of the Duke of Wellington, generally contented to deal with a present difficulty. He was determined to carry Emancipation, because he saw that the Clare election had made it impossible to withhold or even to delay it; and, being so determined, he was desirous to avoid encumbering it with any addition which might increase the opposition to it. At the same time he was far from being sanguine of its effect, "with whatever guards or securities it might be accompanied, to pacify the country or to avert rebellion,"[212] which, in his apprehension, was undoubtedly impending; and, under the influence of these combined feelings, he eventually withdrew that clause from the bill. It was accompanied by another bill, disfranchising the forty-shilling freeholders in Ireland. They were a class of voters sunk in the deepest poverty, and such as certainly could not well be supposed capable of forming, much less of exercising, an independent judgment on political matters. Yet this bill is remarkable as having been the only enactment passed since the Revolution to narrow the franchise. It had no opposition to anticipate from English or Scotch members, and was accepted by the Irish members as the price of Emancipation.

No measure that had ever been framed since the Revolution had caused such excitement in the country; but the preponderance of feeling in its favor was equally marked in both Houses of Parliament. In the House of Commons 320 supported it, while only 142 could be marshalled against it. In the House of Lords 213 divided for it against 109. And in April it received the royal assent.

The general policy of removing the disabilities it is not necessary to discuss here. It is quite clear that the Clare election had rendered it impossible to maintain them. And if some of those who judge of measures solely by their effects still denounce this act, as one which has failed in its object of tranquillizing Ireland, many of those who admit the failure ascribe it to the omission to accompany it by one securing a state endowment for the Roman Catholic clergy, pronouncing it, without that appendage, a half measure, such as rarely succeeds, and never deserves success. However that may be, it is certain that the measure, coupled with the repeal of the Test Act of the previous year, was one which made a great and permanent change in the practical working of the constitution of the kingdom, as it had been interpreted for the last one hundred and fifty years. Of that constitution one of the leading features, ever since the Restoration, had been understood to be the establishment and maintenance of the political as well as the ecclesiastical ascendency of the Church of England. On that ascendency the repeal of the Test Act in 1828 had made the first, and that a great, inroad, and the present statute entirely abolished it as a principle of government. So far as political privileges went, every Christian sect was now placed on a footing of complete equality. But so to place them may fairly be regarded as having been required not only by justice and expediency, but by reasons drawn from the history of the nation and from the circumstances under which these disabilities had been imposed. Before the Rebellion no one was excluded from the English Parliament on account of his religion, whether he was a Roman Catholic, a Presbyterian, or a member of any other of the various sects which were gradually arising in the country. It was not till after the Restoration that a recollection of the crimes of the Puritans, when they had got the upper-hand, and the fear of machinations and intrigues, incompatible with the freedom and independence of the people, which were imputed to the Roman Catholics, gave birth to the statutes depriving both Protestant and Roman Catholic Non-conformists of all legislative and political power. The restrictions thus imposed on the Presbyterians and other Protestant sects had, as we have seen, been gradually relaxed by a periodical act of indemnity. Indeed, after the Union with Scotland, it was impossible with any show of consistency to maintain them, since, as it has been already pointed out, after Presbyterianism had been recognized as the established religion of Scotland, it would have seemed strangely unreasonable to regard it as a disqualification on the southern side of the Border. But, as long as the Stuart princes were from time to time disquieting the government by their open invasions or secret intrigues, no such relaxation could with safety be granted to the Roman Catholics, since it could hardly be expected that they would forbear to employ any power which they might acquire for the service of a prince of their own religion. That danger, however, which ever since 1745 had been a very shadowy one, had wholly passed away with the life of the last Stuart lay prince, Charles Edward; and his death left the rulers of the kingdom and advisers of the sovereign free to take a different and larger view of their duty to the nation as a whole.

It was notorious that the number of Non-conformists was large. In the middle of the last century it had received a considerable accession through the institution of the new sect of Wesleyan Methodists; which, through the supineness of the clergy of the Established Church in that generation, had gradually increased, till it was estimated that the various Dissenting sects in England equalled at least half the number of the members of the Established Church. In Wales they were believed to form the majority. In Scotland three-fourths of the people were Presbyterians; and in Ireland the Roman Catholics outnumbered the Protestants in nearly the same proportion. Taking England, Wales, Scotland, and Ireland together, a calculation which reckoned the different sects of Protestant and Roman Catholic Non-conformists united at half the entire population would probably not have erred very widely from the truth.

It must have been the aim of every statesman deserving of the name to weld these different religious parties into one harmonious whole, as far as their civil position went. And measures which had that tendency could not be foreign to the constitution, properly understood. A constitution which confines its benefits to one-half of a nation hardly merits the title of a constitution at all. For every constitution ought to extend its protection and its privileges equally to every portion of the people, unless there be some peculiarity in the principles or habits of any one portion which makes its participation in them dangerous to the rest. It had undoubtedly been the doctrine of Pitt, and of the greater part of those who since his time had held the reins of government, that if any portion of the King's subjects did cherish a temper dangerous to the rest, it was because they were debarred from privileges to which they conceived themselves to have a just right, and that their discontent and turbulence were the fruit of the restrictions imposed on them. In proposing to remove such a grievance Pitt certainly conceived himself to be acting in accordance with the strictest principles of the constitution, and not so much innovating upon it as restoring it to its original comprehensiveness. And so of the measure, as it was now carried, it will apparently be correct to say that, though it did make an important change in the practical working of the constitution, it made it only by reverting to the fundamental principles of civil and religious liberty, to which every subject had a right; which had only been temporarily restrained under the apprehension of danger to the state, and which the cessation of that apprehension made it a duty to re-establish in all their fulness.

But it is by no means clear that in the conduct of the measure the constitution was not violated in one very important point, the proper relation subsisting between a constituency and its representative, by Mr. Peel's resignation of his seat for the University of Oxford. That he was sensible that the act stood in need of explanation is proved by the careful statement of the motives and considerations that determined him to it, which he drew up twenty years afterward. They were of a twofold character. To quote his own words: "When I resolved to advise, and to promote to the utmost of my power, the settlement of that question, I resolved at the same time to relinquish, not only my official station,[213] but the representation of the University of Oxford. I thought that such decisive proofs that I could have no object, political or personal, in taking a course different from that which I had previously taken, would add to my influence and authority, so far, at least, as the adjustment of the particular question at issue was concerned." "I cannot deny that in vacating my seat I was acting upon the impulse of private feelings, rather than upon a dispassionate consideration of the constitutional relations between a representative and his constituents. I will not seek to defend the resolution to which I came by arguments drawn from the peculiar character of the academic body, or from the special nature of the trust confided to its members; still less will I contend that my example ought to be followed by others to whom may be offered the same painful alternative of disregarding the dictates of their own consciences, or of acting in opposition to the opinions and disappointing the expectations of their constituents. I will say no more than that my position was a very peculiar one, that I had many painful sacrifices to make, and that it would have been a great aggravation of them, if it could have said with truth that I was exercising an authority derived from the confidence of the University to promote measures injurious, in her deliberate judgment, either to her own interests or to those of the Church."

No one would willingly censure too severely an act dictated by a sense of honor, even if somewhat overstrained and too scrupulously delicate; but when Mr. Peel speaks of "defending" or not defending his deed, he clearly admits it to be one open to impeachment. And when he forbears to "contend that his example ought to be followed," he seems practically to confess a consciousness that any defence against such impeachment must fail; while the last sentence quoted above involves an assertion that a constituency (in this instance one of the two most important constituencies in the kingdom) could be justified in regarding a measure required by the safety, or at least by the welfare, of the state, as injurious to its own interests; and so far admits a possible severance between the interests of a particular class or body and those of the whole community, which can have no real existence. That, however, is not the point to be investigated here. The charge, as it seems, to which Mr. Peel's deed lays him open is, that by it he lowered the position and character of a member of Parliament from those of a representative to those of a delegate. It was an adoption of the principle laid down for his own guidance by a colleague of Mr. Burke above fifty years before, and indignantly repudiated by that great political philosopher, as proceeding from an entire misapprehension of the rights of a constituency and of a member[214] of Parliament. He told the electors of Bristol that "when they had chosen their member, he was not a member of Bristol, but a member of Parliament; and that if the local constituent should have an interest, or should form an opinion, evidently opposite to the real good of the rest of the community, the member for that place ought to be as far as any other from any endeavor to give it effect;" that a representative "owes to his constituents, not his industry only, but his judgment, and betrays instead of serving them, if he sacrifices it to their opinion." And in so saying he carried with him the concurrence and approval of all his contemporaries whose sentiments on such a question were entitled to weight.

In the States-general of France each member was, by the original constitution of that body, a delegate, and not a representative. He could not even remonstrate against the most oppressive grievance of which the previous instructions of the constituent body had not instructed him to complain; and this limitation of his duties and powers was, undoubtedly, one very principal cause which led to the States-general so rapidly falling into utter disrepute. It was no light thing to take a step which had a tendency to bring down the British Parliament to the level of the despised and long-disused States-general. And it is the more necessary to put the case in a clear and true light, because at the present day there is an evident disposition on the part of constituencies to avail themselves of Peel's conduct in this instance as a precedent, in spite of his protest against its being so regarded, and to fetter their representatives with precise instructions; and a corresponding willingness on the part of candidates to purchase support at elections by a submissive giving of pledges on a variety of subjects, so numerous as to leave themselves no freedom of judgment at all. On the great majority of subjects which come before Parliament, a member of Parliament, if he be a sensible and an honest man, has a far better opportunity of obtaining correct information and forming a sound opinion than can be within reach of any constituency, whose proneness to misjudge is usually in exact proportion to the magnitude of its numbers. Every elector justifiably may, and naturally will, seek to ascertain that between the candidate whom he supports and himself there is a general conformity of opinion; an absolute identity he will never find, and he has no right to ask.[215]

Notes:

[Footnote 182:] £118,776,000. Alison, c. lxxvi.]

[Footnote 183:] See Lord Malmesbury's account of their first interview.—*Diaries of Lord Malmesbury*, iii., 218.]

[Footnote 184:] "Parliamentary Debates," series 2, ii., 632.]

[Footnote 185:] Mr. Brougham gave his opinion that if the Duke of York, or any other member of the royal family, had been named, it would have been offensive to the Queen; but the measure adopted he regarded as of a neutral character. (Mentioned by Lord Liverpool, "Life of Lord Liverpool," iii., 55.)]

[Footnote 186:] "Minutes of Cabinet," dated 10th and 14th February, 1820, forwarded the King by Lord Liverpool ("Life of Lord Liverpool," iii., 35-88).]

[Footnote 187:] "Life of Sir J. Mackintosh," by R.J. Mackintosh, ii., 110, 116.]

[Footnote 188:] "Lives of the Chief-justices," iii., 171.]

[Footnote 189:] In a letter on the subject to Lord Liverpool, the Duke goes the length of calling the proposed bill "an experiment which, should it fail, must entail the dreadful alternative of the entire ruin of the landed interests of the empire, with which he is decidedly of opinion that the nation must stand or fall."—*Life of Lord Liverpool*, iii., 434.]

[Footnote 190:] At one time it was the fashion with writers of the Liberal party to represent Lord Liverpool as led by Lord Castlereagh in the earlier, and by Canning in the later, part of his administration; but Lord Liverpool's correspondence with both these ministers shows clearly that on every subject of foreign as well as of home policy he was the real guide and ruler of his cabinet. Even the recognition of the independence of the South American provinces of Spain—which is so often represented as exclusively the work of Canning—the memorandum on the subject which Lord Liverpool drew up for the cabinet proves that the policy adopted was entirely his own, and that as such he adhered to it resolutely, in spite of the avowed disapproval of the Duke of Wellington and the known unwillingness of the King to sanction it; and it may be remarked (as he and Lord Castlereagh have sometime been described as favoring the Holy Alliance), that the concluding sentence of his letter to the Duke on the subject expresses his hostility, not only to that celebrated treaty, but to the policy which dictated and was embodied in it. (See Lord Liverpool's memorandum for the cabinet and letter to the Duke of Wellington, December 8, 1824.)—*Life of Lord Liverpool*, iii., 297-305.]

[Footnote 191:] See ante, p. 222.]

[Footnote 192:] "With much prudence or laudable disinterestedness," says Hallam ("Constitutional History," ii., 532).]

[Footnote 193:] The last time had been in 1790, when there had been a majority of 187 against it.—*Peel's Memoirs*, i., 99.]

[Footnote 194:] 237 to 193.]

[Footnote 195:] "Peel's Memoirs," i., 68.]

[Footnote 196:] "Wellington's Civil Despatches," iv., 453.]

[Footnote 197:] See his letter to Peel, March 23 ("Peel's Memoirs," i., 92-100).]

[Footnote 198:] The entry of this bill in Cobbett's "Parliamentary History" is: "The House of Commons testified a very extraordinary zeal in unravelling the Popish Plot, and, to prevent mischief in the interval, passed a bill to disable Papists from sitting in either House of Parliament," to which the Lords, when the bill came up to their House, added a proviso exempting the Duke of York from its operation. An. 1678; October 26 to November 21.—*Parliamentary History*, iv., 1024-1039.]

[Footnote 199:] In the House of Commons the majority for Sir F. Burdett's resolution was six—372 to 266. But, in the House of Lords, Lord Lansdowne, moving the same resolution, was defeated by forty-five—182 to 137.]

[Footnote 200:] See Fitzgerald's letter to Peel ("Peel's Memoirs," i., 114).]

[Footnote 201:] "Peel's Memoirs," i., 121.]

[Footnote 202:] See "Lord Anglesey's Letters," *ibid.*, pp. 126, 147.]

[Footnote 203:] As early as the year 1812, on the negotiations (mentioned in a former chapter) for the entrance of Lord Grenville and Lord Grey into the ministry, the Duke of York mentioned to both those noblemen that the Regent had an insuperable objection to the concession of Emancipation. And it seems probable that it was the knowledge of his sentiments on that point that greatly influenced the course which Lord Liverpool subsequently pursued in regard to that question.—See *Life of Lord Liverpool,* i, 381.]

[Footnote 204:] Speech on moving the second reading of the bill in the House of Lords, February 19, 1829 ("Hansard," xx., 389).]

[Footnote 205:] Speech on the first reading of the bill, February 10 ("Hansard," xx., 208).]

[Footnote 206:] Speech on the first reading ("Hansard," xx., 198).]

[Footnote 207:] An amendment was proposed by Lord Chandos to add the office of Prime-minister to these three, on the ground that if a Roman Catholic were Prime-minister "he might have the disposal of all the patronage of the state and the Church vested in his hands." But Mr. Peel pointed out that the law of England "never recognized any such office as that of Prime-minister. In the eyes of the law the ministers were all on an equality." And the position, such as it was, being a conventional one, was not necessarily connected with the office of First Lord of the Treasury. "In a recent instance his late right honorable friend, Mr. Canning, had determined to hold the office of Prime-minister with that of Secretary of State. And when Lord Chatham was Prime-minister, he did not hold the office of First Lord of the Treasury." At the same time he explained that the impropriety of intrusting a Roman Catholic with Church patronage was already guarded against in the bill, a clause of which provided that "it should not be lawful for any person professing the Roman Catholic religion directly or indirectly to advise the crown in any appointment to or disposal of any office or preferment, lay or ecclesiastical, in the united Church of England and Ireland, or of the Church of Scotland."—*Hansard,* xx., 1425.]

[Footnote 208:] Many years afterward the restriction as to the Lord Chancellorship of Ireland was abolished.]

[Footnote 209:] The plan which Pitt had intended to propose was to substitute in lieu of the Sacramental test a political test, to be imposed indiscriminately on all persons sitting in Parliament, or holding state or corporation offices, and also on all ministers of religion, of whatever description, etc., etc. This test was to disclaim in express terms the sovereignty of the people, and was to contain an oath of allegiance and "fidelity to the King's government of the realm, and to the established constitutions of Church and state."—Letter of Lord Grenville, given in *Courts and Cabinets of George III.*, and quoted by Lord Stanhope, *Life of Pitt*, iii., 270. This plan seems very preferable to that now adopted, since it removed every appearance of making a distinction between the professors of the different creeds, when the same oath was to be taken by all indifferently.]

[Footnote 210:] The question had been discussed with the highest Papal authorities more than once since the beginning of the century. In 1812 Mgr. Quarantotti, the prelate who, during the detention of the Pope in France by Napoleon, was invested with the chief authority in ecclesiastical affairs at Rome, in a letter to the Vicar-apostolic, Dr. Poynter, formally announced the consent of the Papal See to give the King a veto on all ecclesiastical appointments within the United Kingdom; and, after his return to Rome, Pio VII. himself confirmed the former title by a second addressed, by his instructions, to the same Dr. Poynter, which letter, in 1816, was read by Mr. Grattan in the House of Commons, it being throughout understood that this concession of the veto to the King was conditional on the abolition of the disabilities and the endowment of the priesthood. And in 1825, after Lord Francis Egerton's resolution had been carried in the House of Commons, Dr. Doyle, one of the most eminent of the Roman Catholic bishops in Ireland, in an examination before a committee of the House of Lords, expressed the willingness of the Roman Catholic clergy to accept a state provision, if it were permanently annexed to each benefice, and accompanied with a concession of an equality of civil rights to the Roman Catholic laity.—See *Life of Lord Liverpool*, ii, 145; *Diary of Lord Colchester, March* 17, 1835, iii., 373; *Peel's Memoirs*, i., 306, 333 *seq.*]

[Footnote 211:] The sum to be thus employed seems to have been intended to be £300,000 a year.—*Peel's Memoirs*, i., 197. On the whole question of the payment and Peel's objections to it, see *ibid.*, pp. 197, 306.]

[Footnote 212:] See his "Civil Despatches," iv., 570. In February, 1829, he said to Lord Sidmouth, "It is a bad business, but we are aground." "Does your Grace think, then," asked Lord Sidmouth, "that this concession will tranquillize Ireland?" "I can't tell; I hope it will," answered the Duke, who shortly discovered, and had the magnanimity to admit, his mistake.—*Life of Lord Sidmouth*, iii., 453. It is remarkable that the question of endowing the Roman Catholic clergy was again considered by Lord John Russell's ministry in 1848. A letter of Prince Albert in October of that year says, with reference to it: "The bishops have protested against Church endowment, being themselves well off; but the clergy would gratefully accept it if offered, but dare not avow this."—*Life of the Prince Consort*, ii., 186.]

[Footnote 213:] This first extract refers in part to the proposal which he made to the Duke to resign his office as Secretary of State, and to support the Emancipation as a private member, a design which he only relinquished at the Duke's earnest entreaty. The second extract refers to the seat in Parliament alone.—See *Peel's Memoirs*, i., 310, 312.]

[Footnote 214:] Speech to the electors of Bristol on being declared by the sheriffs duly elected member for that city, November 3, 1774.—*Burke's Works*, iii., 11, ed 1803.]

[Footnote 215:] It is worth pointing out, however, that, as if it were one of the natural fruits of the Reform Bill, the Liberal Committee of the Livery of London in 1832 passed a series of resolutions asserting the principle of delegation without the slightest modification; one resolution affirming "that members chosen to be representatives in Parliament ought to do such things as their constituents wish and direct them to do;" another, "that a signed engagement should be exacted from every member that he would at all times and in all things act conformably to the wishes of a majority of his constituents, or would at their request resign the trust with which they had honored him."—*Annual Register*, 1832, p. 300; *quoted by Alison*, 2d series, v., 355.]

CHAPTER IX

Demand for Parliamentary Reform.—Death of George IV., and Accession of William IV.—French Revolution of 1830.—Growing Feeling in Favor of Reform.—Duke of Wellington's Declaration against Reform.—His Resignation: Lord Grey becomes Prime-minister.—Introduction of the Reform Bill.—Its Details.—Riots at Bristol and Nottingham.—Proposed Creation of Peers.—The King's Message to the Peers.—Character and Consequences of the Reform Bill.—Appointment of a Regency.—Re-arrangement of the Civil List.

One of Pitt's great measures of domestic, apart from financial or commercial, policy having become law, it seemed in some degree natural to look for the accomplishment of the other, a reform of the House of Commons, which, indeed, after the conclusion of the war, had been made at times the subject of earnest petition, being one in which a far greater number of people had a lively interest than that excited by Catholic Emancipation. The Englishmen who had advocated that measure had been striving for the adoption of a principle rather than for a concession from which they could expect any personal benefit, since very few in any English or Scotch constituency were Roman Catholics, or desired to return a Roman Catholic representative. But thousands in every county, including the whole body of citizens of some of the largest and most flourishing towns, felt a personal concern in the attainment of Parliamentary Reform, as the measure which would give them, and which could alone give them, that voice in the affairs of the kingdom to which they felt themselves entitled, but which they had never yet enjoyed.

And before the end of the next session the prospect of the early success of their aspirations was greatly increased by the death of the King. George IV., who in his early manhood had attached himself to the Whigs with an ardor and ostentation altogether unbecoming his position as heir to the throne, had formally separated himself from them after the death of Fox in 1806, and had gradually come to regard their adversaries with a favor as exclusive as he had formerly shown to themselves. But the Duke of Clarence, who now succeeded to the throne, had always shown a leaning toward the Whigs, who of late had been commonly regarded as the reforming party. While the war lasted, and during the few remaining years of the reign of George III., no active steps toward Reform were taken in Parliament; but under George IV. more than one borough convicted of gross and habitual corruption, as has been mentioned, was disfranchised. Grampound was so punished in the time of Lord Liverpool, and its members were transferred to Yorkshire, so as to give that largest of the counties four representatives; and it may be remarked that this arrangement caused the Prime-minister to suggest an improvement in the details of an election—which was afterward universally adopted—when, in reply to a remark on the great inconvenience that was found to exist in taking the poll at once in so large a county as Yorkshire, he hinted at the possibility of obviating that difficulty by allowing polls to be taken in different parts of the county. And, since the Duke had been in office, two more boroughs, Penrhyn and East Retford, had also been disfranchised; though the Reformers failed in their endeavor to get the seats thus vacated transferred to Manchester and Birmingham. With the accession of the new sovereign, however, they became more active. They found encouragement in other circumstances also. Many of those who were commonly called the Ultra Tories had been so alienated from the Duke's government by the Emancipation Act, that they were known to be ready to coalesce with almost any party for the sake of overturning his administration. Moreover, as forty years before, the French Revolution of 1789 had caused great political excitement in England, so now the new French revolution of July acted as a strong stimulus on the movement party in this as well as in other countries; and altogether there was a very general feeling that the time for important changes had come. The Duke of Wellington was not blind to the prevalence of the idea; and, being by no means willing to admit that his own policy of the preceding year had in the least contributed to strengthen it, he conceived it to be his duty to discountenance it by every means in his power; but the steps which he took with that object only invigorated and inflamed it. As Prime-minister, he inserted in the speech with which the new sovereign opened his first Parliament in the autumn after his accession a general panegyric on that "happy form of government under which, through the favor of Divine Providence, this country had enjoyed for a long succession of years a greater share of internal peace, of commercial prosperity, of true liberty, of all that constitutes social happiness, than had fallen to the lot of any other country of the world." And in his own character, a few nights afterward, he added a practical commentary on those sentences of the royal speech, when, in allusion to Lord Grey's expression of a hope that the ministers would prepare "to redress the grievances of the people by a reform of the Parliament," he repudiated the suggestion altogether, avowing that the government were contemplating no such measure, and adding that "he would go farther, and say that he had never read or heard of any measure up to that moment which in any degree satisfied his mind that the state of the representation could be improved or rendered more satisfactory to the country at large than at that moment. He was fully convinced that the country possessed at that moment a Legislature which answered all good purposes of legislation to a greater degree than any Legislature had ever answered them in any country whatever.... And he would at once declare that, as far as he was concerned, as long as he held any station in the government of the country, he should always feel it his duty to resist any measure of Reform when proposed by others."

Such uncompromising language was, not unnaturally, regarded by the Opposition in both Houses as a direct defiance, and the challenge was promptly taken up both in and out of Parliament. It happened that at this moment the ministry was extremely unpopular in the City; not, indeed, on account of his hostility to Reform, but in consequence of the recent introduction by the Home-secretary of a police force in London, on the model of one which the Duke himself, when Irish Secretary, had established in Dublin. The old watchmen had been so notoriously inefficient that it might have been expected that the change would have been hailed with universal approval and gratitude, but it met with a very different reception. Many of the newspapers which had not yet forgiven the passing of Catholic Emancipation made it a ground for the strongest imputations on the Duke himself, some of them even going the length of affirming that he aimed at the throne, and that the organization of this new force was the means on which he reckoned for the attainment of his object. No story is too gross for the credulity of the populace. To hear of such a plot was to believe it; to believe it was to resolve to defeat it; and at the beginning of November the government received several warnings that a plan was in agitation to raise a formidable riot on Lord Mayor's Day, when the King and the Duke himself were expected to dine with the Lord Mayor. The Lord Mayor even wrote to the Duke to suggest the prudence of his coming "strongly and sufficiently guarded," and the result of this advice was certainly strange. The Duke cared little enough about personal danger to himself, but he regarded himself as specially bound by his office to watch over the public tranquillity, and to do nothing that might be expected to endanger it. He was at least equally solicitous that a new reign should not open with a tumult which could in any way be regarded as an insult to the King; and, under the influence of these feelings, he took the responsibility of giving the King the unprecedented advice of abandoning his intention of being present at the Guildhall banquet. Such a step had an inevitable tendency to weaken the ministry still farther by the comments which it provoked. Even his own brother, Lord Wellesley, did not spare his sarcasms, pronouncing it "the boldest act of cowardice he had ever heard of;" while the Reformers ascribed the unpopularity which it confessed to the Duke's declaration against any kind or degree of Reform; and, to test the correctness of this opinion, Mr. Brougham, who, in the House of Commons, was the most eloquent champion of Reform, gave notice of a motion on the subject for the 16th of November. Before that day came, however, the ministry had ceased to exist. On the preceding evening it had been defeated on a proposal to refer to a select committee the consideration of the Civil List, a new settlement of which was indispensable at the beginning of a new reign, and on the morning of the 16th the Duke resigned, not only advising the King to intrust the formation of the new cabinet to Lord Grey—who was universally recognized as the head of the Whig party—but recommending his Majesty also to be prepared to consent to a measure of moderate Reform, which, though he could not bring himself to co-operate in it, he was satisfied that the temper of the House of Commons, if not of the people out-of-doors also, rendered unavoidable.[216] The advice was taken. Lord Grey had no difficulty in forming a ministry in which the Whigs were aided by the junction of several of the more moderate Tories, who had regarded Canning as their leader; and from the very beginning Parliamentary Reform was proclaimed to be the one great object of his government. It would be more correct to call it a Reform of the House of Commons, since there was no idea of interfering with the House of Lords, even in those parts of it which were of a representative character, the Scotch and Irish peers. But, by whatever title the ministerial policy was designated, no one misunderstood what was intended; and as Parliament was, after a few days, adjourned over the Christmas holidays, the recess was spent by a sub-committee of the cabinet in framing a measure.

The great extension of our trade, which was the fruit partly of his wise commercial policy, and partly of the long war; the rapid and prodigious growth of our manufactures, developed by the inventive ingenuity of our mechanics and engineers, had given a consideration and influence to the commercial, manufacturing, and moneyed classes which could not be disregarded. The land-owners, who had previously almost monopolized the representation, no longer constituted the wealthiest class of the community. Pitt himself had raised a banker to the peerage. More recently, men closely connected with the commercial classes had become cabinet ministers, one of whom had even subsequently sacrificed office to his feeling of the propriety of enfranchising a single town, Birmingham. But there were other towns at least equal in importance to Birmingham which were unrepresented, and it was clearly impossible to maintain a system which gave representatives to boroughs like Gatton, Old Sarum, or Corfe Castle—where the electors scarcely outnumbered the members whom they elected—and withheld them from large and opulent manufacturing centres like Manchester, Leeds, and Sheffield. The enfranchisement, therefore, of these towns, and of others whose population and consequent importance, though inferior to theirs, was still vastly superior to those of many which had hitherto returned representatives, was so manifestly reasonable and consistent with the principles of our parliamentary constitution, that it was impossible to object to it. And their enfranchisement unavoidably led to the disfranchisement of the smaller boroughs, unless the House of Commons were to be enlarged to a number which was not likely to tend to the facilitation of business. Indeed, in the opinion of the framers of the bill, the House was *already too large*, and they proposed to reduce its number by upward of sixty—a step to which it is probable that many of those whose opposition contributed to defeat it subsequently repented of their resistance. Nevertheless, the line adopted by the Duke of Wellington's ministry showed that there was still a large party to whom reform on a large scale was altogether distasteful; and accordingly the bill which, under the influence of these considerations, Lord Grey's administration brought forward in the spring of 1831, gave rise to the fiercest struggles in both Houses of Parliament that had been witnessed for many generations. One Parliament was dissolved; two sessions of that which followed were opened in a single year; once the ministry itself was dissolved, though speedily reconstructed; and three bills were framed, each in some degree differing from its predecessor in some of its details, though all preserved the same leading principles of disfranchising wholly or partially the smaller boroughs; of enfranchising several large and growing towns; of increasing the number of county representatives; and of enfranchising also some classes which previously had had no right of voting. It would be a waste of time to specify the variations in the three bills. It is sufficient to confine our attention to that which eventually became law. Fifty-six boroughs were wholly disfranchised; those in which the population fell short of a certain number (2000), and where the amount of assessed taxes paid by the inhabitants was correspondingly small. Thirty more were deprived of one of their members, being those in which the population was between 2000 and 4000. And the seats thus vacated were divided between the towns which since the Revolution had gradually grown into importance, the suburbs of the metropolis, and the counties, the majority of which were now divided into two halves, each half returning two members, as many as had previously represented the whole. The boundaries of the boroughs, too, were in most cases extended.

More important, perhaps, in its influence on subsequent legislation was the alteration made in the qualifications which constituted an elector. Hitherto the franchise, the right of voting at elections, had been based on property. The principle had not, indeed, been uniformly adhered to in the boroughs, where, as Lord John Russell, in the speech with which he introduced the bill, pointed out, a curious variety of courses had been adopted. "In some," as he described the existing practice, "the franchise was exercised by 'a select corporation;' that is to say, it was in the possession of a small number of persons, to the exclusion of the great body of the inhabitants who had property and interest in the place represented. In ancient times, he believed, every freeman, being an inhabitant householder resident in the borough, was competent to vote. As, however, this arrangement excluded villeins and strangers, the franchise always belonged to a particular body in every town—a body undoubtedly possessed of property, for they bore the charges of their members, and on them were assessed the subsidies and taxes voted by Parliament. But when villeinage ceased, various and opposite courses seemed to have been pursued in different boroughs. In some, adopting the liberal principle that all freemen were to be admitted, householders of all kinds, down to the lowest degree, and even sometimes beyond, were admitted. In others, adopting the exclusive principle that villeins and strangers were no part of the burgesses, new corporations were erected, and the elective franchise was more or less confined to a select body." But all these diversities and varieties were now swept away, and a uniform franchise was established, all tenants whose rent amounted to £10 receiving the franchise in boroughs, while by a kindred amendment, which was forced on the ministers at a very early stage of the measure, tenants at will whose tent amounted to £50 became entitled to vote in the counties.

The arrangements for taking the poll were also greatly changed. Instead of the fifteen days which had of late been allowed for a county election, two were now thought sufficient.[217] In boroughs the time was abridged in a similar proportion, and the arrangement was facilitated by a division of counties into several convenient polling districts, so that no elector should require to travel more than a few miles to record his vote.

This last change was universally accepted as a great practical improvement, from its tendency to lessen the expense of election contests, which had risen to an enormous and ruinous height. But every other part of the scheme was viewed with the greatest repugnance, not to say dread, by the Opposition; and every one of the bills was fought step by step in the House of Commons. The first bill was only carried by a majority of one; the second was absolutely rejected by the House of Lords; and on the third the ministers, after carrying it triumphantly through the Lower House, were defeated in the Upper House on a point of detail, which, though of no great importance in itself, they regarded as an indication that the peers, though they had consented to read it a second time, would insist on remodelling it to a great degree, and, if they were not allowed to do so, would again reject it altogether.

Meanwhile, the people were wrought up to a pitch of frenzy absolutely unprecedented. Never had agitators, among whom some of the ministers themselves were not ashamed to appear, been so unscrupulous in their endeavors to excite discontent. One cabinet minister wrote inflammatory articles in the newspapers; another publicly called the legitimate opposition of the peers "the whisper of a faction." And their exertions soon bore fearful fruit. In London some of the peers who had been most prominent in their objections to the bill were hooted and pelted, and one, Lord Londonderry, was nearly murdered. The King and Queen were insulted by mobs in the Park, some of the rioters even openly threatening the Queen with death, because she was believed to be favorable to the anti-Reformers. In some of the most important provincial towns the discontent broke out into actual insurrection. At Bristol a tumultuous mob, whose numbers were swelled by crowds of the worst ruffians of the metropolis, sought to murder the Recorder, Sir Charles Wetherall, when he came down to that city to hold the quarter-sessions; and, when defeated in their attack on him, stormed the Mansion House, and set it, with the Bishop's Palace and other public buildings, and scores of private houses, on fire, several of the rioters themselves, who had got drunk, perishing in the flames. A similar mob rose in arms at Derby, but did less mischief, as there the magistrates knew their duty better. But Nottingham almost equalled Bristol in its horrors. Because the Duke of Newcastle was a resolute anti-Reformer, a ferocious gang attacked and set on fire the fine old Castle; and, not content with committing fearful ravages in the town, roamed over the adjacent district, attacked the houses of many of the leading country gentlemen, plundering and burning the dwellings, and in more than one instance murdering some of the inhabitants.

The King had hitherto borne himself between the contending parties in the state with scrupulous fairness to both. Though, he had, probably, been taken by surprise by the sweeping character of the changes his ministers had proposed, he had given them a frank support, consenting, even at a moment's notice, to dissolve the Parliament after the unfavorable division in the House of Commons on the first bill; but he had, at the same time, warned them that he would never consent to employ any means of coercion to overbear the free decision of the House of Lords. And he had more than once rejected as unconstitutional their solicitations to allow them to make peers with that object. At last they endeavored to compel his consent by resigning their offices, though the ground for so decided a step can hardly be deemed sufficient, since the provocation which they alleged was only Lord Lyndhurst's success in carrying an amendment to take the enfranchising clauses of the bill before those of disfranchisement, so as to give the latter a more gracious appearance, as if the boroughs to be extinguished were made to suffer, not so much for their own positive unworthiness as in order to make room for others which had become of undeniably greater importance. The King took the strictly constitutional line of accepting their resignation and intrusting the Duke of Wellington with the task of forming a new administration, warning the Duke, at the same time, that he considered himself now pledged to grant a large measure of Reform; but the Duke found the task impracticable, and then, as the only means of averting farther insurrectionary tumults, which bore no slight resemblance to civil war, and might not impossibly end in it, the King did at last consent to permit the creation of a sufficient number of peers to insure the passing of the bill. But he could not overcome his repugnance to the measure as a severe blow to the constitution—one which would in effect be tantamount to the extinction of the independence of the Upper House as a legislative body; and, thinking no means unjustifiable that would avert the necessity of such a creation, he conceived the idea of authorizing his private secretary, Sir Herbert Taylor, to request the chief peers on the Opposition side to absent themselves from the division on the third reading. It seemed to him, and indeed to many of them, the only thing that could be done. Their judgment of the character and eventual consequences of the ministerial bill was unaltered; but they saw the violence of the public feeling on the subject, and the danger to the state of too stubborn and uncompromising a resistance to it, and, yielding loyal obedience to their royal master's wish, they retired from the House without voting. Those who remained passed the bill, and in the beginning of June, 1832, it became law.

We have ventured in a previous chapter to call in question the propriety of the conduct of the King's father, George III., in using his personal entreaties to influence the House of Lords against the India Bill of Mr. Fox. The transaction which has been related here is the second and only other instance since the Revolution of a sovereign having recourse to such a device to sway the votes of members of either House. But the circumstances were so entirely different, nay, so diametrically opposite, that an opinion of the impropriety of the sovereign's deed in the former case imposes no obligation on the ground of consistency to censure it in the later instance. The interference of George III. was designed to thwart and defeat his ministers on a measure of which he had not previously intimated any disapproval. William IV., on the other hand, was exerting himself to support his ministers, not, as it seems probable, without some sacrifice of his own judgment. His father acted as he did to avert an inroad on his prerogative and independence, which he had been persuaded to apprehend, but the danger of which can hardly be said to have been proved beyond all question; so that even those who think the result of his action fortunate for the nation cannot defend the action as one that on any constitutional principle can be justified. The son, at a far more critical moment, adopted the course which he did adopt as the only means which he saw of extricating the state and the nation from an alternative of great calamities: the extinction of, or at least a deep wound to, the legislative independence of the House of Lords, by the following of a single precedent[218] which had ever since been universally condemned; or, on the other hand, a continuance of outrages and tumults which had already disgraced the nation in the eyes of the world, and which, if renewed and continued, could not fail to imperil the safety of the state. Such a motive may certainly be allowed to excuse the irregularity of the act.

When, however, we come to consider the proposal to create peers, which drove the King to take such a step, that is a question on which, while it is still more important, it is also more difficult to form a satisfactory judgment. It was denounced by the Duke of Wellington and other peers as utterly unconstitutional and revolutionary; as a destruction of the great principle of the equality of the two Houses; as a denial to the peers of their right to form and act upon their own deliberate judgment; and as a reduction of their position to that of a body existing merely to register the decrees of the other House. Indeed, that it had this character was admitted by Lord Grey himself, with no abatement beyond such mitigation as might be found in the idea that it was only intended to affect their decision on a single question. So far it may be said that even while defending it he condemned it; *Habemus confitentem reum*. But the task of a ruler or legislator is often but a choice between difficulties, or even between manifest evils. And, even if an act or course be admitted to be intrinsically evil, taken by itself, yet, if the evil which it is calculated or designed to avert be a greater evil still, the defence is complete, or, at all events, sufficient. And this, in fact, is the principle of the justification which Lord Grey alleged. He was, perhaps, unconsciously referring to a passage in Mr. Hallam's great work on "Constitutional History" (then very recently published), in which, while discussing Sunderland's Peerage Bill, and admitting that "the unlimited prerogative of augmenting the peerage is liable to such abuses, at least in theory, as might overthrow our form of government," he proceeds to point out that in the exercise of this, as of every other power, "the crown has been carefully restrained by statutes, and by the responsibility of its advisers;"

but that, while "the Commons, if they transgress their boundaries, are annihilated by a proclamation" (that is, by a dissolution) "against the ambition, or, what is much more likely, the perverse haughtiness of the aristocracy, the constitution has not furnished such direct securities.... The resource of subduing an aristocratical faction by the creation of new peers could never be constitutionally employed, except in the case of a nearly equal balance; but it might usefully hang over the heads of the whole body, and deter them from any gross excesses of faction or oligarchical spirit. The nature of our government requires a general harmony between the two Houses of Parliament."[219] In the present case no one could impute the difference between the two Houses to any "perverse haughtiness" on the part of the peers. But the difference existed, and was too deeply founded on the cautious principles of the Tory party to be surmountable by ordinary means. It was certain also that the Commons would not give way; that, without danger to the public peace, they could not give way. And this was, in fact, Lord Grey's contention: that a crisis had arisen in which compulsion must be exercised on one or other of the disagreeing parties; and that coercion of the peers by an augmentation of their number, or a threat of it, was the only compulsion practicable. In upholding this position, however, it must be remarked that he was betrayed into the use of language which was as great a violation of constitutional and parliamentary principle and usage as the action which he was recommending; language, too, which was quite unnecessary to strengthen his argument. He accused the Lords of "opposing the declared and decided wishes both of the crown and the people;" of "acting adversely to the crown;" and this introduction of the sovereign's name to overawe the assembly was unconstitutional in the highest degree. For, constitutionally, the sovereign has no right to signify his opinion, nor, indeed, any recognized means of signifying it but by giving or withholding his royal assent to measures which the two Houses have passed. On any bill which has not yet been passed by them he has, as has been already implied, no legitimate means whatever of expressing his judgment. The time has not come for him to do so. Moreover, the statement was, probably, not believed by any one to be strictly true, for it was pretty generally understood that the King would have preferred a far more moderate measure. But, indeed, in the very speech in which the Prime-minister made this use of the King's name he presently added an observation which was a sufficient condemnation of his previous language. For, in denouncing the "vile attacks which had been made on his Majesty in the public press," and disclaiming all share in them (a disclaimer which however true of himself, could not, it is believed, have been uttered with equal truth by all his colleagues), he pointed out that "it ought always to be recollected that it is contrary to the principles of the constitution to arraign the personal conduct of the sovereign." It follows, as a matter of course, that it is equally contrary to those principles to allege his personal opinions in either House on any measure before it, since, if alleged, they must be open to criticism; unless, indeed, the mere allegation of the royal sentiments were to be taken as decisive of the question, in which case all freedom of discussion would be at once extinguished.

But this irregularity, into which the Prime minister was apparently betrayed by his desire of victory, must not be allowed to affect our verdict on the main question; and, now that the lapse of time has enabled us to contemplate dispassionately the case on which he had to decide, it will, probably, be thought that his justification of his conduct in recommending a creation of peers is fairly made out. That, under any pressure short of that, the peers would have again rejected the Reform Bill, or at least would have pared it down to much smaller proportions than would have satisfied the popular demand for Reform, may be regarded as certain; and equally certain that such a line of conduct would have led to a renewal of disgraceful and dangerous tumults. The minister, therefore, as has been said before, had to choose between two evils. It was a grievous dilemma; but those who had to deal with it (even while it may be admitted that they cannot be held wholly free from blame, as having themselves contributed by their own language to the popular excitement and irritation)[220] may be excused for thinking the wound inflicted on the constitution, by thus overbearing the voice of one House of Parliament on a single occasion, less formidable in its immediate fruit, and more capable of being remedied and retrieved, than that which would have followed from a renewal of insurrectionary tumults, even if they should have come short of actual civil war.

One critic of these transactions[221] whose experience and high reputation entitle his opinion to respectful consideration, after reminding his readers that, "although Parliament is said to be dissolved, a dissolution extends, in fact, no farther than to the Commons, and that the Peers are not affected by it; no change can take place in the constitution of their body, except as to a small number of Scotch representative peers," proceeds to argue that, "so far as the House of Peers is concerned, a creation of peers by the crown on extraordinary occasions is the only equivalent which the constitution has provided for the change and renovation of the House of Commons by a dissolution. In no other way can the opinions of the House of Lords be brought into harmony with those of the people." But it may be feared that this comparison is rather ingenious than solid. Indeed, the writer himself limits such an expedient as a creation of peers to insure the passing of a particular measure to "extraordinary occasions." But a dissolution of the House of Commons is so far from being so limited, that it is the natural and inevitable end of every House of Commons after an existence which cannot exceed seven years, and which is very rarely so protracted. And though it may be, and probably has been, the case that a House of Commons has passed measures to which it had no great inclination, lest it should provoke a minister to a premature dissolution, yet no submission on its part can long postpone it; and a threat or apprehension of a dissolution would certainly fail to overcome the opposition of the House of Commons, or of a party within it, if the measure before them seemed open to serious objection. The presumed or presumable immortality of the one body, and the limited existence of the other, seem to constitute so essential a difference between them as must prevent the measures adopted toward one being fairly regarded as any guide to a justification of those employed in the case of the other.

The Reform Bill of 1832 has sometimes been called a new Revolution, and to some extent it deserved the name; for it was not, like the Catholic Emancipation Act, a mere restoration of privileges to any class or classes of the people which had once been enjoyed by them, and had subsequently been withdrawn, but it was a grant of a wholly new privilege to places and to classes which had never enjoyed it; while it was manifest that the political power thus conferred on these classes involved a corresponding diminution of the powers of those who had hitherto monopolized it. It was also the introduction of a new principle. The old doctrine of the constitution had been, that the possession of freehold property, as the only permanent stake in the country, was the only qualification which could entitle a subject to a voice in the government and legislation of the kingdom. The new doctrine was that, as others besides owners of land contributed to the revenue by the payment of taxes, those who did so contribute to a sufficient amount had a right to a voice, however indirect or feeble, in the granting of those taxes; and so far it was the extension and application to subjects at home of the principle for which Lord Chatham and Burke had contended sixty years before in the case of the American Colonies, that taxation and a right to representation went together; a principle which, many ages before, had been laid down by the greatest of our early kings as the foundation of our parliamentary constitution and rights. But this principle, however generally it may have been asserted, had hitherto been but very partially carried out in practice, and the old borough system had been skilfully devised by successive kings and ministers to keep the political power in the hands of the crown and the aristocracy. It was with that object that most of the boroughs which were first allowed to return members under the Tudors had been enfranchised,[222] a great noble or landholder, whose affection to the government could not be doubted, being often able to obtain the promotion of some village or petty town in the neighborhood of his estates to the dignity of a parliamentary borough, and thus acquiring a great addition to his political and social importance by his power of influencing the election. No one could deny that the existence of such boroughs was an abuse, or at least an anomaly, rendered the more conspicuous as time went on by the denial of representatives to towns which contained as many thousands of citizens as they could boast single burgesses. At the same time it was equally undeniable that the aristocracy, generally speaking, exerted their influence advantageously for the state. A peer or great squire who could return the members for a borough took a worthy pride in the abilities and reputation of those whom he thus sent to Parliament; especially the leaders of the two parties sought out promising young men for their seats; and it has often been pointed out that, of the men who in the House of Commons had risen to eminence in the country before the Reform Bill, there was scarcely one who had not owed his introduction to Parliament to the patron of one of those boroughs which were now wholly or partially disfranchised; while on one or two occasions these "rotten boroughs," as, since Lord Chatham's time, they were often derisively called, had proved equally useful in providing seats for distinguished statesmen who, for some reason or other, had lost the confidence of their former constituents. So, when Bristol had disgraced itself by the rejection of Burke, Malton had averted the loss with which Parliament and the country were threatened by again, through the influence of Lord Rockingham, returning the great statesman as their representative. So, to take a later instance, Westbury, under the influence of Sir Manasseh Lopes, had provided a refuge for Sir Robert Peel, when the course which he had taken on Catholic Emancipation had cost him his seat for Oxford. And these practical uses of these small boroughs—anomalies in a representative system, as they were called in the debates on the subject, and as they must be confessed to have been—were so important, that some even of those who felt compelled by their principles to vote for their parliamentary extinction have, nevertheless, confessed a regret for the sacrifice, lamenting especially that it has, in a great degree, closed the doors of the House of Commons against a class whose admission to it is on every account most desirable, the promising young men of both parties.

In one point of great importance the framers of the Reform Bill of 1832 proved to be mistaken. They justified the very comprehensive or sweeping range which they had given it by their wish to make it a final settlement of the question, and by the expression of their conviction that the completeness with which it had satisfied all reasonable expectations had effectually prevented any necessity for ever re-opening the question. Their anticipations on this head were not shared by their opponents, who, on the contrary, foretold that the very greatness of the changes now effected would only whet the appetite for a farther extension of them; nor by a growing party, now beginning to own the title of Radicals, which till very recently had only been regarded as a reproach, and who, even before the bill passed,[223] expressed their discontent that it did not go farther, but accepted it as an instalment of what was required, and as an instrument for securing "a more complete improvement." And their expectations have been verified by subsequent events. Indeed, it may easily be seen that the principles on which one portion of the bill—that which enfranchised new classes of voters—was framed were such as, in shrewd hands, might easily be adduced as arguments in favor of the necessity of reconsideration of the question from time to time. So long as the right of voting was confined to owners of property, or members of corporate bodies, the line thus laid down was one which was not liable to be crossed. But the moment that tenancy was added to ownership, and a line was drawn distinguishing electors from non-electors, not by the nature of their qualifications, but by the amount of their rent, detail was substituted for principle; and the proposer or maintainer of the rule that the qualification should be a yearly rental of £10 might be called on to explain why, if £10 were a more reasonable limit than £15, £8 were not fairer than £10. Or again, if the original argument were, that a line must of necessity be drawn somewhere, and that £10 was the lowest qualification which seemed to guarantee such an amount of educated intelligence in the voter as would enable him to exercise the franchise conferred on him judiciously and honestly, such reasoning would from time to time invite the contention that the spread of education had rendered £8 tenants now as enlightened as £10 tenants had been some years before. And thus the measure of 1832, instead of forever silencing the demand for Reform by the completeness of its concessions, did in fact lay the foundation for future agitation, which has been farther encouraged and fed by farther submission to it, and which its leaders, who have so far triumphed, show no purpose to discontinue. To discuss whether such extensions of the franchise as have already been adopted, and those farther steps in the same direction which are generally understood to be impending, will eventually be found compatible with the preservation of our ancient monarchical constitution, is a fitting task for the statesmen and senators whose duty it is to examine in all their bearings the probable effects of the measures which may be proposed. But the historian's business is rather "to compile the records of the past" than to speculate on the future.[224] And the course which was too perilous or difficult for Mr. Hallam to undertake we will follow his example in avoiding. But it cannot be denied that, if the Reform Bill of 1832 transferred the chief political power of the state from the aristocracy to the middle classes, a farther lowering of the qualification for the exercise of the franchise must transfer it from the middle to the lower classes; and that those who view such transfer with alarm, and deprecate it as fraught with peril to all our ancient institutions, maintain their opinions by arguments as old, indeed, as the days of the Roman republic,[225] but which have not lost strength by lapse of time, if indeed, they have not been fortified by events in the history of more than one modern nation.

Even before the introduction of the first Reform Bill one measure had been passed of constitutional importance, though the concurrence of both parties in its principle and details prevented it from attracting much notice. Two daughters who had been born to the King and Queen had died in their infancy, and the royal pair were now childless; and, as some years had elapsed since the birth of the last, it was probable that they might remain so. The presumptive heiress to the throne was, therefore, the daughter of the deceased Duke of Kent, the Princess Victoria, our present most gracious sovereign, and, as she was as yet only eleven years of age, it was evidently necessary to provide for the contingency of the death of the King before she should attain her majority. A Regency Bill for that purpose had, therefore, been prepared by the Duke of Wellington's cabinet, and had been introduced by Lord Chancellor Lyndhurst in the House of Lords before the resignation of the ministry. It could not be so simple in its arrangements as such bills had sometimes been, since there was more than one contingency possible, for which it was requisite to provide. It was possible not only that William IV. might die within the next seven years, but also that at his death he might leave a child, or his widow in a state which warranted the expectation of one, the latter case being the more difficult to decide upon, since no previous Regency Bill furnished any precedent for the ministers' guidance.

The first point, however, to be settled was, who was the most proper person to administer the affairs of the kingdom as Regent, in the event of the heiress to the crown being still a minor at the King's death. It was a question on which it was evidently most desirable that no difference of opinion should be expressed. And, in fact, no difference existed. The leaders of both parties—the Duke and his colleagues, who had framed the bill, and Lord Grey, with his colleagues, who adopted it—agreed that the mother of the young sovereign would be the fittest person to exercise the royal authority during the minority; and, farther, that she should neither be fettered by any limitations to that authority, nor by any councillors appointed by Parliament nominally to advise and assist, but practically to control her. It was felt that a Regent acting for a youthful daughter would need all the power which could be given her; while, as she could never herself succeed to the throne, she could be under no temptation, from views of personal ambition, to misuse the power intrusted to her.

At first sight it seemed a more difficult and delicate question what course should be pursued with reference to the possible event of the King dying while the Queen, his widow, was expecting to become a mother. As has been said above, no precedent was to be found in any former bill; yet it seemed to be determined by the old constitutional maxim, that the King never dies. Not even for a moment could the throne be treated as vacant, and, therefore, it was proposed and determined that in such a case the Princess Victoria must instantly be proclaimed Queen, and the Duchess of Kent must instantly assume the authority of Regent; but that, on the birth of a posthumous child to the Queen Dowager, the Princess and the Duchess, as a matter of course, should resume their previous rank, and Queen Adelaide become Regent, and govern in the name of her new-born infant and sovereign. The strict constitutional correctness of the principle elaborately and eloquently expounded to the peers by Lord Lyndhurst was unanimously admitted, and the precedent now set was followed, with the needful modification, when, ten years afterward, it became necessary to provide for the possibility of Queen Victoria dying during the minority of her heir. The parent of the infant sovereign, Prince Albert, was appointed Regent, with the cordial approval of the nation; the dissent of the Queen's uncle, the Duke of Sussex who, with a very misplaced ambition, urged instead the appointment of a Council of Regency, of which he hoped to become the most influential member, only serving to make the unanimity of the rest of the Parliament more conspicuous.

A somewhat kindred question, inasmuch as it affected the personal arrangements, if they may be so termed, of the sovereign, was settled in the same session, and on a new principle. What was called the Civil List had hitherto been placed on a footing which was at once unintelligible and misleading. The expression was first used at the Revolution, and was applied not only to that portion of the revenue which was devoted to the personal expenses of the sovereign, but also to many branches of the civil expenditure of the state, with which, in fact, he had no concern whatever. Not only the salaries of the great officers of the household, but those also of the ministers, ambassadors, and of the judges, were paid out of it, as well as those of many place-holders of various classes, and pensions to a large amount. Amounts embracing such a variety of miscellaneous and unconnected expenses could hardly be expected to be kept with regularity, and there was lavish waste in every department. Burke's bill had rectified some of the abuses, and had also pointed out the way to some other reforms which were gradually adopted; but still numbers of charges were left untouched, and there was scarcely any one subject which afforded more topics to unscrupulous demagogues than the amount of the Civil List, which the ignorant multitude were constantly assured that the King enjoyed to squander on his own pleasures, though, in fact, the greater part of it was expended in the service of the state, and was entirely free from his control. Only a portion of the sum which went under this name was voted annually by the Parliament. A portion was derived from the Crown Lands, from duties known as Droits of the Crown and Droits of the Admiralty, etc., the amount of which fluctuated, and with which Parliament was admitted to have no right to interfere. But the working of the whole was satisfactory to no one—neither to the King himself, nor to those who upheld the right of the Parliament to have a predominant control of every branch of expenditure of the public money. The feeling that the whole of the royal income and expenditure should be placed on a different footing was general, and the fall of the Duke of Wellington's ministry had been immediately caused by the success of a proposal that, before fixing the new sovereign's Civil List, Parliament should refer the matter to a committee, that inquiry might be made into every part of it. Lord Grey's ministry were bound to act in conformity with a resolution on which they had, as it were, ridden into office; and the arrangement which they ultimately effected was one in which common-sense and the royal convenience and comfort were alike consulted. That portion of the Civil List of his predecessor which was voted by Parliament amounted to nearly £850,000 a year; but, besides that sum, George IV. enjoyed the income already mentioned as derived from Crown Lands, Droits, etc., while a farther large sum was furnished by the ancient revenue of the crown of Scotland, and another was received from Ireland. The ministers now proposed that all these sources of income should be handed over to the Treasury, and that the Civil List should henceforward be fixed at £510,000, being at the same time relieved from all the foreign and extraneous charges on it which had invidiously swelled the gross amount, without being in any way under the control of the sovereign, or in any way ministering to his requirements, either for personal indulgence or for the maintenance of the state and magnificence imposed on him by his position.

Such a change was on every ground most desirable. It was clearly in accordance with our parliamentary constitution that grants of money made by the Parliament should express distinctly and unmistakably the objects to which they were really to be applied; and that the charges of departments connected with the government, the administration of justice, or the foreign service of the country, should not be mixed up with others of a wholly different character, so as to make what was, in fact, the expenditure of the nation wear the appearance of being the expenditure of the sovereign. Moreover, the assignment of many of the charges to the Civil List even gave a false character to the appointments themselves. If a sovereign was to pay ambassadors and judges out of what seemed to be his private income, the logical conclusion could hardly be avoided that he had a right to lower those salaries, or even to diminish the number of those appointments. And it may even be said that the less any real danger of such a right being so exercised was to be apprehended, the more unadvisable was it to retain an arrangement which in theory could be described as liable to such an abuse.

Notes:

[Footnote 216:] But it may be remarked that till very recently the people out-of-doors had ceased to show any great anxiety about Reform. Two or three years before, Lord Althorp, who, in Lord Grey's ministry, was Chancellor of the Exchequer and leader of the House of Commons, told Peel that the people had become so indifferent to it, that he never meant to bring forward the question again, and in the last seven years only fourteen petitions had been presented to Parliament in favor of it. In reality, such a feeling in the people would have been eminently favorable to a calm framing of a Moderate measure; but this indifference was soon changed into a more violent and widely diffused excitement than there was any record of since the days of the Popish Plot; that excitement, however, according to the confession of the historian of the Whig ministry and the Reform Bill, himself an ardent reformer, being "no spontaneous result of popular feeling, but being brought about by the incessant labors of a few shrewd and industrious partisans forming a secret, but very active and efficient, committee in London."—Roebuck's *History of the Whig Ministry*, etc., ii., 309.]

[Footnote 217:] In 1835 the two days were reduced to one.]

[Footnote 218:] The creation of twelve peers, in the reign of Queen Anne, to secure a majority in favor of the Peace of Utrecht.]

[Footnote 219:] "Constitutional History," iii., 331. See the whole passage.]

[Footnote 220:] Lord John Russell had publicly described the language of the Tory Peers in the debate on Lord Lyndhurst's amendment as "the whisper of a faction." And many articles of most extreme violence which appeared in the *Times* about the same time were generally believed to have been written (in part at least) by the Lord Chancellor, Lord Brougham.]

[Footnote 221:] "Constitutional History of England," by Sir J.E. May, 1., 262.]

[Footnote 222:] Elizabeth enfranchised no fewer than sixty-two in the course of her reign, "a very large proportion of them petty boroughs, evidently under the influence of the crown or the peerage."—Hallam, *Constitutional History* i., 360.]

[Footnote 223:] Sir A. Alison, "History of Europe," xxiii., 55, quotes a paragraph from the *Examiner* newspaper, which says: "The ground, limited as it is, which it is proposed to clear and open to the popular influence, will suffice as the spot desired by Archimedes for the plant of the power which must ultimately govern the whole system. Without reform, convulsion is inevitable. Upon any reform farther reform is inevitably consequent, and the settlement of the constitution on the democratic basis certain."]

[Footnote 224:] Hallam, "Constitutional History," c. xvi., *in fin.*]

[Footnote 225:] "Semper in republicâ timendum est ne plurimum valeant plurinn."—Cicero.]

CHAPTER X

Abolition of Slavery.—Abridgment of the Apprenticeship.—The East India Company's Trade is Thrown Open.—Commencement of Ecclesiastical Reforms.—The New Poor-law.—State of Ireland.—Agitation against Tithes.—Coercion Bill.—Beginning of Church Reform.—Sir Robert Peel becomes Prime-minister.—Variety of Offices held Provisionally by the Duke of Wellington.—Sir Robert Peel Retires, and Lord Melbourne Resumes the Government.—Sir Robert Peel Proposes a Measure of Church Reform.—Municipal Reform.—Measures of Ecclesiastical Reform.

Apart from the consideration of the abstract principle, on which the advocates of Parliamentary Reform had insisted, of the light of many classes hitherto unrepresented to representation, they had also dwelt on the practical advantage which might be expected to ensue from the greater degree in which public opinion would henceforth be brought to bear on the action of the Houses, and, by a natural consequence, on the administrative government also. And the bill had hardly passed when this result began to show itself, not only in transactions of domestic legislation, but in others which affected our most remote dependencies, both in the East and West. We have seen in a previous chapter how Wilberforce, after twenty years of labor and anxiety, reaped the reward of his virtuous exertions in the abolition of the slave-trade. But he had not ventured to grapple with the institution which gave birth to that trade, the employment of slaves in our West India Islands. Yet it was an evil indefensible on every ground that could possibly be alleged. It was not only a crime and an injustice, but it was an anomaly, and a glaring inconsistency, in any British settlement. The law, as we have seen, had been laid down as absolutely settled, that no man within the precincts of the United Kingdom could be a slave; that, even had such been his previous condition, the moment his foot touched English soil he became a free man. By what process of reasoning, then, could it be contended that his right to liberty according to English law depended on what portion of the British dominion he was in—that what was incompatible with his claims as a human being in Kent ceased to be so in Jamaica? The sentiment that what was just or unjust in one place was just or unjust in every place; that a man's right to freedom did not depend on the country of his birth or the color of his skin, had naturally and logically been widely diffused and fostered by the abolition of the slave-trade. It was but a small step from admitting that there could be no justification for making a man a slave, to asserting that there was an equal violation of all justice in keeping one in slavery; and this conclusion was strengthened by tales, which were continually reaching those most interested in the subject, of oppression and cruelty practised by the masters, or oftener by their agents and overseers, on the unfortunate beings over whom they claimed power and right as absolute as any owner could pretend to over any description of property. They made so general an impression that, ten years before the time at which we have now arrived, a society had been formed in London whose object was the immediate extinction of slavery in every British settlement; and Canning, then Secretary of State, had entered warmly into the general object of the society; not, indeed, thinking the instant abolition practicable, but inducing Parliament to pass a body of resolutions in favor of at once improving the condition of the slaves, as the best and necessary preparation for their entire enfranchisement;[226] and the next year, 1824, the subject was recommended to the attention of the Houses in the King's speech, and an Order in Council was issued enjoining the adoption of a series of measures conceived in the spirit of those resolutions, among which one was evidently meant as a precursor of the slaves' entire emancipation, since it gave the "negro who had acquired sufficient property" a title "to purchase his own freedom and that of his wife and family." And it was, probably, from regarding it in this light that the planters (as the owners of estates in the West Indies were generally called) selected that provision as the object of their most vehement remonstrances. But, though they were not so open in their remonstrances against the other clauses of the order, they did worse, they disregarded them; and the stories of the ill-treatment of the slaves were neither less frequent nor less revolting than before.

Fresh Orders in Council, avowedly designed as the stepping-stones to eventual emancipation, were issued; and one which reached the West Indies at the end of 1831 was, unhappily, so misconstrued by the slaves in Jamaica, who regarded it as recognizing their right to instant liberation, that, when their masters refused to treat it as doing so, they broke out into a formidable insurrection, which was not quelled without great loss of life and destruction of property. The planters were panic-stricken; many of them, indeed, were almost ruined. The colonial Legislatures,[227] which had been established in the greater part of the islands, addressed the ministers with strong protests against the last Order in Council; and the mischief which had confessedly been already done, and the farther mischief which was not unreasonably dreaded, were so great that the cabinet consented to suspend it for a while; and the House of Commons made a practical confession that the planters were entitled to sympathy as well as the slaves, by voting nearly a million of money to compensate those of Jamaica for their recent losses.

But out-of-doors the feeling rather was that the insurrection had been caused, not by the unreasoning though natural impatience for freedom entertained by the negro—whom Canning had truly described as "possessing the form and strength of a man, but the intellect of a child"—but by the slackness and supineness of the local Legislature, too much under the influence of the timid clamors of the planters to listen to the voice of justice and humanity, which demanded to the full as emphatically, if somewhat less vociferously, the immediate deliverance of the slave. The object, however, thus desired was not so free from difficulty as it seemed to those zealous but irresponsible advocates of universal freedom; for, in the first place the slaves were not the only persons to be considered; the planters also had an undoubted right to have their interests protected, since, however illegitimate property in human beings might be, it was certain that its existence in that portion of the King's dominions had been recognized by Parliament and courts of justice for many generations, and that suddenly to withdraw a sanction and abrogate a custom thus established, and, as it might fairly be believed, almost legalized by time, would be not only ruinous to the planters, who would have no other means of cultivating their lands, but, as being ruinous to them, would also manifestly be most unjust. Even in the interests of the slaves themselves, instant emancipation before they were fit for it might prove to them a very doubtful blessing. The state, too, and the general interests of the kingdom had to be considered, for the shipping employed in the West India trade, and the revenue derived by the Imperial Exchequer from it, were both of great amount. It was a very complicated question, and required very cautious handling; but it was plain that the people were greatly excited on the subject. One or two of the ministers themselves had deeply pledged themselves to their constituents to labor for the cessation of slavery; and eventually, though by no means blind to the difficulty of arriving at a thoroughly safe solution of the question, the ministry decided that "delay was more perilous than decision," and they brought in a bill, in which they endeavored to combine the three great objects—justice to the slave, by conferring on him that freedom to which he, in common with all mankind, had an inviolable right; justice to the slave-owner, by compensating him fairly for the loss of what (however originally vicious the practice may have been) he was entitled by long usage and more than one positive law to regard as property; and a farther justice to the slave, that justice which consists in being careful so to confer benefits as to do the greatest amount of good to the recipient. The first object was attained by enacting that those who had hitherto been slaves should be free; the third was arrived at by making the freedom thus given, not instantaneous, but by leading them to it, and preparing them for its proper and useful enjoyment, by a system of apprenticeship. The slave was to be apprenticed to his master for seven years, receiving, partly in money and partly in kind, a certain fair amount of wages, and having also one-fourth of his time absolutely at his own disposal. And the second was secured by granting the planters the magnificent sum of twenty millions of money, as compensation for the injury done to them; or, in other words, as purchase-money for the property they were compelled to surrender. The apprenticeship system did not wholly succeed. The slaves were not sufficiently enlightened to appreciate the character of the new arrangement; and, as the light in which it appeared to them was rather that of deferring than of securing their emancipation, it made them impatient rather than thankful. In the majority of cases it proved difficult to induce them to work even three-fourths of their time, and eventually the planters themselves were driven to the conclusion that it was best to abridge the period of apprenticeship. By the act of the colonial Legislatures themselves it was shortened by two years, and the emancipation was completed on the 1st of August, 1838.

Still, though on this single point the success of the scheme did not fully correspond to the hopes of those who had framed it, it was one which did great honor to their ingenuity as well as to their philanthropy (Lord Stanley, as Colonial Secretary, being the minister to whose department it belonged). And the nation itself is fairly entitled to no small credit for its cordial, ungrudging approval of a measure of such unprecedented liberality. Indeed, the credit deserved was frankly allowed it by foreign countries. To quote the language of an eloquent historian of the period, "the generous acquiescence of the people under this prodigious increase of their burdens has caused the moralists of other nations to declare that the British Act of Emancipation stands alone for moral grandeur in the history of the world."[228] And, in respect of the personal liberty of the subject, it may be said to have completed the British constitution; establishing the glorious principle, that freedom is not limited to one part of our sovereign's dominions, to these islands alone, but that in no part of the world in which the British flag is erected can any sort of slavery exist for a single moment.

The abolition of the political authority of the East India Company, which took place some years after the time at which we have arrived, and which will be mentioned in a subsequent chapter, would make it unnecessary to mention the renewal of its charter, which took place at this time, were it not that the force of public opinion again made itself felt in some important limitations of its previous rights. The monopoly of the trade with China which the Company had hitherto enjoyed was resented as an injustice by the great body of our merchants and ship-owners, who contended that all British subjects had an equal right to share in advantages which had been won by British arms. The government and Parliament adopted their view, and the renewed charter extinguished not only that monopoly, but even the Company's exclusive trading privileges in India itself, though these, like the rights of the West India planters over their slaves, were purchased of it by an annuity for forty years, which was estimated as an equivalent for the loss of profit which must result to the proprietors of the Company's stock from the sudden alteration. It cannot be said that any constitutional principle was involved in what was merely a commercial regulation, or relaxation of such regulations. Yet it may not be thought inopportune to mention the transaction thus briefly, as one important step toward the establishment of free-trade, which, at the end of fifty years from the time when Pitt first laid the foundation of it, was gradually forcing itself on all our statesmen, as the only sound principle of commercial intercourse between nations. The laborious historian of Europe during these years finds fault with the arrangements now made, but only on the ground that they did not go far enough in that direction; that, while "everything was done to promote the commercial and manufacturing interests of England, nothing was done for those of Hindostan;"[229] that, "while English cotton goods were admitted for a nominal duty into India, there was no corresponding advantage thought of to the industry of India in supplying the markets of the country." The objection was not unfounded; but the system of which it complains was too one-sided to be long maintained, and in less than ten years a great financial reform had swept away the great mass of import duties, and so far had placed the Indian manufacturer on the same level with his fellow-subjects of English blood.

The disturbances which agitated the first years of the reign of William IV. were not caused solely by the excitement attendant on the passing of the Reform Bill. There had been extensive agricultural distress in England, which had shown itself in an outbreak of new crimes, the burning of ricks in the farm-yards, and the destruction of machinery, to which the peasantry were persuaded by designing demagogues to attribute the scarcity of employment. But statesmen of both parties were agreed in believing that a great deal of the poverty which, especially in the agricultural counties, had become the normal condition of the laborer, might be ascribed to the pernicious working of the Poor-law, which subsisted with scarcely any alteration as it had been originally enacted in the reign of Elizabeth. There was even reason to doubt whether the slight changes which had been made had been improvements. If they had been in the direction of increased liberality to the poor man who needed parish relief, and had to some extent lessened his discomforts, they had at the same time tended greatly to demoralize both him and his employer, by introducing a system of outdoor relief, which, coupled with the practice of regarding such relief as a legitimate addition to wages, led the former to feel no shame at underpaying his workmen, and the workman to feel no shame at depending on the parish for a portion of his means of subsistence. It was not to be wondered at that under such a system the poor-rates gradually rose to the prodigious amount of seven millions and a quarter of money; or that the rate-payers began to clamor against such a state of things, as imposing on them a burden beyond their power to bear. It was evident that it was an evil which imperatively demanded a remedy; and accordingly one of the first objects to which Lord Grey's Cabinet turned its attention after the completion of the Reform Bill was the amendment of the Poor-law.

The scheme which in the spring of 1834 they introduced to Parliament was the first instance of the adoption in this country of that system of centralization which has long been a favorite with some of the Continental statesmen, but which is not equally in harmony with the instincts of our people, generally more attached to local government. But, if ever centralization could commend itself to the English mind, it might well be when a new law and a new principle of action were to be introduced, in the carrying out of which uniformity of practice over the whole kingdom was especially desirable. Accordingly, the government bill proposed the establishment of a Board of Commissioners to whom the general administration of the Poor-laws over the whole kingdom was to be intrusted. They were to have power to make rules and regulations as to the mode or modes of relief to be given, subject to the approval of the Secretary of State, that thus the establishment of one uniform system over the whole country might be secured. Power was to be given to unite several parishes into one union, and to erect large workhouses for the several parishes thus massed together;[230] and every union was to be under the management of boards of guardians, elected by the rate-payers of the different parishes, with the addition of the resident magistrates as ex officio guardians. Lord Althorp, who introduced the bill, admitted that such extensive powers as he proposed to confer on the Board of Commissioners were "an anomaly in the constitution," but pleaded the necessity of the case as their justification, since it was indispensable to vest a discretionary power somewhere, and the government was too fully occupied with the business of the nation, while the local magistrates would be destitute of the sources of information requisite to form a proper opinion on the subject. The commissioners alone, being exclusively devoted to the subject, and being alone in possession of all the information that could be collected, were really the only body who could fairly be trusted to form correct opinions on it.[231] The fact of the creation of such a board being "an anomaly," or, as it might rather have been called, a novelty in the constitution, does not seem an insuperable objection, unless it were also inconsistent or at variance with the fundamental principles of the constitution, and that can hardly be alleged in this instance. It is true that local management, whether its range were wide or narrow, whether covering the business of a county or limited to a single parish, had been the general rule; but, like every other arrangement for the conduct of affairs of any kind, that local management was inherently subject to the supreme authority and interference of Parliament. Nor, as the maintenance of this Parliamentary authority, as the supreme referee in the last resource, was provided for by the subordination of the commissioners for the approval of their regulations to the Secretary of State, does it seem that the arrangement now proposed and adopted can be said to have been inconsistent with constitutional principle. And the necessity for some change of that nature was clearly made out by the abuses which, undeniably, had been suffered to grow up under the old system.

If the habitual condition of the Irish peasant were to be taken into account, it would be correct to say that there was less distress at this time in England than in Ireland; but there was still greater discontent, and infinitely more of dangerous disturbance. Catholic Emancipation had stimulated the agitators, not pacified them; they regarded it as a triumph over the English government; and, being so, as at once a reason for demanding, and a means of extorting, farther concessions. But this notion of theirs, when inculcated on the peasantry, bore terrible fruit, in such an increase of crime as had probably never been known in any country in the world. In the provinces of Leinster, Munster, and Connaught murders, deeds of arson, and rapine were of far more than daily occurrence.[232] Lord Althorp asserted in the House of Commons that more lives had been sacrificed in Ireland by murder in the preceding year than in one of Wellington's victories. And what was, if possible, a still worse symptom of the disposition of the common people, was exhibited in the impossibility of bringing the criminals, even when well known, to justice. Jurors held back from the assizes, witnesses who had seen murders committed refused to give evidence. The Roman Catholic prelates, and the higher class of the Roman Catholic clergy—most of whom, greatly to their credit, exerted themselves to check this fearful progress of wickedness—found their denunciations unheeded; while O'Connell, in his place in the House of Commons, used language which to an ignorant and ferocious peasantry looked almost like a justification of it, affirming it to be caused wholly by the "unjust and ruinous policy of the government" in refusing to abolish tithes. It was not the first time that the existence of tithe had been alleged as an Irish grievance. In the three southern provinces by far the greater portion of the tenantry were Roman Catholics, and they had long been complaining that they were forced to pay for the support of the Protestant clergyman of their parish, whose ministrations they could not attend, as well as for the maintenance of their own priest, whose livelihood depended on their contributions. According to strict political economy, there could be no doubt that the burden of the tithe fell, not on the tenant, but on the landlord, in the calculation of whose rent the amount of tithe to which each holding was liable was always taken into consideration; and that being the true doctrine, it was equally plain that in reality the Protestant clergy were paid, not by Roman Catholics, but by Protestants, since it was not disputed that by far the greater part of the land-owners in every province were Protestants.[233] But an ignorant peasant is no student of political economy or of logic; and the fact that the payment of the tithe passed through his hands was in his eyes, an incontrovertible proof that it came out of his pocket. The discontent had gradually begotten an organized resistance to the payment, and the mischief of allowing the continuance of such a state of feeling and conduct, which was manifestly likely to impair the respect for all law, made such an impression on the government that, in the royal speech with which he opened the session of 1832, the King recommended the whole subject to the consideration of Parliament, urging the Houses to inquire "whether it might not be possible to effect improvements in the laws respecting this subject."

In compliance with this recommendation, committees were appointed by both Houses; and the result of their investigations was a recommendation that a new arrangement should be made, under which the tithe should be commuted to a rent-charge. Accordingly, the next year the ministers proceeded to give effect to this recommendation. But they reasonably judged that an alteration of a particular law in compliance with the clamor raised against it would be a concession pregnant with mischief to the principle of all government, if it were not accompanied, or rather preceded, by a vindication of the majesty of all law; and therefore the first measure affecting Ireland, which they brought in in 1833, was a "Coercion Bill," which empowered the Lord-lieutenant not only to suppress the meetings of any assembly or association which he might consider dangerous to the public peace, but also to declare by proclamation any district in which tumults and outrages were rife to be "in a disturbed state;" and in districts thus proclaimed no person was to be permitted to be absent from his house from an hour after sunset to sunrise. Houses might be searched for arms, martial law was to be established, and courts-martial held for the trial of all offences except felonies; and the *Habeas Corpus* Act was suspended for three months. O'Connell and his party protested with great vehemence against such an enactment, as a violation of every right secured to the subject by the constitution. And a bill which suspended the ordinary courts of justice must be admitted to have been incompatible with the constitution as commonly understood and enjoyed. But if the measure thus proposed was extraordinary, the state of affairs which had led to its proposal was so also in a far greater degree. The records of no nation had ever presented such a fearful catalogue of crimes as was now laid before the Parliament, and at such a crisis the statesmen to whom the tranquillity of the country and the safety of the citizens were intrusted were undoubtedly called upon to go back from the letter of the constitution to that which is the primary object of every constitution—the safety of those who live under it. *Salus populi suprema lex*. And the argument of necessity was regarded, and rightly regarded, by both Houses of Parliament as a sufficient and complete justification of even so exceptional an enactment.

And concurrently with this enactment, which, however indispensable for the repression of crime, no one could deny to be severe, the ministers endeavored also to remove the causes of discontent by a large measure of Church reform, not confining their aim to settling the tithe question, but dealing with the whole question of the Irish Church in such a way as to lay down, as an undoubted principle of the constitution, the doctrine that the Church existed for the benefit of the nation; that its property was bestowed on it for the same object; and that, consequently, the nation, or in other words the Parliament, had a perfect right to deal with its property and endowments of all kinds, always keeping the same end in view, the general advantage of the whole nation. Proceeding on these maxims, they introduced a Church Reform Bill, in which, perhaps, the most remarkable circumstance of all was, that the evil which had been the original cause of their taking up the subject at all was the last thing settled, not, indeed, being finally arranged for four years; while the principal detail in the way of reform which was completed in this first session was one which, however reasonable, had hitherto received but little attention, and had certainly provoked no great outcry. It could not be denied that the Episcopal Establishment in Ireland was out of all proportion to the extent of the country and the number of the Protestant population, or of the parishes. The entire population in communion with the Church fell short of 900,000. The number of parishes scarcely exceeded 1400. But over this comparatively scanty flock were set no fewer than eighteen bishops and four archbishops; while England, with 12,000 parishes, was contented with twenty-four bishops and two archbishops. It was proposed to consolidate these bishoprics into ten, the archbishoprics into two, a reduction which could hardly fail to commend itself to all. But with this reduction was combined a variety of other details relating to the Episcopal revenues, to the right of the bishops to grant leases, and other matters of finance, which the ministers proposed so to remodel as to create a very large fund to be at the disposal of the state. On this point the greater part of the ministerial scheme was wrecked for the time. They succeeded in carrying that part of it which consolidated the bishoprics, and in inducing the House of Commons to grant, first as a loan, which was originally turned into a gift, a million of money to be divided among the incumbents of the different parishes, who were reduced to the greatest distress by the inability to procure payment of their tithes, the arrears of which amounted to a far larger sum.

But the assertion that any surplus fund arising from redistribution of the Episcopal revenues ought to belong to the state, not only called forth a vigorous resistance from the whole of the Tory party at its first promulgation, but, when the subject was revived the next year, and one of the supporters of the ministry, Mr. Ward, proposed a resolution that any such surplus might be legitimately applied to secular purposes, it produced a schism in the ministry itself. The resolution was cordially accepted by Lord John Russell, but was so offensive to four of his colleagues, Mr. Stanley and Sir James Graham being among the number, that they at once resigned their offices. The breach thus made was not easily healed; and before the end of the session other dissensions of a more vexatious and mortifying character led to the retirement of the Prime-minister himself. All attempts to deal with the tithe question failed for the time, four more years elapsing before it was finally settled. But, curtailed as it was, the bill of 1833 still deserves to be remembered as a landmark in constitutional legislation, since it afforded the first instance of Parliament affirming a right to deal with ecclesiastical dignities and endowments, thus setting a precedent which, in the next reign, was followed with regard to the Church of England.

Lord Melbourne succeeded Lord Grey at the Treasury; but every one saw that the ministry was greatly weakened. The King, too, had become greatly dissatisfied both with their general policy, especially in regard to the Irish Church—which he took an opportunity of assuring the Irish bishops he was unalterably resolved to uphold—and also with the language and conduct of one or two individual ministers, to which it is not necessary to refer more particularly; and when, on the death of Lord Spencer, father of Lord Althorp, the Chancellor of the Exchequer, which took place in November, 1834, it became necessary for Lord Melbourne to propose to him a re-arrangement of some of the cabinet offices, he at once dismissed the whole body of the ministers. It was a somewhat singular step to take, for they had not been defeated in Parliament, and he did not himself allege any special dissatisfaction with anything which they had yet done, though he did apprehend that some of them would press upon him measures disadvantageous to "the clergy of the Church of England in Ireland," to which he had an insuperable objection; and, moreover, that the subject would cause fresh divisions in the ministry, and the resignation of one or two more of its most important members. He had, indeed, six months before, given a practical proof of his distrust of the ability of Lord Melbourne and the colleagues who remained to him to carry on the government of the kingdom satisfactorily, by desiring the new Prime-minister to enter into communication with the leaders of the Opposition, "to endeavor at this crisis to prevail upon them to afford their aid and co-operation toward the formation of an administration upon an enlarged basis, combining the services of the most able and efficient members of each" party.[234] Nor had he relinquished the idea of bringing about such a coalition, till he learned that both Lord Melbourne and Sir Robert Peel considered the differences which divided them to be too deeply founded on principle to render their union in one administration either beneficial to the state or creditable to themselves. And it may be said that the letter in which Lord Melbourne had in November announced to his Majesty the death of Lord Spencer, and the necessity for new arrangements which that event had created, by the expression that "in these new and altered circumstances it was for his Majesty to consider whether it were his pleasure to authorize Viscount Melbourne to attempt to make such fresh arrangements as might enable his present servants to continue to conduct the affairs of the country, or whether his Majesty deemed it advisable to adopt any other course," and that "Lord Melbourne earnestly entreated that no personal consideration for him might prevent his Majesty from taking any measures or seeking any other advice which he might think more likely to conduce to his service and to the advantage of the country," did not only contemplate, but to a certain degree even suggested, the possibility of his Majesty's preferring to have recourse to fresh advisers.

    The King's subsequent acts and their result, however, certainly took the kingdom by surprise. He applied to the Duke of Wellington to undertake the formation of a new ministry; and the Duke, explaining to the King that "the difficulty of the task consisted in the state of the House of Commons, earnestly recommended him to choose a minister in the House of Commons," and named Sir Robert Peel as the fittest object for his Majesty's choice. Sir Robert was in Italy at the time; but, on receiving the royal summons, he at once hastened to England, the Duke of Wellington in the mean time accepting the offices of First Lord of the Treasury and Secretary of State, as a provisional arrangement, till he should arrive in London.

Sir Robert reached England early in December; and though, if "he had been consulted beforehand, he would have been inclined to dissuade the dismissal of the last ministry as premature and impolitic," he did not consider it compatible "with his sense of duty" to decline the charge which the King laid upon him, and at once accepted the office of Prime-minister, being fully aware that by so doing he "became technically, if not morally, responsible for the dissolution of the preceding government, though he had not had the remotest concern in it."[235] In the formation of his ministry he so far endeavored to carry out the views which the King had suggested to Lord Melbourne in the summer as to invite the co-operation of Mr. Stanley (who, by the death of his grandfather, had recently become Lord Stanley) and Sir J. Graham, who, as has been mentioned before, had retired from Lord Grey's cabinet. A new name, that of "Conservative," had recently been invented for the more moderate section of the old Tory party; and it was one which, though Lord Grey had taunted them with it, as betraying a sense of shame at adhering to their old colors, Peel was inclined to adopt for himself, as characteristic of his feelings and future objects; and perhaps he thought it might help to smooth the way for a junction with him of those who would flinch from proclaiming so decided a change in their opinions as would be implied by their becoming colleagues of one who still cherished the name of Tory. But they declined his offers; and consequently he was forced to select his cabinet entirely from the party of anti-Reformers. He dissolved Parliament, a step as to which it seemed to him that the universal expectations of, and even preparation for, a dissolution, left him practically scarcely any option;[236] but he soon found, as, indeed, he had feared he should find, the attempt to establish a Conservative government premature. The party of the late ministry, following the example set by Mr. Fox in 1784 with better fortune, divided against him in the House of Commons on every occasion, defeating him in every division; and at the beginning of April he retired, and Lord Melbourne and his former colleagues resumed their offices with very little change.

They had, as was natural, not been contented with opposing the Conservative ministry in its general policy, but in both Houses they had attacked it with great energy. They had begun the battle in both Houses in the debate on the address, in which they selected three points in the recent transactions for special condemnation, affirming that in every one of them the royal prerogative had been unconstitutionally exercised—the dismissal of the late ministry, the dissolution of Parliament, and the appointment of the Duke of Wellington to a variety of offices. In the House of Commons the attack was led by Lord Morpeth and Lord John Russell; in the House of Lords by Lord Melbourne himself. It was urged that, though the prerogative of the sovereign to dismiss his ministers was undoubted and inalienable, yet the Houses had a clear right to sit in judgment on any particular exercise of it; and that the circumstances of the late ministry having been but recently formed, of its possessing in a conspicuous degree the confidence of the great majority of the House of Commons, and of its being occupied at the moment of its dismissal with matters of high national concern, justified the House in calling on the new ministers to show valid reasons for its sudden dismissal. As to the dissolution, it was asked what misdemeanor the late House of Commons had committed? No difference had occurred between it and the other House of Parliament. It had passed no hostile vote against any administration. It had been in existence but a very short time. All these circumstances, they affirmed, made it reasonable for the Houses to express to his Majesty their disapprobation of the dissolution. Lord Morpeth argued, moreover, that the right of the House of Commons to inquire into such an exercise of the royal prerogative was proved by the example of Mr. Pitt, who, in 1784, had introduced into the speech from the throne a paragraph inviting Parliament to approve of the recent dissolution; and what Parliament could be asked to approve of, it manifestly had an equal right to censure. But the most vehement of the censures of the Opposition were directed against what Lord Morpeth called "the most unseemly huddling of offices in the single person of the Duke of Wellington; an unconstitutional concentration of responsibility and power, at which there was hardly an old Whig of the Rockingham school whose hair did not stand on end." He admitted that in the present instance the arrangement had only been provisional and temporary, and that "no harm had been done;" but, he asked, "what harm might not have been done? If the country had been suddenly obliged to go to war, who would have been responsible for the Foreign Department? If an insurrection of the negroes had occurred, who was responsible for the Colonial Office? If in Ireland any tithe dispute had arisen, who was responsible as Home-secretary?" And Lord Melbourne, though a speaker generally remarkable for moderation, on this subject went much farther; and, after urging that, "if one person held the situation of First Lord of the Treasury, and also that of Secretary of State for the Home Department, it would not only place in his hands without any control the appointment to every great office in the state, but a person so situated would also have the pecuniary resources of the state at his disposal without check or investigation," he proceeded to assert that "an intention to exercise those offices would amount to a treasonable misdemeanor." He did not, indeed, go so far as his late Attorney-general, Sir J. Campbell, who, in vexation at his loss of office, had even threatened the Duke with impeachment; but, though he admitted that the Duke had been free from the guilty intention of exercising the authority of these offices, he suggested that "the Lords ought to pass some resolution calculated to prevent so great a breach of the constitution from being drawn into a precedent."

On the first point thus raised, for the dismissal of the late ministry without any such cause as is usually furnished by an adverse vote of one of the Houses of Parliament, Peel frankly admitted that his acceptance of office rendered him constitutionally responsible, though, as he also said, it was notorious that in fact he had, and could have had, no previous knowledge of it; but he denied that any constitutional question whatever was involved in it, since the King's right was denied by no one; and he could, therefore, only consent to discuss it as a question of policy and expediency. And, looking at it in this light, he regarded his defence as easy and complete. He contended that the events of the past year, the resignation of several of the subordinate ministers, and finally of Lord Grey himself, and the proposal which had been made to him (Peel) and several of his friends to coalesce with Lord Melbourne, rendered the act by which the late government had been removed perfectly justifiable on the part both of the King and of himself; that the King was justified in thinking a wholly fresh arrangement preferable to a re-arrangement of Lord Melbourne's cabinet; and he himself in obeying his sovereign's commands to form a new administration.

The wisdom and propriety of the dissolution, too, could only be examined as a question of expediency; but in this instance every consideration not only recommended but compelled it. "When he undertook the arduous duties now imposed upon him, he did determine that he would leave no constitutional effort untried to enable him satisfactorily to discharge the trust imposed in him. He did fear that if he had met the late Parliament he should have been obstructed in his course, and obstructed in a manner and at a season which might have precluded an appeal to the people. It was the constant boast of the late government that the late Parliament had unbounded confidence in them. And, if that Parliament was, as had been constantly asserted, relied upon as ready to condemn him without a hearing, could any one be surprised at his appeal to the judgment of another, a higher and a fairer tribunal, the public sense of the people?" Precedent, too, was in his favor on this point, since, "whenever an extensive change of government had occurred, a dissolution of Parliament had followed;" and he referred to the year 1784, and to 1806, when the administration of which Lord Grey was the leading member at once dissolved the existing Parliament on coming into office; though he believed "the present to be the first occasion on which a House of Commons had been invited to express its dissatisfaction at the exercise of the prerogative of dissolution."

To the strictures of Lord Melbourne and Lord Morpeth on the Duke of Wellington's temporary assumption of a combination of offices, it was replied by Sir Robert and the Duke that, though there might be inconvenience from the assumption of all those powers by one individual, it was so far from being unconstitutional, that it was a common practice for the Secretary for one department to act for another during intervals of recreation, or periods of ill-health; that there was ample precedent for such a proceeding. In the last week of the life of Queen Anne, the Duke of Shrewsbury had united three of the greatest posts of the kingdom, those of Lord Treasurer, Lord Chamberlain, and Lord-lieutenant of Ireland, with the sanction of that great constitutional lawyer, Lord Somers. And in 1827 Mr. Canning had retained the seals of the Foreign Office for some weeks after his appointment as First Lord of the Treasury. Moreover, there was actually a law which provided that when the office of Chancellor of the Exchequer is vacant the seals of that office shall be delivered to the Chief-justice; and under this rule, in the latter part of the reign of George II., Chief-justice Lord Mansfield had continued finance-minister for above three months. And, as to the practical result of what had been done in the present instance, the Duke affirmed, what, indeed, was universally admitted, that the arrangement had from the first been understood to be merely temporary; that no inconvenience had resulted from it; indeed, that "not a single act had been done in any one of the offices which had not been essentially necessary for the service of the country."

The first two points on which the ministry was assailed it seems superfluous to examine, since it is clear that the position taken up by Sir Robert Peel is impregnable: that, on every view of the principles and practice of the constitution, there was no doubt of the right of the sovereign to dismiss his ministers or to dissolve the Parliament at his pleasure; and that those acts can only be judged of by a consideration of their expediency. Inexpedient, indeed, the dismissal of the preceding ministry is generally considered to have been, even in the interest of the Conservatives themselves. But inexpedient the dissolution can hardly be pronounced to have been, since, though the new election failed to give them a majority in the House of Commons, it beyond all doubt greatly strengthened their minority. On the other hand, though it cannot be denied that the House of Commons has a perfect right to express its disapproval of any or every act of the minister, it is not so clear that Lord Morpeth's invitation to it to express its dissatisfaction with this particular act of dissolution was, on general principles, expedient or safe; since such a vote is making a perilous approach to claiming for the House the right of being asked for its consent to its own dissolution, a claim the admission of which had been one of the most fatal, if not the most fatal, of all the concessions of Charles I.

As to the Duke of Wellington's assumption of a variety of offices, it is probable that when he first proposed to the King to confer them on him, he anticipated no objection whatever from any quarter, since he had so little idea of there being any impropriety in holding two offices, were they ever so apparently incongruous, if his Majesty should have directed him to do so, that seven years before, when he became Prime-minister, he had at first designed permanently to retain the command of the army in conjunction with the Treasury, and had only been induced to abandon the intention by the urgent remonstrance of Sir Robert Peel; and, constitutionally, there does not seem to be any limitation of the sovereign's power to confer offices, to unite or to divide them. Indeed, the different Secretary-ships of State seem to owe their existence entirely to his will, and not to any act of Parliament. He can diminish the number, if he should think fit, as he did in 1782, when, on the termination of the American war, he forbore to appoint a successor to Lord George Germaine, in Lord Rockingham's administration; or he can increase the numbers, as he did in 1794, when he revived the third Secretaryship, which he had suppressed twelve years before, without any act of Parliament being passed to direct either the suspension or the revival. He can even leave the most important offices vacant, and intrust the performance of their duties to a commission, as was done in this very year 1835, when the Great Seal was put in commission, and the duties, for above two years, were performed by commissioners, who had other duties also to discharge; and these instances may, perhaps, warrant the conclusion that the distribution of the different posts in what is generally known as the cabinet is dictated by considerations of what is practicable and expedient rather than by any positive and invariable rule or principle.

Yet it does not follow that, because the constitution was not violated or endangered by such an arrangement, the leaders of the Opposition did other than their duty in calling attention to it. Unquestionably, it is historically true that the liberties of the people owe their preservation, growth, and vigor to the jealous watchfulness to check the first and slightest appearance of any attempt to encroach upon them, which has been constantly exercised from the very earliest times by an almost unbroken series of fearless and independent patriots. And in this instance the very novelty of such an arrangement as had taken place did of itself make criticism a duty; though it may also be thought that the critics acted wisely in contenting themselves with calling notice to it, and abstaining from asking Parliament to pronounce a formal judgment on it, since any express censure would have been unwarranted either by the facts of the case or by any inference to be drawn from previous usage, while an approval of it would wear the appearance not only of sanctioning, but even of inviting a repetition of an arrangement which, if ever attempted to be carried out in actual practice, must tend to grave inconvenience, if not to discredit.

Lord Melbourne resumed office, and, being strengthened by the manifest inability of the opposite party to command the confidence of the House of Commons, began to apply himself with vigor to the carrying out of several measures of internal reform, some of which involved not only the property but the long-established rights of very considerable bodies, and, as so doing, have an importance in a constitutional point of view, besides that arising from their immediate effects. Peel had been equally alive to the desirableness, so cogent as almost to amount to a moral necessity, of introducing reforms into more than one old institution, such as should bring them more into harmony with the spirit of the age, remodelling or terminating some arrangements which were manifest abuses, and others which, though, if dispassionately examined and properly understood, they, perhaps, were not really grievances, yet in their operation caused such discontent and heart-burnings that they were as mischievous as many others far more indefensible in theory. And, short-lived as his administration had been, he had found time to frame and introduce an extensive measure of Church reform, not only dealing with the question of tithes, the levy and collection of which in some of their details had long been made subjects of bitter complaints by the farmers, but including also provision for the creation of two new bishoprics, those of Ripon and Manchester. No part of his measure was more imperatively called for by the present circumstances of the nation, or of greater importance in its future operation. There had been no increase in the number of bishops since the reign of Elizabeth; but since her time not only had the population of the entire kingdom been quadrupled, but some districts which had then been very scantily peopled had become exceedingly populous. These districts had hitherto been almost destitute of Episcopal supervision, which now was thus to be supplied to them. But the new legislation did more. It might be expected that the growth of the population would continue, and would in time require a farther and corresponding increase of the Episcopate; and the erection of these new dioceses was, therefore, not only the supplying of a present want, but the foundation of a system for increasing the efficiency of the Church which should be capable of gradual progressive expansion, as the growth of the population in various districts might be found to require additional facilities for supervision. And the judgment with which the new arrangement met the requirements of the community may be regarded as proved by the circumstance that now, after the lapse of nearly half a century, it is maintained in active operation, and is admitted by all parties not only to be of the greatest practical benefit, but also to have a moral effect scarcely less valuable in the degree in which it has stimulated the application of private munificence to the great work of Church extension.

But before Lord Grey quitted office his government had also called the attention of Parliament to the necessity of a large municipal reform, which, indeed, it seemed to them that the Reform Bill had bound them, in all consistency, to introduce. In the speech with which the King had closed the session of 1833, he had informed the Houses that he had "directed commissions to be issued for investigating the state of the municipal corporations throughout the United Kingdom, the result of whose inquiries would enable them to mature some measure which might seem best fitted to place the internal government of corporate cities and towns upon a solid foundation in respect of their finances, their judicature, and their police." He reminded them that they had recently passed acts "for giving constitutions upon sound principles to the royal and parliamentary boroughs of Scotland," and warned them that "their attention would hereafter be called to the expediency of extending similar advantages to the unincorporated towns in England which had now acquired the right of returning members to Parliament." The commission of which his Majesty thus spoke had now presented its report, strongly condemnatory of the existing system in almost every point of view; of the constitution and mode of election of the existing corporations, and of their government of the towns over which they presided. It declared that "even where they existed in their least imperfect form, and were most rightfully administered, they were inadequate to the wants of the present state of society." But they charged them also with positive offences of no venial kind. "They had perverted their powers to political ends, sacrificing local interests to party purposes. They had diverted from their legitimate use revenues which ought to have been applied for the public advantage, wasting them in many instances for the benefit of individuals; sometimes even employing for purposes of corruption funds originally intended for charitable uses." And they asserted that this too common misconduct of these bodies had engendered "among a great majority of the inhabitants of the incorporated towns a general and just dissatisfaction with their municipal institutions, a distrust of the self-elected municipal councils, and of the municipal magistracy, tainting with suspicion the local administration of justice." And therefore they "felt it their duty to represent to his Majesty that the existing municipal corporations of England and Wales neither possessed nor deserved the confidence and respect of his Majesty's subjects; and that a thorough reform must be effected before they could become what they ought to be, useful and efficient instruments of local government."

It would be superfluous here to repeat the story of the rise of the boroughs, whose gradual acquisition of charters, with privileges and powers of various degrees, has been sufficiently investigated by Hallam.[237] What the Parliament had now to deal with was the way in which the system worked in the nineteenth century; and here it must be confessed that the report of the commissioners, severe as it was, did in no degree exaggerate the prevailing evils. The corporations had gradually become self-elected oligarchies of the worst kind. It must be admitted that, in perverting their authority to political purposes, they might plead the excuse that they were but following the example set them by the ministers of William III., who introduced into their bill for restoring the corporations which James II. had suppressed clauses manifestly intended to preserve the ascendency of the Whig party, "by keeping the Church or Tory faction out of"[238] them. But no such palliation (if, indeed, that had any right to be called a palliation) could be alleged for their abuse of the trusts committed to them; abuse which, if committed by single individuals, would have been branded, and perhaps punished, as malversation and fraud of the deepest dye. A sufficient specimen of the kind and extent of their misdeeds in one branch of their duties was afforded by a single paragraph of Lord John Russell's speech, in which he affirmed that, in some of the reports of their management of charitable estates committed to their care, it was proved that "the property, instead of being employed for the general benefit of the town, had been consumed for the partial benefit of a few individuals, and not unfrequently in the feastings and entertainments in which the mayor and other corporators had been in the habit of indulging. In some not very large boroughs these expenses had amounted to £500 and £600 a year; and the enjoyment had been confined to freemen of only one party." And the perpetuity of this mismanagement was in most instances secured by the members of the corporation themselves electing their new colleagues on the occasion of any vacancy.

To put an end to this discreditable state of affairs, the government had prepared a very sweeping scheme of reform, though that it was not too sweeping was proved by the approval with which not only its principle but most of its details were received by the greater part of the Opposition; the leading principle being, to quote the words of the minister in introducing the bill, "that there should be one uniform government instituted, applicable to all; one uniform franchise for the purpose of election; and a like description of officers in each, with the exception of some of the larger places, in which there would be a recorder, or some other such magistrate. The first thing to be amended was the mode of election to the corporation, which was now to be intrusted to all such rate-payers in each borough as had paid poor-rates for three years, and resided within seven miles of the place." Lord John Russell had considered, he said, "whether this franchise should be limited to those paying a certain amount of rates; to the ten-pound householders, for instance, to whom the parliamentary franchise was confined;" but he decided on proposing to extend it to *all* rate-payers, because, according to the established principle, to the known and recognized principle of the constitution, it is right that those who contribute their money should have a voice in the election of the persons by whom the money is expended. The old modes of acquiring the freedom of a corporation, such as birth, apprenticeship, etc., were to be abolished, as also were all exclusive rights of trade, vested rights, however, being preserved. The next point to be decided was the composition of the corporation which these rate-payers were to elect, and the ministerial proposal was that each corporation should consist of a mayor, aldermen, and councillors, possessing a certain amount of property as a qualification, and varying in number according to the population of the borough; the larger towns being also divided into wards, with a certain number of common-councilmen and aldermen to be chosen in each ward. The mayor was to be a yearly officer; of the aldermen and councillors a certain number were to retire each year, being, however, capable of re-election. The mayor was to be elected by the councils, and was to be a magistrate during his year of office. And the body thus constituted was to have the entire government of the borough; of its police, its charities, and generally, and most especially, of the raising and expenditure of its funds,[239] which had been too often dealt with in a manner not only wasteful, but profligate. Cases had been brought forward in which "corporations had been incurring debts year by year, while the members were actually dividing among themselves the proceeds of the loans they raised." The revenue derived from charitable estates had been "no less scandalously mismanaged." And the bill provided for the appointment of finance committees, trustees, auditors, and a regular publication of all the accounts, as the only efficient remedy and preventive of such abuses. The whole police of the town and administration of justice was also to be completely under the control of the council; and for the appointment of magistrates the council was to have the power of recommending to the crown those whom they thought fit to receive the commission of the peace; and in the large towns it should have power also to provide a salary for stipendiary magistrates. Another clause provided that towns which could not as yet be included in the bill, since they had never been incorporated, might obtain charters of incorporation by petition to the Privy Council.

Such were the general provisions of this great measure of reform; a bill similar in principle having already been enacted for Scotland, and another being shortly after passed, with such variations of detail as the differences in the circumstances of the country required, for Ireland. Some of the clauses, especially those which preserved the vested rights of freemen and their families, and which required a certain amount of property or rating qualifications in the town councillors, were not originally included in the bill, but were inserted as amendments in the House of Lords; and it may be remarked that the result of the discussion in that House afforded a proof of the sagacity of those peers who, though conscientiously opposed to the Reform Bill, preferred allowing it to pass by their own retirement from the final divisions to driving the minister to carry his point by a creation of peers, since the avoidance of such an addition to their numbers as had been threatened enabled them now to force the adoption of these amendments on a reluctant minister. And it seems difficult to deny that the first was required by justice, and that the second was most desirable in the interests of the measure itself. Without it the town councillors, from among whom the mayor was to be chosen, might have been selected from the poorest, the least educated, and least independent class of the rate-payers. In some boroughs, or in some wards of many boroughs, it may be regarded as certain that they would have been so chosen; and such an admixture of unfit persons would have tended to bring some degree of discredit on the whole council, while to the successful inauguration of a new system the establishment of a general feeling of respect for it and confidence in it was of primary importance. The danger, too, of so ill-judged a selection would have been greatest in the larger boroughs, those being, at the same time, the very places in which the occasional difficulty of maintaining order and tranquillity made it even more necessary than in smaller towns that the council should enjoy the esteem and confidence of their fellow-citizens.

The principle that every man who contributed to the rates had a right to claim a voice in the election of those who were to expend them, which the minister laid down as the justification of the clause conferring the municipal franchise on all the rate-payers, was strongly contested by Sir Robert Peel, though neither he nor those of his party in the Upper House proposed any alteration of the bill in this respect; but he pointed out that, though Lord John affirmed it to be the known and recognized principle of the constitution, he had not acted on it in the Reform Bill; and it is certainly open to question whether the adoption of some limitation would not have been an improvement on the present measure. The doctrine established in this instance by Lord John gave a preponderance at every municipal election to mere numbers, since the poorest class is everywhere the most numerous, and its admission led almost inevitably to a reduction of the parliamentary franchise at some future day, though certainly at this time, and for many years afterward, Lord John was far from contemplating any alteration of the Reform Bill, but, on the contrary, took every opportunity of proclaiming his adherence to it as a final solution of the question.

But though in this particular it is possible that the bill might have been improved, it must be allowed to have been a measure very creditable to its framers. Few reforms have been conceived in a more judicious and more moderate spirit; few have been so carefully limited to the removal of real and proved abuses, and the prevention of their recurrence, while avoiding any concessions to the insidious demands of revolutionists, or the ill-regulated fancies of metaphysical theorists. It was a reform strictly in accordance with some of the most important principles of the constitution, as they have been gradually developed by the practical experience of successive generations. It combined with felicitous skill representative with local government; it secured uniformity in working, and that peculiarly English principle of publicity, without which the best-devised system cannot long be preserved from degeneracy.

The Church reforms in England and Ireland, which were carried out about the same time, cannot be said to have involved any constitutional principle, though one of them greatly extended the principle of religious toleration and indulgence to the Dissenters of various sects. No alteration had been made in the Marriage Act of 1754, which declared it indispensable to the validity of a marriage that it should be performed in a church and by a clergyman of the Established Church. And it was not strange that this should be felt as a grievance by those who were not in communion with that Church. But some of the Dissenting sects had an additional cause of discontent in the words of the marriage service, which gave a religious character to the ceremony, while they regarded it as a civil contract. In his short administration Sir Robert Peel had recognized the validity of the arguments against the unmodified maintenance of the existing law, and had framed a measure calculated, in his view, to give the Dissenters the relief their title to which could not be denied. But his bill had been extinguished by his retirement. And Lord John Russell now availed himself of the machinery of another measure, which he introduced at the same time, to make the relief somewhat wider and more effective.

Hitherto there was no record of births and marriages beyond that which was preserved in the registers of different parishes, which in former years had in many instances been carelessly and inaccurately kept. But at the beginning of 1836, the ministers, justly urging that it was important, in a national point of view, both with regard to the security of titles to property, and to that knowledge of the state of population the value of which was recognized by the establishment of the practice of taking a decennial census, that there should be a general register of all such occurrences, introduced a bill to establish a registry and registrar in every Poor-law union, with a farther registry for each county, and a chief or still more general one in London for the whole kingdom, subject to the authority of the Poor-law Commissioners. And by a second bill they farther proposed that the registries to be thus established should be offices at which those who desired to do so might contract purely civil marriages. Previous clauses in it provided that members of any sect of Protestant Dissenters might be married in their own chapels, and by ministers of their own persuasion. After enactments removing all the civil disabilities under which Nonconformists had labored for one hundred and fifty years had been placed on the statute-book, it was clearly inconsistent in the highest degree to retain still more offensive and unreasonable religious disabilities, and to deny to them the right of being married by their own ministers, according to the rites most agreeable to their consciences or prejudices. And though some of the details of the ministerial measure were objected to and slightly altered in its passage through Parliament, the general principle was admitted by the warmest friends and most recognized champions of the Established Church, who wisely felt that a bulwark which is too ill-placed or too unsubstantial to be defended, is often a treacherous source of weakness rather than strength, and that a temperate recognition of the validity of claims founded on justice was the best protection against others which had no such foundation, and that measures such as these adopted in a spirit of generous conciliation could only strengthen the Church by taking at least one weapon from the hands of its enemies.

Another of the measures relating to the Church, of which Peel had prepared a sketch, had for its object the removal of a grievance of which the members of the Church itself had long been complaining, the mode of the collection of tithe. It would be superfluous here to endeavor to trace the origin of tithes, or the purposes beyond the sustentation of the clergymen to which they were originally applied.[240] They had undoubtedly been established in England some time before the Conquest, and the principle that the land should support the National Church was admitted by a large majority of the population; it may probably be said with something nearly approaching unanimity on the part of those who really paid it, namely, the land-owners. The objection to the tithe system was founded rather on the way in which it worked, operating, as Lord John Russell described it, as "a discouragement to industry; a penalty on agricultural skill; a heavy mulct on those who expended the most capital and displayed the greatest skill in the cultivation of the land." The present mode of levying the tithes forced the clergy to forbearance at the expense of what they deemed to be their rights, or led them to enforce them at the expense of the influence which they ought to possess with their parishioners, compelling them to lose either their income by their indulgence, or their proper weight and popularity in the parish by the exaction of what the law gave them for "the support of themselves and their families." And this dilemma was felt so keenly by the clergy themselves, that it had become a very general feeling with them that, "if any sort of commutation could be devised, they would be delighted to be delivered from this objectionable mode of payment." Indeed, Sir Robert Peel, whose measure of the preceding year had been chiefly directed to the encouragement of voluntary commutations, had stated to the House that there were already two thousand parishes in the kingdom in which a commutation between the clergyman and his parishioners had been agreed upon, and established as a durable settlement by separate acts of Parliament. Indeed, arrangements of this kind existed very generally; the parishes in which the tithe was taken in kind being comparatively few, and the plan usually adopted being for the occupier of land to pay the incumbent a fixed annual sum bearing a certain proportion to his rent. But arrangements which were optional were, of course, liable to be rescinded; and Peel desired to establish a system which should be universal and permanent. And with this view he had designed the appointment of a temporary commission, one member of which should be nominated by the Primate, as the representative of the Church, under whose supervision the tithes of every parish in the kingdom should be commuted into a rent-charge, regulated partly by the composition which had hitherto been paid, and partly by the average price of grain—wheat, barley, and oats. It was no new idea, since as far back as 1791 Pitt had proposed a general commutation of tithes for a corn rent, and had submitted a plan with that object to the Primate, though circumstances of which we have no accurate knowledge prevented him from proceeding with it.[241] Objections[242] were taken to this last part of the arrangement, chiefly because it would render perpetual the terms of existing compositions, the extreme augmentation of them which was provided for in the bill being only ten per cent., while it was notorious that the majority of incumbents had shown such liberality in these matters that the compositions rarely amounted to two-thirds of the sum to which they were legally entitled. And it was hardly denied that the measure did involve some sacrifice of the extreme legal rights of the clergy; but it was urged and generally felt by the most judicious friends of the Church that the peace and harmony which might be expected to be the fruit of the measure was worth some sacrifice, and the bill was passed with very general approval; a bill on similar principles, with such variations as were required by the differences between the two countries, being also passed for Ireland.

The last measure on ecclesiastical subjects was also chiefly of a financial character, though its details were calculated, some directly, others indirectly, to produce benefits of a still more important nature. The condition of the property of the bishops and the ecclesiastical chapters had long been a subject of censorious remark. The various dioceses differed greatly in extent, as did, therefore, the labors of the diocesans. Some sees contained above 1000, one (London) even above 1200 parishes; others contained under 150. The revenues of some were very large, in one or two instances approaching £20,000 a year, while those of others scarcely exceeded £1000 or £1500 a year, thus affording incomes palpably inadequate to the support of the Episcopal dignity; so inadequate, indeed, that they were generally supplemented by the addition of some better endowed deanery or canonry. It was universally felt that such a deficiency and such a mode of supplying it were in themselves a scandal, which was greatly augmented by the system of translations to which it had given birth. The poorer bishoprics would hardly have been accepted at all had they not been regarded as stepping-stones to others of greater value; and the hope of such promotion had in some cases the not unnatural, however deplorable, effect of making the bishop anxious to please the minister of the day, to whom alone he could look for translation, by parliamentary subserviency; and the still more mischievous result (if possible) of rendering the whole Bench liable to the same degrading suspicion; while the canonries and prebends in the different chapters, whose revenues also varied greatly, were in every diocese so numerous that they had become nearly sinecures, the duties rarely exceeding residence for a month, or, at the outside, six weeks in a year.

These abuses (for such they could not be denied to be) had attracted the attention of Sir Robert Peel, who had appointed a commission, of which many of the highest dignitaries of the Church were members, and who, after very careful investigation and deliberation, presented a series of reports on which the ministry framed its measure. They proposed, as has already been mentioned in connection with the labors of Sir Robert Peel, an amalgamation of four of the smaller bishoprics at their next vacancy, in order hereafter to provide for the addition of two new ones at Manchester, or Lancaster, and Ripon, without augmenting the number of bishops. Lord Melbourne apparently feared to provoke the hostility of some of the extreme Reformers, who had recently proposed to deprive the bishops of their seats in the House of Lords, if he should attempt to increase the number of the spiritual peers; though, as their number had been stationary ever since the Reformation, while that of the lay peers had been quadrupled, such an objection hardly seemed entitled to so much consideration. Another clause was directed toward the establishment of greater equality between the revenues of the different bishoprics, a step which, besides its inherent reasonableness and equity, would extinguish the desire of promotion by translation, except in a few specified instances. Various reasons, sufficiently obvious and notorious, rendered the two archbishoprics, and the bishoprics of London, Durham, and Winchester, more costly to the occupants than the other dioceses; and these were, therefore, left in possession of larger revenues than the rest, proportionate to their wider duties or heavier charges. But all the others were to be nearly equal, none exceeding £5500, and none falling below £4500; while the five richer sees were also the only ones to which a prelate could be translated from another diocese. It followed, almost as a matter of course, that the practice of allowing a bishop to hold any other preferment was to cease with the cessation of the cause that had led to such an abuse.

Another part of the bill provided for the suppression of such canonries or prebends as might fairly be considered superfluous. Four were considered sufficient for the proper performance of the duties of each cathedral; and the extinction (after the lives of the present holders) of the rest was designed to form a large fund, to be at the disposal of the Ecclesiastical Commissioners,[243] and to be applied by them chiefly to meet the wants of the more populous parishes in different large towns, for which it had hitherto been difficult to make any provision,[244] by contributing to the erection of additional churches, by increasing the incomes of the incumbents in cases where it was insufficient, or in any other way which the practical experience of the members of the commission might suggest. One very important reform of a different kind was also provided for in the abolition of pluralities, the bill prohibiting the holding of two livings by the same person except they were within ten miles of each other. The measure was objected to by Sir Robert Inglis, who had represented Oxford as the peculiar champion of Protestant and Church principles ever since 1829, and by a party which shared his views, as one calculated to be "fatal to the best interests of the Church." They looked on the property of the Church and everything connected with it as invested with so peculiar a character, that they not only contested the right of Parliament to take any step to diminish its revenues or to change the employment of them, but they even "disputed its right to deprive one class of the clergy of any portion of their revenues for the purpose of distributing it among another." But the distinction thus made between Church property and that of any other public body seems one which can hardly be supported. The purposes for which ecclesiastical chapters or officials have been endowed with possessions and revenues are undoubtedly of a more sacred character than the duties imposed on lay corporations; but that consideration cannot be regarded as affecting the tenure of those possessions, or as inconsistent with the doctrine that they are national property, bestowed by the nation on the Church for the service and advantage of the people; deeply interested not only in the maintenance of an Established Church, but in that Church being in the highest possible degree efficient for its holy objects. Being so bestowed and appropriated, that property must, on every principle of the constitution, be subject to the control of the national Parliament. And surely that control could never be more legitimately exerted than in carrying out the recommendations of a commission which numbered among its members several of the prelates of the Church, whose profession and position were a guarantee for their anxiety to preserve all the rights of the Church which contributed to its credit or efficiency; while their matured experience enabled them better than any other men to judge how to reconcile the maintenance of its dignity with the extension of its usefulness.

Notes:

[Footnote 226:] The second resolution affirmed that "this House looks forward to a progressive improvement in the character of the slave population, such as may prepare them for a participation in those civil rights and privileges which are enjoyed by other classes of his Majesty's subjects." (Stapleton's "Life of Canning," iii., 98, where also large extracts from the minister's speech are given.)]

[Footnote 227:] Trinidad, St. Lucia, and Demerara were the only British islands which had not separate Legislatures.]

[Footnote 228:] Miss Martineau. "History of the Thirty Years' Peace," book iv., c. viii.]

[Footnote 229:] Alison, "History of Europe," 2d series, c. xxxi., sec. 74.]

[Footnote 230:] In the debate on the Registration Bill, in 1836, Lord John Russell stated that two hundred and twenty eight unions had already been formed in England and Wales, and that it might be calculated that when the whole country was divided into unions the entire number would amount to something more than eight hundred.]

[Footnote 231:] See Lord Althorp's speech, of parts of which an abstract is given in the text.—*Parliamentary Debates*, xxii., April 17.]

[Footnote 232:] Lord Althorp made the following frightful statement of the crimes committed in the province of Leinster alone in the last three months of 1832 and the first three of 1833: 207 murders, 271 cases of arson. The assaults attended with grievous personal injury were above 1000; burglaries and robberies, above 3000.]

[Footnote 233:] It was often asserted that fourteen-fifteenths of the land in Ireland belonged to Protestants, but this estimate was, probably, an exaggeration.]

[Footnote 234:] "Memoirs of Sir Robert Peel," ii., 3, 19.]

[Footnote 235:] "Memoirs of Sir Robert Peel," pp. 31, 32.]

[Footnote 236:] "One important question I found practically, and perhaps unavoidably, decided before my arrival, namely, the dissolution of the existing Parliament. Every one seemed to have taken it for granted that the Parliament must be dissolved, and preparations had accordingly been made almost universally for the coming contest."—*Peel's Memoirs*, ii., 43.]

[Footnote 237:] "Middle Ages," ii., 31 *seq*. See also Stubbs, "Constitutional History," i., 82-92 *et seq*.]

[Footnote 238:] See Hallam's "Constitutional History," ii., 155.]

[Footnote 239:] This was a matter of no small importance. The number of boroughs included in the bill was 183, having a population of about two millions. Their annual income was stated by Lord John Russell to be as nearly as possible £2000 a year for each, being £367,000; but their annual expenditure exceeded that amount by £10,000, being £377,000; "besides which there was a debt of £2,000,000 owing by these bodies."]

[Footnote 240:] See Hallam, "Middle Ages," ii., 205-207.]

[Footnote 241:] "Life of Pitt," ii., 131. Lord Stanhope imagines that the plan was relinquished in consequence of discouraging comments by the Archbishop (Dr. Moore).]

[Footnote 242:] These objections were founded on the following calculations, or something similar to them. The tithe was the tenth of the produce. In letting estates it was estimated that a farm ought to produce three rents; in other words, that a farm let at £1 an acre ought to produce yearly £3 an acre. One-tenth of three pounds, or 6s., therefore, was what the clergyman was entitled to claim. Out of this, however, he had to defray the cost of collection, which might, perhaps, be one shilling, leaving him five shillings. But the average of compositions over the whole kingdom was under 2s. 9d., or eleven-twentieths of what he was entitled to; and if augmented by ten per cent., it would not exceed three shillings.]

[Footnote 243:] The fund so created was expected to amount to £130,000 a year.]

[Footnote 244:] As instances of the want of church-room in such towns, Lord John cited the dioceses of London, Chester, York, Lichfield, and Coventry, containing a population of 2,590,000 persons, with church accommodation for only 276,000, or one-ninth of the population; the Commissioners, from whose report he was quoting, reckoning that church-room ought to be provided for one-third.]

CHAPTER XI

Death of William IV., and Accession of Queen Victoria.—
Rise of the Chartists.—Resignation of Lord Melbourne
in 1839, and his Resumption of Office.—Marriage of
the Queen, and Consequent Arrangements.—The
Precedence of the Prince, etc.—Post-office Reform.—War
in Afghanistan.—Discontent in Jamaica.—Insurrection
in Canada.—New Constitution for Canada and other
Colonies.—Case of Stockdale and Hansard.

The reforms mentioned in the preceding chapter were the last measures of the reign of William IV. In the summer of the next year, 1837, he died, and was succeeded in his British, though not in his Hanoverian, dominions by our present gracious sovereign, who had only just arrived at the age which entitled her to exercise the full authority of the crown. The change was calculated to strengthen the crown, by enlisting the chivalrous feelings of all that was best in the nation in the support of a youthful Queen, and in a lesser degree it for a time strengthened the ministry also; but, with respect to the latter, the feeling did not last long. For the next three years the summers were very unfavorable to the farmer; the harvests were bad; the inevitable accompaniment of a rise in prices had caused severe and general distress, and distress had produced clamorous discontent, and in some districts formidable riots. It had been greatly aggravated in the manufacturing counties by the operations of the trades-unions, which had gradually put forth pretensions to regulate the wages and other conditions of work, and had enforced them with such tyrannical violence, not flinching from the foulest crimes, that in many instances they had driven the masters to close their factories rather than submit to their mandates; and in others had compelled the workmen themselves to discontinue their labors, thus spreading destitution among thousands whose earnings, if they had been allowed to consult their own wishes, would have been amply sufficient for the support of their families;[245] and the evil had grown to such a height, that in 1838 a committee was appointed by the House of Commons to investigate the whole subject of trade combinations. But the turbulent spirit excited by this distress did not now confine itself to single outbreaks of violence, but, under the guidance of some demagogues of a more methodical turn of mind than usual, developed itself in a systematic organization having for its object what they called "the people's charter," which aimed at a total revolution of the existing parliamentary system, with the avowed design that, when adopted, it should eventually lead to an entire reconstruction of the government. The Chartists, as they called themselves, had advocates even in Parliament, who presented their petitions to the House of Commons, and tried, though unsuccessfully, to give them importance by the appointment of a committee to investigate the character of the reforms which they demanded. They were not, however, contented with peaceful modes of pressing their demands, but, in the course of the summer of 1839, broke out in formidable riots in different parts of the country. At Birmingham they set fire to different parts of the town, carrying on their work of pillage and destruction to such a pitch that the Duke of Wellington compared the condition of the town to one taken by storm in regular warfare; and at Newport, in Monmouthshire, they even planned and carried out an attack on the troops quartered in the district. But this violence led for a time to the suppression of the movement, the leaders in the Newport riots being convicted of high-treason; and, though the government forbore to put the extreme severities of the law in force against them, those who remained unconvicted had been taught by their example the danger which they incurred by such proceedings; and some years elapsed before a series of revolutionary troubles on the Continent again gave a momentary encouragement to those in this country who sympathized with the revolutionists, and prompted them to another attempt to force their views upon the government and the people.

It had nearly, however, been another ministry on whom the task of quelling these riots had fallen. Though, as has been already said, Lord Melbourne's cabinet derived a momentary strength from the accession of a young Queen, the support it thus acquired did not last; and in May, 1839, having been defeated on a measure of colonial policy, which will be mentioned hereafter, the cabinet resigned. The Queen intrusted the task of forming a new administration to Sir Robert Peel, who undertook it with a reasonable confidence that he should be able to hold his ground better than formerly, now that the retirement of his predecessors was their own act, and admitted by them to have been caused by a consciousness of the divisions among their supporters and their own consequent weakness. He had the greater reason for such confidence, since two of the colleagues of Lord Grey who had refused his offers in 1834, Lord Stanley and Sir James Graham, were now willing to unite with him; and he had almost completed his arrangements, when he was stopped by an unexpected, though not altogether unprecedented, impediment. It will be recollected that, in 1812, some of the arrangements for the formation of a new administration on the death of Mr. Perceval were impeded by a doubt which was felt in some quarters whether the new ministers would be allowed to remove one or two officers of the household, to whom the Regent was generally understood to be greatly attached, but who were hostile to the party which hoped to come into power, though it was afterward known that these officers had felt themselves bound to retire as soon as the arrangements in contemplation should be completed.[246] Sir Robert Peel was now met by a difficulty of the same kind, but one which the retiring ministers had the address to convert into a real obstacle. The Queen, who had warm affections, but who could not possibly have yet acquired any great knowledge of business, had become attached to the ladies whom Lord Melbourne had appointed to the chief places in her household. It had never occurred to her to regard their offices in a political light; and, consequently, when she found that Sir Robert considered it indispensable that some changes should be made in those appointments, she at once refused her consent, terming his proposal one "contrary to usage and repugnant to her feelings." Sir Robert, however, felt bound to adhere to his request for the removal of some of the ladies in question; for, in fact, they were the wives and sisters of his predecessors, and a continuance of their daily intercourse with the Queen might reasonably be expected to have some influence over her Majesty's judgment of the measures which he might feel it his duty to propose. Such a difficulty could not have arisen under a male sovereign; but Lord Melbourne himself had departed from the ordinary practice when he surrounded his royal mistress with ladies so closely identified with his cabinet. It is very possible that he had originally made the appointments without any such design, from the careless indifference which was his most marked characteristic; but he cannot be so easily acquitted when, in reply to the Queen's application to him for advice on the subject, he, being joined in his assertion by Lord John Russell, assured her that Sir Robert Peel's demand was unjustifiable and unprecedented. Supported by the positive dictum of the ministers on whose judgment she had hitherto been bound to rely, the Queen naturally adhered to her decision of refusing to permit the removal of the ladies in question, and the result was that Sir Robert Peel declined to take office under circumstances of difficulty beyond those to which every new minister must of necessity be exposed, and Lord Melbourne and his colleagues resumed their posts. The transaction was, of course, canvassed in both Houses of Parliament. Sir Robert Peel and the Duke of Wellington, who was the spokesman of the party in the House of Lords, defended their refusal to undertake the government on any other condition than that for which they had stipulated, on the ground that the authority to make such changes in the household as they had proposed was indispensable, as a proof of their possession of her Majesty's confidence; while Lord Melbourne, with a strange exaggeration, defended the advice which he had given her Majesty by the assertion that to have complied with Sir Robert Peel's proposal would have been "inconsistent with her personal honor." Other arguments on the same side were based on the alleged cruelty of separating her Majesty "from the society of her earliest friends, her old and constant companions;" an argument which was disposed of by Lord Brougham's remark, that till she had become Queen (not yet two years before) she had had no acquaintance with them whatever.[247]

But it is needless to dwell at any length on the case, in which all subsequent historians and political critics, however generally prepossessed in favor of the Liberal ministers, have given up their position as untenable. Her Majesty herself kept strictly on the path of the constitution in guiding herself by the counsels of those who, till their successors were appointed, were still her responsible advisers. But the course which they recommended was absolutely irreconcilable with one fundamental principle of the constitution—the universal responsibility of the ministers. In denying the right of the incoming ministers to remodel the household (or any other body of offices) in whatever degree they might consider requisite, they were clearly limiting the ministerial authority. To limit the ministerial authority is to limit the ministerial responsibility; to limit the ministerial responsibility is to impose some portion of responsibility (that portion from which it relieves the minister) on the sovereign himself, a dangerous consequence from which the constitution most carefully protects him. In fact, that the advice Lord Melbourne gave was indefensible was tacitly confessed by himself, when, on the recurrence of the same emergency two years later, he was compelled to recommend a different course;[248] and the ladies whom Sir Robert had considered it necessary to remove anticipated their dismissal by voluntary resignation. It may be added that, at the close of this same year, Lord Melbourne himself insisted on nominating the private secretary to the Prince whom the Queen was about to marry, though no one could pretend that offices in his household were as important as those in that of the sovereign; and though, if there was any post in which the Prince might have been supposed to have a right to an unfettered choice, that might have been supposed to have been the office of his private secretary.[249]

Her Majesty's marriage with Prince Albert of Saxe-Coburg, her first cousin—one tending as greatly to the happiness of herself and the advantage of the nation as any royal marriage recorded in history—took place in the beginning of 1840; and in the preparatory arrangements—matters of far greater consequence to the Queen's feelings than any appointments in the household—the ministry, by singular mismanagement, contrived to force the consideration of other constitutional questions on Parliament in such a way that the conclusions which were adopted, however inevitable, could hardly fail to be mortifying and vexatious to her Majesty, in whose cup of happiness at such a moment special care ought rather to have been taken to prevent the admixture of any such alloy. In the matter of the annuity to be settled on the young Prince, the Opposition must, indeed, share the blame with the minister. If it was unpardonable carelessness in the latter to omit the usual practice of previously consulting the leaders of the Opposition on the amount of the grant to be proposed, it was not the less impolitic and unworthy of such men as the Duke and Sir Robert Peel to show their disapproval of the inattention by a curtailment of the grant. The sum proposed, £50,000 a year, was fairly justified by the fact of its being the same which twenty-four years before had been settled on the Prince's uncle, Leopold, on his marriage with the Princess Charlotte. Indeed, if there were to be any difference, the circumstances might have been regarded as warranting an increase rather than a diminution of it. Money was certainly more plentiful in 1840 than in 1816, and the husband of an actual Queen occupied, beyond all question, a higher position than the husband of the heiress-presumptive, who might never become Queen, and who, in fact, never did. We cannot think, therefore, that the reduction of £20,000, which Sir Robert Peel proposed and carried, was reasonable or becoming, but regard it as neither called for by the circumstances of the kingdom, nor as befitting its liberality, nor as in harmony with its practice.

But on the two other questions—one immediately affecting the constitution, and the other not absolutely unconnected with it—no defence of the minister seems available. At the opening of Parliament in 1840, her Majesty commenced her speech by the announcement of her intended marriage, describing the bridegroom simply as "the Prince of Saxe-Coburg and Gotha," the same expression which she had used in addressing the Privy Council a few weeks before. That description of him had at once struck her uncle, Leopold—who, since the death of his English wife, the Princess Charlotte, had become King of Belgium—as so imperfect and insufficient, that, on reading her address to the Privy Council, he at once wrote to her to point out that it would have been desirable to mention the fact of the Prince being a Protestant,[250] and that the omission would inevitably cause discontent. But, in spite of this warning, Lord Melbourne refused to advise the Queen to insert a statement of the Prince's religion in her speech, though it was by no means superfluous on such an occasion, since, if he were a Roman Catholic, a marriage with him would have incurred a forfeiture of the crown. The Duke of Wellington, on the other hand, regarded it as a positive duty to require that the fact of the Prince being a Protestant should be mentioned, so as to show the care of Parliament to prevent any constitutional precautions from being overlooked, such statement having, indeed, been usually made on similar occasions. When he, therefore, moved an amendment to insert the word "Protestant" in the description of the Prince, Lord Melbourne did not venture to divide the House against it; but still his management gave an ungracious appearance to the transaction, as if there had been in any quarter an unwillingness to recognize the fact of the Prince's Protestantism till the recognition was forced on the government by the action of the Parliament.

The third question, as affecting the relative ranks and positions of the different members of the royal family, cannot be said to have been wholly unconnected with the provisions of the constitution; and the mismanagement of the minister was, perhaps, even more sure to attract notice in this case than in the other, since to introduce into a bill a clause which had no connection whatever with its title had something of the appearance of a deliberate slight to the two Houses. A bill to naturalize the Prince was, of course, indispensable. But into it the ministers, without any notice, had introduced a clause enabling him "during his life to take precedence in rank after her Majesty in Parliament and elsewhere as her Majesty might think fit and proper, any law, statute, or custom to the contrary notwithstanding." It was admitted that no such precedence had been given to Prince George of Denmark, nor to Prince Leopold. And there were obvious difficulties in the way of conferring such a life-long precedence, because, as Lord Brougham had pointed out, it was possible that the Queen might die without issue, in which case the King of Hanover would become King of England also, and his son the Prince of Wales; and it would have been an inconceivable anomaly that a foreign naturalized prince should take precedence of the Prince of Wales, whose special rank and importance was recognized in many acts of Parliament. This objection was so clearly insuperable, that Lord Melbourne consented to alter the clause so as to give the Prince precedence only "after the heir-apparent." But even this concession failed to satisfy the objectors, the King of Hanover, among others, positively refusing to waive his precedence over any foreign prince. And eventually the minister withdrew the clause altogether, and the bill, as it was passed, was confined to the naturalization of the Prince. Lord Melbourne had thus contrived to make the Queen and Prince appear as if they were desirous to induce the two Houses by a sort of trick to confer on the Prince a precedence and dignity to which he was not entitled, and to render the refusal of Parliament to be so cajoled a fresh cause of mortification to the royal pair. The course that was eventually adopted is understood to have been suggested by the Duke of Wellington—to withdraw the affair altogether from the cognizance of Parliament, and to leave it to the Queen to confer on the Prince whatever precedence she might choose, as it was certainly within her right to do. And so, a few days after the bill had passed, she did by letters-patent give him precedence next to herself "on all occasions and in all meetings, except when otherwise provided by act of Parliament," as, seventeen years later, she, in the same way, with the cordial approval of the whole nation, conferred on him the title of Prince Consort. And apart from its convenience, as avoiding all unseemly discussions, this would seem to have been the most natural and proper mode of settling such a matter. The Queen is the fountain of honor in this kingdom, and at her own court she can certainly confer on any of her own subjects whatever precedence she may think fit, while it may be doubted whether any act of a British Parliament could give precedence at a foreign court. It was, probably, not in his character of Duke of Cumberland, but as an independent sovereign, that the King of Hanover maintained his claim to superior precedence; and it was plain that the most illustrious subject could not possibly at any court be allowed to rank above a king. With reference to its possible effect on the subsequent relations of Peel and his followers with the court, it was, perhaps, well that a few months later they had the opportunity of proving that no personal objection to the Prince himself had influenced their course in these transactions, by giving a cordial assent to the ministerial proposal of conferring the Regency on him in the event of the Queen giving an heir to the throne, and dying while he was still a minor. The principle was the same as that which had guided the arrangements for a Regency ten years before; but it was not inconceivable that Parliament might have hesitated to intrust so large an authority to so very young a man, and him a comparative stranger, such as the Prince still was, had the leaders of the Opposition given the slightest countenance to such an objection.

Lord Melbourne's ministry was hardly strengthened by the circumstances under which it resumed office. Yet the close of the same year witnessed a reform of which it is hardly too much to say that no single measure of this century has contributed more to the comfort of the whole mass of the people, with which it has also combined solid commercial benefits. Hitherto the Post-office had been managed in a singular manner, and the profit derived from it had been treated as something distinct from the ordinary revenue of the kingdom. In the reign of Charles II. it had been given to the Duke of York, and the grant was regarded as conferring on him such extensive rights, that when, some years afterward, an enterprising citizen set up a penny post for the delivery of letters in the City and its precincts, the Duke complained of the scheme as an infraction of his monopoly, and the courts of law decided in his favor. That grant ceased, as a matter of course, on the Duke's accession to the throne; and in the reign of

Queen Anne a portion of the Post-office proceeds was appropriated, with the general consent of a grateful country, to reward the great achievements of the Duke of Malborough, a perpetual charge on it of £5000 a year being annexed to the dukedom. In those days the postage of a letter was twopence for short distances, and threepence for any distance beyond eighty miles.[251] But those charges had been gradually increased; about the middle of the century the lowest charge was fixed at fourpence, rising in proportion to the distance, till the conveyance of a single letter from one extremity of the kingdom to the other cost eighteen-pence. Such a rate could not fail to be very profitable; and by the beginning of the present reign the yearly profit exceeded a million and a half of money. The heaviness of the charge, however, had latterly attracted attention, and had been the cause of many complaints, as being a great discouragement, and, in the case of the poorer classes, a complete obstacle to communication. However, neither the ministers nor the Parliament had succeeded in devising any remedy, since a system affording so large a return was not a thing lightly to tamper with, when those who complained suddenly found a practical leader in Mr. Rowland Hill, who published a pamphlet on the subject, in which he affirmed the cost of the conveyance of each letter even for such a distance as from London to Edinburgh to be infinitely less than a farthing; and that, consequently, all the rest of the postage was a tax for the purposes of revenue. When this fact was once established, it needed no argument to prove that to increase the tax paid by each recipient of a letter in proportion to the distance at which he lived from the writer was an indefensible unfairness; and, after much investigation and discussion, Mr. Hill succeeded in converting the ministers to his view. Accordingly, the Budget for 1839, introduced by Mr. Spring Rice, then Chancellor of the Exchequer, contained a clause which reduced the postage for every letter weighing less than an ounce to a uniform charge of a penny, to be prepaid by means of a stamp to be affixed to each letter by the sender. It was not without plainly-expressed reluctance that the scheme was consented to by the Opposition; nor can their hesitation be considered as unreasonable, in the very unsatisfactory condition of the finances of the kingdom at the time. The balance-sheet of the preceding year showed a considerable deficiency. There was a large unfunded debt; and even Mr. Hill's most sanguine calculations admitted a probable loss to the Post-office of £1,200,000 for the first year or two; though he expressed his confidence that eventually the correspondence of the kingdom would be found to increase so largely as to make up for the greater part, if not the whole, of the deficiency. His anticipations were far outran by the reality.

In 1839 the Postmaster-general estimated the number of letters sent yearly by the post at less than twenty-five millions. They are now upward of a thousand millions, a number the conveyance of which (with the addition of newspapers, whose circulation had also been greatly augmented by a recent reduction of the tax to a penny) would have severely taxed the whole carrying power of the kingdom before the introduction of railroads. Nor have the benefits of the new system been confined to ourselves. Foreign nations have followed our example, though not quite in the same degree, till an international postage is at length established throughout the whole of the civilized world. And it has not been only the happiness of private individuals that has been augmented by this facility of communication. In its gradual development it has largely promoted the extension of trade of every kind, and, by facilitating a commercial intercourse between nations, it cannot but contribute to the maintenance of friendship and peace.

The full advantages of this reform could not be seen at first; but, even had it been appreciated as fully as we appreciate it now, no approval of it could have counterbalanced the general dissatisfaction with which the ministry was regarded. At home the finances were falling into great disorder, the expenditure of the year greatly exceeding the income; while the feeling that their Irish policy was dictated by a wish to purchase at any price the support of O'Connell, was still more injurious to them, for he was already beginning to renew agitation in Ireland, inaugurating a new association, which, though its purposes were faintly veiled for a time under the title of the Precursor Association, was understood to point at a repeal of the Union; while the ministers, though they denounced such a measure as ruinous to every part of the kingdom, seemed willing to give it practical encouragement by a bill which they introduced, which bore the name of a Registration Act for Ireland, but which was not confined to that object. On the contrary, it contained a provision for lowering the qualification for the franchise by one-half; so that it was, in fact, a new Reform Bill for Ireland,[252] calculated greatly to increase his influence by the number of voters of the poorer classes whom it would create. The bill was defeated, but the odium of having proposed it remained.

But, besides these home difficulties, there were troubles abroad, both in the East and in the West. In the East, the complications inseparable from a dominion like that of ours in India, where constant expansion seemed to have become a law of its existence, had involved us in a war with a new enemy, the warlike Afghan nation; in the West, both Jamaica and Canada were in a state threatening insurrection. Indeed, the troubles in Jamaica had been the immediate cause of that resignation of the ministry in 1839 which has already been mentioned. Measures adopted in the English Parliament with reference to the termination of that apprenticeship system which, as we have seen, formed a part of the bill for the abolition of slavery, and another for the regulation of the prisons in the island, had given such offence to the colonial Assembly, never very manageable, that the members passed a resolution that their legislative rights had been violated, and that they would abstain from all exercise of their legislative functions, except such as might be necessary "to preserve inviolate the faith of the island with the public creditor, until" (by the rescinding of the resolutions, etc., of which they complained) "they should be left to the free exercise of their inherent rights as British subjects." And this resolution was seconded by an insulting protest, in which they drew an offensive comparison between the state of crime in the island and that which prevailed in Great Britain, taunting the British Parliament with the murders and acts of incendiarism which terrified Ireland night and day, with the murders of Burke and Hare in Scotland, with the law of divorce and *crim. con.* trials in England, and "a Poor-law which has taken millions from the necessities of the destitute to add to the luxuries of the wealthy." The Governor dissolved the Assembly, but that which succeeded re-adopted the resolutions of its predecessor, and the ministers, in consequence, brought in a bill "to suspend the existing constitution of the island for a limited number of years, and to provide that during that interval its legislative functions should not be exercised by a Governor, a Council, and a House of Assembly, but should reside in the Governor and Council alone." The emergency was too great and undeniable, the remedy proposed was also too unprecedented in its stringency, to be dealt with without the gravest deliberation; and the House of Commons accordingly gave the matter the patient consideration which became both it and themselves. They allowed the island to appear by counsel against the bill, and listened for many hours to an elaborate defence of the conduct of the Assembly, which if it failed to change the intention of the ministers, convinced Sir Robert Peel and his party that their measure was doubtful in its justification and impolitic in its severity. He pointed out that "the bill was neither more nor less than one for the establishment of a complete despotism—one which would establish the most unqualified, unchecked, unmitigated power that was ever yet applied to the government of any community, in place of that liberal system which had prevailed for upward of one hundred and fifty years." And, though he did not for a moment question the power of Parliament to pass such a measure, he greatly doubted the policy of such an exertion of it. A somewhat similar measure affecting Canada they had been compelled to enact in the preceding year, and he feared lest "it might seem to be coming to be a practice of Parliament to suspend a constitution every session." And he quoted a speech of Canning, delivered fifteen years before, in which that eloquent statesman, a man by no means inclined to a timorous policy, had declared that "no feeling of wounded pride, no motive of questionable expediency, nothing short of real and demonstrable necessity, should ever induce him to moot the awful question of the transcendental power of Parliament over every dependency of the British crown. That transcendental power was an ordinance of empire, which ought to be kept back within the penetralia of the constitution. It exists, but it should be veiled. It should not be produced on trifling occasions, or in cases of petty refractoriness or temporary misconduct."

And Sir Robert, "looking at all the papers before the House, could not say that there was here any vindication for bringing forward this transcendental power." He asked whether "they had ever treated with so much severity a conquered colony amid the first heat of animosity after the contest." And he traced the history of our government of the island back to the time of Charles II., pointing out (as Burke had formerly argued with respect to our Colonies in North America) that "Jamaica owed its colonization by British subjects to the conquest that was made of it by the arms of Cromwell; that its first English population was composed of those who, disgusted with the excesses of the civil wars, there found a refuge," and who had carried with them that attachment to liberty which, as early as 1678, had led them successfully to repel the attacks made on the privileges of their House of Assembly by the ministers of Charles II. He warned the House, also, that if this measure were passed, "a sympathy for the people of Jamaica would be excited throughout the other West Indian possessions of the crown." And, while fully admitting that the conduct of the Assembly had been "foolish and unjustifiable," he still recommended that it should be treated in a conciliatory spirit, which as yet had not been shown toward it.

The government carried their proposal by a majority of no more than five in a very full house, a success which they regarded as a defeat, and, as has been already mentioned, resigned. But as the state of the question and of the island did not admit of delay, on their resumption of their offices they introduced a fresh measure, which the Conservatives again curtailed of its most severe clauses, and which, in the form in which it was eventually passed, gave the Assembly time to reconsider its conduct, and, without the humiliation of confessing itself guilty, to give a practical recantation of their offensive resolutions, by resuming its work of legislation, any farther delay of which would on many subjects be very mischievous to the island itself. The distinct assertion by both parties of the power of the Parliament to inflict even the severest penalty enabled the Houses to take this conciliatory course without loss of dignity; while the stern disapproval of the conduct of the Assembly which the Conservative leader had expressed, even when pleading for a milder treatment of it, convinced the colonists that any protracted contumacy would be dangerous, and would deprive them for the future of all title to even the modified protection which on this occasion had saved them.

In the discussion of these transactions, Peel, as we have seen, had alluded to the affairs of Canada, which had been of a still more serious complexion; since there the discontent of the colonists in the Lower Province had developed into armed insurrection. We have seen that, from the first moment after the country had passed into our possession, there had been almost constant dissensions between the old French colonists and the English immigrants who crossed over both from England and from the colonies on the southern side of the St. Lawrence in the early part of the reign of George III. The desire of terminating these divisions, which had their root in a difference of religion as well as of race, the French settlers being Roman Catholics, had been one of the chief motives which had led Pitt in 1791 to divide the country into two provinces.[253] And for many years the scheme was fairly successful; but, toward the end of the reign of George IV., the political excitement caused by the agitation in England of the question of Catholic Emancipation, and subsequently of Reform, spread across the Atlantic to the Canadas; and the French portion of the colonists, who almost monopolized the representation in Lower Canada, began to urge the adoption of changes utterly inconsistent with the existing constitution of the colony. In the hope of compelling the compliance of the home government with their demands, in 1832 and the following years they refused to vote the necessary supplies; and, gaining courage, as it were, from the contemplation of their own violence, and under the guidance of a leader of French extraction, a M. Papineau, who scarcely concealed his hope of effecting the complete severance of the Lower Province from the British dominion, they proceeded to put forth farther demands, which they regarded as plausible from the apparent resemblance of the changes which they required to the system of the English constitution, but which, to use the words in which Sir Robert Peel described them, would have established "a French republic." The most important of them were that the Upper or Legislative Council should, like the Assembly, be rendered elective, instead of, as had hitherto been the case, being nominated by the crown. And another asked that the Executive Council should be made responsible to the Assembly, in the same manner as in England the ministers of the crown were responsible to Parliament. As it was at once shown that the ministry at home had no intention of granting these demands, Papineau collected a band of malcontents in arms, with whom he took possession of one or two small towns, and ventured even to measure his strength with the Commander-in-chief of the province, Sir John Colborne, one of the most distinguished of Wellington's comrades and pupils. His force was utterly routed, and he himself fled across the frontier to New York. A similar outbreak, excited in the Upper Province by a newspaper editor, was crushed with equal ease and rapidity.[254] And the next year, 1838, Lord John Russell brought forward a bill to suspend the constitution of the colony, and to confer on a new Governor, who was at once to proceed thither, very ample powers for remodelling the government of the province, subject, of course, to the sanction of the home government. In the previous year he had succeeded in carrying some resolutions announcing the determination of Parliament not to concede the demands of the Assembly of the Lower Province, which have been already mentioned. And the reasons which he gave for this course are worth preserving, as expressing the view recognized by Parliament of the relations properly existing between the mother country and a colony. It was on a proper understanding of them that he based his refusal to make the Executive Council in Canada responsible to the Assembly. He held such a step to be "entirely incompatible with those relations. Those relations require that his Majesty should be represented, not by a person removable by the House of Assembly, but by a Governor sent out by the King, responsible to the King, and responsible to the Parliament of Great Britain. This is the necessary constitution of a colony; and if we have not these relations existing between the mother country and the colony, we shall soon have an end of these relations altogether." And he pointed out the practical difficulties which might reasonably be apprehended if such a change as was asked were conceded. "The person sent out by the King as Governor, and those ministers in whom the Assembly confided, might differ in opinion, and there would be at once a collision between the measures of the King and the conduct of the representatives of the colony."

The plan of sending out a new Governor free from any previous association with either of the parties, or any of the recent transactions in the colony, was, probably, the wisest that could have been adopted. Unfortunately, it was in some degree marred by the choice of the statesman sent out, Lord Durham, a man of unquestioned ability, but of an extraordinarily self-willed and overbearing temper. He drew up a most able report of the state of the provinces, combined with recommendations of the course to be pursued toward them in future, so judicious that subsequent ministers, though widely differing from his views of general politics, saw no better plan than that which he had suggested; but, unhappily, the measures which he himself adopted, especially with respect to the treatment of those who had been leaders in the late rebellion, were such manifest violations of law, that the government at home had no alternative but that of disallowing some of them, and carrying a bill of indemnity for others. He took such offence at their treatment of him, though it was quite inevitable, that he at once resigned his appointment and returned home. But the next year the Queen sent down a message to the Houses recommending a union of the two provinces (a measure which had been the most important, and the very foundation, of his suggestions), and Lord John Russell introduced a bill which, as he described its object, he hoped would "lay the foundation of a permanent settlement of the affairs of the entire colony." The main feature of the government policy was the formation of "a legislative union of the two provinces on the principles of a free and representative government," and the establishment of such a system of local government as amounted to a practical recognition of the principle so earnestly repudiated, as we have seen, by Lord John Russell a year or two before. It was not, perhaps, fully carried out at first. Lord Sydenham, who had succeeded Lord Durham, reported to the home government, as the result of a tour which he had taken through a great part of the country, that in the whole of the Upper Province, and among the British settlers of the Lower Province, "an excellent spirit prevailed, and that he had found everywhere a determination to forget past differences, and to unite in an endeavor to obtain under the union those practical measures for the improvement of the country which had been too long neglected in the struggle for party and personal objects." But of the French Canadians he could not give so favorable a report. Efforts were still made by some of the old Papineau party to mislead the people; but he was satisfied they would not again be able to induce the peasantry to support any attempt at disturbance. It was natural that that party should still feel some soreness at the utter failure of their recent attempts and the disappointment of their hopes; and affairs took the longer time in being brought into perfect order and harmony through a strange mortality which took place among the first Governors-general. Lord Sydenham died the next year of lockjaw, brought on by a fall from his horse; Sir Charles Bagot was forced to retire in a state of hopeless bad health after an administration equally brief; two years later, Sir Charles Metcalfe, who succeeded him, returned home only to die; and it was not till a fourth Governor, Lord Elgin, succeeded to the government that it could be said that the new system, though established five years before, had a fair trial.

Fortunately, he was a man admirably qualified by largeness of statesman-like views and a most conciliatory disposition for such a post at such a time; and he strictly carried out the scheme which was implied by the bill of Lord John Russell, and to a certain extent inaugurated by Lord Sydenham, selecting his advisers from the party which had the confidence of the Legislative Assembly, and generally directing his policy in harmony with their counsels; so that under his government the working of the colonial constitution was a nearly faithful reproduction of the parliamentary constitution at home. Such a policy was in reality only a development of the principle laid down by Pitt half a century before, and warmly approved by his great rival, that "the only method of retaining distant colonies with advantage is to enable them to govern themselves."[255] And since that day similar constitutions have been established in our other distant dependencies as they have become ripe for them—in New Zealand, the Cape, and the Australian colonies—almost the only powers reserved to the home government in those colonies in which such constitutions have been established being that of appointing the governors; that of ratifying or, if necessary, disallowing measures adopted by the colonial government; and, in cases of necessity, that of prescribing measures for the adoption of the local Legislatures, and even of compelling such adoption, in the event of any persevering opposition. The act of 1850, which established a constitution in Victoria, went even farther in the privileges it conferred on the colonists, inasmuch as it gave power to the Legislative Council to alter some of its provisions, and even to remodel the Legislative Council and Assembly. It may be doubted whether this last concession did not go too far, since in more than one important instance the government of that great colony has availed itself of it so liberally as to render it necessary to pass a fresh act of Parliament to enable her Majesty to give her royal assent to some of the changes which the Assembly had enacted.[256] Indeed, it cannot be said that the system has worked in every part or on every occasion quite as well as might have been hoped; nor can it be denied that the colonies have occasionally claimed a power of independent action in opposition to the home Parliament in a way to try severely the patience of the home government. After the British Parliament had adopted the policy and system of free-trade, the Canadian Assembly adhered to the doctrine of protection so obstinately that it actually established a tariff of import duties injurious to the commerce of the mother country, and apparently intended as a condemnation of its principles. But its contumacy showed how wholly different was the spirit of the British government from that which had prevailed in the last century; for though the home government had unquestionably the right of disallowing the offensive tariff, it forbore to exercise it; and, probably, by this striking proof that it considered a complete recognition of the principle of local self-government more important than any trifling financial or commercial advantage, contributed greatly to implant in Canada and all the colonies that confidence in the affectionate moderation of the home government which must be the strongest, if not the only indissoluble, bond of union.

On the whole, it is hardly too much to say that no more statesman-like, and (if sentiment may be allowed a share in influencing the conduct of governments) no more amiable spirit animates any act of our modern legislation than is displayed in these arrangements for the management of our colonies. They are a practical exemplification of the idea embodied in the expression, "the mother country." A hundred years ago, Burke sought to impress on the existing ministers and Parliament the conviction that, "so long as our Colonies kept the idea of their civil rights associated with our government, they would cling and grapple to us, and no force under heaven would be of power to tear them from their allegiance." In the case of which he was speaking his warning, as we have seen, fell on deaf ears; but the policy of the present reign is a willing and full adoption of them, on a far larger scale than even his farseeing vision could then contemplate. Within the century which has elapsed since his time the enterprise of Britain has sent forth her sons to people another hemisphere; and they, her children still, cling to the parent state with filial affection, because they feel that, though parted from her by thousands of miles and more than one ocean, they are still indissolubly united to her by their participation in all the blessings of her constitution, her generous toleration, her equal laws, her universal freedom.

On one transaction of these years the leaders of the Opposition were found acting in close agreement with the ministers. We have seen how, in the early part of the reign of George III., the House of Commons threw the sheriffs of London into prison, on account of their performance of what they conceived to be their duty as magistrates; and in 1840 it subjected the same officials to the same treatment on a question of the same character—the extent of the privilege of the House of Commons to overrule the authority of the courts of law. The question was in appearance complicated by the institution of several suits at law, and by the fact that the House was not consistent in its conduct, but allowed its servants to plead to the first action, and refused the same permission in the second, when the result of the first trial had proved adverse to them. The case was this: some inspectors of prisons has presented a report to Parliament, in which they alleged that they had found in Newgate a book of disgusting and obscene character, published by a London publisher named Stockdale. The House of Commons had ordered the report to be printed and sold by Messrs. Hansard, the Parliamentary publishers, and Stockdale brought an action against Messrs. Hansard for libel. Chief-justice Denman charged the jury that "the fact of the House of Commons having directed Messrs. Hansard to publish their reports was no justification to them for publishing a Parliamentary report containing a libel;" and Stockdale obtained damages, which were duly paid. Stockdale, encouraged by this success, when, in spite of the result of the late trial, Hansard continued to sell the report, brought a fresh action; but now the House forbade the publishers to plead to it; and, as they obeyed the prohibition, and forbore to plead, the case eventually came before the Sheriff's Court; fresh damages were given, and, in obedience to the writ of the Queen's Bench, the sheriffs seized Hansard's goods, and sold them to satisfy the judgment. Lord John Russell, as leader of the House, moved to bring to the Bar of the House all the parties concerned in the action—the plaintiff, his attorney, the sheriffs, and the under-sheriffs. He was opposed by nearly all the legal members of the House except the crown lawyers, Sir Edward Sugden especially warning the House that "a resolution of the House was of no avail in a court of justice;" while others taunted the House with want of courage in not proceeding against the judges themselves, rather than against their officers, which in this case the sheriffs were.

There could be no doubt of the importance of the question, since it was no less, as the Attorney-general, Sir J. Campbell, put it, than a question whether Parliament or the courts of law had the superiority; and now Sir Robert Peel, as leader of the Opposition, came to the support of Lord John Russell, declaring his opinion to be, first, that "the House possessed every privilege necessary for the proper and effectual discharge of its functions;" secondly, that "the publication of evidence which had led the House to adopt any course was frequently essential to justify that course to the nation;" and thirdly, that "to judge of the extent of their privileges, and to vindicate them by their own laws, belonged to the House alone." And he pressed strongly on the House that it was "the duty of the House to fight the battle to the last," though he confessed that "it was with pain that he had come to the determination of entering into a contest with the courts of law." On one point the judges agreed with the House of Commons. The House committed the sheriffs; but, when they sued out their *habeas corpus*, the judges decided that the return of the Sergeant-at-arms that they were committed by the House for breach of privilege was a sufficient return. Stockdale brought fresh actions. But meantime the case was arousing a strong excitement in the country.[257] The singular hardship of the position of the sheriffs excited general sympathy: if they obeyed the House of Commons, which prohibited them from paying over to Stockdale the damages which they had received for him, the Court of Queen's Bench would be bound to attach them for disobedience to its order. If they obeyed the Queen's Bench, the House would imprison them for breach of privilege. And the national feeling is always in favor of the strictly defined authority of the courts of law, rather than of the somewhat indefinite claims of Parliament to interpret, and even to make, privilege. Another consideration, probably, weighed a little with the champions of the House—that their power of imprisonment ended with the session. As matters went on, it was found that even the Attorney and

Solicitor-general differed as to the course to be pursued; and eventually Lord John Russell consented to adopt the advice which had been given by a former Attorney-general, Sir F. Pollock, and to bring in a bill to legalize all similar proceedings of Parliament in future, by enacting that a certificate that the publication of any document had been ordered by either House should be a sufficient defence against any action. The introduction of such a bill was in some degree an acknowledgment of defeat; but it can hardly be denied to have been not only a judicious step, but the only one practicable, if the contest between Parliament and the courts of law were not to be everlasting; and it met with general approval. If it was a compromise, it was one that satisfied both parties and both ends. It upheld the authority of the courts of law, and at the same time it practically asserted the reasonableness of the claim advanced by the House of Commons, by giving it for the future the power which it had claimed. Nor were people in this day inclined to be jealous of the privileges of Parliament, so long as they were accurately defined. They felt that it was for the advantage and dignity of the nation that its powers and privileges should be large; what they regarded with distrust was, a claim of power of which no one knew the precise bounds, and which might, therefore, be expanded as the occasion served.

Notes:

[Footnote 245:] Fifty-two mills and 30,000 persons were thrown out of employment for ten weeks at Ashton in 1830 by the turning out of 3000 "coarse spinners," who could clear at the time from 28s. to 31s. per week. The following passage is extracted from an oath said to have been administered by the combined spinners in Scotland in 1823: "I, A B, do voluntarily swear, in the awful presence of God Almighty, and before these witnesses, that I will execute with zeal and alacrity, as far as in me lies, every task or injunction which the majority of my brethren shall impose upon me in furtherance of our common welfare, as the chastisement of *knobs*, the assassination of oppressive and tyrannical masters, or the demolition of shops that shall be deemed incorrigible." —*Annual Register*, 1838, pp. 204-207.]

[Footnote 247:] The question was examined with great minuteness by Lord Brougham a fortnight after the ministerial explanation. See "Parliamentary Debates," 3d series, xlvii., 1164.]

[Footnote 248:] It is stated on good authority that Lord Melbourne, in private conversation, justified or explained the line he had taken by his consideration for his friends,

scores of whom would have had their hopes blighted by his retirement.]

[Footnote 249:] See "Life of the Prince Consort," i., 55.]

[Footnote 250:] "Life of the Prince Consort," i., 57.]

[Footnote 251:] Macaulay's "History of England," i., 386.]

[Footnote 252:] This is the name which the Liberal historian of the time, Miss Martineau, gives it. "The so-called Registration Bill was, in fact, an unannounced new Reform Bill for Ireland."—*History of the Peace*, book v., c. vi.]

[Footnote 253:] See *ante*, p. 127.]

[Footnote 254:] In one instance the rebels were aided by a party of citizens of the United States, who, without any sanction from their own government, seized an island on the St. Lawrence belonging to us, and attacked some of the Canadian villages. And this led to the discussion of a question of international combined with constitutional law, which Lord Campbell thus describes: "'Whether, if the subjects or citizens of a foreign state with which we are at peace, without commission or authority from their own or any other government, invade the English territory in a hostile manner, and levy war against the Queen in her realm, we are entitled to treat them as traitors?' The Canadian courts held that we could not, as they had never acknowledged even a temporary allegiance to our sovereign. And of this opinion was Sir William Follett. But, after reading all that is to be found on the subject, I come to the conclusion that they owed allegiance when, as private individuals, they voluntarily crossed the English frontier; that it was no defence for them to say that they then had arms in their hands and intended to murder the Queen's subjects."—*Life of Lord Campbell*, ii.,119. It certainly would have been no *defence*; but would it not have taken their conduct from under the definition of *treason*, and made it an act of *piracy*?]

[Footnote 255:] See Fox's words, quoted by Lord Stanhope.—*Life of Pitt*, ii., 90.]

[Footnote 256:] A couple of years after the period which is the boundary of the present work, this Canadian constitution of 1841 was superseded by a measure uniting Canada, Nova Scotia, and New Brunswick in one federal government, with, as the act recites, "a constitution similar in principle to that of the United Kingdom." The act farther provided for the admission of other dependencies of the crown in North America, Newfoundland, Prince Edward Island, British Columbia, and Rupert's Land into the union, and established as the constitution of the whole one scarcely differing from that of 1841, with the exception that both the Houses of the Legislature—called in the act the Senate and the House of Commons—were to be representative bodies, and that powers were conferred on them so absolutely free and independent, that it was thought necessary to add a clause providing that their "privileges, immunities, and powers were never to exceed those at the passing of the act held, enjoyed, and exercised by the Commons House of Parliament of the United Kingdom of Great Britain and Ireland, and by the members thereof."]

[Footnote 257:] Lord Campbell, in his autobiography, puts the transaction, in the phase at which it had now arrived, in a very serious light: "Next came a proceeding which placed me in a most difficult position; and the public never knew the danger which then existed of a convulsion unexampled in our history. The sheriffs sued out a writ of *habeas corpus*, directed to the Sergeant-at-arms, commanding him to produce before the Court of Queen's Bench the sheriffs of Middlesex, alleged to be illegally in custody, with the cause of their detention. Wilde, the Solicitor-general, was strong for refusing to make any return to the writ, and for setting the Court of Queen's Bench at defiance. Had I concurred in this opinion it would certainty have been acted on. The consequences would have been that the Sergeant-at-arms, even with the mace in his hand, would have been sent to Newgate by the Court of Queen's Bench. The House must have retaliated by committing the judges. The crown would then have had to determine on which side the army should be employed, and for a time we must have lived under a military government" (ii., 129). The noble and learned autobiographer does not explain why it should have been indispensable to employ the army on either side.]

CHAPTER XII

Sir Robert Peel becomes Prime-minister.—Commercial Reforms.—Free-trade.—Religious Toleration.—Maynooth.—The Queen's University.—Post-office Regulations.—The Opening of Letters.—Naturalization of Aliens.—Recall of Lord Ellenborough.—Reversal of the Vote on the Sugar Duties.—Refusal of the Crown to Sanction a Bill.—The Question of Increase in the Number of Spiritual Peers.—Repeal of the Corn-laws.—Revolution in France, and Agitation on the Continent.—Death of Sir Robert Peel.—Indifference of the Country to Reform.—Repeal of the Navigation Laws.—Resolutions in Favor of Free-trade.—The Great Exhibition of 1851.

The transactions mentioned in the last chapter were among the last events of Lord Melbourne's ministry. He had for some time been aware of his impending defeat in the House of Commons, and, greatly to his credit, had endeavored to make the return to office easier to his successors by the friendly counsels he had given to the Queen on the subject.[258] A dissolution of Parliament in the summer of 1841 only weakened his party, and in September he resigned, and was succeeded by Sir Robert Peel, who, comparatively short as was his tenure of office,[259] found it long enough to establish for himself a reputation as the greatest financier of Europe since the days of Pitt. It may be worth remarking that, in the "Memoirs of the Prince Consort," it is mentioned that in the course of his administration Peel found reason to change his judgment on the question of which House of Parliament it was the more desirable for the Prime-minister to be a member. Canning had more than once asserted his conviction that the public business would be more satisfactorily conducted when the Prime-minister was a commoner, founding his opinion chiefly on the paramount importance of financial questions, the discussion of which is almost confined to the House of Commons, and conceiving it to be supported by the history of the administration of Pitt, from whom, indeed, he had imbibed the idea; and in former years Peel had more than once expressed his concurrence with that view of the subject. But, from papers which were intrusted to him for the execution of his great work, Sir Theodore Martin learned that Peel had subsequently found reason to come to the opposite conclusion, not from any change in his view of the relative importance of the different departments of administration, but solely because "the amount of work imposed upon the first minister in the House of Commons, in addition to what he had to go through elsewhere, was too great for any human strength. In the House of Lords the Prime-minister would escape the necessity for being in a position to vindicate all the details of administration, and to answer the multiplicity of questions on all sorts of subjects, the putting of which has almost degenerated into a vice. He had, therefore, come to the conclusion that it was there he ought to be."[260] And, indeed, the subjects which demanded the care of the minister, and attracted the attention of Parliament, were constantly increasing in number, variety, and importance to the very end of his administration. Not only were the financial difficulties of the country, the depressed state of agriculture and commerce (the result of a succession of bad harvests), sufficient causes for grave anxiety, but the terrible war, of which mention has already been made, which we had now been carrying on for nearly three years in Afghanistan, and which, before the end of this very year, was about to be signalized by a disaster such as had never before befallen a British army, threatened to kindle the flames of war in Europe also, from the share which the intrigues of Russia had had in fomenting the quarrel; and the same danger was more than once in the course of the next five years imminent, from the irritation with which France regarded us, and which, commencing in Syria, while Lord Melbourne was still at the helm, lost no opportunity of displaying itself, whether in transactions in the remote Pacific Ocean or the old battle-field of the two nations, the Spanish peninsula; and finally, these embarrassing perplexities were crowned by the appalling visitation of famine, which, at the end of the fourth year of the administration, fell upon Ireland with a severity surpassing any similar event in modern history.

With all these multiform difficulties the new minister grappled with unflinching courage, and with conspicuous success. Peace was preserved abroad, and financial prosperity was restored at home. Into the details of his measures devised for this last-mentioned object, though the leading features of his administration, and those on which his fame chiefly rests, it would be beside the purpose of the present work to enter. It is sufficient to say here that, in the spirit of Pitt's great financial reform of 1787, he revised the whole of the import duties of our commercial tariff, especially reducing the duties on raw material;[261] making up the deficiency so caused by an income tax, which he described as a temporary imposition, since he doubted not that the great increase of lawful trade, which would be the consequence of the reduction of duties, would soon enable the revenue to dispense with a tax to the objections of which he was not blind. In recommending this great change to the House, he laid down as the soundest maxim of financial legislation, in which "all were now agreed, the principle that we should buy in the cheapest market and sell in the dearest," a doctrine which, when more fully carried out, as it was sure to be, led almost inevitably to the great measure for which his administration is most celebrated, the repeal of the Corn-laws. There could be no doubt that, in the most modified application of it, it struck at the root of the principle of protection, which had hitherto been the fundamental principle of our finance, and made a farther extension of it inevitable.

And, as he had been one of the leading members of the ministry which carried Catholic Emancipation, so he now proceeded on the same path of religious toleration; and, in the session of 1844, successfully recommended to the House of Commons a bill which had already been passed by the Lords, repealing a number of penal acts affecting the Roman Catholics, which, though they had long been practically obsolete, still encumbered, and it may be said disgraced, the statute book, and were, so to say, a standing degradation of and insult to the Roman Catholic body. One of them, passed in the reign of William and Mary, still forbade any Roman Catholic to come within ten miles of London, to have either sword or pistol in his house, or to possess a horse worth more than five pounds. Another, enacted under Elizabeth, still made every Roman Catholic who omitted to take certain oaths guilty of high-treason, though no attempt to administer those oaths had been made since the Revolution. Another, of the time of Charles I., deprived any Roman Catholic who should send his son to a foreign school of all protection of the law; he could neither sue nor defend an action. It may fairly be said that the credit of Parliament and of the nation was concerned in the abrogation of laws so ridiculously oppressive, and not the less obnoxious for being practically invalid. And in the same spirit another measure was framed and carried by the Lord Chancellor, whose object was the confirmation of religious endowments belonging to different sects of Protestant Dissenters, and their protection from vexatious and unjust litigation, by making a continued possession of any kind of endowment or property for twenty years a valid title.

These enactments may be regarded as indispensable supplements to the repeal of the Test Act and Catholic Emancipation. They were the coping-stone of the great edifice of religious toleration, of which the former acts had laid the foundation. And the next year Peel carried out still farther the same principle, by a measure which could not fail to be regarded as an especial boon in Ireland, since the great majority of the population of that kingdom were of the Roman Catholic persuasion. It has been seen that when the troubled state into which the Continent was thrown by the French Revolution threw hinderances in the way of the Irish students designed for the Roman Catholic priesthood going to one of the great Continental colleges, such as St. Omer or Salamanca, for their education, Pitt established for them a college at Maynooth, for the endowment of which Parliament was annually asked for a grant of about £9000. The sum had long been felt to be altogether inadequate to the requirements of the foundation. As early as the year 1807, Lord Liverpool, then Home-secretary, had contemplated a large increase of the grant, though the weakness of the government, then presided over by the Duke of Portland, prevented him from carrying out that and other measures which he had conceived in a kindred spirit. Moreover, the grant was rarely proposed without giving rise to a warm debate raised by a party whose too tender consciences forbade them to sanction any measure appearing to foster a religion from which they dissented. And to remedy the two evils (the one arising from the want of a sufficient provision, the other from the spirit of religious controversy, for which the House of Commons was certainly very ill-calculated), Peel, in 1845, proposed to treble the grant, so as to put the college on a more satisfactory footing, by providing sufficient incomes for the professors, and a revenue adequate to the respectable maintenance of an increased number of pupils; and also to place the charge for the future on the Consolidated Fund, by which step its yearly discussion in Parliament would be altogether avoided. The measure was vigorously resisted, partly on the religious ground already mentioned, and partly by an argument, urged with some plausibility, that the design with which the college had originally been founded had not been realized; that, in fact, it had not proved a benefit to the country, but rather the reverse, by tempting into the service of the Roman Catholic Church a humbler and poorer class of students than could devote themselves to it when the preliminary education involved the expense of a protracted residence in a foreign country. But the obvious advantages of the change prevailed over these considerations, and the bill was carried by large majorities.[262]

And now that the long cessation of controversy on the subject—which, indeed, has been not the least beneficial fruit of this bill of 1845—permits a candid consideration of it in all its bearings, it will probably be thought that Parliament had not often come to a wiser decision, one more dictated by judicious liberality of sentiment, and more imperatively required on every ground of statesman-like policy. If the countervailing objections and advantages be calmly weighed, it may almost be said that there was no alternative between enlarging the endowment and putting it on a new footing, or suppressing the college altogether. In its existing condition it was notoriously inadequate to fulfil the design of its founder; and any establishment visibly inadequate to its design tends to bring the design itself into some degree of contempt. Yet even if it should be granted that there might have been no fair ground of complaint if the college had never been founded, to close it after its benefits, however scanty, had been enjoyed for half a century, could not fail to have been regarded as an unpardonable injustice and injury. The other alternative, therefore, was practically the only one that remained; and in embracing it Peel was but carrying out the original principle on which the college was founded. It had been intended to be efficient; through lack of means it had proved inefficient. The obvious and just remedy was to supply such increased means as to create or bestow the efficiency originally aimed at. And it was a felicitous idea to place the charge for the future on such a footing as to combine with such an increase an avoidance of the irritation which its yearly discussion had never failed to excite.

And at the same time, to carry still farther the principle of religious toleration, or rather of religious equality, he induced the Parliament to found a new university, consisting of three colleges, one in each of the three provinces of Ulster, Munster and Connaught (Leinster, as having Trinity College and Maynooth, being regarded as already sufficiently provided with university education), which should be open to students of every religious denomination, and at which, while every kind of secular education, both literary and scientific, should be given, the stirring up of religious controversy and animosity should be guarded against, by the absence of any theological professorships. He did not, indeed, design that the still greater benefits of religious education should be withheld from the pupils, but he proposed to provide for that object by confiding their religious education to the care of the clergy of each persuasion, some of whom in each town which was the seat of a college—Belfast, Cork, and Galway—might be trusted for willingness to superintend it. It was hoped that one fruit of this scheme, and that by no means its least valuable result, would be that the association of pupils of various creeds in their studies and amusements from an early age would lead them to maintain, in their more mature years, the harmony of which the foundation had thus been laid in their youth; and that thus the religious animosities which were the principal obstacle to the prosperity of the country would be softened, and in time extinguished. And this object has been achieved to a great extent, though the disfavor with which the Roman Catholic Church regards any educational system which is not under the superintendence of its priesthood has prevented the scheme from attaining the full development which was hoped for. The number of students of each of the principal sects—the Church of Ireland, the Roman Catholics, and the Presbyterians—steadily increases.[263] Members of each religious body are among the professors in each college, and all accounts represent the most perfect harmony and cordiality as existing throughout the whole body.

Yet, important as was the principle contained in these measures, none of them, perhaps, caused such excitement at the moment as an exercise by the government of what was, in point of fact, one of its most ancient, as well as most essential, powers: the occasional opening of letters which passed through the post, in compliance with a warrant of the Secretary of State. England had at all times been the refuge of those unquiet spirits who, in pursuit of their schemes of rebellion and revolution, had incurred the displeasure of their own governments, and had too easily found accomplices here. And in the course of the summer some notorious offenders of this class found a member of the House of Commons to present a petition, in which they complained that some letters which they had posted had been stopped and opened by the officers of the Post-office. The member who presented the petition appears to have fancied it an unprecedented and wholly unlawful exercise of authority; but Sir James Graham, the Home-secretary, not only at once avowed that the statement was true, and that he had issued his warrant for the opening of the letters mentioned, but also showed that the power to issue such an order was reserved to the Secretary of State in all the statutes which regulated the proceedings of the Post-office. The clause in the act which conferred the power had been originally framed by Lord Somers, a statesman certainly as little open as any of his time to the suspicion of desiring to encroach on the rightful liberty of the subject; and it had been exercised from time to time in every reign since the Revolution. It was a power intrusted to the Secretaries of State for the public safety, and exercised by them on their own responsibility. The practice and its justification were assailed in both Houses of Parliament by members of the extreme Liberal party; but, though no distinct motion on the subject was made, the general feeling of both Houses was plainly evinced, that it was a power which might at times be highly useful for the prevention of crime, or for the hinderance of conspiracies which might be dangerous to the general welfare and tranquillity, and that the constitutional responsibility attaching to every minister for every official act was a sufficient security against its being improperly used.[264]

And it will, probably, be generally admitted that this was the statesman-like view of the subject. There is no doubt that the practice in question does infringe the great constitutional right of every individual in these kingdoms to absolute freedom of communication with his friends. But the most important and the most cherished constitutional rights must possess something of elasticity. It must be necessary at times to go back to the original object for which those rights have been conferred and secured. That original object is the safety and welfare of the whole body corporate—of the entire nation. And if that safety and welfare at times require the sacrifice, a wise ruler will not hesitate to demand it of the people, or to impose it on them for their own good. So another principle of the constitution is the absolute freedom of action for all the subjects of the sovereign; yet that principle is infringed by more than one statute: Factory Acts, which limit the hours of even voluntary labor; Education Acts, which compel the parent to a certain line of conduct toward his children; each in their way substitute another rule for that entire freedom of action which, as has been said before, is the fundamental principle of the constitution; but they make the substitution on the reasonable ground that the course of action which they compel is for the benefit, not only of the individual constrained, but of the whole community of which he is a member, and for whose welfare all laws and constitutions exist.

One of the grounds of complaint against the exercise of this power, which had been alleged by some of the opponents of the government, had been that Sir James Graham's conduct had been dictated by an unworthy subservience to some of the despotic sovereigns of the Continent. The fact was indignantly denied in the House of Lords by the Duke of Wellington; and in the course of the session a remarkable proof was afforded how little influence such motives had on the decisions of our government, when they acquiesced in the passing of a bill which was a virtual repeal of the Alien Act, which had existed for more than half a century, and of which more than one Continental sovereign would certainly have desired the retention. Of late, indeed, it had been so modified, that practically it had become little more than a dead letter; and now, in 1844, without being formally repealed, it was virtually abrogated by an act which enabled all foreigners to obtain letters of naturalization, which conferred on them every right of British subjects, except those of becoming members of Parliament,[265] or of the Privy Council.

Generally speaking, few governments had enjoyed more of the confidence of the nation than Peel's did in 1844; yet in this year it was exposed to two remarkable mortifications. The charter of the East India Company, as framed by Pitt in subsequent events, which has led to the entire extinction of the political power of the Company, makes anything beyond this brief mention of the transaction superfluous at the present time.

The other mortification of the ministry to which allusion has been made fell upon it at home in the Parliamentary discussion of the Prime-minister's financial measures, on which his judgment was usually regarded as pre-eminent, and on which a large majority of the House was generally disposed implicitly to follow his guidance. Sir Robert was not, indeed, himself Chancellor of the Exchequer, that office being filled by Mr. Goulburn, but it was certain that the Budget was inspired by a deference to the Prime-minister's views. And, among the arrangements which it proposed, one consisted of a relaxation of the sugar-duties, which was regarded with dread by those interested in the West Indies, as a farther step in the direction of free-trade, and as depriving them of the modified protection which they were as yet enjoying. To preserve that protection to them, Mr. Miles, the member for Bristol, proposed an amendment which, after an animated debate, was carried by a majority of twenty. Three months before, on the Factory Bill and the question whether the hours of labor should be limited to ten or to twelve, the minister had also found himself defeated, though by a much smaller majority; but in that case the defeat had been the less pronounced from the inconsistency of the votes on the different limits.[266] And he extricated himself from that difficulty by abandoning the bill altogether, and introducing a new one, not without angry resistance on the part of Lord John Russell and other members of the Opposition. They denounced such a manoeuvre as alike unconstitutional and unparliamentary; while he, on the contrary, insisted that the House had always jealously retained the right of reconsidering its own decisions. In that instance, however, the introduction of a new bill might have been regarded as the simplest mode of harmonizing the variety of views which had been represented by the discussion of and votes on the ministerial proposal and the amendments; but no such expedient was practicable in this case, that of the sugar-duties. A defeat on an important clause in the Budget by a majority of twenty was a far more serious matter; it was such a blow as had generally been reckoned sufficient to require a resignation of a ministry. But on this occasion Peel did not feel himself called on to take that step; nor was he inclined to dissolve Parliament, which some regarded as his only legitimate alternative, though he had little doubt that, if he did so, he should be supported by the confidence of the country. After careful reflection, the course on which he eventually decided was to adhere to the principle of a relaxation of duties, but to consent to a moderate variation from his original proposal as to the amount. And in pursuit of this plan, on the next discussion of the Budget, he proposed an amendment to that effect, making the adoption of it by the House a test of its confidence in the administration. Lord John Russell opposed the amendment with great vehemence, pronouncing the acceptance of it, if it should be accepted, and the House should thus consent "to retract its previous vote, a lamentable proof of subserviency, which would disgrace it with the country." What Sir Robert now asked was, substantially, that they should now declare that to be expedient which they had declared to be inexpedient only three nights ago; and Lord Palmerston insisted that the proper course to be taken by the government was to resign; while Mr. Labouchere, who had also been a member of Lord Melbourne's cabinet,[267] though he admitted that there might be "circumstances under which a minister might without impropriety ask the House to reconsider a vote," denied that the present was such a case, and especially denounced the importation of the question of confidence or no confidence in the ministry into the discussion as "dangerous and unconstitutional." Another section of the Opposition agreed in taking the same line; Mr. Disraeli (then beginning to lay the foundations of his reputation and influence) strongly denouncing the conduct of the minister, as degrading both to his own supporters and still more to the whole House, and recommending him to say frankly to both, "We have gauged your independence, and you may have a semblance of parliamentary freedom as far as this point, but the moment you go farther, you must either submit to public disgrace, or we must submit to private life." The end of the discussion was, that the minister prevailed by a majority a trifle larger than that which had defeated him before. This is not the place to discuss the difference between one principle of taxation and another; but the question whether a minister when defeated is justified in asking either House of Parliament to reconsider its vote, seems one that could only have been raised in a House under the influence of unusual excitement of some kind. The charge that such a request was unconstitutional only serves to show how loosely the words "constitution" and "unconstitutional" are often used even by those from whom precision of language might most be expected; for Sir Robert Peel's proposal that the House should retract its vote was not unprecedented, the very same demand having been made in 1833 by Lord Althorp, then Chancellor of the Exchequer of Lord Grey's ministry, of which those very men were members who were now loudest in denouncing the conduct of the present government. And on that occasion it is worth remarking that, though Lord Althorp's demand was resisted in one or two quarters, he was vigorously supported by Sir Robert Peel, on the ground that, though to rescind one night a vote passed on a former one might be not altogether free from objection, it would be a far greater evil that questions of importance should be held to be in all cases finally decided by a single vote, passed, it might be, in a thin House, or in obedience to some sudden impulse.

And this seems to be the view of the case commended not only by constitutional and parliamentary practice, but by common-sense. It would be strange, indeed, when the questions submitted to the British Parliament and the decisions of that Parliament on them are so often of paramount importance to the whole world, if the Parliament should be the only body in the world denied the right of revising its own judgments, the only one whose first resolution is so irrevocable that even itself may not change or modify it. To rescind a recent vote is, no doubt, as Sir Robert Peel said, a step not wholly free from objection. It should be an exceptional act, as one which, if often repeated, would give an appearance of capricious fickleness and instability to the opinions of Parliament, calculated to impair that respect for it which the whole state and nation are deeply concerned in upholding; but to refuse, under any circumstances, to confess a change of judgment, would lay the Parliament open to an imputation at least equally dangerous to that respect—that of an obstinacy which refuses to confess the possibility of being mistaken, or to hear reason. It would not be well, therefore, that the abrogation of a previous vote should become an ordinary practice; but it would be equally undesirable that any fixed or unchangeable rule should be interposed to prevent a second discussion of an important question, with the possibility of its leading to a reversal of the opinion first expressed.

In the same year (1844) the ministers felt compelled to raise a constitutional point of singular refinement, which had the effect of arresting the progress of a bill, in which one part of the kingdom took a lively interest, which a division in its favor proved to be fully shared by the House of Lords.[268] It has been already mentioned that in the last year of the preceding reign a bill had passed for creating, when opportunity offered by the sees affected becoming vacant, two new bishoprics at Ripon and Manchester, the incomes of which were to be provided by the union of some of the smaller existing bishoprics, Gloucester with Bristol, St. Asaph with Bangor. But the Welsh regarded with great disapproval any reduction of the number of bishoprics in the principality, and Lord Powis now brought in a bill to repeal so much of the act as provided for the union of two Welsh sees, urging not only their great extent, which he stated at 3000 square miles of very mountainous country, but the fact that the population of North Wales was steadily and largely increasing. The bill, as has been intimated, was favorably received by the Lords, who passed the second reading by a majority of twelve; but, before it could be read a third time, the Duke of Wellington, as leader of the ministry in that House, announced that the bill was one which touched the prerogative of the crown, and therefore could not be proceeded with without the consent of her Majesty, which he was not authorized to express.

As the matter was explained by the Chancellor, Lord Lyndhurst, the manner in which the bill touched the royal prerogative was this: as, during the vacancy of any see, its temporalities belonged to the crown, any alterations in a see affected the direct pecuniary interests of the crown, and he, as Speaker of the House, doubted whether he should be justified in putting a question which so touched the royal prerogative without the sovereign's consent. A committee which was appointed to investigate the case fully confirmed the view thus taken by the ministers, and the bill was dropped.

It was, however, an exercise of the royal prerogative which was received by the House in general with great dissatisfaction. Certainly, since the Civil List and royal income had been placed on their present footing, it was only by a very forced construction that the pecuniary interests of the sovereign could be said to be affected. And it seemed a very insufficient plea for evoking the exercise of a power which, as it was said, had certainly never been exerted before since the accession of the Hanoverian dynasty. Nor was it made more acceptable by the explanation of Lord Brougham, who on this occasion came to the support of the minister, that the refusal of the crown's consent at this stage was "a warning, as it were, a polite and courteous communication between the sovereign, as guardian of the privileges of the crown, and the two Houses of Parliament, that if they passed a certain bill it would not receive the royal assent;" for, though the right to refuse the royal assent to any bill was incontestable, it had not been exercised since the time of William III., and to put it in force for the protection of an imaginary interest of the crown itself would have been so unpopular an exercise of it that no administration could have ventured to advise it.

One of the arguments which the Duke of Wellington brought forward in the discussion, and which, probably, contributed to induce him thus to strangle Lord Powis's bill, has had an influence on subsequent legislation. He urged that its adoption—since the resolution to establish bishoprics at Manchester and Ripon was one which every one desired to carry out—would increase the number of bishops, "and thus make an organic change in the constitution of the House of Lords." It is not very clear how the addition of a single spiritual peer could have that effect. But the Duke had dwelt upon the same argument before in the debate on the proposed union of the sees affected, urging that there was such a jealousy of the Church in many quarters, and especially in some of the large towns, that it would be very undesirable to pass any measure the effect of which would be to increase the number of Episcopal peers. Even if there was any general reluctance at that time to see such an increase (a fact which was by no means ascertained), it may be doubted whether it was founded on any sufficient reason. It is not easy to see why, when there is no limit to the augmentation of the number of lay peers, it should be judged impolitic or unjust to make even so small an addition to the number of spiritual peers. At the Restoration the spiritual peers were, probably, more than a fifth of the entire House. From the great number of subsequent creations of lay peers they were now less than a sixteenth, so that there could be no ground for apprehending that a slight re-enforcement of the Episcopal bench would disturb the balance, or give the Church an undue preponderating weight in the decisions of the House. The difficulty, however, such as it appeared to the Duke then, has had such weight with subsequent administrations, that a new principle has been established of creating bishoprics which shall not at first confer seats in the Upper House till their holders become entitled to them by seniority. As they are peers from the moment of their consecration, it may be doubted whether this creation of peers, without seats in Parliament, does not deserve the name of "an organic change in the constitution," far more than the addition of one or two ecclesiastical peers to the Episcopal bench; and also whether it has not established a dangerous principle and precedent; the disconnection of bishoprics from seats in Parliament, in even a single instance, seeming to furnish an argument in favor of the exclusion of the whole order, a measure which, if unjust and injurious to the Church, would be at least equally injurious to Parliament itself, and to the whole state.

But all questions of this kind were presently lost sight of in the excitement produced by the measure which more than any other has stamped Sir Robert Peel's administration with a lasting character, the repeal of the Corn-laws. Many statesmen, even of those who were most in favor of free-trade in other articles of commerce, made an exception in the case of corn, partly from a feeling of the necessity of encouraging agriculture, and partly from a conviction of the danger of in any way contributing to create or increase a dependence on foreign countries for the food of the people. Both Whigs and Tories were generally thus agreed on the necessity of maintaining the principle of protection; the dispute between the two parties being whether it were best achieved by a fixed duty on imported corn, or by what was commonly known as a sliding scale: a scale, that is, which varied inversely with the price of the grain itself, rising as the price in the home market fell, and falling as it rose. In the manufacturing districts a different feeling had prevailed for some years. In the first years of the present reign severe distress in Manchester and others of the chief manufacturing towns had led to the formation of an association whose chief object was sufficiently indicated by its title of the Anti-Corn-law League. At first Mr. Villiers, the member for Wolverhampton, was its principal spokesman in the House of Commons, but at subsequent elections two manufacturers of great eloquence obtained seats, and year after year urged the entire repeal of all duties on corn with great earnestness, though for some time their arguments made but little impression on the House. Their motions were rejected in 1842 by a majority of 300; in 1843 by one exceeding 250; in 1844 by above 200; and in 1845 by one of more than 130 in a much smaller House. But this last division had scarcely been taken when an unprecedented calamity—the almost entire failure of the potato crop, which was attacked in nearly every part of both islands by a new disease, the cause of which is not to this day fully ascertained—suddenly changed the aspect of the subject. To the English farmer and laborer it was a severe loss; to the Irish farmer it was ruin; to the Irish peasant famine. The grain harvest, too, was generally deficient. And it was evident that rigorous measures, promptly taken, were indispensable, if a large portion of the peasantry in the southern and western provinces of Ireland were not to be left to perish of actual starvation. In the face of so terrible an emergency Peel acted with great decision. On his own responsibility he authorized the purchase of a large supply of Indian corn from the United States, hoping, among other indirect effects of such a step, to accustom the Irish to the use of other kinds of food besides the root on which hitherto they had too exclusively relied.[269] And he laid before his colleagues in the cabinet a proposal to suspend the existing Corn-law "for a limited period," a measure which all saw must lead to its eventual repeal. It would be superfluous now to recapitulate the discussions which took place, the various alternative proposals which were suggested, or the dissensions in the cabinet to which his proposal gave birth; the resignation of the ministry, and its subsequent resumption of office, when Lord Stanley and Lord John Russell had found it impossible to form an administration. It is sufficient to say that, as soon as Parliament met, Sir Robert brought forward a bill to reduce the duty on corn to four shillings, a price only half of the lowest fixed duty that had ever been proposed before, that reduction, too, being a stepping-stone to the abolition of all duties, at the end of three years, beyond a shilling a quarter, which was to be retained, in order to acquire an accurate knowledge of the quantity of grain imported. The diminution, however, of this duty was not the whole object of his new measure. It included other arrangements which would serve as a compensation to the agriculturists, by relieving them from some of the peculiar burdens to which the land was subjected; and it contained, farther, a reduction or abolition of import duties hitherto levied on many other articles, especially on such as "formed the clothing of the country," on the fair ground that if the removal of protection from the agriculturist were "a sacrifice for the common good," the commercial and manufacturing interests might justly be required to make a similar sacrifice for the same patriotic object.

Though opposed in both Houses with unusual bitterness, the ministry carried their measure, which, indeed, in all probability, even if the destruction of the potato crop had not come to accelerate the movement, could not have been long delayed, the continual and rapid increase of the population adding yearly strength to the arguments of those who denounced the imposition of any tax which had the effect of increasing the price of the people's food. But, however inevitable it may have been, we are not the less compelled to regard it as indirectly bringing about a great constitutional change, or rather as consummating that which had been commenced by the Reform Bill. Till the year 1832 the territorial aristocracy had exerted a predominating influence in the government of the state. The Reform Bill, which deprived the wealthier land-owners of the greater part of their power at elections, struck the first blow at that influence. The abolition of the Corn-laws inflicted on it a still more decisive wound, by its extinction of the doctrine that there was any such peculiar sacredness about the land and its produce as entitled them to protection beyond that enjoyed by other kinds of property. Placing in that respect the commercial and manufacturing interest on a level with the landed interest, it made us, in a farther and a somewhat different sense from that in which Napoleon had used the phrase, a nation of shopkeepers.[270]

The repeal of the Corn-laws had another result: it divided the Conservative party, and, as a necessary consequence, led to the downfall of the ministry. The same session which witnessed its success in carrying that repeal witnessed also its defeat on a coercion bill, which they regarded as indispensable for the "protection of life in Ireland," where actual murders had reached the appalling amount of nearly three hundred in two years. The ministry at once resigned, and Lord John Russell had no difficulty in forming an administration, now that the question of the Corn-laws was finally settled. It was, however, no bed of roses to which the new ministry succeeded; the famine in Ireland exceeded the worst anticipations; and, though prodigious efforts were made by the government and Parliament to relieve it, though large sums were placed at the disposal of the Lord-lieutenant, aided by contributions from private sources in England to an enormous amount; though the small remnant of the import duty on corn which had been left on it by the measure of the preceding year was taken off, and the navigation laws suspended, in order that no obstacle interposed to the acquisition of food from every available quarter, it was estimated that more than half a million of people perished through actual famine or the diseases which scarcity brought in its train.[271] A severe monetary crisis was one not unnatural result of this distress, so severe that the Funds fell to a price below any that had been quoted for many years, and the reserve in the Bank of England to an amount lower than it had been at any period since 1828. And these difficulties had hardly been surmounted when a new revolution in France overturned the dynasty of Louis Philippe and established a republic. The revolutionary contagion spread to Italy, where, indeed, the movement had begun. The Pope—Pius IX.—who had but lately succeeded to the tiara, was forced to flee from Rome in the disguise of a foreign courier, after his Prime-minister had been murdered by the mob. Germany was scarcely less disturbed. The administration of Metternich, who had governed Austria with authority little less than absolute for nearly forty years, was overthrown in a tumult in which he himself escaped with difficulty from the violence of the populace; dangerous riots took place at Munich, at Berlin, and at the capitals of most of the smaller principalities, and for some time everything seemed to portend the outbreak of a general war, likely to be the more formidable as being a war of the revolutionary and republican against the monarchical principle. Happily, that danger was averted. The only war which broke out between different nations was a brief contest in the north of Italy, which the superior numbers of the Austrian armies and the skill of Marshal Radetsky, a veteran who had learned the art of war under Suvarof nearly sixty years before, decided in favor of Austria, and which in the spring of 1849 was terminated by a peace on less unfavorable terms to Sardinia than she could well have expected. And in the same season tranquillity was re-established even at Rome, which, from the peculiar character of the Papal power, contained special elements of provocation and danger.

But, though peace was thus generally maintained, these various events had produced a ferment of spirits which required some time to calm down, and so greatly embarrassed the government, that in the spring of 1852 Lord John Russell's administration was dissolved, and a new ministry was formed by Lord Derby[272]. But the causes which had overthrown his predecessor remained to weaken him; so that for some time it seemed impossible to form a ministry which afforded any promise of stability. Such a rapid succession of changes as ensued had had no parallel since the first years of George III. Between February, 1852, and February, 1855, the country had no fewer than four different Prime-ministers, a fact which was at once both the proof and the parent of weakness in every administration. Lord John Russell had attempted to procure a factitious support in the country by stimulating a fresh demand for parliamentary reform. A year or two before, he had provoked the dissatisfaction of the "Advanced Liberals," as they called themselves, by insisting on the finality of the Reform Bill of 1832, and by advising his followers "to rest and be thankful" for what had been then obtained. But now he began to advance an opinion that that act required "some amendments to carry into more complete effect the principles on which it was founded." He inserted an intimation of that doctrine in the Queen's speech; and endeavored to give effect to it by bringing in a bill to lower the franchise, having, it seems, persuaded himself that a five-pound franchise would create a more Conservative class of voters.[273] He had scarcely introduced it when the fall of his ministry led to its abandonment;

but, though it was coldly received by the House of Commons, the idea was taken up by the other political parties, who can hardly be acquitted of having used the question merely as an instrument of party warfare, trying, with an unstatesmanlike indifference to the danger of re-awakening the old frenzy on the subject, to rouse the nation to take an interest in it; but trying in vain. The nation was no longer in the same temper as it had displayed twenty years before. The Reform Bill of 1832 had been demanded and carried with a frantic vehemence of enthusiasm such as could only have been excited by real defects and grievances. But those grievances had been removed and redressed. And the bulk of the people could take no interest in schemes whose sole end seemed to be either to satisfy the theories of some political doctrinaires or to embarrass an adversary; till at last, as Reform Bill after Reform Bill was framed, brought in, and defeated, or dropped, it became plain, "as the Prince Consort noted in a private memorandum at the end of 1859, that what the country wanted, in fact, was not reform, but a bill to stop the question of Reform."[274] And, at last, the prevalence of this feeling Lord John Russell could not conceal even from himself, but confessed to Lord Palmerston, then Prime-minister, who had always silently discouraged the movement, that "the apathy of the country was undeniable; nor was it a transient humor. It seemed rather a confirmed habit of mind. Four Reform Bills had been introduced of late years by four different governments, and for not one of them had there been the least enthusiasm. The conclusion to which he had come was, that the advisers of the crown of all parties having offered to the country various measures of reform, and the country having shown itself indifferent to them all, the best course which could now be taken was to wait till the country should show a manifest desire for an amendment of the representation."[275]

There was, however, in these years one subject in which the country did take a real interest; that was the development and extension of the principles of free-trade. On that the national view had become so decided that in 1848 the Parliament even abolished the navigation laws, which had subsisted so long, the first act on the subject dating from the reign of Richard II., that the adherence to the principle contained in them of confining both the export and the import trade of the kingdom, with but few exceptions, to British shipping, seemed almost an essential article of the constitution. It was the dearer, too, to the national prejudices, from the sense universally entertained of the paramount importance of maintaining the pre-eminence of our navy, and from the belief that the commercial marine was a nursery for the royal fleets, with which they could not dispense. But latterly the laws had become unpopular even with some of those who had formerly been supposed to derive the greatest benefit from them. Many of our colonies had complained of their operation, and several of the ablest of our colonial governors had recommended their repeal. They had been found, too, to present frequent and considerable difficulties in our commercial negotiations with other countries, and many naval officers of large experience and sound judgment expressed a decided belief that they were of no practical use to the naval service. The result of a long and able debate was that the laws were repealed, with the exception of that portion of them which preserved the monopoly of the coasting trade to our own seamen and vessels, that exception being chiefly dictated by considerations connected with the prevention of smuggling.

The ground on which the ministers relied in proposing this repeal of laws so ancient was that, when protection had been removed from every other trade, those concerned in these different trades had an irresistible claim for its removal from the shipping. And on general principles, both of commerce and statesmanship, the claim was, as they urged, irresistible, unless some object of greater importance still than uniformity of legislation—namely, the national safety, bound up as it unquestionably was in the perpetual pre-eminence of the national navy—required an exception to be made. But for the maintenance of our maritime supremacy it was, as Burke had preached three-quarters of a century before, better to trust to the spirit of the people, to their attachment to their government, and to their innate aptitude for seamanship, which they seem to have inherited from the hardy rovers of the dark ages, and which no other nation shares with them in an equal degree. And if that may safely be trusted, as undoubtedly it may, to maintain the supremacy of our warlike fleets, the preponderance of argument seemed greatly on the side of those who contended that our commercial fleets needed no such protection; to which it may be added that exceptions to a general rule and principle are in themselves so questionable, that the burden of proof seems to lie upon those who would establish or maintain them. But the advocates of free-trade were not content even with this triumph, though it might have been thought a crowning one, and in the course of the next year they succeeded in carrying a resolution which (though Lord Derby and the opponents of the act of 1846 were now in office) was not resisted even by the ministry, being, in fact, the result of a compromise between the different parties; and which asserted that "the improved condition of the country, and especially of the industrious classes, was mainly the result of recent legislation, which had established the principle of unrestricted competition, ... and that it was the opinion of the House that this policy, firmly maintained and prudently extended, would, without inflicting injury on any important interest, best enable the industry of the country to bear its own burdens, and would thereby most surely promote the welfare and contentment of the people." Such a resolution was, in fact, the adoption of free-trade as the permanent ruling principle of all future commercial legislation. And even before the adoption of this resolution, the feeling in favor of free-trade had been greatly strengthened by the Great Exhibition, which not only delighted the world for six months with a spectacle of such varied and surpassing beauty as even its original projector, the Prince Consort, had not pictured to himself, but which had also the farther and more important effect of instructing the British workman in every branch of manufacture, by bringing before his eyes the workmanship of other nations; and, as we may well believe (though such a result is not so easily tested), of improving the mutual good-will between rival nations, from the respect for each which the experience of their skill and usefulness could not fail to excite.

Notes:

[Footnote 258:] On the 20th of February, 1840, Baron Stockmar writes: "Melbourne told me that he had already expressed his opinion to the Prince that the Court ought to take advantage of the present movement to treat all parties, especially the Tories, in the spirit of a general amnesty." To the Queen his language was the same: "You should now hold out the olive-branch a little." —*Life of the Prince Consort*, i., 83.]

[Footnote 259:] He became Prime-minister in September, 1841, and retired in June, 1846—four years and three-quarters afterward.]

[Footnote 260:] "Life of the Prince Consort," i., 266. It may be remarked that, in spite of the opinion thus expressed by Sir Robert Peel, of those who, since his retirement in 1846, have held the same office, the majority have been members of the House of Commons. The peers who have since been Prime-ministers have been Lord Aberdeen and Lord Derby; the members of the House of Commons have been Lord John Russell, Lord Palmerston, Mr. Disraeli, and Mr. Gladstone; though it may be thought that in his second ministry Mr. Disraeli showed his concurrence in Sir Robert Peel's latest view, by becoming a peer in the third year of his administration.]

[Footnote 261:] Lord Stanhope tells us "the remedial resolutions moved by Pitt in the House of Commons, as abolishing the old duties and substituting new ones in a simpler form, amounted in number to no less than 2537."— *Life of Pitt*, i., 330. Peel, in his speech, March 21, 1842, states that he reduces or takes off altogether (wherever the duty is trifling, but is practicable) the duty on 750 articles of import.]

[Footnote 262:] In the Commons by 307 to 184; in the Lords by 226 to 69.]

[Footnote 263:] The following statements of the members of colleges and of the three denominations for 1879, 1874, and 1869 appear in the last *Queen's University Calendar*:

	1879.	1874.	1869.
Church of Ireland	201	189	211
Roman Catholics	223	188	161
Presbyterians	388	249	227
Other denominations	88	87	83
	--	--	--
	900	713	682]

[Footnote 264:] In the course of the session, in order to tranquillize the public mind on the subject, secret committees were appointed by both Houses of Parliament to investigate the subject, from whose inquiries it appeared that, since the days when the government was endangered by the plots of the Jacobites, the power had been very sparingly used. The most conspicuous instance of its employment had been in the case of Bishop Atterbury, several of whose letters had been opened, and were produced in Parliament to justify the bill of "pains and penalties" which was passed against him. The power had been confined to Great Britain till the latter part of the last century, when it was judged desirable to extend it also to the Lord-lieutenant of Ireland. But, since the Peace of Amiens, the number of letters opened in a year had not, on an average, exceeded eight; nor was there the least ground for suspecting that a single one had been opened except on such information as fully warranted suspicion.

The practice, however, was not confined to our own government. In the second volume of the "Life of Bishop Wilberforce" a page is given of his diary, dated July 18, 1854, which records a conversation in which the Duke of Newcastle and Lord John Russell took part, and in which it is mentioned that the French government, under the administration of M. Guizot, opened letters, and that the practice was not confined to monarchical or absolute governments, for "the American government opens most freely all letters." And, with reference to this particular case, the Duke of Newcastle said that "Sir James Graham really opened Mazzini's letters on information which led to a belief that a great act of violence and bloodshed might be prevented by it." —*Life of Bishop Wilberforce*, ii., 247.]

[Footnote 265:] A subsequent act, passed since the date at which the present history closes, has repealed even this exception. By the 33d Victoria, c. 14 ("Law Reports," p. 169), it is enacted that "an alien, to whom a certificate of naturalization is granted, shall in the United Kingdom be entitled to all political and other rights, powers, and privileges, and be subject to all obligations to which a natural born British subject is entitled as subject in the United Kingdom," etc.; and at the general election of 1880 the Baron de Ferrieres, a Belgian nobleman, who had been naturalized in 1867, was elected M.P. for Cheltenham.]

[Footnote 266:] In one instance—on the question whether twelve should be the number of hours, as proposed by the Government—the majority against that number was 186 to 183. But immediately afterward a majority of 188 to 184 decided against Lord Ashley's alternative proposal of ten hours.]

[Footnote 267:] As President of the Board of Trade. He afterward was raised to the Peerage as Lord Taunton.]

[Footnote 268:] The second reading was carried in the House of Lords by 49 to 37.]

[Footnote 269:] See "Peel's Memoirs," ii., 173.]

[Footnote 270:] It has been observed that till the Corn-laws were repealed there had been no instance whatever of any person who had been engaged in trade becoming a cabinet minister. Since that time there have been several, some of whom only relinquished their share in houses of business on receiving their appointments, and some who are generally understood to have continued to participate in the profits of trade while members of an administration.]

[Footnote 271:] Alison, quoting the General Report of the Census Commissioners, estimates the deaths caused by famine and the diseases engendered by it at the appalling number of 590,000, and states the sums advanced under different acts of Parliament to meet the emergency at £7,132,268.—*History of Europe*, vii., 274, 276, 2d series.]

[Footnote 272:] The same statesman who has previously been mentioned as Lord Stanley, and whom the death of his father had recently raised to the House of Peers.]

[Footnote 273:] In 1853 he said to Lord Clarendon, speaking of a new bill which he was pressing on Lord Aberdeen, then Prime-minister, "I am for making it as Conservative as possible, and that by a large extension of the suffrage. The Radicals are the ten-pound holders. The five-pound holders will be Conservative, as they are more easily acted upon." — *Life of the Prince Consort*, ii., 503. It was the same idea that inspired some of the details of the Reform Bill subsequently passed by Lord Derby's third ministry.]

[Footnote 274:] "Life of the Prince Consort," iv., 395.]

[Footnote 275:] "Life of the Prince Consort," v., 56.]

CHAPTER XIII

Dismissal of Lord Palmerston.—Theory of the Relation between the Sovereign and the Cabinet.—Correspondence of the Sovereign with French Princes.—Russian War.—Abolition of the Tax on Newspapers.—Life Peerages.—Resignation of two Bishops.—Indian Mutiny.—Abolition of the Sovereign Power of the Company.—Visit of the Prince of Wales to India.—Conspiracy Bill.—Rise of the Volunteers.—National Fortifications.—The Lords Reject the Measure for the Repeal of the Paper-duties.—Lord Palmerston's Resolutions.—Character of the Changes during the last Century.

The frequency of ministerial changes at this time has already been mentioned, and the first of them took place at the beginning of 1852, under circumstances which throw some light on a question which has never been exactly defined—the duty of the different members of a cabinet to one another, to the Prime-minister, and to the sovereign.

Queen Victoria had a high idea of her duties and responsibilities. From any legal responsibility she was aware that she was exempt; but she did not the less consider that a moral responsibility rested on her not to be content to give her royal sanction as a mere matter of form to every scheme or measure which might be submitted to her, but to examine every case for herself, to form her own opinion, and, if it differed from that of her ministers, to lay her objections and views fairly before them, though prepared, as the constitution required, to act on their decision rather than on her own, if, in spite of her arguments, they adhered to their judgment. And in carrying out this notion of her duty she was singularly aided by the Prince, her husband, a man of perfectly upright character, of great general ability, and who, from the first moment of his married life, regulated his views of every question, domestic and foreign, by its bearing on English interests and English feelings, to which he early acclimatized himself with a remarkable readiness of appreciation.

In the administration of Lord John Russell, Lord Palmerston was Foreign Secretary, and during its latter years foreign affairs occupied more of the attention of the country than matters of domestic policy.

The revolution of 1848, which overthrew the Orleans dynasty, had produced in France a state of affairs but little removed from anarchy, which was scarcely mitigated by the election of Prince Louis Napoleon to the Presidency of the new republic for four years, so constant was the opposition which the Republican party in the Assembly offered to every part of his policy. They even carried their opposition so far as to form a deliberate plan for the impeachment of his minister and himself, and for his arrest and imprisonment at Vincennes. But he was well-informed of all these dangers, and on the morning of the 2d of December, 1851 (the day, as was commonly believed, having been selected by him as being the anniversary of his uncle's great victory of Austerlitz), he anticipated them by the arrest of all the leading malcontents in their beds; which he followed up by an appeal to the people to adopt a new constitution which he set before them, the chief article of which was the appointment of a President for ten years.

No one could avoid seeing that what was aimed at was the re-establishment of the Empire in his own person. And so arbitrary a deed, as was inevitable, produced great excitement in England and anxious deliberations in the cabinet. Their decision, in strict uniformity with the principle that rules our conduct toward foreign nations, was to instruct our ambassador in Paris, Lord Normanby, to avoid any act or word which could wear the appearance of an act of interference of any kind in the internal affairs of France. But, on Lord Normanby reporting these instructions to the French Foreign Secretary, M. Guizot, he learned, to his surprise and perplexity, that Lord Palmerston had interfered already by expressing to the French ambassador in London, M. de Walewski, his warm approval of the President's conduct;[276] and Lord Normanby, greatly annoyed at being directed to hold one language in Paris, while the head of his department was taking a widely different tone in Downing Street—a complication which inevitably "subjected him to misrepresentation and suspicion"—naturally complained to the Prime-minister of being placed in so embarrassing a situation.

Both the Queen and the Prime-minister had for some time been discontented at the independent manner in which Lord Palmerston apparently considered himself entitled to transact the business of his department, carrying it so far as even to claim a right to send out despatches without giving them any intimation of either their contents or their objects. And the Queen, in consequence, above a year before,[277] had drawn up a memorandum, in which she expressed with great distinctness her desire to have every step which the Foreign Secretary might recommend to be taken laid clearly before her, with sufficient time for consideration, "that she might know distinctly to what she had given her royal sanction;" and "to be kept informed of what passed between him and the Foreign Ministers before important decisions are taken," etc., etc. And, after such an intimation of her wish, she not unnaturally felt great annoyance at learning that in a transaction so important as this coup d'etat (to give it the name by which from the first it was described in every country) Lord Palmerston had taken upon himself to hold language to the French Ambassador "in complete contradiction to the line of strict neutrality and passiveness which she had expressed her desire to see followed with regard to the late convulsions at Paris, and which was approved by the cabinet."[278] The Prime-minister seems to have taken the same view of the act, and remonstrated with Lord Palmerston, who treated the matter very lightly, and justified his right to hold such a conversation, which he characterized as "unofficial," in such a tone and on such grounds that Lord John considered he left him no alternative "but to advise the Queen to place the Foreign Office in other hands."

A careful and generally impartial political critic has recently expressed an opinion "that Lord Palmerston made good his case;"[279] but his argument on the transaction seems to overlook the most material point in it. Lord Palmerston's own defence of his conduct was, that "his conversation with Walewski was of an unofficial description; that he had said nothing to him which would in any degree or way fetter the action of the government; and that, if it was to be held that a Secretary of State could never express any opinion to a foreign minister on passing events except as the organ of a previously consulted cabinet, there would be an end of that easy and familiar intercourse which tends essentially to promote good understanding between ministers and government;" and he even added, as a personal justification of himself as against the Prime-minister, that three days afterward Lord John Russell himself, Lord Lansdowne (the President of the Council), and Sir Charles Wood (the Chancellor of the Exchequer) had all discussed the transaction with M. de Walewski at a dinner-party, "and their opinions were, if anything, rather more strongly favorable than his had been."

This personal aspect of the case it is impossible to discuss, since there are no means of knowing whether the ministers mentioned would have admitted the correctness of this report of their language. If it were confessed to be accurate, it would only show them to have been guilty of equal impropriety, and to a great extent justify him as against the Prime-minister, whose condemnation of his language, if he were conscious that he had held the same himself, would be inexplicable. But it certainly does not justify him in respect of her Majesty or the cabinet collectively, since the Queen's complaint was, not that he held unofficial conversations as a private individual, and not as "the organ of a previously consulted cabinet," but that the tenor of the conversation which he had held was in direct contradiction to the tone which the cabinet had decided should be taken on the subject; that his language was calculated to draw the government into a course of action which it had been deliberately resolved to avoid. And, in spite of the deference due to Lord Palmerston's great experience, it is hard to see how a conversation between our Foreign Secretary and the French Ambassador on an action, the result of which is as yet undecided, can be wholly unofficial, in the sense of having no influence on the conduct of affairs, or, as he expressed it, "in no degree or way fettering the action of the government."

The result was, as has been mentioned before, that the Prime-minister recommended the removal of Lord Palmerston from his office, and that he was removed accordingly. And this conclusion of the case seems to show that the statement of the position of the Prime-minister in the cabinet is rather understated by Mr. Gladstone in one of his essays,[280] where he says: "The head of the British government is not a Grand Vizier. He has no powers, properly so called, over his colleagues; on the rare occasions when a cabinet determines its course by the votes of its members, his vote only counts as one of theirs." He admits at the same time that "they are appointed and dismissed by the sovereign on his advice." And surely to have the right of giving this advice is to have the greatest possible power over his colleagues; not power, perhaps, to change their opinions (though it possibly at times has had power to prevent the expression of them), but power to compass their immediate removal from the administration, as was exercised in this instance, and as had been exercised by Pitt with regard to Lord Thurlow. That a difference of opinion, even on an important subject, is not always regarded as a sufficient cause for such a dismissal; that a Prime-minister, especially if conscious of his strength, occasionally consents to retain colleagues who differ from him on some one subject, the same work to which we are partly indebted for our knowledge of the details of this affair—the "Life of the Prince Consort"—furnishes two remarkable instances in which the Prime-minister, then Lord Palmerston himself, submitted to be overruled. We read there that on one occasion, when "Count Persigny sought the active intervention of England by the way of 'moral support' to a demand" which France proposed to address to Austria, "Lord Palmerston and Lord John Russell (then Foreign Secretary) were disposed to accede; but a different view was taken both by her Majesty and by the cabinet, and Count Persigny's request was accordingly declined."[281] On this occasion, it is true, he was yielding to an overwhelming majority of his colleagues (her Majesty's approval must, of course, have been expressed subsequently to their decision). But in another instance we find the same Prime-minister consenting to the introduction of a bill by one of his colleagues, Mr. Gladstone, then Chancellor of the Exchequer, of which he disapproved so highly that, after it had been passed by a very slender majority of the House of Commons,[282] he expressed to the Queen a hope that the closeness of the division "might encourage the House of Lords to throw out the bill when it should come to their House, and that he was bound in duty to say that, if they should do so, they would perform a good public service;" and after they had rejected it by a majority of eighty-nine, he pronounced that "they had done a right and useful thing," reporting to her Majesty, as a corroboration of this opinion, and as a proof that it was largely shared by the public out-of-doors, that "the people in the gallery of the House of Lords are said to have joined in the cheers which broke out when the numbers of the division were announced."[283] And on a third occasion also he bore with the same colleague's opposition to a measure which he and all the rest of the cabinet justly thought of vital importance to the best interests of the country, the fortification of our great seaports, allowing him to object for a time in private, and even to threaten public opposition to it the next year, since he felt assured that his opposition, if carried out, which he doubted, would be wholly ineffectual.[284]

The personal interest in politics which this laudable habit of judging of everything for herself naturally engendered in the Queen's mind led, however, to the adoption by her Majesty, in more than one instance, of a course at variance not only with all historical precedent, but, with deference be it said, with constitutional principle, sanctioned though it was by more than one ministry. When the First Napoleon, after his elevation to the head of the French government as First Consul, proposed, by an autograph letter to George III., to treat with that sovereign for the conclusion of peace between the two nations, Pitt, to whom his Majesty communicated the letter, had no difficulty in deciding that it would be unseasonable for the King "to depart from the forms long established in Europe for transacting business with foreign states,"[285] and, under his guidance, the cabinet instructed Lord Grenville, as Foreign Secretary, to address the reply to the First Consul's letter to the French Foreign Secretary, M. de Talleyrand.

But this reign has witnessed several departures from the old and convenient rule. Its violation was not begun by her Majesty, but by the Emperor Nicholas of Russia in the year preceding the Crimean war. He wrote to the Queen herself to discuss some of the points in dispute, and she answered his letter with her own hand.[286] The outbreak of war which soon ensued prevented any continuation of that correspondence; but the close alliance which that war for a time produced between England and

France, strengthened as it was by an interchange of visits between the royal and imperial families, which led to the establishment of a strong mutual friendliness and regard, led also to an occasional interchange of letters on some of the gravest questions affecting the policy of the two nations. The correspondence was sanctioned by successive English cabinets, every letter which the Queen either received from, or sent to, any foreign prince on political affairs being invariably communicated by her either to the Prime-minister or to the Foreign Secretary; and they, in one instance, even suggesting to her Majesty to write to Louis Napoleon[287] with an object so delicate as that of influencing the language with which he was about to open his Chambers.

But we must think the line recommended by Pitt to George III. both more constitutional and more safe. A letter from one sovereign to another on political subjects cannot be divested of the character of a state-paper, and for every state-paper some one must be responsible. The sovereign cannot be, but for every one of his actions the ministers are. And it follows, therefore, that they are thus made responsible for documents of which they have not been the original authors; of which, were it not for the courtesy of the sovereign, they might by possibility be wholly ignorant; and with parts of which, even with the knowledge which that courtesy has afforded them, they may not fully coincide, since they could hardly venture to subject a composition of their royal mistress to a vigorous criticism. Such a correspondence, therefore, places them so far in a false position, and it runs the risk of placing the sovereign himself in one equally false and unpleasant, since, if the opinions expressed or the advice given fail of their effect, the adviser is so far lowered in the eyes of his correspondent and of the world.

As has been incidentally mentioned, in the spring of 1854 war broke out with Russia, nominally on account of the Sultan's refusal to concede some of the Czar's demands concerning the condition of the Greek Church in Palestine, but more really because, believing the Turkish empire to be in the last stage of decay, he hoped by hastening its destruction to obtain the lion's share of its spoils. And for the first time for two centuries an English and French army stood together in a field of battle as allies. In the field our armies were invariably victorious, inflicting severe defeats on the enemy at Alma and Inkerman, and wresting from them the mighty fortress of Sebastopol, in the Crimea, which hitherto they had believed to be absolutely impregnable. Our fleet was, if possible, still more triumphant, destroying Bomarsund and Sweaborg, in the Baltic, without the Russian ships daring to fire a single gun in their defence, while their Black Sea fleet was even sunk by its own admiral, as the only expedient to save it from capture. And in the spring of 1856 the war was terminated by a treaty of peace, in which, for the first time since the days of Peter the Great, Russia was compelled to submit to a cession of territory. But (it may almost be said) to the credit of the nation these successes, glorious and substantial as they were, made at the time scarcely so great an impression on the people as the hardships which, in the first winter of the war, our troops suffered from the defective organization of our commissariat. Want of shelter and want of food proved more destructive than the Russian cannon; presently our gallant soldiers were reported to be perishing by hundreds for lack of common necessaries; and the news awakened so clamorous a discontent throughout the whole of the United Kingdom as led to another change of ministry, and Lord Aberdeen was succeeded by Lord Palmerston. While a war on so large a scale was being waged there was but little time to spare for the work of the legislator, though it is not foreign to our subject to relate that in 1855 the last of those taxes which the political economists denounced as taxes on knowledge, the tax on newspapers, was abolished. Originally it had been fourpence; in 1836 Mr. Spring Rice, Chancellor of the Exchequer in Lord Melbourne's ministry, had reduced it to a penny; and now, with a very general acquiescence, it was abolished altogether.

The entire abolition of a tax is not properly to be called a financial measure, that epithet belonging rather to those which aim at an augmentation of revenue by an increase in the number of contributors to a tax, while lessening the amount paid by each. But the abandonment of the tax in question should rather be regarded as a sacrifice of revenue for the instruction of the people in political knowledge; a price paid to enable and induce the poorer classes to take a well-instructed interest in the affairs of the state and the general condition of the country. And, viewed in this light, the abolition of this tax must be allowed to have been a political measure of great importance, and to have contributed greatly to the end which was aimed at. Till 1836 a daily paper, costing sevenpence, was the luxury of the few; and the sale even of those which had the largest circulation was necessarily limited. But the removal of the tax at once gave birth to a host of penny newspapers, conducted for the most part with great ability, and soon attaining a circulation which reached down to all but the very poorest class; so that the working-man has now an opportunity of seeing the most important questions of the day discussed from every point of view, and of thus acquiring information and forming a judgment on them which the subsequent extension of the franchise makes it more than ever desirable that he should be able to form for himself. Every movement in that direction renders it the more necessary to raise the intelligence of the great mass of the people to a level which may enable them to make a safe and salutary use of the power placed in their hands. And no mode of implanting a wholesome political feeling in the masses can equal candid political discussion: discussion one ruling principle of which shall be to teach that the greatest differences of opinion may be honestly entertained; that, with scarcely an exception, the leading men of each party, those who have any title to the name of statesman, are animated with an honest, patriotic desire to promote the best interests of the nation; and that the elucidation of truth is not aided by unreasoning invective and the undeserved imputation of base motives.

One of the last topics discussed by Mr. Hallam was the introduction of a bill to limit for the future the prerogative of the crown in a field in which its exercise had previously been unrestrained, the creation of peers;[288] and among the last which we shall have to examine was one of an exactly opposite character, though relating to the same subject, the creation of a life peerage. In the winter of 1855 Sir James Parke, one of the Barons of the Exchequer, was created Lord Wenslydale, by letters-patent which conferred the title limiting it also to the new peer's own life. The professed object of the measure was to strengthen the judicial power of the House of Lords. But it was not denied that the limitation of the peerage conferred on him for his own life (a limitation which made no practical difference to Sir James himself, since he had no children) was intended to raise the question whether the crown could or could not create a life peerage with a seat in the House of Lords. A creation so limited was so novel, or at all events so long disused a proceeding, that it inevitably provoked examination and discussion. And, as it was found that the lawyers in general regarded it as indefensible, at the beginning of the session of 1856 Lord Lyndhurst brought the matter before the House of Lords by a motion for the appointment of a committee of privileges to investigate and report upon it. There were two aspects of the case which naturally came to be considered in the debates on it which ensued: the advantages or disadvantages, in other words, the political expediency, of such a form of letters-patent, and their legal or constitutional propriety. It was, of course, with the latter alone that the committee of privileges had to deal. And this part of the question was examined with great legal and antiquarian learning, though, as was almost inevitable, it was argued as a party question, except, indeed, by the lawyers. They, with the exception of the Chancellor, Lord Cranworth, who had advised the measure, were unanimous in their condemnation of it; the Whig peers, Lord Brougham and Lord Campbell, then Chief-justice, being as positive in their denial of the right so to exercise the prerogative as those on the Opposition side of the House, Lord Lyndhurst or Lord St. Leonards.[289]

The arguments against the measure were chiefly these: The objectors drew a distinction between what was legal according to the strict letter of the law, and what was constitutional; contending that there might be exercises of the prerogative which could not be affirmed to be illegal, but which no one would deny to be altogether inconsistent with the principles and practice of the constitution, since a great part of the constitution rested on unwritten law, on long-continued usage, *Lex et consuetudo Parliamenti*. And they affirmed that this measure was so opposed to that usage, that "no instance had occurred within a period of four hundred years in which a commoner had been raised to a seat in the House of Lords by a patent of peerage containing only an estate for life;"[290] one most essential, if not the most essential character of the peerage being that it was an hereditary dignity, and one which combined with its rank an hereditary seat in the House of Lords. That one or two instances of life peerages were to be found in the annals of the Plantagenet kings was not denied, though none exactly similar in character.[291] But Lord Lyndhurst argued that precedents which had occurred "at a time when the constitution of the country was neither understood nor fully formed" were entitled to but little respect; and Lord Derby, limiting the age of valid precedents a little more strictly, "said frankly that he had no respect for any precedent affecting the prerogatives of the crown that dated farther back than the year 1688." And since that time, or indeed since the time of Henry VIII., it was certain that no life peerage had ever been granted, except by Charles II., James II., and George I. and II., to some of their mistresses, instances wholly beside the present case, since, of course, none of those ladies could claim seats in the House of Lords. Indeed, it was believed that both Mr. Pitt, at the time of the Union, and Lord Grey, in 1832, had considered the question, and had both decided against the propriety of advising a creation of life peerages.

In defence of the measure Lord Granville refused to admit the distinction between what was legal and what was constitutional; if a measure were both legal, that is, warranted by the letter of the law, and also expedient, these two concurrent qualities, he contended, made it constitutional. He denied, also, that any legal prerogatives of the crown could be held to have lapsed through disuse; *nullum tempus occurrit Regi*; and he challenged any peer to assert that the sovereign had lost the right of refusing his royal assent to a measure passed by the two Houses, merely because no sovereign since William III. had so exercised his royal prerogative. And against the authority of Mr. Pitt and Lord Grey he quoted that of Lord John Russell, who, in 1851, had offered a life peerage to an eminent judge, who, though he had declined the offer, had been influenced in his refusal by no doubt of the right of the crown to make it.

On the expediency of the measure its opponents had urged that it would effect a remodelling of the House of Peers, a total change of its constitution, by the introduction of a second and distinct class of peerages;

and Lord Campbell, with a not unbecoming jealousy for what he regarded as the interests of his brother lawyers, argued that it would "henceforth prevent any lawyer, however eminent he might have been as an advocate, whatever services he might have rendered to the state in the House of Commons, whatever fame or fortune he might have acquired, from aspiring to an hereditary peerage, or to becoming the founder of a family, since, to make a distinction between the Chancellor and the Chief-justice, between one Chancellor or Chief-justice and another, when coming into the Upper House, as to the tenure of their honors, would be intolerable; all must be under the same rule, 'no son of theirs succeeding.'" And Lord Lyndhurst closed his argument by drawing a comparison between the House of Lords and the French Senate: "It was but a few weeks since he had read an official comment in the *Moniteur*, coming from the highest source, on the inefficiency, the want of patriotism, energy, and the backwardness to fulfil the high destinies to which they were called, that characterized that illustrious body, the Senate of France. He had no disposition to cut down our tribunal to that life interest on which the Senate of France is based, as he believed the hereditary character of the House of Lords to be one from which great and important advantages are derived.... The hereditary principle," he added, "is intwined in every part of our constitution; we in this House enjoy our hereditary rights in common with the crown; we mutually support and assist each other, and we form a barrier and defence to protect both those branches of the constitution against any by whom they may be assailed."

As Lord Granville had made the expediency of any measure the quality which, combined with legality, was sufficient to establish its constitutional character, he naturally labored this point with especial diligence. He dwelt upon the great importance of strengthening the judicial element in the House, since it was the great ultimate court of appeal. He produced a letter of the great Chancellor, Lord Eldon, which quoted instances in which various administrations had found difficulties in the way of introducing eminent lawyers into the House, because their want of adequate fortune to support the rank had disinclined them to encumber their descendants with an hereditary peerage. He showed also that that difficulty had made so great an impression on their own Chairman of Committees, Lord Redesdale, that on one occasion he had intimated a feeling in favor of allowing "the Law, in the same way as the Church, to be, to a certain extent, represented in the House by the holders of certain offices, who should be admitted to that House as Peers of Parliament during the continuance of holding such office" (to which argument Earl Grey added another, that the instance of bishops, who were but life peers, proved that the holders of life peerages were not considered inferior to hereditary peers).

He dwelt, too, on the evil consequence of the Lords "placing themselves before the country as seeking to limit the prerogative of the crown, when that prerogative was exercised with a view to remedy something that was weak, and to remove a certain imminent danger." What the danger was he certainly did not explain. But Lord Grey, in supporting him, took wider ground, and, applying the argument derived from Lord Eldon's letter to other professions, extolled the idea of instituting life peerages as one whose effect would be "more easily to open the doors of the House to men whom it was desirable should be admitted—to distinguished officers; to eminent writers; to members of the House of Commons, who in their different lines might have rendered good service to the state, but who, though possessing means amply sufficient to support their rank during their own life, yet, from having only a life income, or a numerous family to be provided for, might be unable to accept an hereditary peerage without injury to their family. In such instances," he contended, "it would be most desirable to grant peerages for life only. Such a proceeding would, he was convinced, by no means disincline others in different circumstances to accept hereditary titles, nor indispose the ministry to confer them. Nor did he see any reason for fearing that the practice of creating life peerages would be more likely to be abused for the purpose of increasing the power of the minister than the creation of hereditary peerages."

The committee of privileges was appointed, and reported it as the opinion of the members that "neither the letters-patent by themselves, or with, the addition of the usual writ of summons, could entitle the grantee to sit and vote in Parliament." And the House, by a majority of ninety-two to fifty-seven, adopted their report. The ministers yielded to its judgment, and ennobled Lord Wenslydale by a new patent in the usual form, as Lord Derby had suggested. But Lord Derby desired to show that his objection had been founded on principle only; and, as he was willing to admit that, apart from the principle involved, "some advantages in certain cases, and under certain modifications, might arise from peerages for life," he proposed the appointment of a select committee "to consider the expediency of making provision for the more efficient discharge of the duties of the House as a court of appeal." The committee was appointed, and, after careful consideration, recommended the creation of two new offices, to be held by two law lords, as "Deputy Speakers of the House of Lords," who should be judges of at least five years' standing, and should be enabled "by authority of Parliament to sit and vote in the House, and enjoy all the rights and privileges of a peer of Parliament under a patent conferring a peerage for life only, if the crown may have granted or shall grant the same to such persons in preference to an hereditary peerage, provided always that not more than four persons shall have seats in the House at one time as peers for life." Such an arrangement would have introduced a new practice, but not a new principle, since the annexation of a seat in the House of Lords to certain offices had existed from time immemorial in the case of the bishops. And the bill was carried in the House of Lords, but defeated in the Commons by a motion to refer it to a committee, which was adopted by a small majority, in a not very full House,[292] toward the end of the session.

Those who look at the question apart from all preference of one minister or one party to another will, probably, be of opinion that the decision of the committee, that a life peerage thus created by the crown could not confer a seat in Parliament, was conformable to the most legitimate view of the constitution. It was, indeed, matter of history that in the Middle Ages the crown had exercised its prerogative in many ways which it had since abandoned. Boroughs had been enfranchised, and again disfranchised, apparently from no motive but pure caprice; writs of summons had been withheld from peers.[293] But no one would have justified the repetition of such acts now. And common-sense, as well as recognized usage, favored the doctrine that long disuse was a sufficient and lawful barrier against their revival. That the power of conferring life peerages with a seat in Parliament—of which, perhaps, the only undeniable instances were the cases of the brothers of Henry V., whose royal blood would in those days, probably, have been held to warrant an exception in their favor—had not been exercised for full four hundred years, was admitted; and the assumption that so long a disuse of a power was tantamount to a tacit renunciation of it, is quite compatible with a loyal and due zeal for the maintenance of other parts of the prerogative which have suffered no such abatement.

If, however, we consider the expediency of the measure, or, in other words, the possible advantage that might ensue from the existence of a power to create life peerages with a seat in Parliament, opinions will probably be more divided. We have seen that Lord Derby allowed that there might be advantages in such an exercise of power under certain limitations; and the existing system does, undoubtedly, appear open to improvement in certain cases. At present the only mode of rewarding naval or military commanders who have performed brilliant and useful service, or a Speaker of the House of Commons, whose public career, though less showy and glorious, may at times have been scarcely less valuable, and has certainly been by far more irksome, is the grant of a peerage with a pension for lives. Without the peerage they cannot have the pension.[294] And, consequently, many most distinguished officers, whose conspicuous merits well deserved conspicuous honors, have gone unrewarded except by some promotion of knighthood, which carries with it no substantial benefit;

while the descendants of some of those who have been ennobled have openly lamented that the only mode which could be found of honoring their fathers proves a punishment to their heirs, by encumbering them with an empty title, which they are unable adequately to support, and practically closing against them avenues to possible wealth and distinction which custom pronounces derogatory to their rank. So, not to mention the names of living worthies, no reward could be found for Sir W. Parker, that brave and skilful seaman who conducted a British fleet two hundred miles up a Chinese river, and crowned his exploits by the capture of a mighty city, which had never before beheld a European flag; nor for Inglis, who, when the safety of our Indian Empire hung upon his gallantry, successfully sustained a siege whose hardships and dangers are surpassed by none in ancient or modern history. Many will, probably, be of opinion that it is not for the honor of England that such services should want due recognition; and that for men like those life peerages with liberal pensions would be an appropriate recompense. It would, of course, be impossible to limit the number of them beforehand, but it would also be needless, since the nature of the services by which alone they could be deserved would act of itself as a sufficient limitation.

One of the expedients which had been mentioned in this discussion had been the annexation of peerages to certain offices, to which it had been regarded as an unanswerable objection that this would be the creation of an absolutely unheard-of tenure, the peer thus created being able at pleasure to lay down his peerage, or even, it might be, being removable. But before the end of the session an emergency arose which induced Parliament to sanction the principle, novel though it was, that an official peerage, if a bishopric may be so called, might be laid down with the sanction of Parliament when the holder was no longer able to discharge its duties. Two of the most eminent members of the Episcopal bench, Dr. Blomfield, Bishop of London, and Dr. Maltby, Bishop of Durham, had become wholly incapable of discharging their duties, the one having been struck down by paralysis, and the other being almost blind. And they now proposed to the Prime-minister that he should make some arrangement by which they might be allowed to relinquish their offices, retaining a certain portion of the income of their sees as a retiring pension. There was no precedent for such an arrangement, but the necessity of the two cases was so manifest, the injury which the Church must suffer if the superintendence of two such important dioceses were to be neglected, was so palpable, and the conditions of the retiring pensions asked were so moderate and equitable, that Lord Palmerston had no hesitation in sanctioning the introduction of a bill to give effect to the arrangement proposed.

It did not pass without vigorous resistance from more than one quarter. The Bishop of Exeter complained of it as incompatible with the great Church principle, that a bishop could only resign his office to the archbishop of his province; others opposed it as a violation of the common law, which forbids any bargain being made for the resignation of an office; while some, referring to the prohibition of simony (a word, perhaps, as much misunderstood and as often misapplied as any in the language), denounced the arrangement that the retiring prelates were to have pensions as simoniacal.[295] The most reasonable objection made to the proceeding was, that such exceptional legislation to meet an isolated case tended to establish a dangerous precedent, and that, as there were other men of great age on the bench, it would be better to effect the end now aimed at by a large general measure providing means for the retirement of all clergymen, those of inferior rank as well as bishops, whom age or infirmity might incapacitate. But the general feeling was against delay. The bill passed, and served in some degree as a model for that general measure which was soon afterward introduced, and which, as was suggested on this occasion, provided for an arrangement similar in principle being carried out whenever a priest holding any kind of ecclesiastical preferment should become disabled for the performance of its duties.

There can be no doubt that such legislation was absolutely necessary in the interests of the Church, taking that expression to include, not the clergy alone, but the whole congregation of Churchmen. But it introduced a remarkable change into the system of ecclesiastical peerages, and, so far, into the constitution of the House of Lords. What was resigned by the two prelates was not the peerage (they had still the right to be styled "my lord"), but the seat in the House of Lords, which was a part, and which had hitherto been regarded as an inseparable part of it, or, at least (as it should, perhaps, rather be said, since the recent regulation that the junior bishop should not have a seat was a clear violation of that principle), which hitherto no one had been able to dissociate from the peerage after it had been once enjoyed.

The treaties which terminated the war with Russia were not concluded till the spring of 1856; and it was well, indeed, that the country had no longer a foreign war on her hands, for a twelvemonth had scarcely elapsed when the very continuation of her existence as a great Eastern power was suddenly imperilled by what, regarded in one aspect, was a mutiny of her troops on a most extensive scale; in another, a civil war, waged by a combination of native princes, Hindoo as well as Mohammedan,[296] for the total extinction of our power, and the expulsion of the British race from Bengal. As early as the first week of February several commanders of regiments and other authorities received warnings of the organization of a wide conspiracy against our power; and in the second week of May the troops at Meerut broke into open mutiny, set fire to the public buildings, murdered their officers, and even their wives and children, and then marched off to Delhi, where the garrison was prepared to receive them with open arms, and to imitate their atrocities. The contagion spread, and in a few weeks nearly all Bengal was in arms. In one or two instances the native chiefs stood by us, but the greater number joined the insurgents, some from the desire to throw off our yoke, but others, probably, from constraint and through fear. Whatever were their motives, before the end of June nearly all the principal cities and fortresses of Bengal, up to the very gates of Calcutta, were in the hands of the insurgents, the chief exception being at the great city of Lucknow, where, though the mutineers got possession of the city, a British garrison held the Residency, in the centre; and, maintaining themselves with heroic fortitude, unsurpassed in all the history of war, for nearly nine months, contributed more than any other body of men to the final suppression of the revolt. It would be beside our purpose here to dwell upon the great deeds by which in that terrible year our army, in all its branches, maintained its old renown; upon the recapture of Delhi; the deliverance of the incomparable defenders and preservers of Lucknow; the exploits of Lawrence, and Inglis, and Havelock, and Outram, and Peel, and Campbell; and, if we are forced to deny ourselves the proud gratification of dwelling on their combined heroism and wisdom, we may for the same reason be spared the pain of recounting the horrid cruelties wreaked in too many instances not only on the officers who fell into the rebels' hands, and on the civil magistrates, but on the helpless women and children. In the first excitement of fear and horror those cruelties were, no doubt, greatly exaggerated, but still enough remains proved to stamp the insurrection as one branding with the foulest disgrace the race which perpetrated and exulted in them.

It was not till the last week of 1858 that the last sparks of rebellion were finally extinguished by the defeat in Oude of the last body of rebels who remained in arms, and the flight of the remnant of their force across the frontier of Nepaul; but, even before that day came, the ministry at home had been led to see the necessity of putting the government of the country for the future on a different footing. It could hardly be doubted that the prompt suppression of a revolt of so unprecedented a magnitude, and the proof given in the course of our operations that the British soldier still maintained the same superiority over the native trooper as in the days of Clive, had heightened our reputation and the belief of our power among the native tribes. But, speedily and decisively crushed though it had been, the revolt had given too terrible a proof of the inconstancy and treachery of the native tribes not to act as a warning to our statesmen; and the reflection that was thus forced upon them showed that a company of merchants, however distinguished by general courage and sagacity they had shown themselves, was no longer qualified to exercise imperial dominion over a territory which now extended over more than a million of square miles, and more than a hundred and fifty millions of native subjects.

Accordingly, in the first week of the session of 1858, Lord Palmerston, as Prime-minister, introduced a bill to transfer the government of British India from the East India Company to the crown. It was natural that the principle of such a measure should be opposed by the Directors of the Company, though it was supported by more than one person who had held high civil office in India; and equally natural that the arrangement of its details should call forth a minute and rigorous examination, and on many points a very determined opposition. We need not, however, say more about this bill, since circumstances prevented its being proceeded with; and the history of those which succeeded it is now only worth referring to as showing the extreme difficulty of the task of framing a government on new principles for a dependency of such vast magnitude and importance.[297]

Lord Palmerston's bill was dropped, in consequence of the fall of his ministry, before the time came for its second reading; but the discussion on it had to some extent smoothed the way for that of his successor, Lord Derby. A great impression on the Parliament, and on the country in general, had been made by a very able speech of Sir G.C. Lewis, Chancellor of the Exchequer. He traced the whole history of the Indian government from the day of Plassy, and substantiated the right of the home government and Parliament to remodel it as they might judge best, by proving that ever since the passing of Pitt's first bill, in 1784, the Company had been constantly subject to Parliamentary control. He showed, too, most convincingly, that a petition which the Company had presented to the House of Commons, deprecating any change in the existing system which should tend to diminish the authority of the Directors, was based on one great fallacy — speaking, as it did, of the Company as one and indivisible, and unchanged in character, functions, and influence, down to the date of the last renewal of its charter, only five years previously; whereas the truth was, that in the one hundred years since Plassy the system had undergone as many changes as the English constitution between the Heptarchy and the reign of Queen Victoria.

He had thus removed some of the obstacles out of the way of the measure of the new government, though Lord Derby would have preferred postponing it till tranquillity should have been restored to the country by the complete suppression of the revolt, had not the large majority[298] which had sanctioned the introduction of Lord Palmerston's bill, in his opinion, "placed the Company in such a situation that they could no longer command the same amount of public confidence and public support as they were entitled to receive previously to that vote of the House of Commons." It may be added that the first bill on the subject which was introduced by his government bore evident marks of the difficulties under which it was framed—difficulties existing from the unexpected suddenness of his accession to office; so that, after a not very short discussion, it was eventually withdrawn, and it was not till the end of June that the measure which was finally adopted was introduced.

The leading enactments of the measure[299] provided that for the future the government of India, described as having been hitherto vested in, or exercised by, the Company in trust for her Majesty, should be vested in her Majesty, and exercised in her name; that one of her Majesty's principal Secretaries of State should have and perform all such powers and duties relating to the government or revenues of India as had formerly belonged to the Court of Directors, as the Court of Proprietors of the Company; that a Council of the Governor-general should be established, consisting of fifteen members, seven of whom should be appointed by the Court of Directors, being persons who were, or had formerly been, Directors of the Company, and eight should be nominated by the crown. And as to both classes, it was provided that the majority should consist of persons who had served or resided in India for ten years at the least, and should not have left India more than ten years when appointed. They were to hold their offices during good behavior, to receive salaries, and to be entitled to retiring pensions, but to be incapable of sitting in Parliament. The appointment of Governor-general and Governor of each Presidency was to belong to the crown. The expenditure of the revenues of India, both in India and elsewhere, was to be subject to the control of the Secretary of State in Council; other clauses provided for the dividends of the Company, for the admission of persons into the civil service; and, with reference to existing establishments, one clause provided that "the Indian military and naval forces should remain under existing conditions of service."

This last clause was strongly objected to by the Queen,[300] as "inconsistent with her constitutional position as head of the army, which required that the Commander-in-chief should be put in communication with the new Secretary of State for India, in the same manner in which he is placed with regard to the troops at home or in the colonies toward the Secretary of State for War.... With regard to the whole army, whether English or Indian, there could, with due regard to the public interest, be only one head and one general command." She yielded her opinion, however, to the resolute objections of the Prime-minister, with whom on this point his predecessor,[301] Lord Palmerston, agreed; but the result proved the superior soundness of her Majesty's view. It was not only a most anomalous arrangement, since the supreme control of all the warlike forces was one of the most inalienable prerogatives of the crown, but it had the strange fault of preserving the double government in the case in which, above all others, unity of system and unity of command were most indispensable. And, what weighed more than either consideration with the generally practical views of English statesmen, it was from the beginning found to work badly, creating, as it did, great and mischievous jealousies between the two divisions, the Royal and the Indian army. It was found that all the generals then in the highest commands in India—Lord Clyde (Sir Colin Campbell having been ennobled by that title), Sir Hugh Rose, and Sir William Mansfield—strongly disapproved of it, and recommended a change; and consequently, in the summer of 1860, Lord Palmerston, who in the mean while had returned to the Treasury, came round to the Queen's view of the subject, and a new act was passed which amalgamated the two armies into one Imperial army, taking its turn of duty throughout all parts of the British empire.[302]

A letter addressed by Lord Palmerston to the Queen in the autumn of 1857, which appears to have been his first statement to her Majesty of the opinion which he had formed of the necessity of abolishing the governing authority of the Company, states the principal arguments in favor of such a measure with great clearness, as arising from "the inconvenience and difficulty of administering the government of a vast country on the other side of the globe by means of two cabinets, the one responsible to the crown and Parliament, the other only responsible to the holders of Indian stock, meeting for a few hours three or four times a year, which had been shown by the events of the year to be no longer tolerable." His disapproval of parts of Lord Ellenborough's policy probably prevented him from alluding to his recall from India by the Directors, in direct defiance of the opinion of the government,[303] though that strange step can hardly have been absent from his mind. But, in fact, the case for taking the whole rule of so vast a dominion wholly into the hands of the Queen's government at home was so irresistible, that it did not require to be strengthened by reference to any individual instances of inconvenience. When the double government was originally established, the English in India were still but a small mercantile community, with very little territory beyond that in the immediate neighborhood of its three chief cities. Of the conduct of the affairs of such a body, still almost confined to commerce, the chief share might not unreasonably be left to the merchants themselves, subject to such supervision on the part of the government at home as was implied in the very name of the department invested with that supervision, the Board of Control, which, as Pitt explained the name, was meant to show that it was not to be, like the measure proposed by the Coalition Ministry, a board of political influence.[304] But the case was wholly altered when British India reached from Point de Galle to the Himalayas, and spread beyond the Ganges on the east, to beyond the Indus on the west; when the policy adopted in India often influenced our dealings with European states, and when the force required for the protection of those vast interests exceeded the numbers of the royal army. India, too, is a country the climate of which prevents our countrymen from emigrating to it as settlers, as they do to Canada or Australia, and where, consequently, the English residents are, and always must be, a mere handful in comparison with the millions of natives. In such a case their government must at all times rest mainly on opinion, on the belief in the pre-eminent power of the ruler; and it was obvious that that belief would be greatly fortified by the sovereign of Britain becoming that ruler.[305] The great rajahs cordially recognized the value of the transfer of power considered in this light, and felt their own dignity enhanced by becoming the vassals of the sovereign herself.

Turning to French affairs, a brilliant French writer has remarked, that his countrymen are, of all peoples, the least suited to be conspirators, since none of them can ever keep a secret. But it was the ill-fortune of Louis Napoleon that he had provoked enmities, not only among his own countrymen, but among the republican fanatics of other nations also, who saw in his zeal for absolute authority the greatest obstacle to their designs, which aimed at the overthrow of every established government on the Continent, and shrunk from no crimes which they conceived to be calculated to promote their object. To free themselves from such an antagonist, the most wholesale murders seemed by no means too large a price. And in the middle of January, as the Emperor and Empress were going to the Opera, a prodigious explosion took place almost beneath the wheels of their carriage, from the effect of which they themselves had a most narrow escape, both being struck in the face by splinters, the aide-de-camp in their carriage also being severely wounded on the head; while their escort and attendants were struck down on all sides, ten being killed and above one hundred and fifty wounded.[306] It was soon found out that the authors of this atrocious crime were four Italians, of whom a man named Orsini was the chief, and that he, who had but recently escaped from a prison in Mantua, had fled from that town to England, and had there concocted all the details of his plot, and had procured the shells which had been his instruments.

It was not unnatural that so atrocious a crime, causing such widespread destruction, should awaken great excitement in France, and in many quarters violent reclamations against England and her laws, which enabled foreign plotters to make her a starting-place for their nefarious schemes. Even in the French Chambers very bitter language was used on the subject by some of the most influential Deputies, for which our ministers were disposed to make allowance, Lord Clarendon, the Foreign Secretary, writing to the Prince Consort that "it was not to be expected that foreigners, who see that assassins go and come here as they please, and that conspiracies may be hatched in England with impunity, should think our laws and policy friendly to other countries, or appreciate the extreme difficulty of making any change in our system."[307]

But a different feeling was roused by a despatch of the French Secretary of State to the ambassador here, which seemed to impute to this country that it deliberately sheltered and countenanced men by whose writings "assassination was elevated into a doctrine openly preached, and carried into practice by reiterated attacks" upon the person of the French sovereign, and asked, in language which had rather an imperious tone, "Ought the English Legislature to contribute to the designs of men who were not mere fugitives, but assassins, and continue to shelter persons who place themselves beyond the pale of common right, and under the ban of humanity? Her Britannic Majesty's Government can assist us in averting a repetition of such guilty enterprises, by affording us a guarantee of security which no state can refuse to a neighboring state, and which we are justified in expecting from an ally. Fully relying, moreover, on the profound sagacity of the English Cabinet, we refrain from indicating in any way the measures which it may seem fit to take in order to comply with this wish. We confidently leave it to decide on the course which it shall deem best fitted to the end in view." Still, though the charge that our Legislature contributed to the designs of assassins was some departure from the measured language more usual in diplomatic communications between friendly powers, under the circumstances this remonstrance might have been borne with. Unluckily, it was not all, nor the worst, that we were called upon to bear. A few days afterward some addresses to the Emperor from different military corps were published in the *Moniteur*, which not only poured forth bitter reproaches against the whole English nation, but demanded to be led to an invasion of the country, "as an infamous haunt for the carrying out of infernal machinations." Political addresses seem to our ideas inconsistent with military discipline; but the army had been permitted, and even encouraged, to make them ever since the days of the Consulate, though such addresses never received the recognition of a publication in the official journal till they had been subjected to careful revision, and, if necessary, expurgation. On this occasion, however, that supervision had been carelessly performed, and the offensive passages were left standing, though, when the Emperor learned the indignation which they had excited even among his well-wishers in England, he instructed his ambassador to apologize for their retention and publication, as an act of inadvertence on the part of the officials whose duty it had been to revise such documents. So far all was well. And had the English ministers replied to the despatch of M. de Persigny in firm and temperate language, they would have escaped the difficulties which eventually overthrew them. There was no doubt that, according to diplomatic usage, a written despatch formally communicated to the Secretary of State required a written reply.

Unfortunately, a written reply was not given. Lord Clarendon was too apprehensive of the mischief which might possibly arise from a protracted discussion, leading, perhaps, to an angry controversy; and under the influence of this feeling contented himself, when the despatch was presented, with giving the ambassador a verbal answer, that "no consideration on earth would induce Parliament to pass a measure for the extradition of foreign political refugees; that our asylum could not be infringed, and that we adhered to certain principles on that subject which were so old and so sacred that they could not be touched;"[308] adding, however, at the same time an assurance that the Attorney-general was already, at his request, examining our law of conspiracy, to see whether it was sufficiently comprehensive or stringent. The purport of this answer was all that could have been desired; but there was a very general impression that the omission to reply by a written despatch was a sacrifice of the national dignity, if not an unworthy submission to scarcely disguised menace; though at the same time there was also a feeling among both parties in Parliament that our laws with respect to the conduct of foreigners residing among us were, perhaps, susceptible of improvement. On the very first night of the session, in allusion to the attack on the French Emperor, Lord Derby had said that "he could wish to hear the opinion of the ministers whether the existing laws of this country were adequate to afford security for the lives of foreign princes against plots contrived in this country; and, if they were not, whether they might not be amended, so as to meet the case of such crimes as had recently been perpetrated, which were so heinous and revolting to every feeling of humanity." And even before that speech the ministers had applied themselves to frame a measure to amend the law, which in the second week of February the Prime-minister himself introduced to the House of Commons.

It was read a first time, though not without some opposition; but before it arrived at the second reading, though only a week afterward, the feeling of the country, reflected in this instance by the House, had become so inflamed, that the measure was not discussed on its own merits, but on the point whether, since no other answer had been given to the French despatch, this must not be regarded as the ministerial answer, and therefore whether it were such an answer as it befitted England to send. Had it been examined on its own merits solely, it could hardly have provoked much adverse criticism. It was entitled, "A bill to amend the law with relation to the crime of conspiracy to commit murder," and it merely proposed to establish in England a law which had long existed in Ireland. Hitherto, as Lord Palmerston explained the matter, England had treated conspiracy to murder as a misdemeanor, punishable with fine and imprisonment. In Ireland it had long been a capital crime; and, though he did not propose to assimilate the English to the Irish statute in all its severity, he proposed to enact that conspiracy to murder should be a felony, punishable with penal servitude, by whomsoever the conspiracy might be concocted, or wherever the crime might be designed to be committed.

The principle of such a law, supported as it was by the precedent of Ireland, could hardly be resisted. And Mr. Walpole, who had been Home-secretary in Lord Derby's ministry, avowed his determination to support the bill, "as being right in principle." But even he limited his promise of support by a condition "that the honor of England should be previously vindicated;" arguing that the French despatch bore the character of a demand, based upon allegations which were contrary to truth, and which, therefore, the ministers were bound to repudiate; and that to pass such a bill without putting on record a formal denial of those allegations would, in the general view of Europe, imply a confession that to them we had no answer to give. And it was this consideration which eventually determined the decision of the House, Mr. Disraeli, who closed the debate on his side, condemned the conduct of the ministers as "perplexed, timid, confused, wanting in dignity and self-respect. In not replying to the despatch, they had lost a great opportunity of asserting the principles of public law." The House, taking his view of their conduct, threw out the bill by a majority of nineteen;[309] and the ministry resigned, and was succeeded by one under the presidency of Lord Derby.

Many of those who on this occasion combined to form the majority had denounced the bill, as an infringement of the principles of our constitution. It is, however, evident that, had it passed, it would not have deserved such a description. It would in no degree whatever have deprived a foreign resident of safety and the protection of English law, so long as he should obey that law; and that is all the indulgence that the constitution ever gave or ought to give. Foreigners had always been amenable to our courts of justice for any violation of the law. And Lord Palmerston's bill not only went no farther than removing a certain class of offences from the category of misdemeanors to that of felonies, but it also imposed no liability in that respect on foreigners which it did not at the same time impose on all the Queen's subjects. Indeed, the bill was so moderate, and the improvement it proposed so desirable, that, in a subsequent discussion in the House of Lords, Lord Campbell, the Chief-justice, expressed a hope that Lord Derby's government would take it up; though Lord Derby, in view of the existing feeling of the country on the subject, prudently forbore to act on that suggestion. But, as one of Orsini's most guilty accomplices, a man named Bernard, was still in London, he caused him to be indicted for murder, as having incurred that guilt as accessary to the death of some whom the explosion had killed. The excitement on the question had, however, not died away when the trial came on; and, though it will, probably, be generally admitted that the evidence was sufficiently clear, Bernard was acquitted.

Lord Derby, however, did not long retain his office. Indeed, the Earl was so conscious that, on questions of general policy, the House of Commons was inclined to views differing from his own, that he would have preferred declining the task of forming a ministry, had he not conceived that, in the difficulty in which the Queen was placed by recent circumstances, he was bound by his duty to make the attempt, even if the result of it were merely to obtain a kind of respite for his sovereign and the country, which might give time for the present excitement of feeling to calm down. He was not deceived in his forebodings of his inability to maintain his position. In the course of the next spring he was twice defeated in the House of Commons—once by the House which he found in existence, and a second time in one which was the fruit of a general election. And in the summer of 1859 Lord Palmerston returned to office, with power increased by the junction of many of those who had helped to overthrow him in 1858, but who now combined with him to strike a similar blow at his Conservative successor.

Yet, brief as was Lord Derby's tenure of power, it was made memorable by the commencement of a movement which cannot be regarded as devoid of constitutional importance, since, though originally it was only designed to supply a temporary re-enforcement to our ancient constitutional forces, the regular army and the militia, it has eventually created a force which, to the great honor of those who constitute it, has become a permanent addition to them. In the great war against Revolutionary France, when it was generally believed that those who held rule in Paris were contemplating an invasion of these islands, Pitt, as we have seen, had encouraged the formation of corps of volunteers, which continued to be of great use till the very end of the war, by performing, in conjunction with the militia, a great portion of the home duties which must otherwise have fallen on the line regiments, and thus disengaging the regular army for service on the Continent. There was now no such formidable enemy to be dreaded as the first Napoleon, but in every part of Europe affairs were in a state so unquiet that every kingdom seemed at times on the very brink of war; and since, if it should once break out, no one could feel confident that we should not be involved in it, or, if we should be, who would be our allies or our enemies, measures of precaution and self-defence seemed as needful now as they had been sixty years before. Our boldest statesmen were disquieted and anxious; and the nation at large, sharing their uneasiness, kindled with the feeling that it was a time to show that the present generation inherited the self-denying patriotism of their fathers. Leaders were not wanting again to prompt the formation of a volunteer force. The government at once saw the value of the scheme. Fortunately, the Secretary for War, Colonel Peel, happened to be an old soldier, a veteran who had learned the art of war under Wellington himself; and he, having great talents for organization, placed the force from its infancy on a sound footing. How thoroughly the movement harmonized with the martial spirit of the nation—to which, indeed, it owed its birth—is shown by the history of the force, which now, above twenty years after its original formation, maintains its full numbers and yearly improves its efficiency. Though there has not for many years been any apprehension of war, above one hundred and twenty thousand men still annually devote no small portion of their time to the acquisition of military discipline and science, and that so successfully, that, by the testimony of the most experienced judges, they have attained a degree of efficiency which, if the necessity for their services should ever arise, would render them valuable and worthy comrades to the more regularly trained army. Lord Derby retired from office while the force was still in its infancy; but Lord Palmerston was equally sensible of its value, and gave a farther proof of his appreciation of the vast importance of measures of national defence by the vigor with which he carried out the recommendations of a royal commission which had been appointed by the preceding ministry to investigate the condition of our national defences. Its report had pointed out the absolute necessity of an improved system of protection for our great dockyards and arsenals, which, from their position on the coast, were more liable to attack than inland fortresses would have been, had we had such. And, in accordance with that warning, in the summer of 1860, Lord Palmerston proposed the grant of a large sum of money for the fortification of our chief dockyards. It was opposed on a strange variety of grounds; some arguing that the proposed fortifications were superfluous, because our navy was the defence to which the nation was wont deservedly to trust; some that they were needless, because no other nation was in a condition to attack us; others that they were disgraceful, because it was un-English and mean to skulk behind stone walls, and because Lycurgus had refused to trust to stone walls for the safety of Sparta; and one member, the chief spokesman of a new and small party, commonly known as the "peace-at-any-price party," boldly denounced the members of the commission as a set of "lunatics" for framing such a report, and the ministers as guilty of "contemptible cowardice" for suggesting to the nation that there was any danger in being undefended. But the ministry prevailed by a large majority;[310] the money was voted, and the nation in general warmly approved of the measure. As Lord Palmerston subsequently expressed it, "the government, the Parliament, and the nation acted in harmonious concert"[311] on the subject.

One of the arguments against it which the objectors had brought forward was, that the ministry was not unanimous in the conviction of the necessity; and we learn from the "Life of the Prince Consort"[312] that Mr. Gladstone, the Chancellor of the Exchequer, was vehement in his resistance to it, threatening even to carry his opposition so far as to resign his office, if it were persevered in. And, as has been intimated on a previous page, this was not the only question on which in the course of this year the Prime-minister did in his heart differ from his Chancellor of the Exchequer, though he did not think it expedient to refuse his sanction to his proposals on a matter belonging to his own department, the Exchequer. The subject on which he secretly doubted his colleague's judgment was one of the proposals made in the Budget of the year. As has already been mentioned, the transaction throws a rather curious light on the occasional working of our ministerial system; and the fate of the measure in the two Houses of Parliament is also deserving of remark and recollection, as re-opening the question, which had not been agitated for nearly a century, as to the extent of the power of the House of Lords with respect to votes of money. In a former chapter[313] we have had occasion to mention the angry feeling on the part of the House of Commons which, in the year 1772, had been evoked by the act of the House of Lords, in making some amendments on a bill relating to the exportation of corn which had come up to them from the Commons. A somewhat similar act had, as we have also seen, revived the discussion a few years later, when the minister of the day had shown a more temperate feeling on the subject. On neither occasion, however, had the question of the privileges of the Lords been definitively settled; and no occasion had since arisen for any consideration of the subject. But the Budget of 1860 contained a clause which, in spite of the deserved reputation of the Chancellor of the Exchequer as a skilful financier, was not regarded with general favor. There was a large deficiency in the revenue for the year; but while, among his expedients for meeting it, Mr. Gladstone proposed an augmentation of the income-tax, he proposed also to repeal the excise duty on paper, which produced about a million and a quarter. It is now known that the Prime-minister himself highly disapproved of the sacrifice at such a time of so productive a tax.[314] And, if that had been suspected at the time, the House of Commons would certainly not have consented to it; even when the ministry was supposed to be unanimous in its approval of it, it was only carried by a majority of nine; and, when the bill embodying it came before the House of Lords, a Whig peer, who had himself been formerly Chancellor of the Exchequer in Lord Melbourne's administration, moved its rejection, and it was rejected by a majority of eighty-nine.

The rejection of a measure relating to taxation caused great excitement among a large party in the House of Commons—so violent, indeed, that the only expedient that presented itself to the Prime-minister, if he would prevent the proposal of some step of an extreme and mischievous character, was to take the matter into his own hands. Had he been able to act entirely on his own judgment, it may, perhaps, be thought that, with his sentiments on the inexpediency of the measure which had been rejected, he would have preferred a silent acquiescence in the vote of the Lords; but he would have been quite unable to induce the majority of his own supporters, and even some of his own colleagues, to adopt so moderate a course; and accordingly he moved the appointment of a committee to examine and report on the practice of Parliament in regard to bills for imposing or repealing taxes. And when it had made its report, which was purely of an historical character, setting forth the precedents bearing on the subject, he proposed three resolutions, asserting "that the right of granting aids and supplies to the crown is in the Commons alone, as an essential part of their constitution, etc.; that, although the Lords had exercised the power of rejecting bills of several descriptions relating to taxation by negativing the whole, yet the exercise of that power by them had not been frequent, and was justly regarded by the Commons with peculiar jealousy, as affecting their rights, etc.; and that, to guard for the future against an undue exercise of that power by the Lords, and to secure to the Commons their rightful control over taxation and supply, the Commons had it in their power so to impose and remit taxes, and to frame bills of supply, that their right, etc., might be maintained inviolate."

In the debate which ensued his chief opponents came from his own party, and even his own colleague, the Chancellor of the Exchequer, displayed a fundamental difference of feeling from his on the subject, a difference which was expressed by one of the most eloquent supporters of the resolutions, Mr. Horsman, M.P. for Stroud, saying that "Lord Palmerston wished to make the independence of the House of Lords a reality, while Mr. Gladstone seemed to desire that it should be a fiction."

Lord Palmerston, indeed, showed the feeling thus attributed to him in a statesman-like declaration that, if "this nation had enjoyed a greater amount of civil, political, social, and religious liberty than, as he believed, any other people in the world, that result had been accomplished, not by vesting in either of the three estates, the Crown, the Lords, or the Commons, exclusive or overruling power over the others, but by maintaining for each its own separate and independent authority, and also by the three powers combining together to bear and forbear, endeavoring by harmonious concert with each other to avoid those conflicts and clashings which must have arisen if independent authority and independent action had been exerted by each or by all." He entered into the history of the question, explaining that, though "each branch of the Legislature retained its respective power of rejecting any measure, the Commons had claimed from time immemorial particular privileges in regard to particular measures, and especially the exclusive right of determining matters connected with the taxation of the people. They claimed for themselves, and denied to the Lords, the right of originating, altering, or amending such measures; but, as long ago as 1671, the Attorney-general, in a memorable conference between the two Houses, had admitted that the Lords, though they could not originate or amend, had, nevertheless, power to reject money-bills;" and this admission he regarded as consistent with common-sense, for "it was well known that, though the Commons contended for the right of originating measures for the grant of supply, and of framing bills with that object, according to their belief of what was best for the public interest, yet such bills could not pass into law without the assent of the Lords; and it was clear that an authority whose assent was necessary to give a proposal the force of law, must, by the very nature of things, be at liberty to dissent and refuse its sanction."

The committee had enumerated a large number of precedents (above thirty) in which, since that conference, the Lords had rejected such bills; but the cases were not in general exactly similar to that now under consideration, since the bills which they had rejected had commonly, if not in every case, been for the imposition and not for the repeal of a tax; and in most cases some question of national policy had been involved which had influenced their vote. But the view which Lord Palmerston pressed on the House was that the present was "a case in which party feelings ought to be cast aside. It was one in which higher and larger interests than those of party were concerned, and in which the course that the House now took would be a precedent to guide future Parliaments." He pointed out, moreover, that the smallness of the majority in the House of Commons had been to the Lords "some encouragement to take this particular step," and that "he was himself led to think that they had taken it, not from any intention to step out of their province, and to depart from the line of constitutional right which the history of the country has assigned them, but from motives of policy dependent on the circumstances of the moment; and therefore he thought it would be wise if the Commons forbore to enter into a conflict with the Lords on a ground which might really not exist, but satisfied themselves with a declaration of what were their own constitutional powers and privileges. It was of the utmost importance in a constitution like ours, where there are different branches, independent of each other, each with powers of its own, and where cordial and harmonious action is necessary, that care should be taken to avoid the commencement of an unnecessary quarrel, and the party that acted otherwise would incur a grave responsibility."

Mr. Gladstone, however, though he ended by expressing his concurrence in the resolution proposed by his chief, used very different language respecting the vote of the House of Lords, characterizing it as "a gigantic innovation, the most gigantic and the most dangerous that had been attempted in our time," since "the origination of a bill for the imposition of a tax, or the amendment of a money-bill, was a slight thing compared with the claim to prevent the repeal of a tax;" and, dealing with assertions which he had heard, that in this instance "the House of Commons had been very foolish and the House of Lords very wise," he asked whether that really described the constitution under which we live. The House of Commons could not be infallible in matters of finance more than in other matters. It might make errors, but he demanded to know whether those errors in finance were or were not liable to correction by the House of Lords. If they were, "what became of the privileges of the Commons?" On the other hand, Mr. Disraeli, as leader of the Opposition or Conservative party, supported the resolutions, and applauded the speech of the Prime-minister, as "a wise, calm, and ample declaration of a cabinet that had carefully and deliberately considered this important subject. It had acknowledged that the conduct of the Lords was justified by law and precedent, and sanctioned by policy," and he maintained that it showed that "the charge made by the Chancellor of the Exchequer was utterly untenable, and had no foundation." And Mr. Horsman, taking a large general view of the legitimate working of the parliamentary constitution, argued that, while it was an undoubted rule that "all taxes should originate with the Commons, as that elective and more immediately responsible assembly that is constantly referred back to the constituencies, the reviewing power of a permanent and independent chamber was no less essential;" and that, considering that "the Reform Bill of 1832 had given a preponderance of powers to the Commons, and that the tendency of any farther Reform Act must be in the same direction, so far from narrowing the field of action for the peers, the wiser alternative might be to adopt a generous construction of their powers, with a view to preserving the equilibrium that is held to be essential to the safety and well-working of the constitution. The House of Commons," he concluded, "is perpetually assuming fresh powers and establishing new precedents. Virtually all bills now originate with the Commons; but this is not the consequence of any aggressive spirit in them, but is the necessary and inevitable result of the historic working of the constitution; and so this act of the Lords was but the natural working of the constitution to meet a definite emergency." The resolutions were passed, the first and third without a division; the second, to which an amendment had been proposed, designed to limit the force of the precedents alleged as justifying the act of the Lords, by a majority of nearly four hundred.[315] In their form and language the resolutions cannot be said to have greatly affected the power claimed by the Lords, and exercised by them in this instance. The first two were simply declaratory of acknowledged principles or facts, and the third intimated no desire to guard against anything but an undue exertion by the Lords of the right which they were admitted to possess. But it can hardly be doubted that the intention even of Lord Palmerston, dictated by the strong feeling which he perceived to prevail in the House of Commons on the subject, was to deter the Lords from any future exercise of their powers of review and rejection of measures relating to taxation, when, perhaps, the Commons might be under less prudent guidance; nor that the effect of the resolutions will correspond with the design rather than with the language of the mover, and will prevent the Lords, unless under the pressure of some overpowering necessity, from again interfering to control the Commons in such matters. At the same time it seems superfluous to point out that one claim advanced by the Chancellor of the Exchequer, who was apparently carried beyond his usual discretion by his parental fondness for the rejected bill, is utterly unreconcileable with the maintenance of any constitution at all that can deserve the name. When there are three bodies so concerned in the legislation that the united consent of all is indispensable to give validity to any act, to claim for any one of them so paramount an authority that, even if it should adopt a manifestly mischievous course, neither of the others should have the right to control or check or correct the error, would be to make that body the irresponsible master of the whole government and nation; to invest it with that "overruling power" which Lord Palmerston with such force of reasoning had deprecated; and to substitute for that harmonious concert of all to which, in his view, the perfection of our liberties was owing, a submission to one, and that the one most liable to be acted upon by the violence or caprice of the populace. He was a wise man who said that he looked on the tyranny of one man as an evil, but on the tyranny of a thousand as a thousand times worse. And for this reason also the resolutions which were now adopted seem to have been conceived in a spirit of judicious moderation, since, while rendering it highly improbable that the Lords would again reject a measure relating to taxation, it avoided absolutely to extinguish their power to do so. Lord Palmerston, it may be thought, foresaw the possibility of an occasion arising when the notoriety that such a power still existed might serve as a check to prevent its exercise from being required. In the very case which had given rise to this discussion he regarded it as certain that the feeling of the majority of the nation approved of the action of the peers; and, as what had occurred once might occur again, it was certainly within the region of possibility that another such emergency might arise, when the Lords might interfere with salutary effect to save the country from the evil result of ill-considered legislation; finance being, above all others, the subject on which a rash or unscrupulous minister may find the greatest facility for exciting the people by plausible delusions. There is, moreover, another reason why it would not only be impolitic, but absolutely unfair, to deprive the Lords altogether of their power of rejection even in cases of taxation; namely, that the Commons, when imposing taxes, are taxing the Lords themselves, as well as the other classes of the community; while the Lords alone of the whole nation are absolutely unrepresented in the House of Commons. There is a frequent cry for a graduated income-tax; and surely if an unscrupulous demagogue in office were to contrive such a graduation as would subject a peer to three times the income-tax borne by a commoner, it would be a monstrous iniquity if the peers were to have no power of protecting themselves in their own House.

In the last sentence of his speech the Chancellor of the Exchequer had "respectfully reserved to himself the freedom of acting in such a way as should appear to offer any hope of success in giving effect by a practical measure to the principle contained in the first resolution." And it was, probably, an exemplification of the power of which he thus bespoke the use that he the next year struck out a scheme for insuring the repeal of the paper-duties, including it in one bill with all his other financial propositions, instead of dividing them in the ordinary way in several distinct bills. It was a manoeuvre which too much resembled the system of "tacking," which had been so justly denounced as one of the most unseemly manoeuvres of faction in the previous century.[316] But, as some of the principal reasons which in the preceding year had led the Lords to condemn the repeal had ceased to exist, and the deficiency of the revenue had been converted into a surplus, they thought it wiser to prove their superiority of wisdom to the House of Commons by showing a more conciliatory spirit, and passed the bill; though the course adopted, which had the effect of depriving the Lords of that power of examination of the details of the financial scheme of the government which they had hitherto enjoyed without any question or dispute, was strongly protested against in both Houses, and by some members who were not generally unfriendly to the administration.

A hundred years had now elapsed since George III. ascended the throne. It had been a period full of transactions of great importance, developing the constitution in such a manner and to such an extent as to make a change in its character but little inferior to those which had been produced by the contests of the preceding century. One principal result of the Revolution of 1688 has been described as having been the placing of the political power of the state chiefly in the hands of the aristocracy. The Reform Bill of 1832, which has been sometimes called a "second Revolution," transferred that power to the middle classes.[317] And what may be called the logical sequence of the later measures is the contrary of that which was designed to flow from the earlier ones. The changes which were effected in 1688 were intended to promote, and were believed to have insured, stability; to have established institutions of a permanent character, as far as human affairs can be invested with permanency. And down to the death of George II. the policy of succeeding ministers, of whom Walpole may be taken as the type, as he was unquestionably the most able, aimed chiefly at keeping things as they were. *Quieta non movere.* The Peerage Bill, proposed by a Prime-minister thirty years after the Revolution, was but an exaggerated instance of the perseverance with which that object was kept in view. But the Reform Bill of 1832, like the Emancipation Act which preceded it, on the contrary, contained in itself, in its very principle, the seeds and elements of farther change.

The Emancipation Act, following and combined with the repeal of the Test Act, rendered it almost inevitable that religious toleration would in time be extended to all persuasions, even to those adverse to Christianity. And the Reform Bill, as has been already pointed out, by the principles on which it based its limitations of the franchise, laid the foundation for farther and repeated revision and modification.[318] The consequence is, that the aim of statesmen of the present day differs from that which was pursued by their predecessors. The statesman of the present day can no longer hope to avoid farther changes, and must, therefore, be content to direct his energies to the more difficult task of making them moderate and safe, consistent with the preservation of that balance of powers to which the country owes the liberty and happiness which it has hitherto enjoyed.

It is in this point of view that the diffusion of education, beyond the blessing which it confers on the individual, is of especial importance to the state. Political theorists affirm that all men have an equal right to political power—to that amount, at least, of political power which is conferred by a vote at elections. Men of practical common-sense affirm that no one has a right to power of any kind, unless he can be trusted to forbear employing it to the injury of his fellow-creatures or of himself. And the only safeguard and security for the proper exercise of political power is sound and enlightened education. It is unnecessary to dwell on this point, because our statesmen of both parties (to their honor) give constant proof of their deep conviction of its importance.

But, in closing our remarks, it may be allowable to point out the political lesson which, above all others, the teachers of the masses should seek to inculcate on their pupils. The art of government, and each measure of government, is, above all other things, the two-sided shield. There are so many plausible arguments which may be advanced on each side of almost every question of policy, that no candid man will severely condemn him who in such disputable matters forms an opinion different from his own. Age and experience are worse than valueless if they do not teach a man to think better of his kind; and the history of the period which we have been considering teaches no lesson more forcibly than this, that the great majority of educated men, and especially of our leading statesmen, are actuated by honest and patriotic motives. And we would presume to urge that more important than a correct estimate of any one transaction of the past, or even of any one measure to influence the future, is the habit of putting a candid, and therefore a favorable, construction on the characters and intentions of those to whom from time to time the conduct of the affairs of the nation is intrusted.

Notes:

[Footnote 276:] "Life of Palmerston," vol. i., c. vii.]
[Footnote 277:] "Life of the Prince Consort," ii, 303.]
[Footnote 278:] *Ibid.*, p. 412.]
[Footnote 279:] Amos, "Fifty Years of the English Constitution," p. 289.]
[Footnote 280:] "Past Gleanings," i., 242.]
[Footnote 281:] "Life of the Prince Consort," iv., 458.]
[Footnote 282:] 219 to 210.]
[Footnote 283:] "Life of the Prince Consort," v., 100.]
[Footnote 284:] *Ibid.*, p. 148.]
[Footnote 285:] "Life of Pitt," by Earl Stanhope, iii., 210.]
[Footnote 286:] "Life of the Prince Consort," iv., 329.]
[Footnote 287:] *Ibid.*, p. 366.]

[Footnote 288:] "Constitutional History," iii., 319, 3d edition.]

[Footnote 289:] It should be added that, on a subsequent occasion, Mr. Roundell Palmer, member for Plymouth (now Lord Chancellor Selborne, and even then in the enjoyment of the highest professional reputation), declared his opinion to be in favor of the legality and constitutional propriety of the proceeding.]

[Footnote 290:] To illustrate this position, Lord Lyndhurst said: "The sovereign may by his prerogative, if he thinks proper, create a hundred peers with descendible qualities in the course of a day. That would be consistent with the prerogative, and would be perfectly legal; but everybody must feel, and everybody must know, that such an exercise of the undoubted prerogative of the crown would be a flagrant violation of the principles of the constitution. In the same manner the sovereign might place the Great Seal in the hands of a layman wholly unacquainted with the laws of the country. That also would be a flagrant violation of the constitution of this country."—Hansard's *Parliamentary Debates*, cxl., February 7, 1856. In the same debate Lord Derby defined "prerogative" as "the power of doing that which is beside the law." Hallam, in discussing the prosecution of Sir Edward Hales, fully recognizes the principle contended for by Lord Lyndhurst, saying that "it is by no means evident that the decision of the judges" in that case "was against law," but proceeding to show that "the unadvised assertion in a court of law" of such an exercise of the prerogative "may be said to have sealed the condemnation of the house of Stuart."—*Constitutional History*, vol. iii., c. xiv., p. 86.]

[Footnote 291:] In the reign of Richard II. the Earl of Oxford had been made Marquis of Dublin for life, but he already had a seat in the House as Earl. Henry V. had originally made the peerages of his brothers, the Dukes of Bedford and Gloucester, life peerages; but these were afterward surrendered and regranted "in the usual descendible form," so that they rather made against the present case than for it. Henry VIII. had created the Prince of Thomond Earl of Thomond for his life, but he had at the same time granted him the barony of Inchiquin "for himself and his heirs forever." It was also alleged that these life peerages had not been conferred by the King alone, but by the

King with the authority and consent of Parliament, "these significant words being found in the patents."]

[Footnote 292:] The division was 153 to 133. Some years afterward, however, a clause in the act, which created a new appellate jurisdiction, empowered the sovereign to create peerages of this limited character, one of the clauses providing that "every Lord of Appeal in Ordinary should be entitled during his life to rank as a Baron by such style as her Majesty may be pleased to appoint, and shall during the time that he continues in office as a Lord of Appeal in Ordinary, and no longer be entitled to a writ of summons to attend, sit, and vote in the House of Lords. His dignity as a Lord of Parliament shall not descend to his heirs." As this act was passed long after the period at which the present volume closes, it does not belong to the writer to examine how far this act, in providing that every Lord of Appeal shall for the time rank as a Baron (the Lords of Appeal being, of course, appointed by the crown), is entitled to be spoken of as introducing a great constitutional innovation, big with future consequences, as it has been described by some writers.]

[Footnote 293:] In one notorious instance, that of the Earl of Bristol (*confer* Hallam, i., 518), in the time of Charles I., the House of Lords had interfered and compelled the issue of the writ; their action forming a precedent for their right of interference in such matters, which in the present case the Lord Chancellor denied.]

[Footnote 294:] The grant of a pension of £1000 a year, with a baronetcy, to General Havelock, and more recently to Sir F. Roberts, are, it is believed, the only exceptions to this rule.]

[Footnote 295:] Bishop Lonsdale, of Lichfield, in reference to Simon Magus, from whose offer of money to the Apostles the offence derives its name, denying that there was any similarity between his sin and the act of purchasing an advowson or presentation, remarked that it might just as fitly be called magic as simony.]

[Footnote 296:] It has been, and will probably continue to be, a matter of dispute whether the first conception and plan of the insurrection originated with the restless boldness of the Mohammedans or the deeper fanaticism of the Hindoos. It is notorious that the prophecy that a century had been assigned by the Almighty as the allotted period of our supremacy in India had for many years been circulated among both; and, though the conspiracy was at first generally attributed to the Mohammedans, the argument that the period from the battle of Plassy, in 1757, to the outbreak in 1857, though an exact century according to the Hindoo calendar, is three years longer according to the Mohammedan computation, seems an almost irresistible proof that the Brahmins were its original authors. Sir John Kaye, in his "History of the Sepoy War," at the end of book iii., c. iii., prints the following note, as furnished to him by Mr. E.A. Reade, a gentleman of long experience in India: "I do not think I ever met one man in a hundred that did not give the Mohammedans credit for this prediction. I fully believe that the notion of change after a century of tenure was general, and I can testify, with others, to have heard of the prediction at least a quarter of a century previously. But, call it a prediction or a superstition, the credit of it must, I think, be given to the Hindoos. If we take the Hejira calendar, 1757 A.D. corresponds with 1171 Hejira; 1857 A.D. with 1274 Hejira; whereas, by the lunisolar year of the Sumbut, 1757 is 1814 Sumhut, and 1857 is 1914 Sumbut."]

[Footnote 297:] It is worthy of remark that, as early as 1829, the Earl of Ellenborough, then President of the Board of Control, had come to the conclusion that the Company was no longer competent to govern so vast a dominion as that of British India had gradually become. In his Diary, recently published (ii., 131), he expresses his firm conviction that, "in substituting the King's government for that of the Company, we shall be conferring a great benefit on India, and effecting the measure which is most likely to retain for England the possession of India;" and from the same work (ii., 61) we learn that Mr. Mountstuart Elphinstone, one of the ablest servants of whom the Company could boast, and who had recently been Governor of Bombay, even while confessing himself prejudiced in favor "of the existing system, under which he had been educated and lived," admitted that "the administration of the government in the King's name would be agreeable to the civil and military services, and to people in England. He doubted whether, as regarded the princes of India, it would signify much, as they now pretty well understood us." See also *ibid.*, p. 414.]

[Footnote 298:] 318 to 173.]

[Footnote 299:] The whole bill is given in the "Annual Register" for the year 1858, p. 226.]

[Footnote 300:] See her letter to Lord Derby on the subject, given in the "Life of the Prince Consort," iv., 308; *confer* also a memorandum of the Prince Consort, *ibid.*, p. 310.]

[Footnote 301:] *Ibid.*, p. 106.]

[Footnote 302:] It should be remarked that the arrangement originally carried out awoke among the European troops of the Company so deep and general a spirit of discontent as at one time threatened to break out in open mutiny; the ground of their dissatisfaction being "the transfer of their services in virtue of an act of Parliament, but without their consent." Accordingly, "on the announcement of the proclamation transferring the possessions of the East India Company to the crown, some of the soldiers of the Company's European force set up a claim for a free discharge or a bounty on re-enlistment." Lord Clyde's recommendation "that a concession should be made" was overruled by the government of India, and "pronounced inadmissible by the law-officers of the crown" in England. The dissatisfaction was allayed for the time by the judicious measures, equally conciliatory and firm, adopted by Lord Clyde, in whom all ranks of both armies felt equal confidence; but eventually the government became convinced of the necessity of granting discharges to every man who wished for one, provided he had not misconducted himself.—Shadwell's *Life of Lord Clyde*, ii., 407-416.]

[Footnote 303:] See *ante*, p. 385.]

[Footnote 304:] Stanhope's "Life of Pitt," i., 173.]

[Footnote 305:] Sir Theodore Martin quotes a passage from a letter of the *Times* correspondent, giving a report of the effect of the proclamation on the natives: "Genuineness of Asiatic feeling is always a problem, but I have little doubt it is in this instance literally sincere. The people understand an Empress, and did not understand the Company. Moreover, they (I am speaking of the masses) have a very decided notion that the Queen has hanged the Company for offences 'which must have been very great,' and that fact gives hope of future justice." —*Life of the Prince Consort*, iv., 337.]

[Footnote 306:] The "Annual Register" says that "neither the Emperor nor the Empress was touched;" but Sir Theodore Martin ("Life of the Prince Consort," iv., 155) says that "the Emperor's nose was grazed, and that the Empress received a blow on the left eye which affected it for some time."]

[Footnote 307:] "Life of the Prince Consort," iv., 156.]

[Footnote 308:] Speech of Lord Palmerston, February 19.]

[Footnote 309:] It is remarkable that it was not a very full House, the numbers of the division being only 234 to 215. Many members absented themselves, being equally unwilling to condemn the bill or to approve the silence of the ministry.]

[Footnote 310:] 268 to 39.]

[Footnote 311:] "Life of the Prince Consort," v., 131.]

[Footnote 312:] "Life of the Prince Consort," i., 99.]

[Footnote 313:] Chapter II., .]

[Footnote 314:] It is known, from two letters from Lord Palmerston to the Queen, published in the "Life of the Prince Consort," v., 100—in one, written before the debate in the House of Lords, he expresses a hope that the smallness of the majority in the House of Commons will encourage the Lords to throw it out, and he "is bound in duty to say that, if they do so, they will perform a good public service;" and in another, the day after the division in the Lords, he writes again "that they have done a right and useful thing," adding that the feeling of the public was so strong against the measure, that those in the gallery of the House are said to have joined in the cheers which broke out when the numbers were announced.]

[Footnote 315:] 433 to 36.]

[Footnote 316:] See the proceedings of 1700 (Macaulay, "History of England," v., 278; and of 1704, Lord Stanhope's "Reign of Queen Anne," p. 168). The Whig and the Tory writer equally condemn the "Tackers."]

[Footnote 317:] In the debate on life peerages ("Parliamentary History," cxl., 356), Lord Grey spoke of "that great transfer of political power from one class to another which was accomplished by the Reform Bill" And Lord Campbell, speaking of Lord Grey himself in connection with that measure, says: "His Reform Bill ought to place him in a temple of British worthies by the side of Lord Somers, for it wisely remodelled the constitution, and it is hardly less important than the Bill of Rights."—*Life of Lord Campbell*, ii., 201.]

[Footnote 318:] A recent writer, professedly belonging to the Radical party, claims for it the credit of "being the legitimate issue of the Reform Bill of 1832." ("The State of Parties," by J.E. Kebbel, *Nineteenth Century*, March, 1881, p. 497.)]

INDEX

ABBOTT, Mr., proposes a census.

Addington, Mr., becomes Prime-minister, See Sidmouth.

Additional Force Bill.

Albert, Prince, marries Queen Victoria.

Alien' Act, the.

Althorp, Lord, introduces a bill for the reform of the Poor-laws; his speech on the condition of Ireland; invites the House of Commons to rescind a vote.

Amelia, Princess, death of.

Archdall, Mr., on Catholic Emancipation, note.

Association, Catholic, suppression of.

BAKER, Mr., moves a resolution on the dismissal of the Coalition Ministry.

Barrington, Lord, moves the expulsion of Wilkes.

Battle, wager of, abolished.

Bernard, trial of, as accomplice of Orsini.

Bishoprics, provision for the increase of; exclusion of the occupants of the junior bishoprics from the House of Peers; resignation of, by aged bishops.

Blucher, Field-marshal, proposes to put Napoleon to death.

Boston, United States, tea ships at, boarded by rioters, and the cargo thrown into the sea.

Bristol, Lord, denounces the appointment of the Chief-justice to a seat in the cabinet.

Brougham, Mr., afterward Lord Chancellor, the chief adviser of the Queen;

defends the ministry for stopping Lord Powis's bill.

Brownlow, Mr., opposes Pitt's commercial reforms.

Buonaparte, Napoleon, detention of.

Burdett, Sir F., carries a motion for repeal of Roman Catholic disabilities.

Burke, Mr. B., opposes the expulsion of Wilkes;

supports Mr. Grenville's act;

complains of the insolence of the House of Peers;

supports the repeal of the bill for taxing the American Colonies;

on annual Parliaments;

brings in a bill for economical reform;

his "short account of a late administration";

asserts the right of the House of Peers to examine the public accounts;

his violent language on the Regency Bill;

member of Lord Rockingham's second ministry;

his view of the attachment of the Colonies to England.

Bute, Earl of, Prime-minister in 1762;

resigns office.

CABINET, character of.

Camden, Earl of, approves the resolution of the House of Commons;

opposes the Royal Marriage Act;

supports Lord Chatham's views on the American question;

moves the Regency bill of 1788.

Campbell, Lord, his "Lives of the Chancellors" referred to;

his denunciation of the Declaratory Act;

and of the Regency bill;

on the Chief-justice in the cabinet.

Canada, disquietude in;

union of the two provinces.

Canning, Lord, grants the right of adoption to the Hindoo feudatories.

Canning, Mr. G., attacks the appointment of the Chief-justice to a seat in the cabinet; becomes Prime-minister;

dies;

his opinion on the question in which House of Parliament the Prime-minister should be.

Caroline, Princess of Brunswick, marries the Prince of Wales;

investigations into her conduct;

she dies.

Cave, Mr., punished for publishing reports of debates.

Census established.

Charlotte, Princess, birth of.

Chartists, rise of;

outrages of, at Birmingham and Newport.

Chatham, Earl of, Secretary of State in 1760;

Lord Privy Seal in 1767; supports Lord Rockingham's resolution on the expulsion of Wilkes;

denies the power of the Parliament to tax America.

Church reform, sketched out by Sir Robert Peel;

earned by Lord Melbourne's ministry.

Clarence, Duke of, opposes the abolition of the slave trade;

his leaning toward the Whigs.

Clarendon, Earl of, omits to reply to the despatch of the French minister.

Clergy, Roman Catholic, question of endowing the.

Colborne, Sir John crushes the insurrection in Canada.

Colonies, general grant of constitutions to, in New Zealand, the Cape, and Australia.

Commons, House of privileges of, with respect to money bills.

Conventicle Act, repeal of.

Conway, General, Secretary of State, introduces a bill of indemnity.

Cornwallis, Lord, surrenders in America.

Corporations, reform of.

Crosby, Brass, Mr, Lord Mayor, commits a messenger of the House of Commons, and is himself committed to the Tower.

Cumberland, Duke of, marries Mrs Horton.

Cust, Sir J, Speaker of the House of Commons.

DASHWOOD, Sir F., his revels at Medmenham Abbey.

Declaratory Act.

De Grey, Mr, Attorney-general, supports the resolutions against Wilkes.

Denbigh, Lord, defends the employment of Hanoverian troops at Gibraltar.

Denman, Lord Chief justice, his charge to the jury in the case of Stockdale v. Hansard.

Disraeli, Mr B, his act for the trial of election petitions;

he denounces Sir Robert Peel for not resigning when defeated on the sugar-duties;

condemns Lord Clarendon's omission to reply to the French despatch;

supports the House of Lords on the paper duties.

Dowdeswell, Mr, opposes the Royal Marriage Act.

Dundas, Mr, moves an amendment to Mr Dunning's resolution.

Dunning, Mr, afterward Lord Ashburton, supports Mr Glenvilles act;

criticizes a resolution on the influence of the crown.

Dunham, Lord, Governor of Canada.

EDUCATION, influence of the penal laws on in Ireland.

Eldon, Lord, on the coronation oath in connection with the Catholic question;

on the detention of Napoleon;

on life peerages.

Elgin, Lord, Governor general of Canada.

Ellenborough, Lord, supports the Additional Force Bill;

becomes a member of the Cabinet;

is recalled from the government of India by the Company.

Emancipation of Roman Catholics designed by Pitt;

concurred by the Duke of Wellington.

Erskine, Lord, as Chancellor, presides over the impeachment of Lord Melville;

resists Lord Sidmouth's Six Acts.

FITZGERALD, LORD E., opposes the English government.

Fitzgerald, Mr Vesey, is defeated in Clare.

Fitzgibbon, Mr (afterward Lord Clare), opposes the convention of delegates in Dublin;

Attorney-general in Ireland, prosecutes the sheriff of Dublin;

supports the Regency bill.

Fitzwilliam, Earl, is dismissed from the Lord-lieutenancy of Yorkshire.

Five Mile Act repealed.

Fox, Mr C., opposes Mr Grenville's act;

on the privileges claimed by the House of Commons respecting money-bills;

note, on Parliamentary reform and annual Parliaments;

urges the appointment as Prime-Minister of the Duke of Portland;

resigns office;

becomes Secretary of State;

his India Bill;

violence of his attacks on Pitt at the beginning of his ministry;

his opinions on Colonial policy;

denies the Prince's marriage;

opposes the Regency bill;

opposes the Alien Act and other bills;

opposes Pitt's commercial reforms;

becomes Secretary of State;

supports the abolition of the slave trade;

dies.

France, new revolution in 1848.

Franklin, Dr, is examined by the House of Commons on Mr Glenville's measures of taxation.

GEORGE III., state of affairs at the accession of;

illness of in 1764;

firmness in the Gordon riots;

becomes deranged;

is attacked on the street;

resists the relaxation of Catholic restrictions;

becomes permanently deranged;

dies;

character of his reign.

George IV. succeeds to the throne.

Gladstone, Mr W.E., opposes the fortification of the dockyards;

proposes to repeal the paper-duties;

carries the repeal of the paper-duties;

desires to weaken the power of the House of Lords.

Gloucester, Duke of, marries Lady Waldegrave.

Gordon, Lord George, the Gordon riots.

Goulburn, Mr. H, is Chancellor of the Exchequer.

Grafton, Duke of, Prime-minister in 1767;

disapproves of American taxation.

Graham, Sir J., as Home-secretary, orders the opening of letters.

Grampound disfranchised.

Granville, Earl, defends life peerages.

Grattan, Mr. H., moves the repeal of Poynings' Act;

opposes Pitt's commercial reforms;

opposes Pitt's Regency bill.

Grenville, Mr. G., becomes Prime minister;

opposes the expulsion of Wilkes;

brings in a bill for the investigation of election petitions;

imposes taxes on the North American Colonies.

Grenville, Lord, introduces the Alien Bill;

opposes the Additional Force Bill;

brings in a bill for the abolition of the slave trade;

refuses a seat in the cabinet in 1812.

Grey, Mr. (afterward Earl), opposes the Regency bill;

opposes the Alien Act;

opposes the union with Ireland;

proposes to diminish the number of members of the House of Commons;

opposes the abolition of slavery;

refuses a seat in the cabinet in 1812;

becomes Prime minister;

his ministry brings in Reform Bill;

defends a proposed creation of peers;

mentions the sovereign's opinion unconstitutionally;

letters from office.

Grey, Earl (son of the preceding), his doctrine on the true principles of colonial government;

on life peerages.

Gower, Lord F.L., carries a resolution for the endowment of the Roman Catholic clergy.

Girizot, M., Foreign Secretary in France.

HALIFAX, Earl of, issues a general warrant against the publishers, etc., of *The North Briton*.

Hanoverian troops, employment of, at Gibraltar.

Hansard, Mr., publishes the Parliamentary debates.

Hardy, General, taken prisoner by Sir J. Warren.

Hill, Mr. Roland, proposes a reform of the Post-office.

Hillsborough, Lord, writes a circular letter to the North American

Colonies.

Hoche, General, sails for Ireland.

Holdernesse, Earl of, Secretary of State in 1760.

Holland, Lord, opposes the Regency Bill.

Holt, Chief justice, his decision on the question of slavery.

Holsmann, Mr., supports the House of Lords on the paper duties.

Humbert, General, taken prisoner in Mayo.

INDIA, Fox's India Bill;

Pitt's India Bill;

Mutiny in;

transfer of the authority of the Company to the crown;

establishment of the Order of the Star of India;

is visited by the Prince of Wales.

Ireland, affairs of;

connection with France;

rebellion in.

JAMAICA, planters in, compensated for the diminution of the value of their property by the abolition of slavery;

disturbances in;

its constitution is suspended.

Judges, new tenure of their office.

KING, the, cannot be a witness in any legal proceeding.

LABOUCHERE, Mr. H., reproaches Sir Robert Peel for not resigning.

Leopold, King of Belgium, points of the insufficiency of the description of Prince Albert.

Lewis, Sir. G.C., speech on the history and power of the East India Company.

Liverpool, Lord, earnest for the universal abolition of the slave trade;

becomes Prime minister;

makes the Catholic question an open question in the cabinet;

brings in, and subsequently withdraws, a "Bill of Pains and

Penalties";

against the Queen;

attacked by apoplexy and dies;

contemplates an increased grant to Maynooth.

Lopes, Sir M., procures the return of Mr. Pool for Westbury.

Louise, Princess, marriage of.

Lowther, Sir John, obtains a grant of Inglewood Forest.

Luttrell, Mr., is declared elected for Middlesex.

Lyndhurst, Lord, carries an amendment on the Reform Bill; introduces a Regency bill.

MACINTOSH, Sir J., applies himself to mitigate the severity of the law.

Mahon, Lord, brings in a bill to diminish the expenses of elections.

Mansfield, Lord, condemns general warrants;

insists on the necessity of a bill of indemnity;

vindicates the supremacy of Parliament;

his house is burnt by the rioters in 1780.

Martin, Mr., wounds Wilkes in a duel.

Massachusetts, riots in.

Maynooth, foundation of a college at;

is enlarged and more fully endowed.

Melbourne, Lord, becomes Prime-minister;

resigns;

resumes office;

mismanages the arrangements for Prince Albert.

Melville, Lord, is impeached.

Metternich, Prince, is driven from Vienna.

Miles, Mr., defeats the government on the sugar-duties.

Moira, Lord, employed by the Regent to negotiate with the Whig leaders in 1812.

Money-bills, power of the House of Lords as to.

Montesquieu, M. de, his opinion of the English constitution.

Montmorin, M., Wilberforce writes to him on the subject of the slave-trade.

NAPOLEON, Louis, is elected President of the French Republic; his *coup d'état*;

conspiracy against.

Navigation laws, the, repeal of.

Nelson, Lord, his victory at Copenhagen.

Newcastle, Duke of, Prime minister in 1760.

New Shoreham, disfranchisement of for bribery.

Newspapers, tax on, reduced and afterward abolished.

Nicholas, Emperor of Russia, writes to the Queen.

Normanby, Lord, ambassador in Paris, complains of Lord Palmerston.

North, Lord, supports the decision in favor of Mr. Luttrell;

opposes Mr. Grenville's act;

opposes Mr. Seymour's bill to limit the *Nullum Tempus* Act;

opposes reform of Parliament;

rejects the demands of Ireland.

Northington, Lord C., defends the embargo on corn;

indicates the supremacy of Parliament.

Nullum Tempus Act, the, extended.

O'CONNELL, Mr. D., is returned for Clare;

is chief of the Catholic Association.

Octennial act for Ireland.

"Olive Branch, the,"

Onslow, Colonel, complains of the publication of the debates.

Orsini, conspiracy of.

PALMERSTON, Lord, is dismissed from the Foreign-office;

introduces the bill for the transfer of the government of India to the crown;

writes to the Queen on the abolition of the authority of the East India Company;

is defeated on the Conspiracy Bill and resigns;

returns to office;

disapproves of the reduction of the paper-duty;

desires to uphold the House of Lords.

Papineau. M., organizes an insurrection in Canada.

Parke, Sir J., is created a peer for life.

Parliament, first meeting of the United.

Peel, Sir Robert, responsible for the change of ministry in 1834;

becomes Home-secretary;

resigns his seat for Oxford and fails to be re-elected;

impropriety of his resignation;

speech on introducing the bill for Catholic Emancipation;

becomes Prime-minister;

declines to form an administration in 1839;

supports Lord J. Russell's resolutions in the case of Stockdale *v.*

Hansard;

his opinion on the question in which House the Prime-minister should be;

becomes Prime-minister in 1841;

revises the commercial tariff;

suspends the Corn-law;

causes its abolition.

Peel, Colonel, organizes the Volunteers.

Peerages, life, legality of.

Peers, the House of, strikes out of a corn bill some clauses giving bounties;

their right to inquire into the public expenditure asserted by Lord Camden and others;

their privileges as to money-bills;

provisions as to Irish peers in the Act of Union;

proposed creation of peers to carry the Reform Bill considered;

the House of Peers rejects the abolition of the paper-duty.

Penal laws, in Ireland;

repeal of;

in the United Kingdom.

Penu, Mr., sent from America to England with "the Olive Branch."

Perceval, Mr., becomes Prime-minister;

proposes a Regency bill;

is murdered.

Percy, Lord, proposes the entire abolition of slavery.

Persigny, M. de, French Secretary of State, his despatch on Orsini's conspiracy.

Pigott, Sir A., brings in a bill on the slave-trade.

Pitt, see Earl of Chatham.

Pitt, Mr. T., denounces the influence of the crown.

Pitt, Mr. W., on the privileges of House of Commons respecting money-bills;

note;

becomes Prime-minister;

his long struggle against, and eventual defeat of the Opposition;

comparisons between his father and him;

his India bill;

his Quebec bill;

his Regency bill;

founds Maynouth;

carries the Irish Union;

resigns on the Catholic question.

Plunkett, Mr., opposes the Irish Union.

Ponsonby, Mr. G., condemns the policy of open questions.

Poor-law, the, reform of.

Portland, Duke of, becomes Prime-minister;

again.

Post-office, reform of;

letters opened by the order of the Secretary of State.

Powis, Earl, brings in a bill to preserve the Welsh sees.

Pownall, Governor, introduces a corn bill.

Poynings' Act;

repeal of.

RADETSKY, MARSHAL, his campaign in North Italy.

Reform of Parliament, Alderman Sawbridge proposes a measure of;

Mr. Pitt brings in a bill for;

agitation for, in 1818;

introduced and carried by Lord Grey's administration;

the people indifferent to farther reform.

Regency bill of 1764;

of 1840;

former Regency bills had been passed in the reigns of Edward III., Richard II., Henry VI., and George II.;

in Ireland;

bill of 1810.

Registration, extension of, 342.

Rice, Mr. Spring, as Chancellor of the Exchequer, introduces Post-office reform;

as Lord Monteagle proposes the rejection of the paper-duty bill.

Roberts, Mr., returning officer for New Shoreham.

Rochfort, Lord, introduces the Royal Marriage Act.

Rockingham, Marquis of, Prime-minister in 1768;

moves a resolution condemning the proceedings against Wilkes;

Prime-minister a second time;

repeals the American taxes;

disapproves of the employment of Hanoverian troops at Gibraltar;

wisdom of his policy toward America;

his speech on the influence of the crown;

becomes Prime-minister a second time.

Rolle, Mr., moots the question of the Prince's marriage.

Romilly, Sir S., opposes the Regency bill;

applies himself to reforms of the law.

Rose, Mr., opposes Sir A. Pigott's bill on the slave-trade.

Russell, Lord J., his opinion on Fox's conduct in Opposition;

on the Regency bill;

carries the repeal of the Test Act;

introduces the Reform Bill;

introduces a bill for municipal reform;

his resolutions in the case of Stockdale v. Hansard;

becomes Prime—minister.

Russia, war with.

SANDWICH, EARL OF, denounces Wilkes's "Essay on Woman."

Sarsfield, General, takes refuge in France.

Savile, Sir G., his bill for the limitation of the *Nullum Tempus* Act.

Seaforth, Lord, reports of the treatment of slaves in Barbadoes.

Seditious Meetings Act.

Shelburne, Lord, denounces the employment of Hanoverian troops at Gibraltar;

becomes Prime-minister.

Sheridan, Mr. R., his language on the Prince's marriage;

opposes the Alien Act;

conceals Lord Yarmouth's intention to resign.

Sidmouth, Lord, as Home-secretary, introduces six bills for the suppression of sedition;

resigns office.

Slavery, abolition of.

Slave-trade, abolition of.

Smith, Mr. W., M.P. for Norwich, on repeal of the Five Mile Act.

Somersett, is released by Lord Mansfield.

Stamp Act, imposed on the American Colonies by Mr. Grenville; repealed by Lord Rockingham.

Stanley, Mr., afterward Lord, and afterward Lord Derby, denounces the Catholic Association;

brings in a bill for the abolition of slavery;

fails in the attempt to form a ministry in 1845;

becomes Prime-minister in 1852;

proposes a committee on life peerages;

becomes Prime-minister;

resigns.

St. Vincent, Lord, opposes the abolition of the slave-trade.

Stockdale, Mr., brings an action against Messrs. Hansard.

Sugar-duties, Sir Robert Peel's ministry is defeated on a reduction of.

Sussex, Duke of, protests against some clauses of the Regency Act.

Sydenham, Lord, Governor-general of Canada.

TANDY, NAPPER, proposes a congress.

Temple, Earl, his interview with George III.

Test and Corporation Acts are repealed.

Thurlow, Mr., afterward Lord Chancellor, on the case of Wilkes;

defends the employment of Hanoverian troops at Gibraltar;

denounces Fox's India Bill;

approves of the King's employment of Lord Temple.

Tone, Wolfe, commits suicide.

Townsend, Lord, Lord-lieutenant of Ireland.

Townsend, Mr. C., re-imposes taxes on North America.

Traitorous Correspondence Bill.

Troy, Dr., petitions for a Roman Catholic college in Ireland.

UNION, the Irish.

Union with Scotland, obstacles to, and advantages resulting from.

VICTORIA, Queen, succeeds to the throne;

marries;

her careful exercise of her duties;

draws up a memorandum for the guidance of the ministers;

writes to foreign sovereigns.

Victoria, the province of, grant of a constitution to.

Villiers, Mr. C., advocates the repeal of the Corn-laws.

Volunteers, rise of the Irish, 158; rise of the English.

WALES, Prince or, son of George III., his conduct and establishment;

marries Mrs. Fitzherbert;

is attacked in the streets;

See George IV.

Wales, Prince of, son of the Queen, visits India.

Walpole, Sir R., the case of;

on election petitions;

refuses to repeal the Test Act;

his general policy.

Walpole, Mr. Spencer, supports the Conspiracy Bill.

Warburton, Bishop of Gloucester, denounces Wilkes.

Ward, Mr., his motion on the appropriation of Church funds.

Wedderburn, Mr., on the case of Wilkes;

supports Mr. Grenville's act;

his opinion on the Riot Act;

the chief legal adviser of the Prince of Wales;

suggests the Traitorous Correspondence Bill;

excites the King to resist the removal of Catholic disabilities.

Wellesley, Marquis, proposed to be appointed Prime-minister.

Wellington, Lord, afterward Duke of, his victories in the Peninsula and in France;

becomes Commander-in-chief;

advises the King to decline dining with the Lord Mayor;

fails in the endeavor to form an administration;

becomes temporary Prime-minister, holding several offices;

condemns the recall of Lord Ellenborough.

Westmoreland, Lord, opposes the abolition of the slave-trade.

Wetherall, Sir Charles, is attacked at Bristol.

Weymouth, Lord, Secretary of State, writes a letter to the Surrey magistrates.

Whately, Archbishop, his opinion on the Lord-lieutenancy of Ireland; note.

Whitbread, Mr., promotes the impeachment of Lord Melville.

Wilberforce, Mr. W., proposes the admission of Roman Catholics to the militia;

devotes himself to the abolition of the slave-trade.

Wilkes, Mr., sets up *The North Briton*;

criticises the King's speech;

is apprehended;

is expelled the House of Commons for printing the "Essay on Woman;"

is elected for Middlesex, expelled, and re-elected;

as Lord Mayor behaves with spirit during the Gordon riots;

procures the expunction of the resolutions against him.

William IV., his conduct on the Reform Bill;

dies.

Windham, Mr., brings in a bill for reenforcing the army.

Wolseley, Sir C., is elected M.P. by a Birmingham convention.

YARMOUTH, Earl of, Lord Chamberlain.